FORGOTTEN WARRIORS

FORGOTTEN WARRIORS

THE LONG HISTORY of WOMEN in COMBAT

SARAH PERCY

BASIC BOOKS

New York

Basic Books
Hachette Book Group
1290 Avenue of the Americas, New York, NY 10104
www.basicbooks.com

Printed in the United States of America

Originally published in 2023 by John Murray Press in Great Britain
First U.S. Edition: September 2023

Published by Basic Books, an imprint of Perseus Books, LLC, a subsidiary of Hachette Book
Group, Inc. The Basic Books name and logo is a trademark of the Hachette Book Group.

The Hachette Speakers Bureau provides a wide range of authors for speaking events. To find
out more, go to hachettespeakersbureau.com or email HachetteSpeakers@hbgusa.com.

Basic books may be purchased in bulk for business, educational, or promotional use.
For information, please contact your local bookseller or Hachette Book Group Special
Markets Department at special.markets@hbgusa.com.

The publisher is not responsible for websites (or their content)
that are not owned by the publisher.

Typeset in Bembo MT Pro by Palimpsest Book Production Limited, Falkirk, Stirlingshire

Library of Congress Control Number: 2023934297

ISBNs: 9781541619869 (hardcover), 9781541619876 (ebook)

LSC-C

Printing 1, 2023

To my family: James, Tatiana and Jonah

Contents

CONTENTS

Illustrations follow page 202.

Introduction:
The Tomb of the Unknown Warrior

THE SWEDISH ISLAND of Björkö nestles alongside many others in the long, crooked-shored Lake Mälaren. When the Vikings sailed the lake and roamed the land, they settled in a significant trading post called Birka. Birka's exact location was lost to history for generations, but in the 1870s it was rediscovered and excavations began. The settlement was studded with burial chambers stuffed with clues about their occupants – amber, textiles, gold, silver and many other treasures.

One prominent burial chamber at Birka stands high between the town and a hill fort, marked by a large boulder. When the nineteenth-century archaeologists found it, they labelled the grave Bj.581. The chamber contained hints of its occupant's identity: weapons, including a sword, an axe, a spear, a battle knife, two shields and twenty-five arrows strong enough to pierce armour. There were the remains of two horses.[1] Clearly, this was the grave of a warrior – and a significant one. A 2002 study examined the warrior's clothing, particularly a tasselled cap, and concluded that the skeleton was 'a cavalry commander under the immediate authority of a royal war leader'.[2] It was obvious that this great Viking warrior had been laid to rest alongside his belongings, his horses and the tools of his trade.

No one really looked closely at the skeleton to confirm it was male. After all, the grave and its treasures indicated that this was a high-status warrior, buried in a marked and prominent position, in a grave full of weapons. There are 1,100 graves on the island. Only Bj.581 and one other have a full complement of weapons.[3] For a hundred years the record held that the warrior in Bj.581 was male.

In the early 1970s bone analysis suggested the skeleton was a woman, but archaeologists appear not to have done much further investigation. In 2013 further bone analysis established the skeleton was female, and DNA analysis published in 2018 confirmed that the bones were a woman's, with two X chromosomes. The team conducting the DNA analysis also examined the relationship between the skeleton and the contents of the grave, and drew the same conclusion as all other previous investigations had, starting in the nineteenth century: 'the person in Bj.581 was buried in a grave full of functional weapons and war-gear (and little else) in close proximity to other burials with weapons, next to a building saturated with weapons, outside the gate of a fortress'.[4] If it looks like a warrior, and is armed like a warrior, it must be a warrior.

Except many critics were unconvinced. Had the authors of the study got the wrong skeleton? Had another skeleton been mixed up in the grave? (No, the evidence is firm on both points.) Maybe the warrior was a woman who was, for whatever reason, buried with lots of weapons but wasn't herself a warrior (but she was buried with none of the usual accoutrements of women, including jewellery; as the authors of the study note with more than a hint of exasperation, 'perhaps she was a farmer, a housewife, a fisherwoman . . . buried with expensive and dangerous things that did not belong to her, and with none of her own possessions').[5] Some people accepted that the skeleton was female, but wondered if she were transgender or non-binary; the authors point out that these categories do not map neatly onto understandings of the past, and that all we can know for sure is that the skeleton is biologically female.[6]

For well over a hundred years, Bj.581 was a clear example of the grave of a prominent warrior. The only feature that caused critics to obsess over whether or not the skeleton was indeed a Viking fighter was its gender. No one had questioned it before, because it was obvious — except if you believed that women weren't warriors. The story of the skeleton in Bj.581 took off around the world because it challenged so many assumptions about women, combat and the history of war.

The woman warrior of Birka is not the only case of mistaken identity masking a woman's military contributions. General Casimir

Pulaski, born in Poland in 1745, was a patriot and fighter exiled for his role in an uprising against the Russians. Like many other ideal-istic believers of the time, he went to America in order to join the Revolution. Pulaski, among his many accomplishments, saved George Washington's life and reformed American cavalry warfare. He died from the wounds he suffered at the Battle of Savannah, and is one of only eight people ever to be granted honorary citizenship of the United States.

There is a monument to Pulaski in Savannah, containing a metal box of his remains. Controversy raged for years over whether the box really contained Pulaski's bones or if they were actually the bones of someone else. So in 1996 a forensic team decided to settle the argument. When they opened the box, one of the scientists said 'you'll just have to shoot me. It's not Pulaski'[7] – because the skeleton was clearly a woman's. For some, this settled the debate. After all, how could the father of American cavalry warfare be a woman?

The argument over whose bones they were continued until 2019, when more sophisticated DNA analysis on the exhumed skeleton of a Pulaski descendant provided a definitive answer. The skeleton was indeed Pulaski's, but his body had many female characteristics. The Revolutionary War hero was either a woman or intersex, a fact hidden throughout his entire life. Women who masqueraded as men to fight often did so with such success that no one ever knew.

The stories of Pulaski and the Viking woman warrior, are, in many ways, the story of women in combat in many other contexts and eras. Women have fought in wars, but their contribution is often forgotten, glossed over or erased by assumptions that women have had little to do with warfare. The military historian John Keegan famously wrote in 1993 that

> warfare is . . . the one human activity from which women, with the most insignificant exceptions, have always and everywhere stood apart . . . Women . . . do not fight. They rarely fight among them-selves and they never, in any military sense, fight men. If warfare is as old as history and as universal as mankind, we must now enter the supremely important limitation that it is an entirely masculine activity.[8]

Martin van Creveld agreed, arguing in 2008 that 'for thousands of years, armed forces [have] been able to fight and kill each other very effectively even though they had hardly any women in their ranks (and without experiencing any particular urge to correct that shortcoming).'[9] Van Creveld and Keegan were writing at a time when the militaries of most major Western powers relied on the combat exclusion, a legal and social mechanism that prevented women from fighting.

Of course, if you take this view of military history, historical evidence of women in combat – like Pulaski or the warrior woman of Birka – must be written off as a mistaken interpretation, or slightly more generously, an exception, a quirky irrelevance that makes for an exciting story but doesn't have any real impact on military history. The useful thing about dismissing these examples is that doing so enables people to argue that the military (at least the important, fighting side of the military) was and has always been all male, so adding women would be an unwelcome and unhelpful innovation. Dismissing women warriors in this way helped maintain the combat exclusion that prevented women from fighting.

The history of the creation and maintenance of the combat exclusion is a history of how patriarchy works. Militaries deliberately excluded women from combat roles when the burgeoning feminist movement was breaking down every other imaginable type of barrier. The creation and maintenance of the combat exclusion required the sort of clear strategic thinking for which militaries are justifiably known. Militaries and their supporters in government worked carefully to construct the most compelling arguments to keep women away from the front lines; they worked hard to make sure that the combat exclusion remained lawful; and they manipulated the definition of combat in order to make sure that even if women entered the military in greater numbers, they could not enter combat. And all this relied on claiming that there were few historical examples of women's capacity for fighting.

From the 1500s through to the end of the nineteenth century the battlefields of Europe were in fact full of women. Military history tends to record these women as camp followers; sometimes, less politely, if you look in the index of a military history book covering this period, under 'women' you are likely to find an entry nearby labelled 'whores'. But in fact these women were often crucial to the machinery of warfare, providing essential supplies (often through pillage), food and drink, and even working as soldiers (often disguised as men). These women were far more militarily important than 'camp followers': they picked up and used weapons, they kept the army they joined fed and watered and they were a part of the military system. But it is easy to glance back at history and assume that the men did all the fighting and the women were simply going along for the ride. If soldiers fight for all that is great and glorious, then the conventional history tells us that these women were there to serve them. Their lives and contributions might be interesting, but not for a history of combat, because what do whores and wives reveal about military history?

As time went on, militaries took great pains to argue that even if it might *look* like women were fighting, they weren't. During the Second World War, British women were tasked with every aspect of operating an anti-aircraft battery. They spotted enemy aircraft, worked out the trajectory – and then men, with the battery for this purpose only, fired the gun. This enabled the British authorities to claim that women were not in combat. As late as the wars in Iraq and Afghanistan, when women were legally barred from combat, militaries maintained the fiction that a woman who received enemy fire and fired back was not a combatant – even when some women received decorations for valour in combat.

Sometimes military history simply diminished the nature of the battles during which women were fighting, as they were not 'proper' wars, the kinds with recognisable battlefields and lots of (male) soldiers. Sieges were by far the most common form of warfare in Europe for three hundred years, between the late fifteenth and early eighteenth centuries; far more common than battles fought on battlefields. The wars on the battlefields may have relied on men to fight, but sieges often involved women. But because the siege is not a 'battlefield' – women were only defending their towns and homes, not striding out to battle – military history does not count them as soldiers.

During the Second World War women worked covertly with

resistance movements. The Australian Nancy Wake, working in France under the auspices of the British Special Operations Executive (SOE), trained a resistance force of 7,000 men, and led them into battle. Pearl Witherington, also an SOE agent, led a 3,000-man resistance force that eventually forced the surrender of 18,000 Germans. But Nancy Wake and Pearl Witherington were not called soldiers, they were British agents, fighting an irregular war with resistance fighters. And if we cannot call them soldiers, we also cannot call them commanders, which they clearly were.

In 1992, after the Persian Gulf War exposed some of the inconsistencies of whether or not women were in combat, or on battlefields, the United States called for a presidential commission to address the topic. The resulting report makes for eye-opening reading. One of the commissioners, Ronald D. Ray, who was a former Marine colonel and Assistant Secretary of Defense under President Ronald Reagan, wrote that

> battles and wars for thousands of years have involved armies of men engaged against each other often fighting for national survival. No military in history has willingly chosen to send women as combatants to fight another nation's male soldiers simply because men are inherently better designed for such savage activity.[10]

Nancy Wake and Pearl Witherington would have found this surprising, and they would not have been alone.

Women have fought in many different time periods and many different places. This is not to say that they have fought in the same numbers and in the same ways as men. Joshua Goldstein, author of one of the definitive books examining gender and war, points out that all women fighters over time probably add up to a number less than 1 per cent of all the warriors in history.[11] If there were so few women fighters, why should we look at them? Are they anything other than exceptions, interesting adjuncts to the main event of military history?

The picture I want to paint for you is not one of a historical battlefield containing a secret legion of previously unknown women soldiers. I am not going to claim that women were the star players and strategists who influenced the big turning points of military history. But I do want to demonstrate that women were part of the warp and weft of war, that they were common on the battlefield, and that they survived and even thrived as part of a machine of war. It is to tell you that there were plenty of examples, if anyone had bothered to look, that showed that women could fight. I want to show you that the history of war is not only a history where women are victims; it's also a history where women have agency, where they make their own choices about combat (even if men sometimes stood in the way). It's a story where rules about female combat suppressed gender equality in society, and a story of the women who fought to change those rules.

But if this history exists, how was it possible for so many militaries to keep the combat exclusion in place as late as the first decade of the twenty-first century, and even in Western societies, where gender equality had opened the door of virtually every other imaginable job to women? Many of the examples of women fighting in the past were dismissed, denied, forgotten and even actively suppressed. When Western governments were forced by the feminist movement in the 1970s to consider the question of whether women should be allowed to fight, they were looking at an idealised version of the world where men fought and women were safe at home. They refused to see a history where so-called women camp 'followers' were following so closely they were actually on the battlefield, providing food and drink and supporting artillery fire. They didn't see women in the thick of battle, fighting alongside men – most often disguised as men, occasionally in their own right, and sometimes (but rarely) even leading those men. Whatever women had done on the battlefields of history was ignored, written off as a notably unusual exception, and sometimes simply forgotten.

Worse still, ignoring or suppressing this history helped perpetuate the exclusion of women from combat. If anyone ever wanted or needed evidence that patriarchy exists and requires active and deliberate maintenance, examining the actions of the militaries in states that were reluctant to open combat to women provides an object lesson. Preventing women from fighting prevented them from taking on military leadership roles, which required combat experience. Military leadership has long been a route to political and societal leadership. But perhaps more importantly, excluding women from combat served as a potent reminder that despite what the feminist movement told women, and told the world, they were not equal. Women were simply too fragile to fight. Men would be too distracted by the presence of a woman (who, after all, couldn't bring much else of use to the battlefield) in order to fight properly; women would disrupt the essential bond between men, between brothers, that allowed for battlefield excellence. Women would be uniquely and horrifyingly susceptible to violence on the battlefield. Even though women could fight all kinds of battles, and win them, the military ensured that they couldn't fight real battles – men would still have to do that for them.

Understanding how keeping women out of combat was part of the playbook of patriarchy isn't just important in historical terms. There is a strong link between authoritarianism and the suppression of gender equality, and consequently a strong link between democratic backsliding and the removal of hard-won women's rights.[12] The right to engage in combat is no different from any other of these rights. In fact, before his 2016 election, it was widely reported that Donald Trump was opposed to women in combat and likely to dial back the extension of combat roles to women. The American decision to open combat roles was a policy choice rather than a law passed through Congress, and so it was entirely possible for him to do so.[13] And underlining Trump's dislike of the policy was the fact that Trump's voters also disliked the idea of women in combat: one study showed that the two strongest factors associated with opposing the deployment of a co-ed unit in combat were support for Trump and support for the Republican Party.[14]

Understanding the history of women warriors is also crucial to defending the principles of gender equality. Picking apart the ways in which the combat exclusion was created and maintained provides unique insights into how male-dominated institutions deliberately and strategically ensure their survival: understanding the playbook of patriarchy in relation to women in combat helps prevent similar strategies from being used again. Moreover, women's demonstrated capacity in combat serves as a profound reminder of women's overall social equality; it is harder to take away women's rights if women are equal on every level with men, and easier if women are not. And as time goes on, women will get more and more chances to demonstrate their leadership in the crucible of combat – and bring that leadership back into society.

This book traces the history of women in combat, pulling these forgotten warriors back into military history. The first part examines the periods of history when women were a commonplace feature on battlefields, mainly focusing on the sixteenth century to the end of the nineteenth. At this time the battlefield was often a place of surprising freedom for women, where usual social rules did not apply, allowing women to live a different kind of life. The second part turns to considering why and how women disappeared from war, and how an all-male battlefield became understood as normal, focusing on the period from the late nineteenth century to the Second World War – a time when social rules, particularly expectations about gender, infiltrated the battlefield, closing off opportunities for women. By the end of this period there was an official 'combat exclusion' explicitly banning women from combat around the world, and the combat exclusion came to be a significant barrier for women in the fight for equality. It was so normal it was rarely questioned, even when there was direct evidence contradicting its historical accuracy. The third part examines how, when and where women returned to combat.

These three parts explain how the so-called combat exclusion is not universal but rather grew, became established with constant nurturing, and has declined. I argue that the combat exclusion is composed of three core beliefs: that the militaries of the past were exclusively male; that such an all-male force is essential for military success; and therefore that combat must be carefully fenced off to prevent women from fighting. These beliefs rest on two convenient fictions: a view that women are incapable of fighting and require protection, and that war can be organised in such a way that there are distinct lines between the front and the rear, so that women can be carefully kept in a safe place. All this, of course, is for women's own good.

If we look at the history of war through the lens of female fighters, it is revealing to note that the idea of combat is more complex than it at first appears. What is combat in war? It may seem obvious: the physical fight with an enemy. But it's not so easy to define. It may be easy to agree that a soldier carrying a weapon on the front line of battle is a combatant. But what about a cook on the front line who picks up a weapon? What about a person piloting a drone? What about personnel on a ship firing torpedoes at sea? An electrician in the army at the front line was a combatant in the early 1980s;[15] a woman military police officer under attack and firing back in the war in Iraq in 2003 was not. British women in the anti-aircraft batteries in the Second World War were explicitly not combatants, while the women who fought behind enemy lines as agents of SOE were officially non-combatants too, even though they were trained in fighting. After the war, they were eligible only for civilian medals of valour, not military citations.

If we could ask a general in the eighteenth century if he had any non-combat soldiers in his army, he might wonder about the premise of the question. There might be some members of the army who didn't fight much, but there were none who assumed they would *never* fight. The people who provided services to the military were usually not soldiers at all. Modern war changed that equation – militaries became vast organisations that required accountants and secretaries and carpenters and electricians and a range of jobs that could remain non-combat – but one of the primary reasons militaries have had to distinguish between combat and non-combat jobs is to make sure women do not end up fighting.

Understanding how and why definitions of combat have evolved, and altered, often deliberately to exclude women, also clarifies the changing nature of war. Arguing that some jobs in the military are 'combat' while others are not, and sticking to this neat division, requires that there are wars with a distinct front line and a safe rearguard, where non-combatants can be kept from the fighting. The history of women in combat is an effective reminder that very few battlefields have actually met this description. Only twentieth-century, industrial war, fought between states and usually far away from home, has really had a division between the front and the rear stark enough that women can be safely kept from the fighting. Once states began again to fight wars that did not have a clear front line

– such as the first Gulf War in 1991 and the wars in Iraq and Afghanistan – the carefully drawn distinctions between combat and non-combat jobs fell apart.

If the category of combat is not as clear as it might seem then neither is the notion of the battlefield. Defining a battlefield as a place where major powers fight directly against each other helped maintain the historical fiction that women did not fight, because it obscured the roles women played on different battlefields – in sieges, as rebels and as resistance fighters. For many women, the battlefield *was* their home, in the case of sieges, or where women lived with an army. The role of women on battlefields historically also reminds us that wars which had a distinct front line are far more rare than the public imagination might suspect, and that keeping people safely on 'the home front' is a luxury for states who can fight wars far from home. Civilian women have long been caught, horribly, 'at the front' even though they are at home – a fact that is all too easy to ignore from the perspective of major powers who have done most of their recent fighting overseas.

The history of women in combat also sheds light on the relationship between strongly held beliefs, such as those about gender, and war. Looking at the history of women warriors also reveals puzzling aspects that a traditional military history may not explain. Strategic studies tells us that when a nation fights a war of national survival, it should mobilise all available resources in order to stave off defeat. But the belief that women were incapable of fighting (or couldn't be seen to be fighting) was so profound that even under the extreme pressure of the Second World War only the Soviet Union was able to mobilise women for combat roles. Nearly a million Soviet women fought under arms, and did so successfully. Other countries either blocked women from combat entirely or manipulated the definitions of 'combat' and 'battlefield' in order to make sure that women weren't technically fighting. In Germany, the Reich preferred to allow boys as young as fourteen to defend Berlin before the mobilisation of adult women was a serious consideration, and in Britain, women were carefully prevented from doing anything that came too close to combat. When women used force it was completely secret, as with the SOE operatives, and was never presented as combat after the war. Gendered beliefs about war, particularly about women's abilities, are so profound that they have been almost impossible to abandon, even when it is strategically better to allow women to fight.

It should come as no surprise that masculinity is tied up with the enterprise of war. But so too is femininity. Prevailing ideas about femininity, particularly what they assume about female capability, go a long way to explaining where, when and how women have been able to fight as soldiers. In fact, war and femininity may have even shaped each other by directing who gets to fight. When the feminine ideal focused on a woman's delicacy, it is perhaps unsurprising that the idea of a female fighting seemed impossible – and abhorrent, because after all a delicate female would not be able to cope on the battlefield. And when this delicate feminine ideal became the ideal for working-class women as well as for their better-heeled sisters in the nineteenth century, then the number of women fighters declined alongside social tolerance for their presence. In fact, many Victorian practices sought to 'civilise' the lower classes by imparting the importance of feminine delicacy.[16] In contexts where the ideal woman was not a delicate flower – usually within particular classes of women in a given era, such as pre-nineteenth-century England or nineteenth-century Russia – plenty of women appeared to be likely fighters. And as we have moved to a feminine ideal that tolerates strength and capacity, it has been far less of a stretch to imagine physically capable females.

The belief that women not only should not but *could not* fight became monolithic in the twentieth century, and the impact of this has been profound and lasting. This is why it is important to examine the intertwined histories of gender and war. How did the historical record become so neglected? When historians of war have recognised the existence of women on the battlefield at all, they have too often assumed that women are merely wives, girlfriends and daughters of the military – in the words of the feminist scholar Jean Bethke Elshtain, they are the 'beautiful souls' that motivate men to fight.[17] If women are not wives, girlfriends and daughters, and they are on or near the battlefield, then they are whores. Worse still, women are presented as *only* victims. Of course, women have been victimised by war to a horrifying degree, in numbers that exceed those of female fighters by a large margin. But what about the stories of women who were on the battlefield, who were architects of their own lives and who pushed to fight, even sneaking around official rules? Their stories are a history of capability, not powerlessness, and of women capable of working on an equal basis with the men around them. Embracing this history can help us build on the legacy of these women warriors, reinforcing gender equality in our world today.

I want to tell the stories of these ordinary women as an important history in its own right: the history of women in combat. In turn, this history will illuminate the history of war, and make it clear that while these women may have been exceptions to the general rule that women did not fight, they were not necessarily 'exceptional'. The women on the battlefields of the past were ordinary, just like the men around them. Sometimes they were exceptionally brave, and sometimes they were cowardly; sometimes they exaggerated their military exploits, and sometimes they underplayed them. If we see women combatants as people who were exceptional, then we assume that the women who fought must also have had some unusual qualities that allowed them to fight but that prevented other women from fighting. The women who fought were able to do so because they were given, or they were able to take, the opportunity to become soldiers. The thing about exceptions is that they can be dismissed as unlikely, or undesirable, to be replicated. And this is precisely what happened to women fighters. In tracing the history of women warriors, we are examining a history that was often (by contemporaries and later observers) dismissed, denied and even actively suppressed, with an impact not only on the military but on wider society.

FORGOTTEN WARRIORS

PART I

Women in War

I

Women Generals

THE BATTLEFIELDS OF history were not always exclusively male. It would seem uncontroversial, though, to say that the generals who commanded those battlefields were nearly always men. The people who started the wars, manoeuvred the troops, made strategic decisions, were men; the generals who caused military history – and world history – to pivot were almost always men.

But only *almost* always. One of the first noteworthy female generals, Boudicca, was a British Celtic queen of the first century CE. For the Romans, Boudicca represented the wild, untamed barbarian. Our only accounts of her come at a remove, from the Roman historians Tacitus (who was not in Britain, though his father-in-law was) and Cassius Dio (who was writing even later than Tacitus). Boudicca was 'very tall, in appearance most terrifying, in the glance of her eye most fierce, and her voice was harsh; a great mass of the tawniest hair fell to her hips, around her neck was a large golden necklace'.[1]

Boudicca's husband was the leader of the Iceni. When he died, he tried to ensure the safety of his family and the Iceni by making his daughters his heirs alongside the emperor. The plan was not a success. The Romans whipped Boudicca, raped her daughters and stole Iceni lands.[2] Infuriated, Boudicca and the Iceni joined forces with a neighbouring tribe and marched on the Roman city of Camulodunum (now Colchester). Boudicca led the troops, and Camulodunum was crushed. The attack was so brutal that it left archaeological traces still visible today. Archaeologists call the layer of Camulodunum's carbonised remains, including buildings, mattresses and food, the 'Boudiccan destruction horizon'.[3]

Boudicca and her army turned to an undefended London, at this stage neither a capital nor fortified.[4] The Roman governor Suetonius Paulinus had abandoned it, fearing he lacked the numbers to defeat the advancing Celts. Boudicca's army gave no quarter. They could 'not wait to cut throats, hang, burn and crucify'.[5] As they had done in Camulodunum, Boudicca's troops burned the city so comprehensively that if you dig deeply enough, you will find a red layer of scorched debris in the London soil dating from the attack.[6] According to Cassius Dio, the Britons

> hung up naked the noblest and most distinguished women and then cut off their breasts and sewed them to their mouths, in order to make the victims appear to be eating them; afterwards, they impaled the women on sharp skewers run lengthwise through the entire body. All this they did to the accompaniment of sacrifices, banquets and wanton behaviour.[7]

Once the Britons had razed London, they moved on to Verulamium (modern-day St Albans). Tacitus claims that here Boudicca's Britons killed 70,000 people.[8] While Boudicca and her army were destroying Verulamium, Suetonius led the Roman army to a strategically superior position, 'a spot encircled with woods, narrow at the entrance, and sheltered in the rear by a thick forest. In that situation, he had no fear of an ambuscade. The enemy, he knew, had no approach but in front'.[9] The Britons had 'brought into the field an incredible multitude', including their wives in wagons, 'where they might survey the scene of action and behold the wonders of British valour'.[10]

Bringing women to the front was not uncommon for the British, but to the Romans it was an alien practice signifying poor discipline. Suetonius had previously faced a different British army on the island of Anglesey: 'On the beach stood . . . a serried mass of arms and men, with women flitting between the ranks. In the style of Furies, in robes of deathly black and with dishevelled hair, they brandished their torches'.[11] The Romans stood firm, 'inciting each other never to flinch before a band of females and fanatics', and were victorious.[12] Any enemy that would bring women to the front, rather than leave them safely at home, was uncivilised indeed.

Our Roman sources say that on the day of the great battle, both Suetonius and Boudicca made speeches. Whether or not this happened we can never know (Suetonius' strategic advantage could only have been diminished by a long period of speechifying during which the Britons may have noticed that they were encircled without hope of escape) and likewise, we can never know what Boudicca said. But it is still fascinating to consider what the Romans *claimed* this female general said. After all, for them, a woman in military command was astonishing, as astonishing as seeing a horse lead men into battle. Dio opens his remarks by pointing out that the loss of two cities and tens of thousands of people in Roman Britain 'was brought upon the Romans by a woman, a fact which caused them the greatest shame'.[13]

According to Tacitus, Boudicca addressed her army, claiming: 'This is not the first time that the Britons have been led to battle by a woman'.[14] He reports that Boudicca told her troops that she 'took the field, like the meanest among them, to assert the cause of public liberty, and to seek revenge for her body seamed with ignominious stripes, and her two daughters infamously ravished'.[15] Boudicca finished her speech with a call to arms: 'On this spot we must either conquer, or die with glory. There is no alternative. Though a woman, my resolution is fixed: the men, if they please, may survive with infamy and live in bondage.'[16]

The disciplined Roman troops in their strategically strong position were too much for the British army, no matter their number. Boudicca's army was slaughtered. The Romans lost 400 men; the British, 80,000.[17] Tacitus claims that Boudicca took poison to kill herself, while a later Roman source claims she took ill and died after the battle.

Usually, the Romans would sell captured women and livestock for a profit, but not in their battle against Boudicca.[18] The 'cattle, falling in one promiscuous carnage, added to the heaps of the slain' where 'neither sex nor age was spared'.[19] Defeat, even temporary defeat, by a woman leader or a *dux femina* was the ultimate humiliation. Even being *subject* to a queen was so humiliating that the only solution was to conquer her;[20] actually being defeated by one required not her conquest but her utter destruction.

Boudicca's rebellion failed. For the Romans, she exemplified the less organised, less civilised and ultimately inferior barbarians they conquered around the world. In Tacitus' account, the Britons are undone by the wagons containing their wives blocking the exit and trapping them among the more disciplined Romans. In other words, Boudicca was defeated because her army violated the distinction between home front and battleground by bringing women to watch the war.[21]

Tacitus' and Dio's accounts of Boudicca's life do not tell us whether or not she was proficient in fighting, or how she was able to command her large army. For the two writers, she was a rebel leader of a rabble successful through good fortune (the targets of the Iceni attacks were unfortified) but ultimately undone by cool, rational strategy and Roman discipline. She was not a proper general in Roman eyes, and the stories of her military command have not come down to us – even though Suetonius' military prowess is often discussed. Suetonius is a man of 'military skill' and 'remarkable firmness'.[22] It is his far-sighted strategy of abandoning London in favour of a strategically useful battleground that wins the day against the Iceni. In our records of Boudicca, she is not so much a general as a curiosity, a symbol of how and why the Britons were unable to resist the superior organisation of the Roman troops. She is simply an exception that proves the rule that women do not fight.

Female generals were unquestionably exceptional. They were sufficiently rare that it is easy, and fast, to rattle off a list. Military command requires extensive military experience, which very few women had, and the ability to persuade men to fight for you, a difficult task for a man with years of military experience, let alone a woman. Female generals were remarkable: they were able to persuade people that a woman could lead men in battle, and they often fought (at least at first) without significant military experience.

Demonstrated military leadership in a woman created a problem for military observers of the day and for later military historians: in what way does one explain how a woman, a weak and feeble woman, rose to lead armies successfully? The apparent answer was that women generals were not only exceptions, but when they did appear, there had to be another reason which explained how such a striking anomaly could be possible. Boudicca was a 'barbarian', and her leadership was a sign of the outlandish and unfortunate practices of an alien race so different from the civilised world that they would even allow women into battle. Other female generals, as we will see, also had their military prowess explained away.

And because female generals were the exception rather than the rule, the way history tells their stories also gives us clues as to how and why it has been so hard to overturn our more contemporary view that women have never played significant roles on the battlefield. If we write women generals off as exceptions, as only able to fight because of some special characteristic, then we diminish them as military leaders and keep them safely to one side of an accepted history. Focusing on the exceptional status of female generals meant that no one ever considered whether these skills might exist in other women, should they be given the chance to lead.

While female *generals* may have been rare, queens and other female rulers have often presided over significant military activity. Queenly leadership was reasonably common. In Europe alone, between 1300 and 1800 thirty women ruled as queens,[23] a number that excludes other female rulers such as Amalie Elizabeth of Hesse-Kassel, a landgravine rather than a queen. Queens did not march onto the battlefield, but military leadership was a normal part of queenship, including organising, procuring and planning at the strategic level. The queens of Europe presided over some remarkable military victories, from the famous, such as Elizabeth I of England's defeat of the Spanish Armada to Isabella of Castile's ten-year war to take Granada, to the less well known in the English-speaking world, for example the many victories of Queen Margaret of Denmark, including her capture of the King of Sweden in 1389. Amalie Elizabeth of Hesse-Kassel had a profound influence on the shape of the Thirty Years War and the famous treaty that ended it.[24] Queen Christina of Sweden had multiple victories during the Thirty Years War and Maria Theresa of Austria defeated Frederick II of Prussia.

Part of rulership was command of the military, for kings *and* queens. And while kings may have been more likely to set foot on the battlefield, this was not always the case. As militaries became more professional so military leadership became more professional too, and it was no longer necessary or desirable to have a monarch on the battlefield.[25] The last British monarch to accompany his troops in battle was George II in 1743. By 1745 European kings no longer fought alongside their men[26] – but there is little doubt that subsequent European monarchs were in overall command of the military, even when they were not on the battlefield itself.

Queens were often no different from kings in their oversight of the military. Queen Christina managed military matters related to conscription, regimental composition, transportation and provisions, as well as sending orders to commanders in the field.[27] Amalie Elizabeth had an army of at least 20,000 men that one observer described as 'always nimble, always ready, and always victorious'.[28] Queen Isabella of Spain was known for her organisational skills, including the management of logistics, military equipment[29] and the call-up of troops.[30] While some of her activities were traditionally feminine – she established the first military camp hospitals[31] – she was also known to ride among her men in armour.[32]

Empress Maria Theresa was intimately involved with the military from the moment she ascended the throne, with an interest in every aspect from dress to discipline and tactics to weapons.[33] As she later explained, the military was the only part of state administration 'for which I harboured a real personal interest'.[34] Maria Theresa's military enthusiasm persisted during her sixteen pregnancies and the rearing of her thirteen surviving children (one of whom was Marie Antoinette). Apparently, she complained that her frequent pregnancies held her back from going to war herself.[35]

The empress noted that the Austrian military, prior to her reign, was haphazardly organised. She wrote:

> Who would believe that there was not the slightest attempt to achieve uniformity among my troops! Every regiment had its own separate drill on the march, on manoeuvres, on deployment. One fired in quick time, another in slow time; the same terms and words of command meant different things to different regiments. No wonder the Emperor was beaten all the time during the ten years before my ascension, no wonder the state in which I found the army was indescribable.[36]

She duly transformed the army. In an era characterised by problems of soldier discipline, including desertion, an English soldier noted that Austrian troops rarely ran away, because they were 'well paid, well dressed, and well fed . . . the troops are aware that the Empress is concerned for their welfare, and this consideration binds them to her service for her own sake'.[37] She also established professional military education, including a military academy that remained at the centre of Austrian military thinking until the end of the First World War.[38]

Queens and female rulers had to carefully navigate a world that equated leadership, intelligence and fortitude with masculinity. Nowhere was this balancing act more pronounced than in military matters, and it explains a tendency on the part of many of these queens to describe themselves as male — a view sometimes shared by observers. Queen Christina of Sweden apparently crossed out *Regina* in the royal genealogy, replacing it with *Rex*.[39] She explained that her father, the great king Gustavus Adolphus,

> wished that in the remainder I should be like a young prince and that I should be taught in all things a prince's virtues and skills. In this my inclinations in a marvellous way supported his purposes because I felt an unconquerable dislike for everything that women talked about or did.[40]

England's Queen Elizabeth I justified her rule by explaining that she was simultaneously a female queen and a male king.[41] Her famous speech at Tilbury, where she is said to have stated, 'I know I have the body but of a weak and feeble woman; but I have the heart and stomach of a King, and a King of England too', neatly demonstrates the bifurcated leadership of her monarchy: a queen who ruled, but also a king who fought.[42] Amalie Elizabeth of Hesse-Kassel was described as a warrior woman, a 'new Penthesilia' and a 'hermaphroditic genius'.[43] Empress Maria Theresa loathed her chief adversary, Frederick the Great (Frederick II) of Prussia, and her loathing took on a masculine form: she once wanted to challenge him to a duel with pistols.[44] Frederick in turn noted that Maria Theresa wore the trousers in her marriage: 'The Emperor gives the impression of a good bluff innkeeper who leaves all his affairs to his wife'.[45]

Queens and other women rulers were most often in leadership roles by accident: they were stepping into the shoes of an absent husband or a son too young to rule, or occasionally because a quirk of inheritance left a woman on the throne. So while queens were military rulers, it was rarely by design. The very few women who actually commanded troops on the battlefield had to seize the opportunity, it was not given to them. And when they seized it, it caused their adversaries to sit up and take notice.

Because female generals were so rare, they often took on enormous symbolic value – sometimes to the point that the symbolism obscured the military accomplishment. Joan of Arc demonstrated military and command skills that far exceeded those of most women – and most men. Her military experience was so unusual that it was, especially to the people of the time, inexplicable without reference to the intervention of God. And so Joan's military accomplishments are often dismissed, taking a back seat to her divine stature.

Joan's story is remarkable because in one so young her military talent and successes were so striking as to be manifestly miraculous. Joan was born during the Hundred Years War between England and France. There were two notable features of her teenage years: the war was going very badly for France, and Joan spoke to saints and angels in her garden. Saint Michael, Saint Catherine and Saint Margaret told her to drive the English from France, and to bring the Dauphin to Reims to be crowned king. The Dauphin, Charles, had inherited the throne but could not be consecrated as king in Reims, the traditional venue for French coronations, because it was in English hands. Joan petitioned and manoeuvred until she finally gained an audience with the local garrison commander, where she proved her credentials by predicting the outcome of a battle near the besieged city of Orléans. This little miracle was enough to prove Joan's bona fides.

The disastrous military position of the French in the Hundred Years War made it possible for the king and his advisers to accept the otherwise ludicrous proposition that a teenage girl could save France. The Hundred Years War was even more interminable than its name suggests – in fact, it lasted longer than a hundred years. The French had no crowned king, and armies had swarmed over the countryside for decades, living off the land and preventing economic activity.[46] When Joan made her offer to the local garrison commander in 1429, the French court had a stark choice: carry on fighting (and mostly losing) a war already nearly a century old, or take a chance on a girl whose divine inspiration seemed to be confirmed by her little miracles. Desperation has, over the centuries, caused many people to change their minds about the military capacities of women.

It is possible that Joan's miraculous intervention in the war was abetted by canny members of the court, who realised that the appearance of a little divine intervention might be enough to give the French armies the confidence they needed to turn the tide of the war.[47] The military situation was sufficiently dire that throwing a teenage girl who heard voices into the mix could hardly make it worse, and doing so might actually give weary soldiers and a weary country the inspiration they needed to fight back. As one commentator noted,

> here is she who seems not to come from anywhere on earth, who seems to be sent from heaven to sustain with her neck and shoulders a fallen France. She raised the King out of the vast abyss . . . she lifted up the spirits of the French to a greater hope.[48]

Unsurprisingly, there were still doubters among the French royal court about an illiterate teenage girl's ability to achieve the Dauphin's coronation and drive the English from France. It was decided that Joan's divine credentials would be established one way or the other if she could, as she claimed, lift the siege of Orléans. Having been provided with armour and provisions, she set off on the first phase of her mission to crown a king and win a war.

The siege of Orléans had started the previous year, on 12 October 1428. Orléans' inhabitants – including the women, who had even pushed advancing Englishmen off the city walls[49] – had ardently defended themselves against the English, but the situation had devolved into a worrying stalemate. It was clear that the intertwined fates of siege and city were pivotal to the outcome of the war between England and France. Had the English successfully taken the city, there was every likelihood they would have been able to take all of France.[50] Demonstrating her extraordinary confidence, Joan warned the English in Orléans of her impending arrival, telling them to go back to your countries, for God's sake . . . If you do not do so, I am commander of the armies . . . I shall have them all killed. I am sent from God, King of Heaven, to chase you out of all France, body for body.[51]

Joan and her soldiers left for Orléans in late April. Driving the English from the city would require taking three strategic fortifications, which Joan and her troops did during the first week of May 1429. The assault on the last of these fortifications, the Tourelles, saw fierce fighting. According to a chronicle of the battle,

> there was a spectacular assault during which there were performed many great feats of arms, both in the attack and in the defence, because the English had a large number of strong soldiers and placed them skilfully in all of the defensible places . . . the French scaled the different places adeptly and attacked the angles at the highest of the strong and sturdy fortifications . . . But the English repulsed them from many places and attacked with artillery both high and low, both with cannon and other weapons, such as axes, lances, pole-arms, lead hammers and even with their bare hands.[52]

Joan was the first to plant her ladder on the walls of the besieged town. She 'immediately took her standard and placed it on the bank of the ditch. At that instant when she appeared, the English trembled and took fright and the soldiers of the king felt their courage rekindled and began to go forward, delivering an assault on the boulevard without encountering any resistance'.[53] Joan was wounded in the fighting, an event she had previously prophesied, but only paused briefly to pray before fighting on.[54] By 8 May Orléans was in French hands.

The French poet and writer Alain Chartier wrote shortly after the victory at Orléans that no mortal man would not wonder at the

> strength and the greatness of these countless, marvellous deeds . . . but why wonder? For what is necessary for leaders in battle that the Pucelle does not have? Perhaps military skill? She has an admirable one. Or a strong spirit? She has the highest one and surpasses all . . . and in fact she herself leads the army into battle against the enemy, she arranges the camps, she urges to war and to battle, bravely demonstrates military skills.[55]

Joan's success at Orléans caused Charles VII to allow her to make military advances along the Loire, en route to Reims (where her visiting saints had told her to bring the Dauphin to his consecration). Reims was a challenging, if not impossible, target, deep within English-held territory. But with Joan in tow, the French proceeded with pace and success up the Loire throughout the month of June, until a decisive battle at Patay saw the English comprehensively defeated. The French army was on the doorstep of Reims by late June, and on 16 July they took the city. Just as Joan's saints had foretold, the Dauphin had his coronation in Reims.

In September 1429 the French army turned towards Paris, where Joan was wounded in the leg by a crossbow bolt, before the army, facing a heavily fortified and well-defended city, was ordered to withdraw. A Parisian official described her as 'the woman who led the army with the other captains'.[56] The defeat at Paris, while not Joan's fault, tarnished her reputation: if she was driven by the divine, had God forsaken her?[57] Nonetheless, she continued to travel with the army and in December 1429 she was ennobled with her family by Charles VII.

The change of the year saw a further change in Joan's fortunes. A truce kept the first part of the year quiet, but after it collapsed, Joan travelled with the army to Compiègne, to defend against English attack. Staying at the rear of her troops in order to protect them,[58] Joan was captured by the English and taken hostage on 23 March 1430. Her enemies were delighted, even more 'than if they had taken 500 soldiers, because they feared no captain or war leader up until that day as they had dreaded the Maid'.[59]

The French explained away Joan's military success by accepting that it was divinely granted. The English, defeated by a teenage girl who terrified them, explained Joan away by calling her a witch and a lawbreaker. The nature of the laws Joan broke help us to see the contours of beliefs about women, and their ordinary capabilities. Why did a girl like Joan pose such a threat?

Undoubtedly part of the threat was political. If Joan's voices were right, and Charles was the rightful, divinely ordained king of France, then it damaged the English claim to rule. But Joan also scared the English. She was a girl at the head of a successful army, and that success could only be supernatural. In fact, Joan was threatening on so many levels that after her capture her demise was a foregone conclusion. The English announced Joan's trial, declaring that

> a woman calling herself Joan *the Maid*, putting off the dress and habit of the female sex (which is contrary to divine law, abominable to God, condemned and prohibited by every law) has dressed and armed herself in the state and habit of man, has wrought and occasioned cruel murders.[60]

The trial lasted about four and half months throughout which Joan stuck to her story: she was inspired by God, and directed by her voices. Joan's inquisitors repeatedly tried to get her to recant, but she held up with intelligence and strength.

On 24 May 1431 Joan's captors decided to use different tactics to get her to recant. She was brought to a scaffold and forced to listen to a priest harangue her for her sins. Exactly what happened next is a matter of debate. We know for sure that Joan recanted many of her previous statements, including her divine inspiration; what we do not know is whether she was fooled into doing so, or did so mockingly, or in such a way that it signalled to her followers that the recantation was false. Whatever happened, the fact of the recantation caused difficulties for the English. A repentant heretic, like Joan, could not be executed. The only grounds for her execution would be if she relapsed.

Joan's commitment to one of her chief heresies, her male dress, was to be her undoing. Joan had been dressed as a woman during her trial, but in late May she returned to her male clothes, for reasons that remain uncertain. Her captors may have plotted to steal her women's attire to force her to don her men's clothes and commit heresy.[61] Or Joan may have abandoned her previous recantation, insisting she still heard her voices, and returning to her accustomed dress.[62] Or it may have been because, as Joan herself insisted, dressing as a man kept her safe from sexual assault. But once she reoffended, she demonstrated her commitment to her heresy – and opened the door to her execution. Once word of Joan's renewed cross-dressing got out, the cleric leading the investigation demanded to see her. During their conversation she insisted again that the voices she heard were real. Now she was a committed heretic twice over. Joan was guilty. On 30 May 1431, a little more than two years after her first military victories, she was burned to death. Her charred body was burned twice more to prevent the crowd from collecting relics. She was nineteen.[63]

Whether or not Joan was indeed prompted by God to save France can never be known. But there is ample evidence of her military skills and impact on the war. Joan was clearly more than a figurehead. She had an array of armour, including helmets for different types of fighting, suggesting that she was expected to do far more than march at the front of the army.[64] Her close companion, Jean, duke of Alençon, wrote that 'in the conduct and disposition of her troops, in deeds of war and the organization of combat and the encouragement of troops, she comported herself as if she were the most adept captain in the world, trained for years in warfare'.[65] Joan developed other military skills, practising fighting on horseback.[66] According to Alençon, everyone marvelled at the fact Joan 'acted so wisely and clearly in waging war, as if she were a captain who had the experience of twenty or thirty years; and especially in the setting up of artillery, for in that she held herself magnificently'.[67]

Joan seems to have been surprisingly skilled in the newly significant use of gunpowder in war. The battle for Orléans involved the greatest use of gunpowder on both sides that had yet been seen, and the presence of so many gunpowder weapons in the English fortifications around the city may have been one of the deterrents preventing a French counter-attack.[68] How could a teenager become so good at gunpowder warfare, the cutting-edge military technology of the day? Military historians speculate that Joan's age and class actually assisted her in understanding this new technology. The fact that she was young and a commoner made her more like the cannoneers around her than a wealthy lord, and perhaps she was simply good at listening to them, as she had listened to her voices.[69]

The question of Joan's divinity has undoubtedly overshadowed her military skill. She performed many miracles off the battlefield: she was able to identify the disguised Dauphin, despite never having seen him before; she correctly predicted the outcome of a battle before it was known; she predicted when and where she would be wounded. There were more miraculous occurrences during her military campaigns, ranging from rapidly healing wounds to a river that magically filled to a high enough level to allow troops to use it.

Although no one knows for sure exactly what Joan looked like, her beauty was at the heart of another of her miracles – one which looks astonishing to modern eyes. The duke of Alençon recalled that 'sometimes he saw Joan get ready for the night, and sometimes he saw her breasts, which were beautiful'. But one of the signs of Joan's divinity was that no man who saw her was tempted by carnal desire, even though she was attractive – clearly a miracle for a lone woman among many soldiers, and a comment on how other such women would likely have been treated on the battlefield.[70]

And indeed, how on earth it was possible for an illiterate teenager to have such military impact was only explicable in two ways to contemporaries. For the French, Joan was a heroine directed by the hand of God. For the English, she was a witch – they agreed that only magic could explain her military skills, but could not countenance that a girl leading the enemy was divinely directed. Those powers had to have come from the devil – or indeed, Joan might not even be human at all. She may have been a 'creature . . . who was in the form of a woman that was named the Pucelle',[71] who used 'used false enchantments and sorcery'.[72] After her execution and before her second burning, Joan's body was displayed to the crowds to prove she was a human woman, so convinced were many that she was some kind of demon.[73]

It is interesting how much Joan's transvestism, her taking on a male role, was her undoing. Five of the seventy charges against her relied on her cross-dressing. One charge stated:

> the said Jeanne put off and entirely abandoned woman's clothes, with her hair cropped short and round in the fashion of young men, she wore shirt, breeches, doublet, with hose joined together . . . tight-fitting boots or buskins, long spurs, sword, dagger, breastplate, lance and other arms in the style of a man at arms.[74]

A theologian wrote at the time that 'if a woman could put on male clothing as she liked with impunity, women would have unrestrained opportunities to fornicate and to practice manly acts which are legally forbidden to them'.[75] Dressing as a man gave a woman the possibility of behaving like a man, and Joan's successful adoption of male skills as well as clothes made her especially threatening. If Joan's military skills were not magical then they were especially dangerous because the Maid demonstrated that a woman was capable of leading troops to victory. If Joan was just a girl with a flair for war, what else might other women be able to accomplish? It was far safer to assume that she was a divine exception to normal femininity, and easy to deny that a teenage girl could have innate military skill. But female generals were not always so easy to dismiss.

While Joan of Arc could be a general because she was divine (or a witch), and Boudicca's generalship was based on luck and only successful until she met a disciplined Roman army, other women were able to take military command because they managed to completely step into the male role of kingship, including its military aspects.

Queen Njinga of Ndongo was a genuine warrior queen and commander.[76] She was born around 1582 in what is now Angola, and came of age during the era of Portuguese colonisation of central west Africa. Njinga first protected, and then expanded, her kingdom, through multiple wars, becoming Portugal's main adversary.[77] She would be celebrated as an extraordinarily powerful queen and general in any other context. But to her Portuguese enemies and other Western observers, Njinga was the uncivilised world personified: sexually aggressive, totally subversive of gender expectations and the sort of terrifying enemy who allegedly ate the hearts of victims.[78] Even though Njinga ruled a kingdom that was perpetually at war for forty years (only slightly less than Queen Elizabeth I),[79] and had the military capacity to be a thorn in the side of a well-equipped and ruthless coloniser for nearly as long, she was written off by Europeans as a curiosity rather than understood as a genuine military leader.

The history of central west Africa during Njinga's life is a history of almost constant warfare – of local people against the Portuguese; of tribes against each other; and even European wars that imposed themselves on Africa through colonial competition. In fact, Angola became a distant battlefield of the Thirty Years War in the 1640s, when the Dutch seized the Portuguese colonial capital of Luanda.[80] Any leader in this period who wanted to survive more than a month would have to have notable political and military skills.

Njinga was born just shy of a hundred years after the first Portuguese incursions into central west Africa, and less than a decade after the founding of the colonial city of Luanda. She came into the world feet first, with the umbilical cord wrapped around her neck (the name 'Njinga' derives from a word for 'to twist, turn or wrap'), a form of entering the world that signalled a person would have an unusual life.[81] Njinga grew up as the favoured daughter of the king in a context of perpetual violence. She was notably skilled with the battle-axe, better than her brother and the other children in the royal household.[82] By the time she was an adult, her European contemporaries noted that she was 'a cunning and prudent *Virago*, so much addicted to Arms, that she hardly uses any other exercise'.[83]

The necessity of developing weapons expertise during childhood reflected the remarkably violent (and perilous) state of affairs in seventeenth-century central west Africa. The realities of the slave trade and Portuguese colonisation ruled out a peaceful existence, which may have been unlikely anyway, given the history of violent transitions of power between leaders in Ndongo.

Njinga's father became king of Ndongo in 1593, and in 1617, after his death, her brother seized power and solidified it by killing the other claimants to the throne. His campaign to eradicate rivals that threatened his rule may have extended to killing Njinga's son and forcibly sterilising her and her two sisters, Funji and Kambu.[84] But the conflict between local leaders created by power struggles was compounded by the presence of colonial interests, attracted by a hugely valuable resource: the slave trade, which had been an important part of local culture and life prior to the Portuguese arrival.[85] And like any hugely valuable resource, slavery at once fuelled conflict and paid for it. In fact, battle was a chief mechanism whereby new slaves could be acquired for the market.[86] In roughly the same decades as Njinga's rule (1621–60) over half a million enslaved people were exported from central west Africa.[87] Leaders like Njinga could gain strategic advantage by seizing and blocking trade routes, not to mention financial benefit. It was hardly a situation that lent itself to peace.

The reign of Njinga's brother Ngola Mbande coincided with several years of particularly brutal war with the Portuguese. Portugal's strategy was to build alliances with local leaders to develop its holdings in the area, creating an almost bewildering array of shifting alliances in a context of military gains and setbacks. The only constants appear to have been the level of violence itself and the perpetually moving and growing slave trade, fuelled by the taking of more and more captives. By early 1621 the Portuguese had taken enough territory, forced enough local leaders into vassalage and pulled so many people into slavery that Ngola Mbande saw the futility of military action and shifted towards diplomacy. He selected his estranged sister Njinga as his envoy, bringing her to centre stage in central west Africa. She was to remain there until her death.

Njinga set off for Luanda at the head of what was perhaps the largest ever delegation to travel through Ndongo to the colonial capital, where they were greeted by a Portuguese military escort complete with gun salutes.[88] Njinga's diplomatic skills were considerable. She persuaded the Portuguese to recognise her brother's rule, successfully arguing that as an unconquered leader, he should not have to pay tribute.[89] Her success relied on a mixture of the usual diplomatic avenues of speech, persuasion and theatre. In her first meeting with the Portuguese governor, he was seated. Njinga knew that the Portuguese forced other leaders to sit on the floor, an overt reminder of the status of the coloniser over the colonised. So instead she arranged her own chair: a member of her entourage knelt before her on all fours, and Njinga sat down.[90] Her seat afforded her equality with the Portuguese and was a potent reminder of her own power among her people. She also made the first of a series of attempts to manipulate her Christian adversaries with promises of conversion to Catholicism.

Njinga's successful agreement with the Portuguese, as with many of the pacts between indigenous peoples and Europeans, was swiftly altered. Soon, Portugal had new demands for Ngola Mbande, including his baptism. Ngola Mbande became profoundly depressed. His mental state may have had much to do with his sister's perpetual taunts: Njinga hurled 'injurious words' at Ngola Mbande until he 'became very emotional and thought of ways of protecting his diminished sovereignty and fearing the audacity of a woman who was still his sister'.[91] In 1624 Ngola Mbande died from poisoning – either self-administered or given by Njinga herself.[92] Njinga had taken the throne she would hold until her death in 1663.

In the style of her predecessors, Njinga consolidated her power by comprehensively eliminating her rivals, including her own nephew, for whom she was regent. He may have died of natural causes,[93] or, more dramatically, Njinga may have engineered his death through an elaborate plot involving her marriage to her nephew's foster father, Imbangala Kasa. At some stage during the wedding ceremony, Njinga allegedly murdered her seven-year-old nephew and dumped his body in a river, in vengeance for her own losses; she then murdered other relatives in attendance.[94]

Njinga's consolidation of power did not lead to peace. The Portuguese had been attempting to make local leaders their vassals, including in Ndongo; Njinga's attempts to negotiate on this front failed and the Portuguese attacked in 1626. They drove Njinga into the eastern reaches of Ndongo and put a puppet king, Ngola Hari, in her place. By 1631, after nearly four years of guerrilla warfare and a marriage alliance with a local warlord, Njinga had seized the neighbouring territory of Matamba (also ruled by a queen), where she ruled for the rest of her life.

Njinga was not just a queen. She was a queen who led from the front during nearly four decades of perpetual war. Njinga's primary military goal was to recapture the territory of Ndongo lost to the Portuguese-installed Ngola Hari, but her disputes with Portugal were manifold – over slavery and its profits; over the boundaries of her lands and the return of what she and her predecessors had lost – and all were fuelled by the humiliation meted out to local rulers by the Portuguese. It is likely that her army routinely consisted of around 8,000 men, perhaps reaching as high as 15,000 or 20,000,[95] and as many as 80,000 while she fought with the Dutch.

For any general, to command troops continually for forty years is a noteworthy accomplishment. To have done so in the cut-throat world of seventeenth-century Angola, where leaders were brutally eliminated by rivals and constantly contended with external colonial forces, is remarkable. Njinga displayed all the qualities associated with excellent generalship. She had physical prowess, tactical skills, a command of strategy with a particular skill in manipulating and maintaining alliances, and the ability to inspire decades-long devotion among her troops.

Njinga spent the first years of her reign largely on the run from the Portuguese after they replaced her with Ngola Hari. In classic guerrilla mode, she fought where she could and ran when she could not fight, and in general exasperated the Portuguese, who were wholly unable to catch her. One of the many occasions when she was on the run from the Portuguese came in her early fifties, but age was no obstacle to eluding her pursuers. At one stage she escaped by climbing down a precipice so steep and vast that apparently a voice at the top could not be heard from the bottom.[96] Even at the end of her long life, when she no longer took to the battlefield in person, if a soldier received a bow from Njinga's hand, he would believe his aim to be faultless and himself to be invincible.[97] She commented to one European missionary, who was impressed by her agility at the age of nearly eighty: 'Excuse me, Father, for I am old, but when I was young I yielded nothing in agility or ability to wound any Jaga [Imbangala], and I was not afraid to face twenty-five armed men'.[98]

Njinga's ability to command troops in her late teens and early twenties suggests to historians that she must have been an effective fighter even at this early age.[99] She very quickly gained battlefield experience, which was probably inevitable given the constant warfare that formed the background of her life and reign. She appears to have commanded troops while her brother was still king, and the Portuguese reported she was blocking key communication routes in the 1620s.[100] Njinga's early rebellions after taking the throne were so successful that the Portuguese governor, Fernão de Sousa, wrote back to Lisbon that he had been unable to collect the tributes he had hoped for, and that many of the local allies he had been counting on had chosen to fight with her instead.[101] Njinga also supervised a complex military system with a command structure, regular units and sophisticated communication systems between commanders and units.[102]

Even when she lost, Njinga appears to have had mastery of strategy, tactics and communications. During her many battles she deployed multiple tactics, from surprise attacks to blocking escape routes.[103] In 1626 the Portuguese managed to push Njinga back to an island in the Kwanza River. She prepared the island with trenches, supplies and outward defences, as well as with a communication system that alerted her when the Portuguese attack began.[104] The Portuguese prevailed, but not because Njinga was an incapable general.

The ability to manage a bewildering array of shifting alliances and perpetual conflict was an essential strategic component of Njinga's rule and military success. She had to work out how to manage relationships with European powers, and how to manoeuvre among local rulers and rivals in order to maintain an overall goal of holding her new territory of Matamba and restoring as much of her lost territory of Ndongo as possible.

Njinga knew how to use her military skills to gain alliance advantages. In 1630, even at a low point of her military power, she used guerrilla tactics to disrupt the slave trade so much that it affected the profitability of the Portuguese colony, forcing the authorities to begin new negotiations with her.[105] Despite the official negotiations, Njinga carried on her guerrilla campaigns and by 1633 her impact on the slave trade was so significant (reducing the export of slaves from 13,000 in 1630 to almost none three years later) that it was impossible for the Portuguese to carry on fighting her.[106]

In the early part of her reign, the Portuguese were the only European power with whom Njinga had to contend. But in 1641 the Dutch West India Company seized Luanda and Njinga seized the chance of a European ally that might help her drive out the Portuguese. At this point she was causing the Portuguese so much difficulty that they identified her as 'the most powerful adversary that has ever existed in this Ethiopia [Africa]'.[107] The Dutch West India Company was aware of the impact an alliance with a character as formidable as Njinga would have on the Portuguese.[108] They were no doubt further enticed by the fact that Njinga's dominance of

Matamba meant she could easily export slaves, selling to the Dutch as many as 13,000 slaves in some years.[109]

Njinga's alliance with the Dutch allowed her to amass an army of 80,000 people, well armed with Dutch munitions.[110] She became the pre-eminent power in the region by the mid 1640s, seizing back much of her lost territory and raising concerns among local leaders. In October 1646 she led an attack against the Portuguese with 4,000 men in a mixed contingent of Dutch and African forces with a combined strength of about 14,300. The battle was a success, with 3,000 enemy killed.[111]

The Portuguese were determined to remove the Dutch from West Africa – but to do so they needed to disrupt the alliance between Njinga and their European enemy. In March 1646, Portugal attacked Njinga with a huge army, including 400 Portuguese officers, 30,000 African soldiers and various weapons including field artillery and archers.[112] Njinga had prepared for the arrival of the Portuguese-led force by building bridges across a river, in order to make them sitting ducks for her soldiers. However, the Portuguese circumvented these and other defences, and, despite an epic battle, won the day.[113] By 1648 they had pushed the Dutch out. Njinga once again escaped, although her sisters Kambu and Funji were captured and Funji was later executed.

From this point on, Njinga's main strategic goal was retaining her possessions rather than driving out the Portuguese. She was by this stage in her sixties and, perhaps, finally reaching a lower ebb of energy. The Portuguese still took Njinga's power seriously. In the early 1650s there was a clear awareness among Portuguese officials both in Luanda and Lisbon that Njinga's military power and personal character made signing a treaty with her far preferable to fighting her.[114]

But Njinga's strategic goal of securing her own territory through the manipulation of external alliances did not disappear when the Dutch left Angola. She decided to find allies in Europe itself – specifically, in the Vatican.[115] Njinga took two Capuchin monks hostage in the late 1640s, in an effort to get messages to Rome, indicating her willingness to have further religious missions in her territories in exchange (presumably) for further support. The

Capuchins were Spanish, and Njinga's religious manoeuvrings gave her a chance to influence politics in the Vatican, to pursue a claim that the Portuguese had unjustly taken her territories.[116]

In fact, the manipulation of her religious beliefs was one of Njinga's most effective tactics in her alliances both with European powers and her own people. When she was acting as the diplomatic envoy for her brother, Njinga was baptised in the cathedral in Luanda under the name Ana de Sousa.[117] Her religious beliefs appear to have been pragmatic, flipping between Christianity and local practices according to political demands at the time, and often combining them for maximum impact.[118] Her devotion to Catholicism undoubtedly increased when it would buy the greatest benefits from Portugal or help gain support from the Vatican. After concluding a final treaty with Portugal in 1656 (another triumph – including her recognition as queen and the release of her sister Kambu, all while avoiding paying further tribute),[119] Njinga organised a public ceremony in front of a church she had built after her conversion to Christianity. In front of a crowd including 2,000 members of her army, she brandished her bow and shouted, 'Who can ever defeat this bow?' Her soldiers replied, 'No one, No one!' Njinga continued, 'Only Maniputo, King of Portugal can defeat it, and now I say to all of you that I have just made peace with him . . . now it is the time that I leave this bow.'[120] She discarded her bow. Njinga was seventy-four, and she had held her kingdom through decades of violence, betrayal and outright war.

In 1663 Njinga succumbed to a final illness. Twenty thousand soldiers and commoners congregated after her death to stage a play that re-enacted her many military victories.[121] She was buried with a fortune worth the same amount as a nobleman's estate in Rome.[122] And while Njinga may have taken power in a context where female rule was unusual, in eighty of the next hundred years women ruled her former kingdom.[123]

Njinga's military leadership, while recognised at the time, caused difficulties for European adversaries shocked by the idea of a woman in military command. As a result, European commentators made much of Njinga's exceptional status: it was true that she was both a military commander and a woman, but she was not a recognisable type of European woman – and therefore certainly not one worthy of emulation. European chroniclers emphasised the deficiencies of her brand of womanhood, in particular dwelling on her sexual excesses and the more grim aspects of her cultural practices, in an effort to explain why it was that a woman could be such a successful leader and general.

Njinga thoroughly subverted European expectations of appropriate womanhood. While Queen Elizabeth I explained to her forces at Tilbury that she had the heart and stomach of a king inside the body of a feeble woman, Njinga announced to her people in the 1640s that she was, in fact, a man; she ordered her husbands to dress as women.[124] A Captain Fuller, who was appointed by the Dutch to assist Njinga in her fight against the Portuguese, took particular note of the queen's gender-bending practices. Not only did she dress as a man, she kept male concubines with women's names and made them dress as women.[125] Antonio Cavazzi, one of the European missionaries who knew Njinga, wrote that she was

> the most barbarous & cruel woman that there had ever been in the world . . . for the space of forty years, each one worse than the last, as will be seen from the story of her life. I will only add that she was a sea of lust, & had more Concubines than the three most famous prostitutes in the world had lovers; she surpassed the Tyrants in barbarity, the lions & tigers in cruelty, the harpies in wrath, & the poisonous snakes in the ferocity she showed in her lair, shedding more blood in peace than others in war.[126]

Njinga's sexual appetites were noteworthy, even to her own people. One member of the court was sufficiently perturbed by her sexuality that he tried to curb her behaviour. Njinga responded by requiring him to watch his son's murder, and then killing him too.[127]

Diminishing female leaders by dwelling on their unusual sexual appetites or practices is a fairly common tactic. Frederick the Great of Prussia once said of Catherine the Great, 'A woman is always a woman, and in feminine government, the cunt has more influence than a firm policy guided by straight reason.'[128] If the sexual excesses of male rulers were deemed to disqualify them from the ranks of political or martial heroes then there would be very few left in the annals of history.

If Njinga's sexuality was not enough to shock outside observers, her reported religious practices were sure to do so — especially because many of her contemporary Western observers were religious missionaries and had a particular stake in portraying her heathen practices in as compelling a light as possible, so as to burnish their own reputations if they succeeded in her conversion. There is evidence that Njinga engaged in ritual sacrifice, which in turn may have included eating the hearts or arterial blood of victims. To conduct the sacrifice, the queen dressed as a man,

> hanging about her the Skins of Beasts, before and behind, with a Sword about her Neck, an Ax at her Girdl, and a Bowe and Arrows in her Hand, leaping according to their Custom . . . when she thinks she has made a show long enough, in a Masculine manner . . . she takes a broad Feather and sticks it through the holes of her boar'd Nose, for a sign of War. She . . . begins with the first of those appointed to be sacrific'd, and cutting off his head, drinks a great draught of his blood.[129]

Ogilby's *Africa*, a compendium guide, noted that Njinga

> and her people lead an unsettled life, roving up and down from place to place . . . before any enterprize undertaken, though of meanest concern, they ask counsel of the Devil; to which end they have an Idol, to whom they sacrifice a living Person, of the wisest and comeliest they can pick out.[130]

The reality of Njinga's religious practices cannot be determined from these accounts alone, but they do indicate how she was perceived outside Angola.

Whether or not Njinga engaged in extensive or occasional canni- balism, and if she did so, whether or not she enjoyed it or simply did it to demonstrate her religious bona fides, is a matter of debate.[131] There is certainly evidence of practices that would have appeared particularly eye-popping to outside observers. The Imbangala religion that Njinga used to prop up her support had an unusual practice of infanticide, where babies were pounded in a mortar in order to make an ointment that would provide invincibility to warriors.[132] Njinga seems to have enthusiastically thrown herself into this prac- tice.[133] Njinga and such practices were entirely alien to Europeans.

Yes, central west Africa had a woman general, but it was also the sort of place where people drank the arterial blood of enemies and made babies into magic paste – in other words, it was not remotely normal and certainly not worthy of emulation.

It is hardly surprising that the more lurid aspects of Njinga's reign dominated the way she was remembered in Europe. After all, she had her race and gender working against her. Rather than focusing on her military exploits and the quite extraordinary facts of her reign, Njinga became a byword for salacious brutality. Her memory in Europe became so associated with the sensational aspects of her story that the Marquis de Sade used Njinga to illustrate a story of how sexually driven women are not only lustful but bloodthirsty, black widows who kill their lovers after sex, destroyers rather than creators.[134] Hegel also used Njinga, unnamed, in his lectures on history, relaying the story of an African ruler from the past who 'is said to have pounded her own son in a mortar, to have besmeared herself with the blood, and to have the blood of pounded children at hand. She is said to have driven away or put to death all the males'.[135] These stories ensured Njinga was remembered not as a general, not for her long reign, not for her skilful manipulation of the Europeans around her, but as a sexually promiscuous barbarian eventually subdued by Christianity.

Njinga's reign was nothing short of extraordinary. Her military skill and ability to command kept her in power for an astonishing period of time, under conditions that were violent and changeable, and which led to constant shifts in power. During Njinga's rule Portugal sent thirteen governors to their colony. After her death the kingdom she had controlled passed to her sister and then to four others, in eighteen years, with each transition ending in bloodshed. To rule for forty years in this context was a transcendent achievement.

A casual glance at the history of war might suggest that women have played virtually no role as military leaders. After all, queens had generals who did the battling for them, and female generals themselves have been very rare. Yet scratch the surface and this silence might actually speak of something else. Female rulers were interested and competent in military matters. Women generals had skill and power. Contemporaries were so overcome at the shock of seeing a woman at the head of an army, however, that they did not record tactics or strategies, or tell many tales of their inspirational leadership, as they would have done while following a great male general. And when such leadership was recorded, it was easily dismissed. Joan of Arc was a witch, Boudicca was a barbarian and Njinga was part of a culture so 'other' as to be almost completely alien to Western observers. Erasing women's military leadership capacity from the historical record made it that much more difficult for women to be taken seriously as military or political leaders.

And while women generals were rare, they were not alone on the battlefield in a sea of men, a sole woman in a band of brothers. In fact, battlefields of the past relied on the labour of women, and this labour has been dismissed as commonly as the exploits of female generals.

2

Camp Followers

IN 1880, VISITORS to the markets of Les Halles in Paris might have noticed an especially striking woman sitting at her vegetable stall. In her mid-fifties, with black hair and unwrinkled skin, she had an expression of 'courage and energy',[1] which was perhaps unsurprising, given her past. Annette Drevon was a *cantinière* in the French army, a woman officially deputised to sell food and drink to the soldiers. At the Battle of Magenta in 1859, Annette was attached to the second regiment of Zouaves. During the battle two Austrian soldiers seized the regimental flag. Annette got it back: she killed the first soldier with a sabre and the second with two shots from her revolver.[2] The regiment's colonel pinned his own Cross of the Legion of Honour to her chest in honour of her actions.[3]

Annette was still serving during the Franco-Prussian War of 1870, where she shot another soldier, this time a German who either insulted her or attempted to steal her Cross; she was sentenced to death but pardoned by Prince Frederick Charles of Hesse, and returned to France. She later received a small pension from Marshal MacMahon, who had commanded the French troops at Magenta, which she used to set up her vegetable stall.[4]

Annette Drevon's story is a useful reminder that for well over 400 years the normal battlefield was full of ordinary women, who were not only essential to the conduct of war but also demonstrated bravery, physical strength and the ability to stand up to tough conditions – all the things military leaders of the late twentieth century fretted that women could not do.

The extraordinary prevalence of war in Europe during the early modern era meant that violence, fighting and death were everywhere. Between the 1690s and the Napoleonic Wars, 16 million people died in combat in Europe and its colonies – and this figure excludes deaths from the Thirty Years War.[5] In the hundred years of the eighteenth century, Europe was only at peace for sixteen, which was actually an improvement on the sixteenth and seventeenth centuries, neither of which managed more than ten years of peace.[6] War was common and the lines between military and civilian life were blurry, sometimes non-existent.

Women were present on the battlefield in droves. At 'no time in European history were so many women engaged in warfare – as spies, foragers, artillery personnel, or soldiers – than between 1500 and 1650'.[7] And even afterwards, throughout the eighteenth century, and as late as the latter half of the nineteenth, women were on battlefields selling food and drink and doing laundry. Often, but not always, they were accompanying their husbands. These women may not have been fighting (although they sometimes did), but they were crucial to the armies they supported. Warfare would not have been possible without them. The simple fact of the presence of so many women, and their evident capabilities, is a sharp rebuke to the more recent discussions swirling around whether women have the stamina, strength and general fortitude to cope with life on the battlefield.

Battlefield women provided services to soldiers – not just to their own husbands – and they were integral to warfare from the early 1500s to the mid-nineteenth century. This period of over 450 years can be divided up according to the number of women accompanying armies and the roles they performed. In the early modern period, roughly from 1500 to 1650, women were part of the 'campaign community', the extremely large military force of the day. After 1650, militaries reduced the overall numbers of women following the army through several mechanisms, including allowing only soldiers' wives in limited number to accompany the army. These women officially and unofficially provided a range of services, in-cluding supplying food, alcohol and other necessities; doing laundry and sewing; and supplementing rations with foraged or stolen food. By the nineteenth century military wives still accompanied the army, but they did so in dwindling numbers. In France, women provi-sioners called *cantinières* (drink sellers) and *vivandières* (sutlers) continued to provide services until the early twentieth century.

Women were able to participate in the armed forces because of the organisation of European armies. The European army in the early modern era was huge, around the same size as a large city. The Swedish forces of Gustavus Adolphus were bigger than the towns of Bordeaux, Turin and Strasbourg.[8] Henri II of France had an army of 50,000 men, and a baggage train nearly the same size; all together, it meant that Henri had more mouths to feed than the city of Milan and almost as many as London.[9] Cities, however, were full of logistical support, with transport links designed to bring food from the country into town. Armies on the move had no such systems, and catering for them was remarkably difficult. An army of 30,000 men required twenty tons of bread a day, which in turn meant it needed 10,000 pounds of flour. To get enough meat required 1,500 sheep or 150 bullocks.[10] An army of 60,000 required 40,000 gallons of beer. Moving all these goods and chattels required wagons and horses, as many as 2,500 for an army of 5,000.[11]

A disorganised state requiring a very large army faced a difficult problem: how to feed everyone. There were three possible solutions, and often all were in play at the same time. The state could provide the army with as much as possible, which often meant coming to an arrangement with a town and using that town's supply lines; the army could 'live off the land' and pillage for what it needed; or entrepreneurial individuals could be allowed to follow the army and sell soldiers the requisite goods. Requiring pillage and allowing small businesses to provide for the army created a scenario in which women were necessary to operations, as they were in the early modern period, or a useful adjunct to them, as they were later on. Women could pillage alongside men, or even instead of them if the men were fighting, and they could provide useful services like laundry, food and drink.

The very large armies of Europe partly owed their size to immense accompanying baggage trains. An army on the march dragged its artillery, but it also carried ovens, cooking pots, giant cauldrons for laundry, and stalls and counters to set up shops, mobile taverns and food stations.[12] The pastors of the town of Bergen op Zoom described the Spanish Army of Flanders in 1622 thus: 'such a small army with so many carts, baggage, horses, nags, sutlers, lackeys, women, children, and a rabble which numbered far more than the army itself'.[13] The Scottish mercenary Sir James Turner, writing in the 1680s, described the baggage train as the Romans did: '*impedimentia*, hindrances'.[14]

The necessity of provisioning (where it was possible) and pillaging for resources (when provisioning failed) meant that women and children were an important part of early modern armies: 'campaign communities'[15] that relied on a large number of non-combatants for success. The army was a city on the move – and like all cities, also contained women and children whose homes were effectively in these mobile military cities. Any distinction between the lines of battle and the home front were hard to make, particularly given that 'living off the land' inevitably brought the campaign community in direct contact with the civilian world.

The baggage train may have been an encumbrance, but without it the army could not survive long enough to fight. Alongside the essential services they provided, women inevitably had sex with the men around them.

The view that 'camp followers' were all whores has obscured the nature of women's military contributions. A cursory glance at military history would seem to confirm this view. After all, in the mid-sixteenth century German armies had *Hurenweibels* – whore sergeants. James Turner describes these 'Rulers or Marshals of the Whores . . . I have seen them ride, keep Troop, rank and file very well, after their Captain . . . and a Banner with them, which one of the women carried'.[16] But a closer look reveals that the whore sergeants were marshalling women for far more than sexual services. A German military observer noted in 1598 that the *Hurenweibel*'s role was to keep the women and children of the baggage train orderly, so that they were 'running, pouring out, fetching food and drink, knowing how to behave mostly with regard to the needs of others, and taking it in turn to do what is necessary according to orders'.[17]

There is no doubt that women on campaign provided sexual services for soldiers, and that their ability to do so is part of the reason they were tolerated by authorities. Providing sexual services for an army on the move theoretically reduced the chances of that same army raping its way through the countryside and hopefully improved sexual hygiene, lowering the impact of venereal disease. Regulated prostitutes accompanied some armies for precisely these reasons, with specific rules and often under military discipline. The Spanish army in the Netherlands in the mid-sixteenth century, for example, allowed four to eight prostitutes for each company of 200 men – although apparently opinion varied about the appropriate number.[18]

But to assume that all camp followers were whores, or worse, that they were *only* whores, reflects just how oddly gender influences our understanding of history. To begin with, not all members of the campaign community were female. Non-combatant men, such as blacksmiths and carpenters, also accompanied armies.[19] The men who served as soldiers likely had a lot of sex. They may even have had sex for money. But their sexual activity didn't define them: they were soldiers who happened to have sex. Women in the campaign community may have been whores, but they were also laundresses, nurses, common-law wives and providers of essential food and drink to soldiers. Just because they had sex (and even if they did it for money) does not mean that sex was all they did.[20] It is, however, a convenient way to dismiss and undermine the importance of their service.

Assuming that camp followers were whores also stems from ideas about social class. Relationships between women in the military camp and soldiers were common; sometimes, women followed their partners to war, and new relationships began in the army itself. But marriage itself was much less regulated in the lower classes that formed the bulk of armies. Informal but long-term relationships were common, and widows often quickly remarried after their husbands died, practices that looked scandalous to the outside world but were both normal and practical in the army itself.[21]

Marriages of convenience also arose. A sixteenth-century German observer wrote:

> The German soldiers, no sooner than an expedition arrives, saddle themselves with frivolous and loose women with whom they contract 'May Marriages' whom they drag here and there just as millers do

their sacks. The soldiers enhance the situation by pretending that in war they cannot get along without women; they are needed to take care of clothes, equipment and valuables.[22]

These relationships often, but not always, ended with the end of the campaign. During the campaign, however, both husbands and wives benefitted: the men received assistance and the women were often safer with the army than as a civilian in the army's path.

Robert Monro, a Scottish soldier serving in Sweden in the 1630s, noted that soldiers' wives were particularly steadfast:

> in my judgment no women are more faithfull, more chast, more loving, more obedient nor more devout, then Souldiers wives, as daily experience doth witnesse, and none have more reason to be so, then some of them, whose husbands doe daily undergoe all dangers of body for their sakes, not fearing death it selfe, to relieve and keep them from dangers.[23]

Following the army was not restricted to the lower classes. Officers' wives were also part of the military community, particularly in the eighteenth and nineteenth centuries. But it is worth noting that military women, whatever their class, defied any stereotype that equated femininity with a flower-like delicacy. Women on campaign had to be, and were, strong and brave in order to survive.

Wives could help their husbands enormously. They were able to

> provide, buy and dress their husbands meat when their husbands are on duty, or newly come from it, they bring in fewel for fire, and wash their linens, and in such manner of employments a Souldiers wife may be helpful to others, and gain money to her husband and her self; especially they are useful in Camps and Leaguers, being permitted (which should not be refused them) to go some miles from Camp to buy Victuals and other Necessaries.[24]

Women even supplied their husbands with sustenance and support while the battle was raging. A Bavarian sergeant said of his wife, who had delivered him food despite heavy artillery fire,

> we were surprised at her boldness, and the officers called out to her to inquire how she had escaped the hail of shot and shell in which

she could so easily have been wounded or killed. 'If my husband is hit,' she said, 'I must look after him, on campaign just as much as at home.'[25]

Just being on the battlefield to deliver food or munitions was brave. Some wives were heroic. A Mrs Stone, 'rather of a small and handsome make', had accompanied her husband during the American Revolution,

> through most of the hardships our armies underwent in America . . . no consideration of fear could make her leave her husband's side, thro' *nine engagements* in which he was concerned; in the course of which she twice helped to carry him off wounded from the field of battle; and it is a fact that can be testified by living witnesses . . . that at the siege of Louissburg [*sic*] at a time when many of our troops were killed, she supplied the living with the powder cartridges of the dead and animated the men in the ranks next to her by her words and actions.[26]

In fact, women played an important role in supporting artillery positions, and may have even stepped in to fire the guns themselves. The American Revolution's Molly Pitcher, who apparently took over her husband's gun when he fell at the Battle of Monmouth, may be the most famous example. Molly Pitcher is likely a composite figure, a post-war invention based on a number of stories of women stepping in for their husbands. Margaret Corbin was with her husband John when he was killed in 1776 and she took his place; while firing the cannon she was seriously wounded, taken captive by the English and left permanently disabled.[27] In recognition of her service she was given both a military pension[28] and sent to serve with the Corps of Invalids at West Point, where she was buried.[29] Enough women clearly took over their husbands' artillery positions that the story of Molly Pitcher resonated.

Women in the military community were part of a multi-generational tradition that included entire families. The British Army during the American Revolution was accompanied by as many as 12,000 children.[30] Boys born to military women invariably became soldiers, and girls usually followed in their mothers' footsteps as military wives or provisioners. Accompanying the army was a way of life, just as soldiering itself was a way of life.[31] And just like soldiers, once the war ended, the women of the camp community could be bereft. As one woman said at the end of the Thirty Years War: 'I was born in war, I have no home, no country and no friends; war is all my wealth and now whither shall I go?'[32] One French *cantinière*, Marie Tête-de-Bois, fought with Napoleon's forces at Waterloo; she was wounded but continued to serve. Marie 'preferred death in the final stand' rather than a return to civilian life and destitution.[33]

In the British Army, wives continued to accompany their husbands up until the Crimean War. *The Times* issued a report from the Crimean front, a snippet that provides a clear picture of the full spectrum of life as an army wife on campaign. The wives were well looked after.

> The men build them snug houses of leafy branches; they make little fortunes as laundresses, and until the pestilence . . . smote the army and fell upon them with extraordinary fatality, they seemed the happiest and most contented beings in the camp, where their services as excellent foragers and washerwomen were fully appreciated.[34]

Military women, whether they were wives, prostitutes or entrepreneurs, performed many of the tasks they would have performed in a regular house in a regular town. As the Duke of Newcastle wrote in 1754, 'the soldiers would be disgruntled, if the women did not accompany them to do the cooking, washing and sewing, and to serve other purposes for which women naturally go with the army'.[35] Laundry appears to have been a crucially important task; even during periods when authorities acted to reduce the number of women accompanying the military, special provision was made for laundresses. During the French Revolution women were banned from military camps, but four laundresses per battalion were allowed.[36] Washington's Continental Army set out price guides for laundresses, right down to 'Stock, Stockings and Handkerchiefs, Six Pence, each'.[37]

Like laundry, nursing was a traditionally female role. It is no surprise that women informally nursed their husbands and other soldiers, and such activity had a real impact on soldiers' lives.

Restrictions reduced the number of wives accompanying British forces during the American Revolution, and this had the knock-on consequence that British soldiers lacked the experienced nurses who accompanied troops in Europe.[38] Even so, the recognition of wifely nursing was so well understood that Lady Christian Henrietta Acland asked for and received permission to enter enemy lines to nurse her husband, wounded in battle in 1777 in America.[39]

For a period of several hundred years, women accompanying the military may have been wives, and they may have been whores, but they were certainly also entrepreneurs who did far more than take in laundry and look after the sick and wounded. Sutlers, or civilian merchants accompanying military forces, sold food, drink, tobacco, soap and other goods to an army on the march.

In fact, the creation of official or semi-official sutlers and laundresses allowed militaries to impose a degree of order on the great mass of wives, girlfriends and other camp followers forming the long and unwieldy tail. In general, militaries had regulations for the number of sutlers that were allowed to accompany a regiment, and even what they were allowed to charge for their services.

In the German military, these women were called *Marketenderin* and wore a blue cockade in their hats to indicate their role (one historian describes their attire as an 'undeniably saucy outfit',[40] but this may say more about the salacious imagination of the historian than the actual outfit). Frederick the Great apparently encountered two *Marketenderinnen* when he went to inspect his army from a hill near Potsdam. The women had set up their stalls on the hill and refused to move on the grounds that Frederick could see his army from anywhere, but their trade depended on a good pitch.[41]

Of course, the lines between wives and entrepreneurs were often blurry. In 1757 Frederick the Great's forces were facing off against Austria. It was a stifling June day, and the enterprising wives of the Prussian regiment broke into an icehouse and sold the ice at a terrific profit to soldiers wilting in the heat – an act that was both profitable for the women and beneficial to the soldiers. The threat of hot weather was serious – 105 Prussian soldiers died from oppressive heat in a battle five years later.[42] The provision of water on the battlefield was not just for refreshment. It was an essential service, as water was necessary for gun crews to swab out cannons before they could be reloaded.[43]

Battle offered women entrepreneurs greater opportunities for profit. It wasn't just ice that soldiers might buy in the midst of the fight. A quick tot of booze was always popular, and soldiers would pay almost any price for alcohol in battle if death was around the corner.[44] During the American Revolution, sutlers could raise the prices as high as they liked, and soldiers would still buy their liquid courage. Commanders, in turn, tried to limit profiteering and alcohol consumption by limiting sutlers.[45]

The French system was particularly well developed and persisted almost until the outbreak of the First World War. The *cantinières* and *vivandières* were employees of the War Ministry from 1792 onwards – but always as civilians. The new French Republic believed that military service was a duty that gave the rights of citizenship, including the vote and the right to hold office,[46] but there was no official enthusiasm for providing these rights to women, so they remained as civilian employees, not soldiers.

Even so, the French *cantinières* and *vivandières* adopted an unofficial uniform themselves in the 1830s, in a bid to persuade the officialdom that they were an integral part of military forces, rather than mere citizens. It included a hat (usually with a red, white and blue cockade) and a feminised version of the regimental uniform, including a jacket and skirt worn over pants and boots.[47] They carried a *tonnelet*, a small, decorative barrel used to store the spirits they sold. The French system persisted throughout the nineteenth century, including during the Franco-Prussian War; and it was the defeat of Napoleon III's Second Empire in that war which spelled the start of a forty-year process of removing the *cantinières* from the army.[48]

Women also provided for men and for the military in a different way. Especially in the early modern army, but even later on, women's labour was important because of their ability to pillage. Pillage was necessary to supplement the poor – or non-existent – rations provided to badly paid troops. A German soldier called Peter Hagendorf kept a diary of his exploits as a soldier for twenty-five years. In it he tots up his wife's pillage tally with pride: 'bedclothing . . . and a large pitcher holding four quarts of wine, as well as finding dresses and two silver belts'. Later on, she acquired 'a ball gown made of taffeta'.[49] A Catholic priest complained about the 'abominable' wives of Swedish soldiers, who cut produce from local gardens 'as soon as a single green leaf peeped out' and even sold it for a profit in the markets.[50] The remarkable Christian Davies worked as a sutler (and also as a soldier while dressed as a man — we'll meet her again in her male disguise in the next chapter) and stole a variety of livestock as well as movable goods she could sell at a profit.[51]

Pillaging sometimes helped a *vivandière* set up business in the first place. In the French Revolutionary army, women or their husbands stole carts, wagons and horses in order to set up shop; and of course, the sale of sundries alongside alcohol and food would help the family business turn a better profit, so theft could add to the wares for sale, too.[52]

Pillaging and foraging was useful throughout the nineteenth century. The British soldier George Bell recalled many incidences of pillage in his memoirs of the Peninsular War. He describes the Irish wives of his regiment, particularly one Mrs Skiddy, 'as broad as a big turtle' and a 'devoted soldier's wife, and a right good one, an excellent forager', who always had something for her husband when all the rest were starving. The exemplary Mrs Skiddy also carried her wounded husband on her back, noting that she did so along with 'knapsack, firelock, and all, as strong as Sampson . . . I carried him half a league'.[53] Bell also describes behaviour that (while profitable) was less laudable. At the end of battles, he notes, 'it was marvellous how quickly the dead, and often the wounded, were stripped on the battle-field by the camp-followers of the two great armies — an unhallowed trade, and no stopping it'.[54]

No matter the role they played, women accompanying the military had to be tough. One German soldier remarked that women usually carried

at least 50 or 60 pounds. Since the soldier carries provisions or other materials, he loads straw and wood on her, to say nothing of the fact that many of them carry one, two, or more children on their back. Normally, however, aside from the clothing they are wearing, they carry for the man one pair of breeches, one pair of stockings, one pair of shoes . . . one pan, one pot, one or two spoons, one sheet, one overcoat, one tent, and three poles. They receive no wood for cooking in their billets, so they pick it up on the way. And to add to their fatigue they normally lead a small dog on a rope or even carry it with them in bad weather.[55]

Women accompanying the military were subject to military discipline, especially when their presence was more organised. In fact, they were easier to punish, because unlike soldiers, women were fairly expendable.[56] Martha May was one of the many women who helped the army fight by providing her husband and other soldiers with food, drink and laundry services. In 1758 Martha was incarcerated by the colonel of her husband's regiment, Henry Bouquet, for apparent insubordination. She wrote to him,

> I beg and hope you'll take it into Consideration that it was the Love I hd for my Poor husband and no [bad] will to Yr Honour, which was the cause of abusing so good a Colonel as you are . . . I have been a Wife 22 years and have Traveld with my Husband every Place or Country the Company Marcht too and have workt very hard ever since I was in the Army. I hope yr honour will be so Good as to pardon me this time that I may go with my Poor Husband one more time to carry him and my good officers water in hottest Battles as I have done before.[57]

We don't know if her petition was a success, but military punishment for women ran on a diverse spectrum. One 'common' punishment British military women faced was the whirligig:

> This was a kind of circular wooden cage which turned on a pivot: and when set in motion, whirled round with such an amazing velocity, that the delinquent became extremely sick and commonly emptied his or her body through every aperture.[58]

'Regiment women' who accompanied British forces abroad could be 'drummed out' of the regiment, just as men could. The consequences of such an action were serious: women who left had no means to secure their livelihood, no source of food and no means of returning home.[59]

And of course, military punishment also meant the lash. The British General Pulteney wrote to the Duke of Cumberland in 1745 of a woman convicted of petty larceny (in other words, pillage):

> her tail was immediately turned up before the door of the house, where the robbery was committed, and the Drummer of the Regiment tickled her with 100 very good lashes, since which time the ladies have behaved like angels. The sex is not the worse for correction.[60]

Women suspected of being mere prostitutes (rather than official or semi-official camp followers) were subject to even more terrible punishment. In 1685 the French authorities ordered that any prostitutes found within two leagues of a military camp should have their nose and ears slit. Eighteenth-century ordinances were equally harsh. A French directive of 1750 states regarding women discovered in the garrison: 'if . . . the women are strangers and are roaming around' then the commander should have the women 'exhibited mounted on wooden horses, shall have them run the switch gauntlet and drive them out of the city'. The wooden horse was designed with sharp edges so it would inflict maximum pain; sometimes, the woman 'exhibited' on it would have heavy weights attached to her feet to intensify the punishment.[61]

The fact that prostitutes would appear near armies (for obvious business reasons) made it important to have official or semi-official permission. But even officially sanctioned camp followers could not escape moral judgement. 'Respectable' women were unlikely to be camp followers, and this class judgement not only left room to respect an officer's wife (she would, after all, have been a lady) but also to judge and sneer at the ordinary women accompanying their husbands and lovers. These women simply did not behave as respectable women did. One officer in Washington's army described the women in the baggage train as 'the ugliest in the world to be collected . . . their Visage dress etc.' along with their children,

> some with two others with three & four children and few with none – I could not help pitying the poor innocent Creatures – their way of living and treatment with the many low & Scandalous examples . . . the furies who inhabit the infernal Regions can never be painted half so hideous as those women.[62]

Accompanying the military placed women in great danger. The baggage train was indeed an encumbrance, especially if a military had to move quickly. A French colonel described one retreat in 1809:

> We were obliged to abandon our artillery and the baggage train. The wounded, the women and children had to stay behind and were pitilessly murdered by the Spanish less than two minutes later, and God knows with what refined cruelty. It still makes me shudder.[63]

Life in the military meant being in the line of fire. A British soldier wrote to his brother in the 1780s describing the dangers:

> the enemy's gun and mortar boats came over last night, and fired . . . on this occasion, a soldier's wife was killed, as she was hastily dressing herself in the tent, in order to seek some place of refuge. Some others were slightly wounded.[64]

After Waterloo, a British sergeant major noted that 'many women were found among the slain . . . as is common in the camp, the camp followers wore male attire, with nearly as martial a bearing as the soldiers'.[65]

Women accompanying the military were in what military historian John Lynn calls the combat zone, which is

> best defined by the intensity and immediacy of danger and by the ability to do direct harm to the enemy . . . the full reality of war lives here. Modern armies regard it as an innovation to send *some* women into combat, but in the campaign community *all* women stood in harm's way.[66]

It would be odd to imagine that the women accompanying an army, exposed as they were to all the dangers of the military world, didn't pick up arms and fight. In 1643, in the earlier stages of the English Civil War, a regiment of troops was recalled from Ireland to support King Charles. Rumours swirled that they were accompanied by a regiment of women, and that 'these were weaponed too; and when these degenerate into cruelty, there are none more bloody'.[67] Indeed, when 120 Irish women were taken prisoner at Nantwich they were discovered to have long knives with them, causing a furore in the press. The dubiously named *True Informer* excitedly reported that the knives in question were half a yard long, with a hook at the end, 'made not only to stab but to tear the flesh from the very bones'.[68] The likeliest explanation for these knives, however, is that the women weren't soldiers; they were camp followers, and they needed the knives to help them with pillage and self-defence.[69]

The women of the campaign community did fight. The Bishop of Albi, on the battlefield of Leucate in southern France to administer to the dying in 1637, came upon the bodies of several women in uniform. 'These were the real men,' he was told by the Castilian soldiers, 'since those who had fled, including certain officers, had conducted themselves like women'.[70]

Madeleine Kintelberger was a *vivandière* accompanying the French Seventh Hussar Regiment at Austerlitz in 1806, along with her soldier husband and their six children. The regiment was under heavy attack from Russian forces when her husband was killed by a cannonball, and her children seriously wounded. Madeleine herself had taken a cannonball to the arm, virtually slicing it off below the shoulder. As the Russian Cossacks approached, she scooped up a sword to defend her children, receiving further wounds in both her arms before the family was taken prisoner. Madeleine was six months pregnant and gave birth in captivity. Her bravery was rewarded with a pension from Napoleon.[71] Examples of *cantinières* fighting are 'legion'.[72]

Even as late as the Crimean War, lines in the combat zone between wives and soldiers were blurry. Lady Errol, whose husband was the Earl of Errol, caused a stir in the Crimea. Fanny Duberly, another army wife, complained that Lady Errol '*always* goes about with a brace of loaded revolvers in her belt!'[73] She rode (along with her French maid) on a mule with the army, and '[b]efore long, their mounts were festooned with the rifles of the men too weak to carry them'.[74] As we will see in the next chapter, these women on the battlefield alongside men undoubtedly made it easier for those women who wanted to be soldiers themselves and dressed as men in order to fight.

While the army relied on women, there is no doubt that the imperfections of a military that could only feed itself through pillage or a 'camp train' was impeded in its duties. Commanders were stuck between the necessity of securing nursing, laundry, food and other services, and the challenges of accommodating a large and unwieldy baggage train. One solution to this problem was to restrict the women who accompanied the military by allowing only a certain number of wives per regiment or company. The British Army went through a series of attempts to reduce the number of wives accompanying their husbands in the army. In 1671 an order of the Coldstream Guards insisted that captains must approve the marriages of soldiers under their command, under threat of being cashiered with loss of pay; this order was extended to the entire army in 1685 and remained official policy for 200 years.[75] Married men were problematic because they might bring wives, or worry about wives at home; unmarried men were problematic because their sexual pursuits led to problems with local women and the spread of sexually transmitted disease. The challenge of what do to with marriage (and therefore with wives) appears to have been common in European armies.[76]

James Wolfe, who would later gain fame as the general who defeated the French in Quebec and drove them from Canada, wrote in 1751 that his 'Officers are desired to discourage Matrimony amongst the men as much as possible. The Service suffers by the multitude of Women already in the Regiment.'[77] Wolfe's vociferous anti-marriage views may have been induced by his own failed courtship of a general's daughter, during which time he recalled, 'I committed more imprudent acts than in all my life before, I lived in the idlest, dissolute, abandoned manner that can be conceived. I have escaped at length, and am once again master of my reason.'[78] Wolfe disapproved of marriage, but his soldiers did not – more than half a dozen of his men married in the same year Wolfe issued his edict.[79]

General Wolfe, as he became, remained irritated by wives throughout his career. A British soldier, John Knox, wrote of his service in Quebec that the many privations, including 'swarming flies, short rations, dysentery and scurvy', were relieved only 'by the almost lethal spirits provided by the women sutlers, whose petticoats and leather stays, hanging up between the trees, drove Wolfe to fury'.[80]

Indeed, British commanding officers of the period appear to have been plagued by marriages (official and clandestine) and wives, warning that

> the long March and Embarkation that will soon follow must convince them that many Women in the regiment are very inconvenient, especially as some of them are not so industrious nor so useful to their Husbands as a Soldier's Wife ought to be.[81]

The regulation of wives did not mean their disappearance. By the 1750s between 4 and 6 women were allowed for each company of 100 men.[82] Women were still present in significant numbers – alongside Wellington's army of 60,000 men in 1813 there were 4,500 British wives, and 700 Portuguese and Spanish *cantinièras* and *vivandières*, all in all about 9 women for every 100 men.[83] In 1817 French military regulations allowed 'as an occasional indulgence and as tending to promote cleanliness and the convenience of the soldier, 4 married women per Troop or Company of 60 men . . . to be resident within the Barracks'.[84]

Whether wives were good or bad, helpful or a hindrance, no doubt depended on the wives – but more importantly on the rules for their participation. The British 95th Rifle Corps seems to have had a pragmatic handle on the situation, stating in its orders of 1801 that 'the marriage of soldiers being a matter of benefit to a regiment, of comfort to themselves, or of misery to both exactly in proportion as it is under good or bad regulations'.[85]

Restricting the women of the regiment to wives not only reduced overall numbers of women accompanying the military but also gave strength to the view that all those unmarried women who had followed the army in years gone by were not respectable. Florence Nightingale insisted that her nurses wear a uniform, writing: 'the rule about wearing the regular dress applies *particularly* to when they are *out of* Hospital. The necessity of distinguishing them *at once* from camp followers is particularly obvious when they are *not* engaged in hospital work'.[86] Once the decision was made to restrict the numbers of regimental women, and regularise their presence with official roles such as nursing, it heralded the end of the band of brothers and sisters. As logistics became more professional and concerns about the respectability of married women heightened, women were no longer necessary nor wanted in the army.

It is no coincidence that Florence Nightingale's nursing innovations began in the Crimean War in 1854, and that 1854 was the last time British wives were allowed to accompany their husbands (in an officially regulated capacity).[87] Many regiments sailed to the Crimea with wives and children – but not all the wives were allowed to come, and the ones that stayed behind were left destitute. Debate raged in Parliament as to whether married soldiers should be allowed, and whether accompanying wives simply induced more marriages and more hardship.[88] Any lingering debate was finished off by the shocking conditions in the Crimea, where hundreds of army wives lay sick in terrible conditions below the military hospital in Scutari.[89]

Another development ensured women would no longer accompany the army. The British Contagious Diseases Acts of the 1860s, designed to control venereal disease, reinforced the idea that camp followers were prostitutes that sapped the army of its strength. In 'the name of controlling venereal disease, maintaining discipline, and guarding the men's health', regimental women lost their legitimacy.[90] Regimental women, despite all they had done, were firmly placed in the category of prostitute – where they would remain in the historical imagination for generations. As we will see, even during the world wars of the twentieth century, the stigma of the camp follower tainted women's military mobilisation.

A growing judgemental morality also put paid to the French system of *cantinières* and *vivandières*. The women entrepreneurs accompanying French forces dwindled in number in the late nineteenth century when moral distaste for alcohol combined with a desire to build a more efficient army.[91] *Cantinières* were also no longer viable because they challenged the increasing French orthodoxy that citizenship was intimately linked to military service: if men got the right to vote because of their participation in the military, why shouldn't the women who also served their country? The authorities solved this problem by increasing male conscription and better organised alternatives for provisions. By 1906 the age of the *cantinière* was over,[92] and citizenship rights were safely restricted to men.

There is no doubt that a horde of women and children, shop stalls and counters, dragged on carts behind the army, was hardly the pinnacle of military organisation. There is also little doubt that the professionalisation of logistics had a dramatic impact on military performance. And while women were important to the function of the army, after the early modern period they were certainly not integral to it. So why are these women more than historical curiosities?

The women of the campaign community, regimental wives, *cantières*, *vivandières* – all demonstrate that women were strong, brave and physically able. They were not delicate, and no one expected the lower-class women who followed the military to be so. The officers' wives of the later nineteenth century may have been more of a surprise, but women were perfectly capable of coping with the rigours of military life, and some even thrived in it. The problems caused by camp followers were not caused by womanhood but by the design of warfare at the time. Women never demonstrated that they were weak, or cowardly, or unable to cope with life on the battlefield. But the system of which they were a part was replaced by a better system.

This peek into the lives of women accompanying the army also reveals something very important about military organisation: the military world prior to the nineteenth century was not an entirely masculine world. The image of a brave male soldier, with his band of brothers, writing letters to his sweetheart at home, is not universal. Prior to the nineteenth century a soldier's sweetheart was probably just around the corner, bringing water or selling food. So much of the way we imagine militaries rests on these images of men, together, in great danger while their wives and girlfriends wait at home. In fact, twentieth-century military culture, from propaganda to training, relied on the separation of women from men. An all-male environment toughened men up, and the image of the sweetheart waiting at home is a powerful propaganda tool. But the women of the campaign community, the *cantinières* and *vivandières*, the wives, the nurses, and the whores: they were part of a band of brothers and sisters. They were necessary to the project of war. And they were perfectly capable of hardship, bravery and violence, just the sort of attributes soldiers themselves required in order to survive in a dangerous military world. But when women left the battlefield, war changed so completely that it became normal to assume that they were absent for a reason. War had progressed so that they were no longer necessary, and it was not proper for them to be there.

3

Under Siege

IN 1472 BEAUVAIS was under siege. The forces of Charles the Bold, Duke of Burgundy, had encircled the French city, which was defended by fewer than 300 men. A young woman called Jeanne Laisnet[1] armed herself with a hatchet and led a band of women to the ramparts. These women 'occupied themselves by loading the cannon, pouring hot water, boiling oil, or molten lead on the heads of the besiegers, supplying the archers with arrows, or performing any other service their strength would allow'.[2] Despite this fierce defence, Charles's men began to climb the ramparts and one attempted to plant a flag to signify victory. Jeanne Hachette, as she became known, chopped off his hands, threw him from the ramparts and snatched the flag.[3] After nine hours of fighting the women were relieved by arriving troops. The battle raged on for nearly a month, and Jeanne and her band of women remained at the heart of the defence. When victory finally came, Jeanne carried the flag she had captured at the head of the French army. Every year since 1473 Beauvais has marked the occasion with a festival, including a procession led by a woman portraying Jeanne Hachette.

Jeanne, like many ordinary military heroes, may or may not have done all that was claimed. But it is true that the women of Beauvais were so critical to the defence of the town that a grateful Louis XI released them from the sumptuary laws. Demonstrating an early French commitment to fashion, and indicating that stereotypes about how best to please ladies have a long history, the king granted the women of the town the right to wear whatever they wanted.[4]

Jeanne Hachette was one of innumerable women who fought while defending against a siege. The predominant form of military action in Europe between 1495 and 1715,[5] between 1550 and 1714

49

sieges were ten times more common than pitched battles.[6] In fact, the military historian Frank Tallett concludes that the style of war in this period was weighted so heavily to sieges that 'it might reasonably be asked why battles occurred at all'.[7] A combination of effective fortification and artillery that was not quite effective enough to be decisive led to stalemates between attacking armies and defending cities. Sieges during this period could last for months or even years.

Sieges were battles of attrition, scenes of constant attack and defence, with astonishingly high death rates. Defending forces could suffer a loss of 50 per cent of their men. After the city of Frankfurt fell in 1631, there were so many bodies that they could not be buried. Instead, they were 'cast by heapes in great ditches, above a hundred in every grave'.[8]

Sieges were the site of appalling atrocities against women. But they were also places where women demonstrated military command, heroism and courage. Women in sieges were both victims and fighters, in part because during a siege the city itself becomes the battleground. There was no safe place to retreat, no real front line. But if sieges were the most common type of war, and commonly involved women, why is it that we have forgotten the role that women played in them? And what sorts of things did they do?

It would be easy to focus on how women were victims of sieges. The fate of women in a city that fell to the enemy was appalling. If a city resisted a besieging army, the army earned the right to pillage the city when it fell.[9] Pillage compensated soldiers for poor pay, and rape was viewed as an unfortunate but natural consequence of war.[10]

Sexual violence was rampant. Contemporary 'paintings and wood-cuts of sixteenth-century urban slaughter depict women's dead bodies strewn in rivers, streets, alleys and on the pavements of public squares'.[11] A German mercenary soldier recorded the aftermath of the siege of Magdeburg in his diary: 'Beyond all measure was wrecked the most dreadful and awful havoc with the plunder, thievery, murder and the violation of virgins and wives that was begun right away'.[12] A 1621 broadsheet commenting on the war in Bohemia exhorted readers to 'weep and pray alike' at how soldiers carried on with the female sex, especially with the maidens whom they rape and abuse such that one is horrified by it. Some beautiful women are forced to swear to serve the soldiers . . . their husbands are forced to lose their lives, even right before the very eyes of their wives. Also sold among the soldiers, and very cheaply, are wives and maids in equal numbers.[13]

The whole business of the siege was deeply sexualised. The ancient Greek historian Herodotus recounts that Sesostris, the Egyptian monarch, placed victory columns in cities he had conquered after the siege:

those of whom he found valiant and fighting desperately for their freedom, in their lands he set up pillars which told by inscriptions his own name . . . and how he had subdued them by his power; but as to those of whose cities he obtained possession without fighting or with ease, on their pillars . . . he drew upon them the hidden parts of a woman, desiring to signify by this that the people were cowards and effeminate.[14]

Throughout history, metaphors of purity, sex, and rape were commonly used to describe siege warfare. During the siege of Hull in the English Civil War, the town could boast of 'our Troops of Virgins, who shewed so much diligence that many of our fortifications may deserve to be called the Virgins Workes'.[15] A poem about the 1550–1 siege of Magdeburg portrayed the city itself as a violated virgin:

White and pure was once my body
Now sword and flame have violated it utterly
Here 'tis half burnt
Here run through
Here a mutilated limb
Here a weal and bruise
'Tis a wonder
The pain does not make me cry out constantly.[16]

The depiction of a city as female may in part have been because women were integral to siege defences, from digging trenches and building ramparts to the defence itself. The lines between townsfolk and garrisoned soldiers were blurry in the extreme. Ordinary people, men and women, fought, starved and fell ill alongside the garrison; if the garrison fell, they fell; if it won, they won.

The first task of a city under siege was to shore up the fortifications: trenches and ditches had to be constructed and often existing fortifications had to be torn down and changed. This required thousands of people: 12,000 built 9 miles of trenches for the city of Lille in 1708.[17] During the siege of La Rochelle in 1628, as many as 250 women at a time worked in organised groups; a contemporary observer reported that 'some carried baskets full of earth on the ramparts of the town, others dug, and made very hollow ditches at the foot of the walls'.[18] Women were commonly paid less than half the male wage for this work.[19] In London, besieged by Cromwell's troops in 1643, women of all classes worked together:

> Raised rampiers with their own soft hands
> To put the enemy to stands;
> From Ladies down to oyster-wenches
> Labour'd like pioneers in trenches
> Fell to their pick-axes and tools,
> And help'd the men to dig like moles.[20]

Women also delivered munitions to the soldiers manning the wall, placing them in the direct line of fire. In the siege of Lyme Regis in Dorset during the English Civil War, the Roundhead Bulstrode Whitelocke recounts that 'the women of the town would come into the thickest of the danger, to bring powder, bullet and provisions to the men, encouraging them upon the works'.[21] Lord Byron, in command of Royalist forces in Cheshire, remarked:

I must not forget the great courage and gallantry the Chester women expressed that day, who all the time the cannon played upon the new breach . . . carried both earth and feather beds, and other materials incessantly, and made up the breach in the very mouth of the cannon. And though eight or ten of them, at the least, were killed and spoiled with great shot, yet the rest were nothing at all dismayed, but followed on their work, with as great alacrity and as little fear as if they had been going to milk their cows.[22]

Simply staying off the ramparts was no guarantee of safety. Inaccurate munitions meant that every inhabitant of a city under siege was at risk, and people could be struck down by artillery anywhere. The immediate threat was a stray cannonball. The more distant, and more horrible, threat was starvation. The French city of La Rochelle had 28,000 inhabitants before the 1628 siege, and was left with only 5,000 afterwards. By the end of the siege, grass, snails and shellfish had all been consumed. People had turned to eating rodents, bread made from straw and jellies out of animal hide. Eventually, they turned to cannibalism.[23] Civilians were trapped in what was often a slowly evolving tragedy. If they stayed inside the city, they faced dwindling food, constant attack and the prospect of horrific violence after the city fell. Yet staying put was not always a choice. Blaise de Monluc, the commander of Siena during its siege of 1553, demanded that 'useless mouths' be expelled from the city and created a list of 4,400 'useless people'. He himself describes their terrible fate:

> which of all the miseries and desolations I have ever seen was the greatest any eyes yet ever beheld . . . these poor wretches were to go through the enemy who beat them back again towards the city . . . they drove them up to the very foot of the walls that they might the sooner consume the little bread we had left . . . but that prevailed nothing, though they lay eight days in this condition, when they had nothing to eat but herbs and grass, and above one half of them perished.[24]

Needless to say, many of the 'useless mouths' were women. There was no escape for civilians because attacking armies had a strong incentive to keep civilians trapped inside fortifications, putting food supplies under maximum stress, in order to persuade the town to surrender. The lines between the civilian space and the battlefield were non-existent.

The awful prospects of a siege inspired whole towns to fight for their survival: women as well as men were drawn into the defence. At the siege of Montauban in 1621, an observer noted that women actively fought against the enemy during a breach of the walls. One 'grabbed a grenade and threw it at the besiegers' and another 'cut off seven or eight pikes of the enemies with her scythe'.[25] Another

> performed the act of an Amazon, for having encountered a man armed with cuirass and helmet, she killed him with a sword that she had and withdrew from the fight only when two wounds in the head

and the thigh forced her to retire. Another girl killed an enemy soldier with her own dagger.[26]

At the siege of Montpellier, after a grenade had wounded a dozen girls, 'one young girl of fifteen or sixteen years saw one of the enemies' scaling the fortification and 'grabbed a pike and stabbed him'.[27] An anonymous chronicler of the siege of Chester in 1645 noted that 'our women are all on fire, striving through a gallant emulation to outdoe our men and will make good our yielding walls or loose their lives'.[28]

Towns were not the only places to suffer under a siege. Castles were often the target of a besieging force, and the nature of household organisation meant that women were often in charge of castles. In the medieval period it was a normal expectation that part of a noble lady's household management was knowledge and direction of military affairs. Christine de Pisan argued that a noblewoman should

> have the heart of a man, that is, she ought to know how to use weapons and be familiar with everything that pertains to them, so that she may be ready to command her men if the need arises. She should know how to launch an attack or defend against one, if the situation calls for it. She should take care that her fortresses are well garrisoned.[29]

In fact, military matters remained part of women's ordinary work throughout Europe from the fifteenth to the seventeenth centuries: a woman might provision her household with sugar and flour, but also with small arms, cannon and gunpowder.[30] And if her husband was away, it would fall to the lady of the house to organise its defence.

As a result, noble or high-born women, living in houses or castles important enough to become a military target, found themselves in command of sieges.[31] The English Civil War was replete with examples of women leading siege defences, on both sides of the conflict. In 1642 Lady Mary Bankes defended Corfe Castle in Dorset from an army of 500 including two large siege engines, the Boar and the Sow; when these failed to win the castle, the besiegers were provided with 'several cartloads of petards, grenadoes and &c for an assault;

£20 were offered to the first man that would scale the wall'.[32] Lady Mary, however, with only her daughters, women and five soldiers, saved the castle by 'rolling over stones and hot embers. They repulsed the assailants and killed and wounded above a hundred men'.[33] A Mrs Purefoy of Caldecot Manor in Warwickshire had a shorter but no less dramatic defence of her household, holding back Prince Rupert and 500 men with only twelve muskets in the house. The 'ladies and their maidservants loaded as fast they were discharged, melting down the pewter plates for bullets when the ammunition began to fail'.[34]

In 1643 the French-born Countess of Derby, Charlotte de La Trémoïlle, found herself in charge of defending against the siege of her Lancashire property, Lathom House. Countess Charlotte was alone with her two daughters. The siege lasted for eighteen weeks, the longest female-led siege defence of the war.[35] Lathom House was more of a castle than a house, with a 'strong wall two yards thick; upon the walls were nine towers flanking each other', each with six pieces of ordnance, all surrounded by a moat eight yards wide.[36]

The long siege of Lathom House was punctuated by repeated negotiations and occasional violence. Sir Thomas Fairfax, in charge of the besieging forces, repeatedly attempted to secure the countess's surrender, while she herself used these negotiations to buy the time necessary to secure the defence of the house and military assistance from Royalist forces. A soldier in the house wrote in his journal of the siege that Charlotte, 'though a woman and a stranger, divorced from her friends, and rob'd of her estate, she was ready to receive their utmost violence, trusting in God both for protection and deliverance'.[37] When the demands for surrender became more strident, Charlotte simply announced: 'Tell that insolent rebel, he shall neither have persons, goods, nor house . . . if providence of God prevent it not, my goods and house shall burn in his sight: myself, children and soldiers, rather than fall into his hands'.[38]

Inevitably the siege included violence. Lathom House came under fire, from mortars and cannons; but its inhabitants were brave. The soldier's journal notes that the 'mortar troubled us all'. As for Charlotte's daughters, he wrote that the 'little ladies had stomach to digest cannon, but the stoutest soldiers had no hearts for granadoes'.[39]

Charlotte and her garrison at Lathom House managed to humiliate the besiegers by capturing their largest mortarpiece, dragging it back inside 'like a dead lion quietly lying'.[40] Throughout all this, 'her ladyship commanded in chief'.[41] The siege ended when the besieging force, plagued by desertions due to poor pay, were forced to retreat.[42] Charlotte joined her husband on the Isle of Man.

Contemporary news reports leave little doubt that Charlotte was central to the defence of Lathom House. A Royalist publication took particular note of her military success, describing her as 'the incomparable Countess of Derby (since her last Sally upon Wednesday fortnight when she took two pieces of cannon, one mortar-piece and more Colours)'.[43] The opposing view was less complimentary but could not avoid crediting Charlotte with military success. A Parliamentary news-sheet declaimed that the surrender of Lathom House had 'cost much blood at several times' and that 'the Countess of Derby (whose house it was)' had 'stolen the Earle's breeches when he fled . . . and hath in his absence played the man'.[44] Unfortunately for the countess, her brave attempts to defend Lathom House were ultimately for naught, as it was destroyed later in the war.

The Countess of Derby had a Parliamentary counterpart, Lady Brilliana Harley. Lady Brilliana's husband was away, and she was in control of the family seat, Brampton Bryan Castle in Herefordshire. Brampton Bryan was a Parliamentary stronghold in predominantly Royalist territory, and as a result an attack on it was inevitable. Lady Brilliana, like the other noblewomen we've met, clearly saw preparing the castle's military defences as part of her role as mistress of the house, ordering muskets, bandoliers and shot.[45] The first call for her to hand over her castle and arms came in March 1642. She bought time through negotiations, but by July Brampton Bryan was surrounded by a force of 700 men and seven 'great iron guns, one . . . called *Roaring Megg*'.[46]

Conditions inside the castle were poor. Lady Brilliana and her three children were accompanied by about fifty soldiers. The besieging forces had stolen the castle's cattle and supplies were running low. One soldier wrote that during the siege, 'our sufferings were great . . . all our bread was ground with a hand mill, our provisions very scarce, the roof of the castle so battered that there was not one dry room in it; our substance without plundered and all our friends fled' and yet 'this noble lady bore all with admirable patience'.[47] The castle was bombarded repeatedly. A week into the siege a large artillery piece shattered the walls and took out one woman's eye, and by the end of the week a key wall in the castle was 'battered almost to a breach and that very near the ground'.[48] Lady Brilliana 'called a council' to plan counter-attacks.[49] The siege continued until early September when the besiegers were called away to assist with the attack on Gloucester. Lady Brilliana acted to remove all the siegeworks to make any subsequent siege harder, and ordered her men to attack a Royalist camp at Knighton. Priamus Davies, a soldier serving in the house, wrote that 'this noble lady who commanded in chief, I may truly say with such a masculine bravery, both for religion, resolution, wisdom and warlike policy, that her equal I never yet saw'.[50] The attack on Knighton resulted in the successful capture of prisoners, arms and horses.

Lady Brilliana's bravery was not enough to protect her against illness. She wrote to her son in October: 'I have taken a very great cold, which has made me very ill these 2 or 3 days, but I hope the Lord will be merciful to me, in giving me health, for it is an ill time to be sick in'.[51] Lady Brilliana died shortly after. She was right to think it was not a good time to be sick. Her body was 'carefully preserved and placed in a high tower of the castle' to await a proper funeral, which was 'prevented by the malice of her implacable enemies'.[52] In fact, when the castle finally fell during a second siege, in 1643, despite negotiations that 'no dishonour' should be brought to the body, 'it was taken up under pretence to search for jewels, but the jewels being gone, the cabinet was raked up again in close cinders'.[53] Loyal soldier Priamus Davies hoped that his mistress's body would 'one day rise against these monsters and usurpers of the name Christian'.[54]

War in France also led noblewomen into military command. Alberte-Barbe de Saint-Baslemont (sometimes called Madame de Saint-Balmon) became famous for military exploits in her husband's extended absences during the Thirty Years War. Over a period of eight years she defended her property, people and neighbours,[55] leading at least two dozen missions with her band of cavalry and soldiers between 1636 and 1643.[56] Madame de Saint-Balmon preferred practical dress, sporting

> a hat with blue feathers; blue is her colour. She wears her hair the way the men do, as well as a doublet, a cravat, men's double cuffs, knee breeches, very low men's shoes . . . a skirt over her breeches; she always has a sword by her side.[57]

De Saint-Balmon was always ready to fight, 'always booted and wearing men's dress under her women's clothes; at the first alarm [of attack] she would remove her skirt' so as to ride to battle.[58] Before the war began she successfully fortified her house, allowing it to become a place of refuge for people living nearby.[59] Her success was so great that at one stage she rescued the French governor of nearby Bar-le-Duc;[60] Louis XIII even offered Madame de Saint-Balmon her own regiment.[61]

During the Fronde, the rebellion against Louis XIV of 1648–53, women played pivotal roles that often began with the defence of their chateaux but sometimes extended to other forms of military command. These women warriors were known as *femmes fortes* or *Amazones*. During the Fronde, if a woman were highly enough born, the defence of her property might blur with the defence of the realm itself; some noblewomen participated in the wider war to further the cause of the rebels. The military exploits of Anne-Geneviève de Bourbon-Condé, the Duchesse de Longueville, included riding at the head of Spanish troops marching on Paris.[62] She also was the primary organiser and financier of troops at Stenay, a key fortress.[63] So great were her contributions at Stenay that its lieutenant, Sommerance, built a temple dedicated to her (the Temple to the Goddess Bourbonie), claiming that her heroism was evident because 'in every war expedition you act like an Alexander or a Caesar, as much in those things that concern the army as in those that concern fortifications and the re-establishment of border areas'.[64]

Anne Marie d'Orléans, the Duchesse de Montpensier, was so highly born that at one stage she was considered a possible bride for Louis XIV himself, and she was probably the wealthiest woman in Europe.[65] Known as La Grande Mademoiselle, reflecting both her elegant height and social status,[66] she was a key figure in the Fronde.

In March 1652 she was sent to Orléans to further the cause of the princely rebels against Louis XIV. She set off in a coach which she quickly abandoned for a horse, because, as she wrote in her memoirs, 'it was very fine . . . and it gave the troops considerable joy to see me'.[67] (The opposing side noted that 'Mademoiselle took the road to Orléans determined to put on an act à la Jeanne d'Arc').[68] Mademoiselle took command of her troops, and forced her way into the city, leaping over ramparts.[69] She prevented the city from falling to the king's forces for six weeks.[70]

She was only getting started in Orléans. In July 1652 she led 400 musketeers into Paris itself. The rebel forces were small, and struggling against a much larger royal army. The king was watching from outside the city. The situation looked dire. Mademoiselle saved the day when she realised that the cannons of the Bastille, ordinarily pointed inwards towards the city itself, could be turned outwards and used to attack Louis' forces.[71] Doing so stopped a likely massacre. Mademoiselle noted that shots frightened the enemy by 'mowing down a row of horsemen; had it not been for that, all the foreign infantry, the *gendarmerie*, and some cavalry . . . would have been destroyed'.[72] She was suitably impressed with herself, writing:

> when I reflected that evening – and when I still reflect – that I had saved that army, I confess it was a source of . . . great satisfaction and great wonderment to me that I had also caused the guns of the King of Spain to rumble through Paris.[73]

Mademoiselle left her presence at the Bastille in no doubt, having deliberately worn a large plumed hat in order to make her tall figure even more visible.[74] After her Paris adventures, she was lauded in verse:

> this adorable Amazon,
> This generous Bourbon blood
> Whose candid heart is so good to us.
> Oh gods! What marvels she has wrought
> Through her skills and her vigils,
> On that day when one favourable stroke of hers
> Saved Paris and its saviour![75]

The 'adorable Amazon', however, found that her fortunes fell with the defeat of the rebels fighting against the king. When the

Fronde finished, Mádemoiselle was not only in disgrace but any chance she had of marrying the king was gone. She was exiled in one of her more dilapidated estates until 1657, and while she eventually returned to court life, she never married.

Women all over the world seized command in sieges. Absent husbands were often part of the story – but so too was maintaining an estate on behalf of a son too young to rule. Lakshmi Bai, the Rani of Jhansi, became drawn into a siege and war during the rebellions in India in 1857 that were a combination of the two – and in so doing became a national heroine and symbol of Indian resistance to British rule.

Lakshmi Bai was born Manikarnika Tambe in approximately 1828,[76] and was renamed Lakshmi on her marriage to the much older Maharaja of Jhansi, Gangadar Rao Newalkar, in 1842. As in most aristocratic marriages, the production of an heir was important. In the context of mid-nineteenth-century India, however, it was crucial. At this time, the English East India Company was the ruling arm of British India. The East India Company maintained a policy called the doctrine of lapse,[77] designed to help eliminate the rule of small princely families. If a family died without an heir (or if the ruler was 'manifestly incompetent') then their right to rule would 'lapse' and the territory in question would revert, happily for the East India Company, to British control.[78]

The Rani and Maharaja were acutely aware of this policy. They had one son, but the child died in infancy. On his deathbed in November 1853, the Maharaja adopted another child, and made sure to do so in the presence of British officialdom, to make clear that the line of descent would carry on after his death.[79] It didn't work. Jhansi was annexed to the territories controlled by the East India Company, and the Rani was given a pension and ordered to leave the palace.

The British, with their meticulous imperial records, are the sources for most of our information about Lakshmi Bai (Indian writing about the events of 1857–8 was suppressed by the colonial authorities, keen to put the rebellion behind them),[80] which means that they reflect the racial views and bias of the colonisers. The English lawyer and writer John Lang wrote:

she was a woman of about middle size – rather stout, but not too stout. Her face must have been very handsome when she was younger, and even now it has many charms . . . the eyes were particularly fine, and the nose very delicately shaped. She was not very fair, though she was far from black . . . What spoilt her was her voice, which was something between a whine and a croak.[81]

The nature of this description is back-handed (one wonders if John Lang was a prize himself, especially because no matter the estimate of her birth, the Rani could not have been much over thirty).

Four years later the potent brew of tensions was about to reach boiling point. In May 1857 the first rebellion of what would become known as the Indian Mutiny (or the First War of Independence) began. In June the rebellion reached Jhansi when the rebelling Twelfth Bengal Native Infantry seized the fort.

What happened next was the subject of considerable debate at the time. The Rani had been administering the territory of Jhansi with the permission of the East India Company.

She wrote to the British to explain that she was being forced to support the rebels, and to ask for advice and assistance. The British authorities were concerned about the fates of the British citizens inside Jhansi. They understood that the Rani was likely the only individual who could guarantee safe passage for the British out of the fort.[82] And, indeed, a promise of safe passage was made in exchange for the British relinquishing their weapons. But the rebels went back on their word. The assembled British citizens – men, women and children – were separated and massacred beyond the city walls.[83] The Rani's precise role was unclear: had she abetted the massacre or fruitlessly sought to prevent it?

She wrote to W. C. Erskine, a British commissioner in India, reporting on the massacre perpetrated by 'faithlessness, cruelty and violence' and lamenting that she had been powerless to stop the killing as she had been trapped in her house by the rebels.[84] While some British officials accepted this story, wider opinion began to run the other way. The public thought that the Rani, who had developed a 'smouldering hatred of the British race'[85] after Jhansi had been lost through the doctrine of lapse, had deliberately engineered the massacre. Thomas Lowe, a British Army doctor, wrote in his memoir that she was the 'Jezebel of India . . . the young, proud, unbending, uncompromising Ranee, and upon her head rest the blood of the slain, and a punishment as awful awaited her'.[86] On the other hand, Sir Hugh Rose, commander of the Central Indian Field Force during the war, called her 'a sort of Indian Joan of Arc'.[87]

The Rani certainly appears to have had the physical capacity to lead troops in the defence of her city. Stories of her childhood include her training with horses, swords and other weapons.[88] She was a woman of physical prowess, apparently weightlifting, wrestling and steeplechasing before breakfast. One eyewitness recalled her practising on horseback, the reins in her teeth and a sword in each hand.[89]

The British government was uncertain enough about the Rani's role in the massacre at Jhansi that they allowed her to manage the district until such time that a new British superintendent could be despatched to the area. The Rani began to prepare Jhansi's defences, organising troops and securing weapons, including casting cannon.[90] She held the fort until March 1858, when a British force arrived in Jhansi to find the fort well defended and a Rani who had finally decided to throw her lot in with the rebels. Most historians agree that at this point Lakshmi Bai would have realised that the British authorities were now convinced that she was responsible for the massacre in 1857, and so her only hope of freedom lay with the rebelling forces.[91] Jhansi and its queen were now under siege by the British.

The British heavily bombarded the castle, but the Rani and other defenders robustly counter-attacked. Lowe described the first few days of battle as a constant back and forth: 'the enemy kept up a very smart fire upon our various works from their guns . . . we had silenced several of their guns, and as often as they were silenced so often did they reopen them to our astonishment'.[92] The British observed women working in the batteries, delivering ammunition, repairing walls and supplying water.[93] The Rani supervised the defence, ordering repairs to damaged fortifications,[94] and according to the British, 'constantly visited the troops and animated them to enthusiasm by her presence and her words'.[95] A Brahmin priest claimed that Lakshmi herself gave the orders to fire on the British, and that when the guns fell silent, 'the Rani tied on her sword . . . and gave a reward to the cannoneer whose cannon had fallen silent. Then she herself stood to fire the cannon'.[96] A surgeon accompanying the British forces wrote that

> that dauntless bravery of the Ranee was a great topic of conversation in camp. Farseeing individuals thought they saw her under an awning on the large square tower of the fortress, where she was said to sit and watch the progress of the siege. Report [*sic*] told she was young and beautiful, and as yet unmarried. Field and opera glasses were constantly directed to the awning in question.[97]

The Rani was holding out hope that another rebel, Tatya Tope, was marching to assist Jhansi. He arrived on 31 March, but ultimately to no avail.

On 2 April the British launched a full assault on the fort. They successfully breached the walls and attacked, fighting at close quarters throughout the city, where the conflict 'was severe . . . at the palace it was desperate. The houses on both sides of the street had been set on fire, and the heat was fearful'.[98] Lowe noted that 'heaps of dead lay all along the rampart and in the streets below, and screams and groans were heard in every house'.[99] When the attackers reached the palace, 'it was apparent that the resistance had only begun. Every room was savagely contested'.[100] He counted the dead: 'In Jhansi, we burnt and buried upwards of a thousand bodies . . . such was the retribution meted out to this Jezebel Ranee and her people for the heinous crimes done by them in Jhansi'.[101]

Lakshmi Bai escaped. The precise means by which she did so are unknown, but in later depictions she is almost always shown leaping from the ramparts on horseback, her adopted son strapped to her back, glorifying both her bravery and her motherhood (given that the adoptive son in question was at least eight years old and the ramparts were famously high, this is a particularly unlikely mode of escape). The Rani fled to nearby Kalpi, where she and the other rebels prepared the defence of the town, only to be defeated again by the British on 22 May. The Rani, alongside the other rebels, had to flee once more.

The rebels' objective was the fortified city of Gwalior, which they swiftly occupied. However, their success was short-lived, as Gwalior too fell into British hands. One observer noted that Lakshmi was 'continually on horseback, armed with sword and pistol, at the head of 300 Horse'.[102] The Rani made one final daring escape, but this time she was not able to flee for long. Her army of 5,000 was attacked by a British-led force, and during the fight the Rani was killed. How she died is unknown, and there are varying stories of her final stand. British commander Sir Hugh Rose noted that 'the whole rebel army mourned her' as she was the 'best and bravest of the rebel leaders'.[103] The myth of the brave Rani, the Indian Joan of Arc, was already occupying the public imagination, Rose noting that 'the high descent of the Ranee, her unbounded liberality to her troops and retainers, and her fortitude which no reverses could shake, rendered her an influential and dangerous adversary'.[104]

It is difficult to separate myth from reality in the stories of the Rani of Jhansi, who was to become a particularly powerful national symbol. But the nature of the legends that sprang up around her only emphasise her martial know-how. One story goes that after her marriage, the Rani trained her maidservants in military skills, including horsemanship and the use of weapons.[105] The legend of the Rani was so compelling that in the Second World War an all-female regiment was created with her name attached. While the regiment never saw combat, its women were trained and ready to fight.[106] Lakshmi Bai's life permeates Indian culture, even after well over a hundred years. The Indian academic and literary critic Harleen Singh relates a story from her childhood: 'I was admonished for getting into a fight with boys and told to check myself or, as the teacher said, "Who do you think you are, the Rani of Jhansi?"'[107]

The Rani of Jhansi differs from her European sisters who fought in and even commanded during sieges. Today, Charlotte de La Trémoïlle and Brilliana Harley are not national heroines. Lakshmi Bai's fight became a symbol for nationalism, and that symbol carried her memory forwards through the centuries – and, arguably, has been used to reinforce a dominant patriarchal culture.[108] Even though the Rani of Jhansi's exploits are remembered today, they are associated with her status as a mother (think of that eight-year-old improbably strapped to her back). The women who led in sieges invariably did so in lieu of the important men in their lives; the ordinary women who carried ammunition and grabbed swords when fighting was necessary did so to defend their homes. In other words, while these women all fought, they did so in ways that could be easily explained in traditional gender terms. And their fighting occurred in a context where there was no distinction between their home and the battlefield, in a traditionally feminine space. Because sieges drew the battle into the homes of ordinary people, they are forgotten – they are not the high heroics of masculine military endeavour. The people who fought in them are largely forgotten, too, and what is remembered are the commanders, their tactics and ability to break the fortress and enter the city (no wonder all the metaphors of seizing a city are sexual).

The question remains, though, that if later military planners were seeking evidence for women's ability to fight, why didn't they look at sieges, where there was plenty of evidence to be had. The answer is that it was just too easily dismissed: the siege was not a 'proper' war; the women were a disorganised if helpful rabble; and it was a woman's duty to step into the shoes of her absent husband or protect her children.

If sieges were the most common type of war for generations, and women commonly fought in them, then the fact that we still perceive 'normal' war to be an encounter between two all-male armies on a battlefield becomes even more problematic. Women fought in sieges, and women *commanded* in sieges – what are those in charge of defences if not generals? Looking at the history of war through the prism of women fighters reveals that even what counts as 'war' looks very different.

Women, no matter whether they were tall, elegant aristocrats with plumed hats, Indian queens or ordinary women protecting their families, were a common part of the most common type of war in the early modern era in Europe. Women in sieges were brave; they were physically able to assist with the building of fortifications and the defence of the town. Women were able to direct military defences.

And their efforts to defend their towns, their homes, were praised. Their bravery was depicted in songs, broadsheets and pamphlets. After the siege of Braunschweig in 1615, the town's women were remembered in verse:

> Some of them ran to the city walls
> and indefatigably among the foe
> threw stones
> and fired balls
> defended themselves with all their might
> with all their weapons well chose
> with water hot
> and burning pitch
> blackening many a man's nose . . .
> 'tis that which many days from now
> will be said of Braunschweig's women.[109]

The heroism of Braunschweig's women, and all the women defending their towns, cities and homes from sieges, resonated in local memory. Official histories of war, however, treat this heroism as an adjunct to the main business of war-fighting as conducted by men. Women fighting in sieges were not organised as regiments, not at the vanguard of the military, and so they could be dismissed. But half a world away, when European women were fighting in sieges, women in Africa were indeed fighting as part of an elite regiment.

4

Women Regiments

IN MARCH 1792, during the aftermath of the first phase of the French Revolution, 304 women petitioned the French National Convention. They made a proposal that seemed only logical in a context where citizens were asked to fight for their new country, and expected to receive rights in exchange. If the *levée* to save the Republic was to be truly en masse, why wouldn't it contain *citoyennes* as well as *citoyens*?

Their leader, Pauline Léon, said,

> We wish only to defend ourselves the same as you; you cannot refuse us, and society cannot deny the right nature gives us, unless you pretend the Declaration of Rights does not apply to women, and they should let their throats be cut like lambs, without the right to defend ourselves.

Léon asked for permission to procure pikes, pistols, muskets and sabres as well as for practising manoeuvres in a suitable public place.[1] The petition was denied. Monsieur Dehussy-Robecourt replied, 'Let us not interfere with the order of nature. It's not the destiny of women to deliver death; their delicate hands are not made to wield iron or to brandish pikes'.[2]

Léon was not the only revolutionary woman proposing a regiment. A couple of weeks after her failure, Théroigne de Méricourt went a step further and called for a regiment of Amazons to aid in the defence of France:

> Women citizens . . . let us not forget that we owe ourselves wholly to the Fatherland . . . let us arm ourselves, this is our right, by nature and even by the law; let us show the men that we are not inferior to them, either in virtues or in courage.[3]

A year later, in May 1793, Méricourt was attacked by a group of women from the opposing Jacobin faction and whipped in public, an attack from which neither her mind nor her body recovered (she was certified insane a year later and lived in asylums until her death in 1817).[4] The same month, an unthwarted Pauline Léon, along with Claire Lacombe, established the Société des citoyennes républicaines révolutionnaires (Society of Revolutionary Republican Women) to fight for the new France and equal political rights. In fact, their main goal was the formation of an armed group of women to protect the state internally: 'we have resolved to guard the interior while our brothers guard the frontiers'.[5] They later declared that 'the Society's purpose is to be armed to rush to the defence of the *patrie*' and women were to swear to 'live for the Republic or die for it'.[6] French women were deliberately pursuing military service as a route to citizenship, a situation which became so threatening to the Jacobin leadership that it was thoroughly suppressed.[7] One deputy remarked, 'soon they will demand belts, complete with pistols'.[8] A report by another official on the women's activities pointed out that 'women are disposed by their constitution to an over-excitation which would be deadly in public affairs'.[9] The same year, the National Convention duly banned the society and all other female political associations, women wearing political symbols and the participation of women in public political debate.[10] The doors were firmly shuttered to women's military participation because of its potential impact on their political participation and the social order. The French were revolutionary, but not so revolutionary they were prepared to have women organise politically and militarily.

In 1806, after Napoleon's invasion, Prussian women proposed a 'corps of Amazons' — they felt 'that the many patriotic pamphlets and songs promoting voluntary military service were intended for them, too. They demand their right as women to defend themselves and their fatherland'. The debate over whether or not the Amazons should be allowed to fight consumed one newspaper so completely that the king put an end to the 'unseemly' discussion. Women who wished to fight were ridiculed,[11] and the only route left open to them was to dress as men, a phenomenon we will explore in the next chapter.

Women wanting to fight together usually made their case in moments of revolutionary fervour, where a society's normal rules were suspended and patriotism drove political activity to the fore, as in France. Resisting an invader, as in Prussia, also inspired women to patriotic military action. During the American Revolution, Prudence Cummings Wright organised a militia of between thirty and forty women to guard a bridge; armed, they arrested a British courier.[12] During the American Civil War a group of women in the Shenandoah Valley proposed to the Confederate leadership that they could form a regiment of defence. Their proposal was politely declined.[13]

European and American women, inspired by patriotic or revolutionary fervour, may have been unable to get a regiment of women off the ground. But in far-away Dahomey in West Africa, a women's regiment was integral to the military success of a martial nation described by one observer as a 'small black Sparta'.[14] Within Dahomey, the women were known as Mino or Agojie. The success of the Dahomean women's regiment tells us a lot about the mindset necessary to allow women to fight.

Inevitably, European observers dubbed the women soldiers of Dahomey 'Amazons' – fierce female fighters of Greek myth who lived in Asia Minor. The name 'Amazon' means 'without a breast' as the Amazons purportedly cut off one breast in order to better shoot their bow and arrow (even though in artistic depictions, they usually have two breasts).[15] These classical Amazons appear in several of the main Greek myths, including the stories of Hercules and Theseus.[16] While there is no evidence that a mass of women like the Amazons ever existed, tantalising pieces of evidence uncovered in graves point to the existence of women soldiers in Asia Minor, as well as north of the Black Sea in modern-day Ukraine, which may have provided the source for the tales of the Amazons that captivated the Greeks.[17] Regardless of the truth, it was obvious to Europeans in Dahomey that these bare-breasted women warriors were closely akin to the classical Amazons. As Frederick E. Forbes, a British naval officer who had gone to Dahomey to persuade the king to end the slave trade, noted, the 'Amazons' he met were 'not deprived, like the ancient female warriors, of their left breast, but are perfect women'.[18]

The mythical status of the Amazonian women's army undoubtedly attracted Europeans keen to see the spectacle. The Victorian explorer and writer Richard Burton got himself sent to West Africa, in part because

> I was looking forward with prodigious curiosity to see 5000 African adult virgins – never having met with a single specimen. I found that most of them were women taken in adultery and given to the King as food for powder instead of being killed. They were mostly elderly and all of them were hideous. The officers are decidedly chosen for the size of their bottoms.[19]

Burton was, in his published writings, more complimentary, but it seems he was disappointed that the reality of the women's army did not match up with the vision that had sent him to Dahomey in the first place; he described the women to his wife as exquisite warrior maidens, making her 'madly jealous . . . I imagined lovely women in flowing robes, armed and riding thoroughbred Arabs'.[20]

Myths aside, by the mid-nineteenth century the kingdom of Dahomey was small, rich and highly militarised. These three factors are closely intertwined. Dahomey (today Benin) occupied a crucial position on West Africa's so-called Slave Coast, and the trade in humans enriched the small state, about the size of Rhode Island, with a population of approximately 250,000.[21] An economy reliant on slavery, as Queen Njinga's was earlier, is also an economy reliant on war, as slaves are taken by force; the presence of a lucrative commodity also creates incentives for local and foreign powers to fight. As a result, Dahomey retained a sizeable military force, recognised by most military observers as maintaining high standards of organisation and training. ('Most' is a crucial qualifier here, as the racist attitudes of many nineteenth-century observers inevitably clouded their judgement.)

Dahomey maintained an army of approximately 15,000 throughout the nineteenth century. The Agojie probably averaged 3,000 to 5,000 women, but may have reached numbers as high as 8,000 to 10,000 women.[22] By the 1890s, when Dahomey's primary adversary was a France scrambling for colonial possessions in Africa, the women probably numbered between 1,000 and 3,000.[23] The women were so impressive that even the accounts of European observers could not discount their impact (although invariably included side notes about the women's physical attributes, particularly their bared breasts and well-oiled physiques, the latter a technique to achieve an advantage in hand-to-hand combat).

Royal Navy Commodore Eardley Wilmot, visiting Dahomey in the mid-nineteenth century to persuade the king to cease trading in slaves, was particularly impressed by the women soldiers, noting of the 5,000-woman force he observed in the mid-nineteenth century that 'they marched better than the men, and look far more warlike in every way: their activity is astonishing'.[24] He also described them as

> fully aware of the authority they possess, which is seen in their bold and free manner as well as by a certain swagger in their walk. Most of them are young, well-looking, and have not that ferocity in their countenance which might be expected from their peculiar vocation.[25]

Later in the nineteenth century, Frederic Martyn, a British man in the French Foreign Legion, described the women's dress. While the women wore a leather belt with their rifle cartridges, 'the upper part of their bodies were [sic] quite nude, but the head was covered with a coquettish red fez . . . these ladies were all exceedingly well developed, and some of them were very handsome'.[26]

Although the historian Stanley Alpern mentions that while there were other armed groups of women in Africa, none were as large, well-organised and around for as long as the Amazons of Dahomey. How was it that Dahomey was able to produce and sustain a regiment of women so successfully as to impress the battle-hardened members of the French Foreign Legion?

The early origins of the women soldiers appear to be an all-female group of king's guards. Dahomey's kings were perpetually afraid of assassination and attack – a common problem of the time. One solution was to ban men from the palace. If rival kings could not enter the palace then they could not overthrow the ruler. European observers commented on the presence of the guards throughout the eighteenth century: it was a significant but not large force, probably never exceeding a thousand women.[27] The female palace guards were well equipped and superior to the men in both training and discipline.[28] The notion of a female guard was not unique in West Africa at the time (and indeed a hundred years later, former Libyan dictator Muamar Ghaddafi had an all-female guard corps also called the Amazons, some of whom were shot while defending him from an assassination attempt in 1998 and stayed with him until the fall of his regime).[29] What was unique was the decision in the nineteenth century to deploy women outside the palace and on the battlefield itself.

One driver was undoubtedly the fact that constant warfare and enslavement meant there was a notable disequilibrium between men and women in Dahomey. Commodore Wilmot thought that the constant state of war meant 'a constant drain upon the male population is required, and it naturally follows that the supply is never equal to the demand; hence the remarkable circumstance of nearly "5000" women being found in the Dahomian [sic] army' (again demonstrating that the presence of women fighters could only be explained by some sort of problem with the men).[30] Wilmot also thought that it was likely that the king had deliberately created a regiment of women as it would encourage the men to fight harder in order to demonstrate they were better.[31]

The women were selected on the grounds of their physical capability. In Dahomey, any young woman was a potential wife for the king, which meant that the state had strong administrative structures to assess all of the kingdom's women. King Gezo required all fathers to bring daughters aged nine and older to be assessed once every three years; the girls with the most physical potential were assigned to military duty (as well as, apparently, disobedient daughters).[32] Initially, many of the women soldiers were slaves, but eventually they were also recruited from free women.[33] The most physically suitable were directed to the guard. Once in the guard, women trained, exercised and developed their skills. In a society at constant war, if there was a shortage of men, it was not a stretch to deploy these women in war outside the palace gates. In 1818 King Gezo made the decision to transform his guard into soldiers. Gezo knew the women could fight, as he had taken power in a coup and had seen at firsthand their defence of his predecessor.[34]

That the solution of women soldiers should propose itself to the Dahomeans was not surprising considering that women occupied influential positions in the kingdom. Richard Burton noted that at 'the Dahoman Court, curious to say in Africa, women take precedence of men'.[35] While this was not quite accurate, Dahomean women certainly appeared to be far more equal than most other women around the world. Dahomey's guiding philosophy was based on a world in which masculine and feminine were in balance, and as a result all roles in the Dahomey court were 'doubled' – a man held a position, but he had a female counterpart. Even the palace's chief eunuch had a female double.[36] Consequently, women had a significant political and social voice, and retained a range of unusually modern rights, including the power to divorce (which lay entirely with the wife), earn money and retain inheritances.[37]

Once the women moved from the palace to the battlefield, they became even better trained and organised, relying on specific exercises, which they would often demonstrate to visiting Europeans. One of the main features of warfare among Dahomey and its neighbours were fortifications comprised of mud walls and lethally sharp thorn barriers. John Duncan, a former British officer, described barriers of the 'most dangerous prickles . . . about seventy feet wide and eight feet high . . . I could not persuade myself that any being, without boots or shoes, would, under any circumstances, attempt to pass over so dangerous a collection of armed plants I had ever seen' – but that the women, 'with a speed beyond exception' did so easily as a demonstration of their prowess.[38] A French naval surgeon watched the exercises with awe, commenting:

> it's difficult to describe, even to imagine, the picture they presented, under a fiery sky, amid the swirl of dust and smoke, the crackling of musketry and the roar of cannons, these four thousand panting women, intoxicated by powder and smoke, moving convulsively with the contorted faces of the damned and uttering the most savage cries. Finally, when all was exhausted, the ammunition and the energies, order and silence were restored.[39]

Another French official was impressed that the exercises were executed with 'cohesion and vigor', by the speed with which the women followed orders and 'above all by the kind of tactics' that lay behind the women's movements: 'I was very surprised to see such a perfect analogy between the movements of this army and those of a European army'.[40] Duncan had a conversation with King Gezo after one of the exercises, as the king wanted to know if British women were also capable of such martial feats, and Duncan rose to the defence of English womanhood by saying that while England had no female soldiers, 'we had females who had individually and voluntarily distinguished themselves'.[41] (King Gezo went one further with the French, offering the French king a seasoned guard of 500 Amazons; the French official in charge of the mission commented that this was indeed a special mark of favour, as Queen Victoria had only been offered women for the royal laundry.)[42]

The women were trained to be cohesive. Like modern military recruits, the Amazons used songs and chants to build *esprit de corps*, including lyrics like 'war is our pastime – it clothes, it feeds, it is all to us'[43] and 'we will return with the intestines of our enemy'.[44] They were also subject to strict military discipline, another way to build cohesion in a military unit. The women were required to be celibate (although they could break this vow with the king). Otherwise, sexual relations would result in execution, sometimes performed by other Amazons; or it could be punished by assignment to the suicidal vanguard troops, the 'gate opening force', which led the charge to usually inevitable death.[45]

Victorian observers often remarked on the agility and physical strength of the women – albeit both race and gender were viewed through the lens of a thoroughly Victorian sensibility. For Europeans, the Agojie's strength and military success invariably could only be as a result of a defect in the men. Burton was fascinated by the women, describing two as 'of abnormal size, nearly six feet tall . . . while the men were smooth, full-breasted, round-limbed and effeminate looking'.[46] He observed after a diplomatic mission in the mid 1860s that

> such . . . was the size of the female skeleton, and the muscular development of the frame, that in many cases femineity [*sic*] could be detected only by the bosom. I have no doubt that this physical superiority of the 'working sex' led the . . . Dahomean race to the employment of women as fighters.[47]

The general consensus was that the women warriors of Dahomey, who were not really women, were more effective fighters than the men, who were, by contrast, unmanly and not proper men. The women 'are as brave, if not braver than, their brethren in arms, who certainly do not shine in that department of manliness',[48] and exceeded the men 'in cruelty and all the stronger passions'.[49] A French hostage held in Dahomey remarked that 'old or young, ugly or pretty, they are marvellous to contemplate. As solidly muscled as the male soldiers, their attitude is as disciplined and as correct'.[50] The Amazons viewed themselves as men, as set apart from the norm of Dahomean society. One of their songs chanted, 'as the blacksmith takes an iron bar and by fire changes its fashion so have we changed our nature. We are no longer women, we are men.'[51]

Europeans also often accompanied their praise of the Amazons with a description of their otherness. Wilmot thought them 'formidable enemies. They fully understand the use of the musket, and load and fire with remarkable rapidity. Their activity is surprising; they would run with some of our best performers in England.' But in the next breath he explained that 'the "Captains" carry the skulls of their enemies in their girdles, and an occasional jaw is also seen'.[52] Frederic Martyn saw a woman's body among the dead.

> This dead Amazon was a very handsome and beautifully proportioned young woman, and her dead face bore a particularly mild and peaceful expression, utterly at variance with the bloodthirsty-looking machete in her girdle and the Winchester repeating carbine lying by her side. She had a very massive ring, made of particularly brassy-looking West African gold . . . not having any sentimental scruples about robbing a dead enemy, I took possession of this ring.[53]

He was impressed with the Amazon, and even more so with the ring: 'it was altogether such a well-made and effective ornament I could not believe it was of native manufacture'.[54]

The women were trained in an astonishing array of weapons and fighting techniques, starting with their fingernails, which they sharpened to points and honed in a brine solution for maximum impact in a hand-to-hand fight.[55] Martyn, the French Legionnaire, saw them fight 'like unchained demons, and if driven into a corner [they] did not disdain the use of their teeth and nails'.[56] Along with hand-to-hand combat, they were also expert in the use of bows and arrows (often poison arrows), muskets, machetes, muskets and other gun-powder weapons, battle-axes, clubs, spears, metal-tipped javelins and, most uniquely, a special razor spring-loaded in a long handle. This weapon was 24–30 inches long, and so sharp it could apparently split a man in two. Whether the razor was designed primarily to remove an enemy's genitalia is up for debate.[57]

The Amazons were well versed in the use of firearms, even though they were usually using weapons and bullets far less up to date than their European adversaries. Forbes noted in the late 1840s that the women 'all take great care of their arms, polish the barrels, and except when on duty, keep them in covers'.[58] They were also effective shots, despite relying on outmoded weaponry; the 'King's body-guard of Amazons distinguished themselves by their good shots'.[59] In the 1890s, while male Dahomean fighters took around fifty seconds to reload and fire, the women could do it fewer than thirty seconds.[60]

Once the women had made the transition from guards to soldiers, they were at the vanguard of Dahomey's wars from around the 1830s onwards: in slaving raids; against other neighbouring kings; and finally, against the colonising French. While the women's skills were universally recognised by outside observers and their adver-saries, the vainglory of the king meant that the women were sent into impossible, even suicidal, military situations. King Gezo and his successor Glele masterminded two attacks, thirteen years apart, on the neighbouring city of Abeokuta. Both ended in failure, and both times because the Dahomeans relied on faulty intelligence and underestimated the resolve and crucially the firepower of the enemy. Abeokuta was supported by the British, and before the first attack the Amazons had argued in the Great Council that the attack was impossible; but King Gezo was determined and the Amazons loyal, and the attack proceeded in 1851.[61] It was a disaster. Dahomean troops stormed the city fortifications with ferocity only to be beaten back by an enemy armed with superior British-supplied guns and tipped off by intelligence that an attack was forthcoming. Some 6,000 women and 10,000 men stormed Abeokuta's walls; while some of the women made it over, it was at huge cost, with 1,200 to 1,600 dead.

After this defeat the crown passed from Gezo to Glele, and by

1864 the new king was desperate to avenge the loss. The army had been rebuilt, and despite its earlier losses numbered about 11,000 male and female soldiers, armed with two cannons.[62] Forbes had observed women taking an oath of loyalty to the king, 'if Abeahkeutah be opened to us, we will conquer or die. Should one only return, let her die'.[63] Unfortunately, Abeokuta was closed, not least because once again its inhabitants knew the Dahomean forces were en route. To make matters worse, outside observers knew an attack was futile without better artillery, as the British had supplied Abeokuta with modern cannon and thousands of muskets.[64] The attack proceeded despite the warnings. Three of the women soldiers successfully breached the walls, only to be captured and their dismembered heads and hands flaunted throughout the city on poles.[65] This time, the losses were even worse, with 2,000 dead and 2,000 captured.[66] The repeat failure didn't deter the kingdom, which attempted and failed a third time to take Abeokuta in the 1870s.

These doomed battles demonstrate two things. First, the women's skills were never in any doubt. Rather, strategic miscalculation and superior firepower meant that they never had a hope. Second, the martial culture of Dahomey ran deep enough that even replacing thousands of lost Amazons was not a problem. The cultural expectation that women should fight meant that a supply of women was there; the systems for recruitment and training meant that they could be successfully converted from civilian to soldier.

The last, and most significant, battles were against France, which was keen to take Dahomey as part of its growing empire in the 'scramble for Africa' of the 1890s. The army of Dahomey was at this point hopelessly (and literally) outgunned. The French rifles were so effective they remained the army's principal weapon until 1939, and French artillery pieces so accurate that they were in use throughout the Second World War.[67] The Amazons were still using muskets, mostly dating back to 1822, very often loaded with something other than a bullet.[68] The French were armed with the Lebel rifle cartridge, the first smokeless powder cartridge. It was highly dangerous. 'To look at the wound caused by the Lebel bullet,' wrote Martyn, 'one would think that they had been inflicted by ammunition not authorised by the rules of civilised warfare, so ghastly were they.'[69]

The Legionnaires, however, were impressed by the women's military skill. Martyn put it directly:

> anyone inclined to sympathise with the Amazons on account of their sex, and look upon the combat between them and our men as unequal, may take from me that their sympathy would be misplaced. These young women were far and away the best men in the Dahomeyan army, and woman to man were quite a match for any of us.[70]

He also relayed that one woman, 'seized and disarmed' by a marine, 'was so far from being beaten that she at once turned on her captor and set about biting his nose off' until finally she 'was cut down by the sword of an officer'.[71]

While the Dahomean troops made some inroads against the French, superior firepower meant defeat was inevitable. A Dahomean attack on the French base in Cotonou in March 1890 was initially successful, but again artillery and machine guns decimated the Dahomean forces, including women whom the French commander dubbed *les harpies* – an impression no doubt encouraged by the fact that one woman was shot as she was about to behead a French corporal.[72] Martyn described the attack of the Dahomean troops:

> our fire literally mowed down the advancing lines, but they came on again and again in the most determined manner, and there is no doubt in my mind that if they had been under capable European leadership we would have found ourselves in the very queerest of queer streets.[73]

The French were victorious, and the Amazons were no more: only fifty or sixty are thought to have survived the conflict.[74]

It is interesting to note that the racial politics of the time meant that none of the European observers from the mid-nineteenth century onwards drew any connection whatsoever between the capabilities of the Dahomey Amazons and the possibilities for European women – even the French, who, at the time of their defeat of the Dahomean army still had *cantinières* on the battlefield. If the women of Dahomey were excellent fighters, Europeans thought it was because of the physical characteristics granted to them by race, not because of the fact that they were carefully selected and extremely well trained.

Unlike European women, they had been socialised from childhood to wrestle, run and survive in the wild; they demonstrated not only what a woman freed from middle-class European ideas about feminine capacity could do, but also what all women who were brought up to believe they could fight were capable of.

A French observer of one of the women's training exercises described the women in a way that unwittingly revealed the degree to which female military prowess could only be explained by racial difference. Watching the women storm the walls, he remarked that they resembled nothing so much as 'an army of demons spewed up by a volcano and covering the ground with its black battalions; nothing in these intrepid creatures recalled the most beautiful and timid half of the human species'.[75]

The French were especially fascinated by their African adversaries. The French press featured breathless articles accompanied by startling pictures of women warriors. One edition of the *Petit Parisien* featured dozens of images, including women warriors wielding muskets while carrying aloft the severed heads of their enemies, and images of human sacrifice.[76] Yet again, women's contributions were dismissed as features of an alien culture rather than accepted as evidence that women were capable of fighting.

Some of the Amazons' military practices did little to dispel this view. The Amazons observed a number of rituals in order to bind new women to the group and bind the group together. New recruits swore a blood oath: a priestess would cut their arms, collecting the blood in a skull, where it was mixed with alcohol and other substances; the women would drink it to pledge their loyalty and receive invulnerability.[77]

More than one French onlooker saw the women engage in a ritual involving an enormous native ox weighing over 440 pounds (200 kg).[78] They would surround the ox so closely that it would disappear from view, and then the women would emerge: 'each Amazon holds in her hand or her teeth a bloody remnant, which she devours raw and throbbing like a ferocious beast'. The women were capable of slaughtering the ox 'in less time than one skins a sheep in a slaughterhouse . . . all that remains of the animal is the skin and the horns. All the rest has disappeared, even the entrails, which the horrible viragoes devour voraciously.'[79]

Hazing practices and rituals are, of course, a key part of military training in nearly every military around the world. And while the Dahomey women's ox ritual may sound particularly gruesome, it is not hard to imagine a 'detached' anthropological observation of Western military hazing. Consider the example of 'blood pinning' in the US Marine Corps in 1997, where metal pins, such as wing insignia, were forcibly pounded into a recruit's chest. Marines were 'lined up against a wall to have their wings driven into their chest' by as many as thirty other Marines:

> In addition to a single or double fist blow to drive the wings in, many of the hazers start off by using their thumbs to twist or gouge the victims' chests, until many of the victims are screaming in pain, their T-shirts soaked in blood.[80]

Gruesome ferocity as a bonding practice was hardly unique to Dahomey, and things were not really any more civilised in the Marines of over a hundred years later.

While the French forces recognised the ferocity of the troops, they also belittled the women's military prowess. The French press couldn't get enough sensational stories of colonial warfare in Dahomey; one account had it that

> the elders are killed; women are disembowelled and children still nursing are stoned. The young boys and girls are seized, bound and kept in reserve, the former for the slave trade and the latter for human sacrifice. Afterwards the fields are deserted, crops ruined and houses destroyed. Such are the crimes committed by the king and his army of ferocious savages.[81]

By the 1890s the Dahomey women had become notorious, a curiosity to be gawped at by white strangers. When the kingdom fell to the French, a troupe of supposed Amazons toured Europe for two years; not one of the members appears to have been genuine, and at least one of its number died far from home, in Prague.[82] Dahomey also had a cultural exhibit at the Columbian Exhibition in Chicago in 1893: the entryway featured a female Dahomean warrior brandishing a severed head on one side and a French officer on the other.[83] A magazine article on the fair remarked that sixty-nine Dahomeans were present 'in all their barbaric ugliness . . . as degraded as the animals which prowl the jungles of their dark land'.[84] The Agojie were no longer the vanguard of their troops but a spectacle; their military prowess was reduced to alien savagery. Women's military contribution had been dismissed, with an extra push downwards by the politics of race.

By the 1960s the Western imagination was at fever pitch. Recognition of the women's fighting capacity was tempered by dismissive comments focusing on descriptions of

> leggy Amazons marching along with beautiful bare breasts swinging in cadence, or tearing off their skirts as they hurled themselves over thorn barriers. Even more titillating, declared the old Africa hands, were the erotic dances the naked Amazons performed . . . when preparing for a raid.[85]

All of this held a grain of truth – the marching, the barriers, the dancing – but modern eyes inserted eroticism and ignored all the comments about military skill. By the 1960s the very idea of women soldiers was so outlandish that they could only be viewed as sexual caricatures.

The Dahomean Amazons were unique – but not because they were uniquely capable. Women, trained for generations to be physically powerful rather than delicate adornments, were an effective fighting force. A society with a strong belief and strong evidence of women's leadership and political skills was open to the idea of deploying women if it became necessary – and keeping them deployed when the women proved to be effective fighters. The Dahomean military, as we will see, made similar decisions to those made in the Western world much later on. But until gender equality reached Western societies at higher levels, even under the most extreme national duress, it would be hard to deploy women in combat. Until then, women had to sneak on to the battlefield in small numbers.

5

Cross-dressing Soldiers

IN 1745 A young man slipped out of his house and ran away to join the British Army. His name was James Grey, and his timing was excellent: the British were engaged in fighting the Jacobite Rising, the last significant armed rebellion on home soil. They needed men, and James joined them as they marched north. His career in the army did not last long. Young James received 500 lashes as a punishment for offending his sergeant, and he ran away again, this time to join the marines at Portsmouth. He sailed on the sloop *Swallow*, bound for the West Indies, and saw action all around the world. He was wounded at least twelve times before he left military service in 1750.

James's career is so commonplace that it does not seem to warrant any further attention. It is not full of noticeable heroics, or even noticeably bad behaviour, and certainly would not warrant inclusion in any military history. His life was a typical military life of the time, punctuated by episodes of danger, brutality and likely exaggeration (surviving 500 lashes strains credulity).

But James was actually a woman called Hannah Snell, and she survived a stint in the army, years at sea and at least twelve wounds, all the while maintaining her disguise as a man. It all started when her husband left her alone and pregnant, and soon afterwards her baby died. So she cut her hair and bound her breasts, and became James Grey to track down her errant husband. For five whole years no one discovered that James was really Hannah. When she finally heard that her husband had been executed in 1750, there was no further point to her military career, so Hannah shed the persona of James Grey and left it all behind. She led an equally colourful life afterwards, earning a living for a time by performing a one-woman show about her exploits. Eventually she was given a military pension by the Royal Hospital, Chelsea.

There were many women like Hannah who fought on the battlefields of Europe and America prior to the nineteenth century. They were wounded; they were killed; they were heroic; they were aggressive; they lived louche and unsavoury lives; they were romantic; and they were cowardly. In short, women soldiered like men, and they lived like men. However, to do so, they had to dress as men.

Women like Hannah Snell were a well-known part of military life across Europe and North America from the seventeenth to the early nineteenth centuries. Military historians have sidelined the stories of cross-dressing women soldiers as curious footnotes to military history, often pointing out that the level of interest in these women vastly outweighs their actual significance on the battlefield and to military history more generally.[1] It is true that they weren't numerous enough to influence the course of battles, or to make the difference between victory and defeat. But cross-dressed women soldiers were recognised as brave and effective fighters. These women are a lot more interesting and significant than their status as mere adjuncts to military history suggests.

The prominence of female cross-dressed soldiers, especially to contemporary observers, demonstrates how different war was, and how different the relationship between women and war was, prior to the nineteenth century. These women fought in real life, in armies all over the world, most prominently between 1650 and 1850. Forgetting them, or treating them as the titillating sideshow to the main event of war, obscures 'what was at one time normal – indeed, the stuff of popular songs' and debases them to something 'curious, rare, exotic, archaic and almost extinct'.[2] We must remember that these women were not just convincing in their guises as men. They were convincing *as soldiers.* They lived in a society where the idea of a woman who could fight alongside men was neither preposterous nor insane. Their world was more open to the idea of female military service than would be the case in much of the world two hundred years later. This chapter explores who these women were, how they fought, and why cross-dressing women (like their sisters performing military support roles in the campaign community) disappeared from the battlefield.

Women who dressed as men in order to become soldiers are known to have fought in the armies and navies of Russia, Britain, the Netherlands, France, various German states and on both sides of the American Civil War. Sometimes their stories are recorded in memoirs or in songs and plays. We also have numbers painstakingly extracted from historical records. Around 119 cross-dressing women are documented as having served in the Netherlands between 1550 and 1840;[3] around 40 in *ancien régime* France;[4] between 30 and 50 in Revolutionary France;[5] 22 in the Prussian army during the wars against Napoleon in the early nineteenth century;[6] over 60 in Britain between 1660 and 1832;[7] and as many as 400 in the American Civil War.[8]

We should note at the outset, however, that it is simply impossible to know exactly how many women fought this way. Official numbers can only represent a part of the whole. After all, these women were in disguise, so by definition we only know about those who were discovered or revealed themselves.

Keeping an accurate count of this type of woman soldier faces another difficulty. Nearly all the official records of women's work in this period are plagued with inconsistency. The expectation of record keepers inevitably shapes the nature of the record. The differentiation between paid work and unpaid domestic support was often blurry. Official mechanisms like surveys and censuses 'systematically defined adult men as workers', regardless of how irregular or unusual that work actually was, but excluded adult women whose work was out of the ordinary or irregular in nature.[9] To officially record a cross-dressed female soldier would require uncovering her disguise, but also differentiating her from other women on the battlefield. As we saw in the last chapter, the pre-nineteenth-century battlefield was full of women in non-combat roles, so the presence of a woman fighter, however disguised, may simply have been ignored, just as the contributions of the women in the camp community were taken for granted.

Many cross-dressed women did escape the notice of the authorities – even at the highest levels of the military. The Revolutionary War hero General Casimir Pulaski, whom we encountered in the Introduction to this book, was 'esteemed as one of the greatest officers in Europe . . . famous . . . for his bravery and conduct in defence of the liberties of his country',[10] according to Benjamin Franklin.

George Washington decided to put Pulaski 'in command of the horse . . . a man of real capacity, experience and knowledge in that service, might be extremely useful. The Count appears by his recommendations, to have sustained no inconsiderable military character in his own country'.[11] Before he came to America, Pulaski had commanded troops in defence of various posts, including a monastery, from Russian onslaught.[12]

In 1929 a profile of Pulaski noted that his life 'is shrouded in mystery, unsettled by controversy as to many of the details, but always tinged with romance', particularly around his youth.[13] Of course, we now know that Pulaski's skeleton, interred underneath a statue in Savannah, Georgia, was discovered well over two centuries later to have been either intersex or female. Pictures of Pulaski suggest he had facial hair, providing support for the view he was intersex. Either way, Pulaski would have had to conceal his biology his entire life. He was slightly built – between five foot one and five foot four, and had a delicate facial structure.[14] Of course, if Pulaski had reasons to disguise either his womanhood or his intersex characteristics, it might have been well advised to cultivate an aura of mystery alongside his demonstrable military skills.

Pulaski had acquired outstanding horsemanship in Poland. It was said 'he could ride at full speed, throw his pistol up in the air, grasp it as it came down, hurl it ahead of him and then leaning over his horse, recover it from the ground without checking his speed'. The American soldiers who tried to copy him got injured.[15] On arrival in the United States, Pulaski immediately proved to be a valuable asset, leading troops against the British in significant engagements including the Battle of Brandywine, after which he was granted permission to raise his own legion of cavalry and light infantry.[16] He had a strong command of strategic affairs, writing to Washington that

> I believe this campaign will be most instructive. The enemy can execute various maneuvres [sic], by which he will try to make us engage in a general combat. It is to our interests to avoid this . . . [but rather that] several detached bodies of troops should constantly observe the movements of the enemy, confuse them as much as possible, and carefully await a very favourable opportunity to make a deliberate attack on the enemy with the support of the whole Army.[17]

Pulaski was killed during the battle for Savannah. Just as there are blurry accounts of his youth so there are two conflicting accounts of his death, both relying on (different) eyewitness testimony. The first has it that Pulaski charged through the city with his cavalry in order to confuse the enemy and raise morale; according to one of his officers, he was fatally wounded in the thigh and chest while they 'sped like Knights into the peril'.[18] The wound turned gangrenous, and according to some accounts Pulaski's body was so odorous that he was buried at sea.[19] The second version sees Pulaski shot in the groin while observing the battle next to a poplar tree, where he was immediately treated by a surgeon who extracted the bullet before placing Pulaski on a ship for evacuation – whence he was buried at sea due to the smell of his wound.[20] Only many years later did one of Pulaski's men reveal a story that the general was buried under a large tree near Savannah,[21] after which the bones were found and exhumed, and later interred in the Pulaski Monument in Savannah itself. The body's exact identity remained unconfirmed until the 2019 DNA analysis confirmed both gender and identity.

As with many historical controversies, the origin of the confusion over Pulaski's body remains a mystery. But it is not too much of a stretch to note that the burial at sea story – which obscured the reality of Pulaski's actual burial – meant there was no body, and therefore no biological evidence that this war hero was anything other than a man. It is not hard to imagine his comrades, on discovering Pulaski's lack of manhood, deciding to 'bury him at sea' and concealing the body elsewhere.

There are intriguing clues dotted throughout the historical record that suggest many more women may have fought than we know about. In 1762 the practice was common enough that in England jesting comments were made that 'there were so many disguised women in the army that it would be better to create a regiment for them'.[22] The revolutionary government in France faced a tide of patriotic *citoyennes* wanting to join the new army, either on their own or as part of a woman's regiment. Some did succeed, in sufficient numbers that women's military service was eventually banned. To achieve this, the revolutionary government used a simple tactic: it prohibited women from wearing trousers in public. In 1800 in the Decree of 16 Brumaire An IX, the Prefect of Police, 'informed that many women are dressing as men, and persuaded that none of them are leaving the clothes of their sex for health reasons', issued a specific ordinance banning the practice without express permission for medical reasons. This order was then shared with the military and civilian authorities, and only applied to women; the upshot was that it clearly prevented cross-dressers from fighting, a ban that persisted until the First World War and remained on the books, astonishingly, until the 1960s.[23]

Popular culture of the time celebrates such women and proves that they were a common feature of military and social life. There are hundreds of ballads from this period written about cross-dressed women going to war.[24] One of the most famous is 'Mary Ambree'. Mary, dressed as a man, ends up leading an attack on the city of Ghent:

> Then she took her Sword and her Target in hand
> And called on those that would be of her Band
> To wait on her person ther [sic] came thousands three
> Was not this a brave bonny Lasse, mary Ambree . . .
>
> The skie she then filled with the smoak of her shot
> And her enemies bodies with bullets most hot
> For one of her owne men a score killed she
> Was this not a brave bonny Lasse, mary Ambree.[25]

Ballads were not the only record of women fighters. The memoirs of women cross-dressers made for highly popular books.[26] Hannah Snell's memoirs fall into this genre, and so too do those of Christian Davies, who ran away to join the military to follow her husband, and Mary Ann Talbot, who was the mistress of a captain and donned men's garb to stay with him. Female veterans of the American Civil War, including Loreta Velasquez and Sarah Edmonds, also wrote their memoirs. Hannah Snell's one-woman show was enthusiastically received. There was plenty of inspiration for any woman interested in joining the military.

Female soldiers were sufficiently accepted that they were even recognised by the machinery of bureaucracy: they were neither treated as an official embarrassment, nor were they hidden under the carpet. Hannah Snell, Christian Davies and a woman soldier called Mary

Lacy all received pensions from the British government, a pattern echoed around Europe[27] and in the United States after the Civil War, as we will see.

When women cross-dressers were discovered, the reaction to their unmasking was nearly always neutral and often supportive: they were lauded as heroines[28] rather than condemned. In Prussia, a young woman called Frederieke Krüger cut her hair, dressed as a man and joined an infantry regiment in 1813. An excited yell in a high-pitched voice in the heat of action apparently gave her away, but her commander allowed her to stay on. She became a non-commissioned officer and received two military honours: the Iron Cross and the Russian Order of Saint George.[29] A woman who had proved herself but was nonetheless discovered did not experience a gender bar to her fighting.

Louise Françoise de Houssay, who fought alongside her husband in France from 1792 to 1795, initially kept her sex a secret. Eventually, however, her whole regiment knew about it. No one seemed to mind. She recalls that one colleague 'introduced me to his family, who bestowed high compliments upon me for my resolution, courage and affection to my husband'.[30] At one battle, she writes, 'we fought desperately for nearly seven hours; our corps lost 130 men; my husband was one of the number'.[31] After her husband's death, Louise was offered a military pension, but her 'too eager' desire to avenge him kept her fighting.[32]

The discovery of a woman cross-dresser in the ranks appears in general not to have caused much of a stir. As has been shown, laundresses, cooks, sutlers, provisioners, wives and girlfriends were so much a part of the military that the idea of a woman actually fighting was not a stretch. Women were integral to the military's success and performed tasks requiring physical strength and courage, so it was not such a big leap to imagine them bearing arms. There was no suggestion that these women were delicate or physically incapable.

Not only were many women, officially 'civilians', integral to the functioning of militaries; there were far fewer strict demarcations between military and civilian life, and between the 'front' and the 'rear'. The 'activities of war – maneuvers, outdoor camps, parades, press-gangs, supply trains – encroached continually on the lower class, men and women alike'.[33] A woman moving into battle in this era had less far to travel than her sisters would in the twentieth century.

The prevailing belief that women were strong and capable in turn relied on a common understanding of gender that was only just beginning to wane in the eighteenth century: the 'one sex' understanding of human physiology assumed that women and men were essentially variations on the same anatomical theme, rather than two distinct sexes. This view was so profoundly held that unexpected bleeding from a man's body was understood to be menstruation, and a woman's ovaries were considered a form of testicles.[34] A woman's body thus held within it the potential of masculinity. A woman 'who excelled at manly pursuits was an overachiever rather than a failure, and cross-dressing in no way implied a sexual interest in women'.[35]

Women in the rest of society in this period were considered to be entirely capable of hard physical labour.[36] Contemporaries 'do not seem to have had any moral objection to women working for their living, quite the opposite in most cases, and one does not read in this period that a woman's place is in the home'.[37] In general, expectations of womanly behaviour were different, particularly for working- and lower-class women: they were not expected to be 'delicate'.[38]

In fact, delicacy was at a significant remove from a world where women were not only physically capable but also capable fighters, as the ballad 'The Gallant She-Souldier' reminds us:

> For other manly practices she gain'd the love of all
> For Leaping and for Running, or Wrestling of a fall
> For Cudgells or for Cuffing, if that occasion were
> There's hardly one of ten Men that might with her compare.[39]

Stories of cross-dressed soldiers in songs and memoirs do not shy away from the fact that these women were violent, successful warriors. A picture of one female cross-dressed warrior, Ann Mills, shows her dangling the head of a French enemy by the hair. Hannah Snell's biography describes her in action:

> Our heroine still maintained her wonted Intrepidity, and behaved in every Respect, consistent with the character of a brave *British* soldier . . . she fired no less than thirty-seven rounds of Shot; and during the Engagement, received six Shot in her Right Leg and five in the Left

> . . . and one so dangerous in the Groin . . . that had she applied for any Aid and Assistance on that Account, she must inevitably have [been] discover'd.[40]

To avoid discovery, Hannah arranged for a local woman, rather than the ship's doctor, to remove the bullet.

Christian Davies was entirely capable of inflicting violence both on and off the battlefield. One night she stole a pig, and a corporal tried to take it from her. In the ensuing altercation the corporal swung his sword at Christian, and 'had the Sinew of my little Finger cut in two; at the same Time, with the Butt End of my Pistol, I struck out one of his Eyes'.[41] Christian is another woman who had enlisted to find her missing husband. As it transpired, he wasn't worth the effort: when she found him, he had a mistress. The news set her 'in a Flame . . . I struck at her with a Knife . . . and cut her Nose off close to the Face, except a small Part of the Skin, by which it hung'.[42]

Women fighting was a common spectacle of the period. Eighteenth-century stage shows featured bouts between couples, where both the male and female fighters were paid according to how many cuts and blows they inflicted. The Irish pair of Robert Barker and Mary Welsh promoted an upcoming fight with an advertisement which gives a vivid sense of the public appetite for such events:

> having often contaminated our swords . . . find ourselves once more necessitated to challenge, defy and invite Mr Stokes and his bold Amazonian virago to meet us on the stage . . . swords, daggers, quarter-staff, fury, rage and resolution will prevail.[43]

No wonder the prospect of a woman on the battlefield was not surprising.

The evidence shows that significant numbers of women fought dressed as men, on many different battlefields. So who were they, and why did they end up fighting in wars? There is no doubt that patriotism, or youthful adventurism, or a combination of both, played a role. The American Revolution, the French Revolution, the Prussian resistance against Napoleon and, slightly later, the American Civil War all saw women inspired by patriotic fervour to join new citizen armies.

Women were integral to the Continental Army during the American Revolution. Some 20,000 'women of the army', mainly wives and other official military followers, were on the campaign and were subject to courts martial for poor discipline.[44] They were accompanied by women who joined the fight disguised as men. Sally St Clair, a woman of French and African descent, was in the Continental Army until her death in the Siege of Savannah (where Pulaski also died).[45] We know that one Samuel Gay, a corporal in the First Massachusetts Regiment, was, according to his records, 'Discharged, being a woman, dressed in mens cloths. Augt 1777'.[46] Deborah Sampson was perhaps the most famous of these American Revolutionary women, because after the war she went on a lecture tour and published her memoirs of her life as a soldier.[47]

The American Civil War saw far more women fighters, between 250 and 1,000, with the proviso that as always the nature of disguise makes exact numbers hard to pin down.[48] High numbers of women were partly simply the result of the sheer size of the fighting forces in the American Civil War, with over 2 million men serving in the Union Army and between 750,000 and 1 million men in the Confederate forces over the course of the war.[49] But it may also be because unlike during the Revolution, when the Continental Army had relied on the services of women (as all eighteenth-century Western armies did), other forms of service for women were blocked. The army now hired (male) labour to do laundry, provide food and even nurse.[50] Women who wanted to serve the military cause may have been pushed into dressing as men in order to do so because there were no other options.

The true scale of women's service in male garb may be impossible to discover. There are multiple accounts of soldiers finding women's bodies among the dead on both sides of the conflict. One Union soldier remarked,

> I've picked up a great many wounded rebs . . . among these were found a female dressed in mens clothes & a cartridge box on her side . . . she was shot in the breast & through the thy and was still alive & as gritty as any reb I ever saw.[51]

The fact that both sides were fighting a bitterly contested war with an almost insatiable need for manpower seems to have reduced the need for physical checks,[52] and in a war where fighters were drawn from the general population, experience and skill was not the pre-requisite it might otherwise have been.[53] One Union soldier described a new recruit encountered on a long march: 'we enlisted a new recruit on the way to Eastport. The boys all took a notion to him. On examination, he proved to have a Cunt so he was discharged.'[54]

A surprising amount can be discovered about the women who served, from the battles where they fought to the wounds that usually uncovered them. Their names are a roll call of the common female names of the day; Mary Ann, Jane, Sarah, Frances, Marian, Jennie, Martha, Catherine, Rebecca, Ida, Lizzie. They took on equally quotidian names in their male identities: Frank, Charley, Henry, Jim, Albert. Many of the women remain anonymous, only mentioned in the memoirs, letters and despatches of the men fighting on both sides of the Civil War.

At least eight disguised women fought at the Battle of Antietam, where on the bloodiest day of the conflict 30,000 were killed; it may have been more, investigations of a grave site near another battle having found a female skeleton among the men. Her identity remains unknown. Of the eight fighters at Antietam, one woman had an arm amputated; one was shot in the neck; and another survived that battle, and the Battle of Fredericksburg, where she was promoted to sergeant only to give birth a month later.[55] There are confirmed accounts of five women fighting at Gettysburg; one lost her leg and two marched in the famous Confederate Army infantry assault called Pickett's Charge. One of these anonymous women could be heard screaming in agony from her wounds on the battlefield.[56] She would not have been alone. The Confederate Army lost more than half of the soldiers who fought that day to injury or death, 6,555 men.[57]

Pregnancy of officers should have been a giveaway that there were disguised women in the ranks: one memo read,

> The general commanding directs me to call your attention to a flagrant outrage committed in your command . . . an orderly sergeant . . . *was to-day delivered of a baby* – which is in violation of all military law and the army regulations. No such case has been known since the days of Jupiter.[58]

But birthing women were hardly unknown. One soldier wrote to his wife, regaling her with the story of the 'very good looking corporal in our regiment' who had fallen ill, before 'this same good looking corporal had been relieved of a very nice little boy and that the corporal and the boy was doing first rate'.[59] His wife wrote back: 'I think it was quite a grand thing about that corporal what a woman she must have been . . . she must have been more than the common run of woman or she could never stood soldiering especially in her condition'.[60]

One Confederate soldier wrote home that 'there were a great many fanatic women in the Yankee army . . . some of whom were killed'.[61] Some of these fanatic Yankee women (as were their Confederate sisters) were no doubt attracted by the pay as much as the cause – women could get money through enlistment bounties and pay of $13 a month as a private, inducements very attractive to poor women with limited prospects.[62] Others may have been seeking safety. At least one woman ran away from prostitution, preferring life as a soldier to life in a Nevada brothel.[63]

Women recorded their own experiences in letters home, and some were unafraid of a soldier's life. Sarah Rosetta Wakeman (Private Lyons Wakeman) wrote to her parents about fighting and marching with a typical soldier's bravado: 'I don't fear the rebel bullets and I don't fear the cannon'. And after a battle, she explained: 'I had to face the enemy bullets with my regiment. I was under fire about four hours and laid on the field of battle all night'.[64]

The case of Jennie Hodgers demonstrates the degree to which it is impossible to say just how many disguised women fought in the Civil War. Hodgers fought with the 95th Illinois Infantry from 1862 until her regiment was discharged from service in 1865. She was totally convincing as Private Albert D. J. Cashier. Cashier did all the usual things a soldier did; the only thing noteworthy about him was his height. At five feet, another soldier remarked, 'they surely must want soldiers very badly, if they take that little fellow at the end of the line'.[65] Private Cashier fought, was captured and escaped (by stealing a gun from one of his guards).[66] Like many young soldiers, he was brave if not foolhardy. According to one of the men in his unit, Albert mounted a barricade and called out, 'Hey! You darn rebels, why don't you get up where we can see you?'[67] Albert even managed to secure a military pension.

No one knew Albert had been born Jennie until 1911, when after admission to hospital following a car accident, his secret was uncovered – but kept secret by the doctors and nurses. Albert's health continued to decline, and eventually he was admitted to an insane asylum. At this point the fact that Albert was once a woman was leaking out to the press, threatening the payment of his pension. An investigation by the pension authorities revealed that the men in her company had no idea that Albert D. J. Cashier was a woman during the war. One deposition stated:

> About two years ago I learned Albert D. J. Cashier is a woman. I never supposed anything of the kind. I know that Cashier was the shortest person in the Co. I think he did not have to shave . . . she was very quiet in her manner and she was not easy to get acquainted with.[68]

But Cashier's comrades rallied, and ensured that the pension remained. Cashier did not have much of a life left to live. One of her friends from the regiment recalled, 'I left Cashier, the fearless boy of 22 at the end of the Vicksburg campaign' and when he went to the asylum, he found 'a frail woman of 70, broken, because on discovery, she was compelled to put on skirts. One day she tripped and fell, hurting her hip. She never recovered.'[69] Cashier died in 1915, but received a funeral with full military honours.

Women soldiers in the Civil War, despite extensive documentation (and photographs), were not officially recognised by Americans later on. In fact, they were totally denied. In 1909 the investigative journalist Ida Tarbell wrote to the adjutant general of the US Army. Tarbell explained, 'I am anxious to know whether your department has any record of the number of women who enlisted and served in the Civil War, or has it any record of women in the service?' Tarbell received the following reply:

> I have the honour to inform you that no official record has been found in the War Department showing specifically that any woman was ever enlisted in the military service of the United States . . . during the period of the civil war. It is possible, however, that there may have

been a few instances of women having served as soldiers for a short time without their sex having been detected, but no record of such cases is known to exist in the official files.[70]

But the office of the adjutant general was either lying or lazy: they did have records of women's military service, including discharge records and pension records.[71]

In fact, Sarah Edmonds, who had fought as Franklin Thompson for two years in the Union Army, had to fight to get a pension. In middle age, Sarah's health was declining (no doubt in part because of her military service) and she needed the money a pension would give her. She had a problem, however; Franklin had deserted. Franklin contracted malaria, requiring hospital treatment, which would have led to discovery. So Franklin fled and returned to life as Sarah to receive medical treatment. Deserters could not get pensions, so Sarah had to persuade Congress to remove the charge of desertion. She did so, with the support of many of her fellow soldiers and even a general, and the Bill to Remove Charge of Desertion from the Record of Franklin Thompson was passed in 1886.[72] The House Committee on Invalid Pensions duly reported to Congress that 'for nearly two years he remained with his regiment, sharing in all its ails and privations, marching and fighting'. They relied on testimony from Franklin's quartermaster, one William Shakspear, who knew of Franklin as 'a strong, healthy and robust soldier'.[73] Sarah Edmonds received a pension until her death in 1898.[74]

But women were not only motivated to fight by patriotism. The majority of the cases of cross-dressing outside a revolutionary context occurred when women became regular soldiers. Soldiering in these cases was just a job. For these women, it is likely that safety was the motivation: a woman was often safer as part of the military, even when dressed as a man and fighting, than on her own in a big city. In Britain, women constituted as many as 86 per cent of those classified as poor in 1755, a percentage which remained constant in 1800.[75] There were not many choices for a poor woman in a big city, beyond descending into prostitution. Like all clichés, the 'fallen woman' existed as a literary trope because it was a common fate. Women could also use the military as a means to escape an unhappy or abusive home life. A woman dressed as a man gained the protection of masculinity;

in the military she also gained the safety of a community, food and pay.

Reconstructing specific motives is challenging, as we have relatively few first-hand accounts. Love looms large as a motive for women who pursued a military career – no doubt because it played sympathetically to a wide audience. A woman in love was a recognised symbol of feminine behaviour – even a woman dressed as a man and fighting a war. Hannah Snell and Christian Davies were both behaving in stereotypical ways, searching for missing husbands. Many of the women fighting in the Civil War joined with their husbands.[76]

No matter what the reason, women fighters all faced the same obstacles: they had to disguise themselves as men convincingly enough that they would not be discovered. The range of potential traps for the young woman cross-dresser was extensive: body shape; bodily functions, particularly the pesky problems created by the need to urinate, and by menstruation; and the fact that young soldiers were known for their lusty pursuit of women.

The first order of business for a young woman wishing to pass as a man was to change her appearance sufficiently that she would be convincing. For some women, this involved binding their breasts tightly, or simply wearing a padded waistcoat, as Christian Davies did.[77] Maintaining this disguise was not easy. Hannah Snell would have had to endure her 500 lashes without anyone noticing her breasts, a feat she claimed to have accomplished because she was tied to the barracks gate, her chest obscured, before the beating. At least one commentator is suspicious that Hannah could possibly have survived the lashes at all, let alone done so without anyone noticing her bosom.[78] Of course, Hannah could have been participating in another fine military tradition – that of embellishing the danger and thrill of one's career – but the stories of her later life in the marines have been corroborated by other historical sources.[79]

Hannah's beating, or even her less remarkable injuries, represent the sort of moment where it was either difficult or impossible for a woman soldier to maintain the charade of a male disguise. But given how rarely people washed or changed clothes, it was perfectly possible to hide a female shape from day to day. Louise Françoise Houssay, who we met earlier fighting alongside her husband, explains:

We messed ten together, and slept all of us in the same room, yet I was not apprehensive of being detected. When I was sensible that everyone else was asleep, I would shift my shirt: besides I had an underwaistcoat and a pair of trowsers, which I never pulled off for fifteen months, when I served in the regiment.[80]

In fact, women were assisted in their disguises because clothes themselves during the eighteenth century were remarkably compelling symbols. Dress was a powerful indicator of social class and gender.[81] A passer-by would quickly ascertain whether a person was a man or a woman, whether rich or poor, simply by looking at what they wore. No woman wore trousers, so trousers created an automatic expectation that their wearer was male. This may explain why, in the ballads and broadsides that feature women warriors, surprisingly little is made of the mechanics of disguise. In the ballad 'Young Flora', the sailor's uniform combined with Flora's bravery seems to have been enough:

> In battle she did run as she stood by her gun
> Like a Britainer she was never afraid
> Three years upon the ocean she sailed with her love
> And was never expected a maid
> It never could be said that young Flora was a maid
> In her jacket and trousers so blue.[82]

Women usually tried to pass as boys or young men to account for their lack of whiskers. Smooth faces were common because soldiers were young. Armies and navies contained many teenaged boys. Even where regulations attempted to control the enlistment of teenagers, as in the American Civil War, they were routinely subverted and boys under sixteen often lied in order to serve.[83] Some women were scrawny enough that womanly curves were not a problem. In an army that also included skinny boys, a lack of physical strength was easier to disguise.

The composition of militaries in the eighteenth and nineteenth centuries gave women another advantage in creating a disguise. Rank-and-file soldiers, both men and women, came from lower-class backgrounds, where poor nutrition meant that people were smaller and scrawnier. One military historian suggests that female cross-dressers grew in numbers when military technology changed in the late seventeenth century. The new Flintlock rifles, which were substantially lighter than the muskets and pikes that preceded them, made a disguise easier.[84]

Women soldiers had to figure out how to appear male. But they also had to *act* male. And as young soldiers, this meant carousing, philandering and chasing young women. Christian Davies knew that she had to maintain her disguise, so she flirted, courted and even went to brothels.[85] Her disguise received a fortunate boost when a young woman claimed that Christian was the father of her child. In her memoir, Christian writes:

> I was so surprised at the impudent Perjury, that I was almost tempted to disprove her . . . and give her up to the law; but on a mature Deliberation I thought it is better to defray the Charge . . . it left me the Reputation of being a Father.[86]

Louise Houssay, in order 'to remove suspicion of any kind', would 'sometimes pay compliments to such Ladies, as I thought deserving of them'. This got her into trouble one day with a jealous member of her regiment, who used

> such abusive language, that I found myself under the necessity of demanding satisfaction for the offence . . . We agreed to go to a private place . . . there we drew, and fought. It was very lucky for me that my antagonist proved to be a bad swordsman; I wounded him in the arm, the blood gushed abundantly, I dressed the wound, and we were reconciled.[87]

Some women were obviously tempted by the opportunity for seducing other women, or, in modern eyes, may have identified as men. The discovery of actual seduction was one of the only circumstances under which women cross-dressers appear to have been punished. In Germany in 1721 a woman called Catherina Linck was arrested and put on trial for sodomy. The tale of how she got there is almost preposterously lurid. Catherina's colourful career appears to have been started in a religious cult run by a female prophetess. After some time among the 'Inspirants' of this group, Catherina dressed as a man and became a musketeer with the extraordinary name of Anastasius Lagranas Caspar Beuerlein.

Catherina's military career was lengthy and chequered. She deserted from the Hanoverians, an offence often punished by execution, and was only saved when her cause was taken up by a Professor Franck, who confirmed that she was actually a woman. Catherina attempted to join other militaries multiple times, including the Royal Prussians, Hessians and the Royal Polish troops, despite the professor's best efforts to save her from herself. She enlisted and then deserted from the Royal Polish troops, and again from the Hessians. Eventually she settled in Halle, working for the university shoemaker, which is where she met and married another woman – also called Catherina. The eventual discovery of her gender, and her forbidden sexual relationship, led to her trial and execution.

Catherina Linck was punished not because she was a soldier but because she persistently dressed as a man with the intention of having sex with other women. A similar story is that of the Dutch soldier Maria van Antwerpen, also known as Jan van Ant and Machiel van Antwerpen, who married two different women while disguised as a man. Like Catherina, she was put on trial because of her marriages, but in her case she was punished by exile. Women who dressed as men to fight, or even just to work, were lauded as industrious or patriotic. Women who seduced other women were not tolerated: this was perceived as a threat to the social order. Cross-dressing seducers took on the very essence of a man: his sexuality and virility.[88] Catherina and Maria were not merely trying to perform the tasks of a man; they were trying to *become* men, and that was not acceptable.

Some women appear to have dressed as men in order to become soldiers; other women appear to have been living as men, and took up soldiering as part of a male disguise. Albert Cashier was living as a man before the war. Sarah Edmonds did so, too.[89] Albert stayed living as a male when the war ended, but Sarah returned to a conventional woman's life. From the vantage point of the twenty-first century, it certainly seems that people like Albert Cashier or Catherina Linck or Maria van Antwerpen were transgender, living life identifying as a man. But it is not always easy to categorise what these women were doing when they dressed as men, and why they did it. Sarah Edmonds lived as a man for two years before the war, to escape an arranged marriage and then because of the increased economic opportunities it afforded her, but lived as a woman afterwards.[90] For many women, the temptation to continue living as men after the war may have been an inducement on its own: after all, men could vote, they could get jobs, they had agency.[91] The issue of gender identity is further obscured by the mores of the time, and another loss created by the lack of attention to women's military history.

Women could dress as men, and even act male, but other outward signs of womanliness were harder to conceal. The question of what women would have done about menstruation is difficult to answer, in part because the taboo nature of the subject meant that women themselves rarely recorded any strategies they used. It is important to remember that not all women soldiers would have been menstruating. Poor nutrition meant that women began menstruating at an older age: the average onset was seventeen in the United States and some Western European countries in the nineteenth century.[92] When under significant physical strain, weight loss, stress and poor nutrition, women can also stop menstruating, and all these factors would likely have applied to women soldiers. So women may simply have had fewer periods, if any, to conceal; moreover, a soldier on campaign could easily produce a plausible wound to explain any bloody rags.[93]

We can't avoid the obvious question: surely urination posed a challenge for any disguise? The fact that young James Gray never stood up to piss against a wall with his comrades might seem, to modern eyes, to be a sure-fire giveaway that he was different. But surprisingly different views of privacy may have helped these women maintain their disguises. When living in close quarters, humans develop a heightened sense of privacy around personal behaviours such as urination. In order to survive living closely together, we ignore each other's bodily functions as much as possible and let those near us simply get on with it.[94] And indeed, when camp latrines existed, they were so unpleasant that many soldiers may have wandered away in order to answer the call of nature.[95] Some women used special devices, for example straws or leather tubes, to allow them to urinate standing up. Christian Davies found it relatively easy, solving the problem 'by Means of a Silver Tube painted over, and fastened about her with Leather Straps'.[96]

Catherina Linck appears to have turned a remarkably creative mind (and mechanical ability) to all the problems caused by a lack of a penis. According to the records of her trial,

> she had a penis of stuffed leather with two stuffed testicles made from pig's bladder attached to it . . . the defendant had made the leather instrument herself while she was with the Hanoverian soldiers, and using her ingenuity, she had used it with several girls while she was a soldier . . . since she had to act like all the other soldiers.[97]

No doubt the success of the false penis encouraged Catherina to think that she could maintain an apparently heterosexual marriage; if she was able to find a young woman innocent enough, she might just be able to persuade her that the leather penis was real. Catherina also kept a leather-covered horn through which she urinated. But her suspicious mother-in-law discovered both when, after some weeks of worrying about her daughter's unusual new husband, she cornered her and ripped off her pants.[98] It was this moment that ended Catherina's life as a man and brought her to trial, and ultimately to execution.

The window of time in which women fought dressed as men is surprisingly precise. From the late sixteenth century to the early nineteenth century (and in the United States, as late as the Civil War) the records contain many stories of women who dressed as men in order to fight. But by the 1850s in Europe, and after the Civil War in America, the women who slipped into militaries dressed as men drop out of history. What caused them to disappear?

The ballads about women cross-dressers began to shift in the early nineteenth century, both presaging and reflecting military and social changes that were increasingly pushing women off the battlefield. From 'Mary Ambree' and 'The Gallant She-Souldier', with their emphasis on fighting and physical strength, and the picture of Ann Mills carrying her Frenchman's head, we turn to a different picture of the female warrior, pretty, delicate and not a fighter.

The ballad 'William and Harriet', dating from between 1819 and 1844, describes a new type of cross-dressed woman. Harriet, who sang 'like a linnet, and appeared like a dove', dresses as a man to run away to sea with her lover William. Their plans of escape fail. With nothing to eat, the two lovers 'folded together intending to die'.[99] It is a far cry from Mary Ambree's command of men in battle at Ghent.

These women warriors became delicate and fragile, mirroring the expectations of their sisters in conventional society.

Parody forms of the warrior woman ballads became more common, mocking rather than praising, and usually with a focus on sexual innuendo. The 'Female Cabin Boy', from the 1830s, illustrates the change:

> So nimble was that pretty maid & done her duty well
> But mark what followed often the thing itself will tell
> The captain with that pretty maid did oftimes kiss and toy
> For he soon found out the secret of the female cabin boy.[100]

And so the bold, brave heroines of the earlier ballads, firmly in charge of their own destinies, disappeared at the same time the door was closing on women's military service.

Conscription, and a more organised bureaucratic military, required minimum standards of health, height and weight for soldiers, and this required a physical examination. Even the best disguise could not withstand systematic physical assessment. And in the new dormitory or barracks housing,[101] it would no longer be possible to hide a female body and its needs. Some cross-dressing did persist, as we will see in the next chapter, but generally in a context where military organisation was poor.

The military of the later nineteenth century became regimented, organised and hyper-masculine. It is perhaps no coincidence that European militaries of this time began to require moustaches as a component of uniform. In Prussia, soldiers either had to have a moustache of a certain shape and size or one had to be drawn on.[102] British soldiers were required to have a moustache between 1860 and 1916. French soldiers were also required to have moustaches, but the style varied from regiment to regiment.[103] Military rules, down to the most arcane, left no space for women as part of the armed services.

With the disappearance of cross-dressing women from the military, women themselves got written out of debates about war and mobilisation, and their previous role was forgotten – or deliberately twisted. In the immediate aftermath of the American Civil War female soldiers were widely praised in the press; after the First World War, when the dominance of the new highly organised and highly male military was clear, women cross-dressers were usually portrayed as sexually loose, insane or lesbians (or some combination thereof). The female soldiers of the Civil War began to be seen through the lens of modern military life, and what historians saw was so outlandish that they dismissed it as incredible, immoral and shocking.[104] Women's contributions were not just forgotten; they were deliberately distorted. As women edged towards political power, their presence as members of the military became more threatening. American Civil War historians Lauren Cook Wike and DeAnn Blanton argue that when women's political participation in the form of suffrage was on the line, the desire to keep them out of the military (and therefore away from the civic rewards of military service) intensified,[105] paralleling the moves in France to remove *cantinières* from the battlefield.

As time went on, the women soldiers were written off as prostitutes. By 1966, Mary Massey was writing that 'many a romantic girl dreamed of being a second Joan of Arc, but those who actually entered the ranks by posing as men were usually viewed by contemporaries as mentally unbalanced or immoral' and that 'there is no question that many and probably most of all the women soldiers were prostitutes or concubines'.[106] Similar deliberate repression occurred over the remembrance of women fighting in the anti-Napoleonic wars in Prussia.[107]

It was also possible to dismiss the fighting of women dressed as men because it was part of an older form of war, less systematic and less effective. The modern military was perceived – not incorrectly – to be a major improvement on the past, better organised, better provisioned and better disciplined. Women could only sneak into the old-fashioned military because of its very weakness: disorganisation and a lack of systematisation. It was progress itself that made it impossible for a woman to disguise herself as a man in order to fight.

Military progress may have closed the door to women fighters, but an increasingly accepted view of femininity locked it. Throughout the industrialising world a growing middle class vigorously championed a model of femininity that privileged delicacy, gentleness and devotion to family and home. Ladies' magazines and conduct books for women and girls reinforced the message, which spread through Europe and the Americas.[108] This middle-class view of respectable femininity was proselytised to working-class women, often through the guise of civilising good works.[109] A proper woman was the pinnacle of feminine delicacy, and therefore both unwilling and unable to fight – and her menfolk would have failed in their duty to protect her if she did.

Changing your life was no longer simply a matter of donning a man's clothes and slipping out of the house to join an army on the march. The closing of the military to women was part of a wider closing down of opportunities of all kinds to women, and the opening up of a world where gender roles and expectations were differently defined.

The military of the nineteenth century no longer had a place for women. It had clear rules for recruitment, and effective, centralised organisation for everything from the provision of uniforms to the provision of food. All roles were to be fulfilled by men, and women were surplus to requirements. Society didn't just see this as military progress but as social progress, because it allowed women to flourish in their natural place: the home.

It is this military, the all-male military in an all-male battlefield, that we have come to regard as normal. Women on the battlefields of the twentieth century now had to overcome not only the view that they might be too delicate and too weak to be useful soldiers: they had to confront a dominant perception that they had never been there in the first place.

PART II
World War

6

The First World War

B<small>Y THE END</small> of the nineteenth century women had largely disappeared from the battlefields of Europe. Wives, disguised women, *cantinières* and other female interlopers had been removed as militaries became more organised. Women were no longer allowed on the battlefield, and usually not even near it, unless they were nurses. There were now sharp dividing lines between the front, where men fought, and the home, where women were safe. These dividing lines were reinforced by a solidified view of gender differences, where physically and emotionally frail women *needed* to be kept safe while their stronger male counterparts were naturally equipped for war.[1] It was only possible to maintain this ideal in smaller wars, where one power was pitted against another and the front was defined, or even more easily, where the war was in a distant empire and the fighting occurred overseas.

The First World War's totality crept up on its protagonists. When world leaders predicted the war would be over by Christmas, they were also failing to predict the level of social mobilisation necessary to maintain a multi-year, ultimately global war, which relied on industrial might and apparently endless reserves of manpower. And it was also in a context where no major war had occurred 'at home' in much of Europe for nearly fifty years.[2] So political and military leaders, having ensured that the battlefield was free of women, suddenly had a problem: they needed manpower, but how could women be mobilised to participate in this all-male activity?

The solution was to draw sharp boundaries between the battle 'out there' and the safety of home; battles were where the men fought and home was where the women supported the men. In fact, the term 'home front' came into existence in 1914, an invention of wartime propaganda,[3] as a counterpoint to 'war front'. In France, it was called the *arrière*, leaving the front 'a zone of pure masculinity' where 'the feminine should cease to exist'.[4] It was the place where women supported the war effort, and it was as distinct as possible from the actual front, where the fighting took place. But this necessitated a careful redrafting of boundaries: women could assist the military, but not be *in* the military; and to make the distinction even sharper, combat was only for men.[5] The formal exclusion of women from combat had begun.

The masculinity of combat was reinforced throughout the war by propaganda that drew an evocative picture of the female home front and the male war front. Both British and American recruiting posters asked women to be 'the girl behind the man behind the gun'. Ideally, the girls were far, far behind – and nearly every major military carefully designed their female support in order to ensure that women were nowhere near combat, even when they went to the front.

The manpower requirements of the war and the newly solidified lines that separated the girls at home from the boys at the front are all the more remarkable because they arose at a time when women were beginning to break through all kinds of barriers, from education to jobs in the professions. Through the suffrage movements, women were more politically and socially organised than ever before. But while women were making strides in society, they were formally closed off from the battlefield.

It is no coincidence that women's new political gains occurred at the same time women were more and more isolated from the military sphere. In most Western democracies, there are tight links between military service and citizenship. Throughout the nineteenth century military service (in most European countries through conscription) earned increasing citizenship rights. In France, the *cantinières* were shuffled from the battlefield because of this relationship;[6] it would have been inconvenient in the extreme to have women earn citizenship this way. The debate on suffrage in the American context was closely tied to the notion of military service – 'bullets for ballots'. Excluding women from military service ensured they were excluded from the vote.[7] Military service to the state was how a citizen contributed to the state; in turn, the state rewarded him (and it was always him) with the right to vote. One reason to guard the battlefield zealously from women was that it would deny them the same route to full democratic rights that men had been able to follow.

The creation of the home front, sharply separated from the front lines, relied on another new distinction. As historian Tammy Proctor explains, the First World War heralded a definitive but puzzling split between 'civilians' and 'soldiers' in the popular imagination: 'after all, what really separated an enlisted civilian male who donned a military uniform and carried a gun from a civilian male who made guns in a war factory under military control?'[8] Civilians were those at home, who required protection, while men fought at the front. This distinction laid the groundwork for dividing military jobs on the basis of whether they were combatant (at the front) or non-combatant (away from it), distinctions that were to dominate twentieth-century warfare and beyond.

While militaries did not realise how many women they would need for the war effort, women themselves, riding the crest of a wave of social and political organisation, were already organising for social, political and even military life. As a result, when war came, women were sometimes better prepared, and certainly more ambitious, for creating organised contributions to the war effort than governments, who were hampered by the view that women should be nowhere near the war. Nearly all the wartime protagonists faced a similar journey from the total exclusion of women from the military towards an organised and limited approach to female mobilisation. But mobilisation was not a top-down affair. In fact, it was made possible because of the efforts of women themselves.

When war finally came, in 1914, women were inspired to create organisations that would help assist with the war effort generally, not just in nursing, which was well established in volunteer organisations around Europe. Women also proposed organisations with a distinctly military flavour. In Britain, the Women's Volunteer Reserve (WVR) intended to defend the nation if Germany invaded, to free men for fighting at the front and to help those who were helpless. Established in December 1914, the WVR was quasi-military: the women drilled twice weekly in an organisation complete with battalions, officers and khaki uniforms. In 1916 its acting colonel wrote that women could do more than assist men – they could replace them. 'I have with me 250 hunting women,' she wrote, 'all hard as nails, and each brought up from girlhood to know and understand horses. Why waste us? The machinery to train and discipline a women's army is ready and waiting.'[9] The British women's organisations garnered themselves a mythical international reputation, with the press excitedly (and incorrectly) reporting that a group of Amazonian suffragettes were landing in France to assist the Allies.[10]

Not all the British women's organisations were so martial. In fact, the Women's Legion, formed in 1915 by Edith Vane-Tempest-Stewart, Lady Londonderry, as a breakaway group from the Women's Volunteer Reserve, was in its set-up and mission 'an implicit criticism of the paramilitary tendencies' of its progenitor.[11] Lady Londonderry later wrote that it was difficult to deal with the WVR because 'we had to contend with a section of She-Men who wished to be armed to the teeth' while reassuring the public that they did not wish to create 'a militant force of warlike Amazons capable of fighting side by side with men in the fighting-line'.[12] The Women's Legion began with a focus on providing cooks for the army, but eventually established administrative, clerical and agricultural sections.[13]

In France, women agitated for the right to support the military as early as 1913, when prominent archaeologist Jane Dieulafoy argued in the press and in public speeches that France should prepare for the coming war by using civilian women to replace male soldiers.[14] She had moderated her position: initially, Dieulafoy had proposed that French women should fight, and that she would fight with them.[15] Dieulafoy had form. She had, very soon after her marriage, dressed as a man to fight alongside her husband in the Franco-Prussian War in 1870, apparently with official permission.[16] After that war she continued in iconoclastic style by dressing as a man, a practice she adopted on archaeological sites in Persia so as to avoid the restrictions of femininity. As we have seen, sporting men's clothes in France required a permit from the authorities: Dieulafoy's obituary in the New York Times describes her as 'author, explorer, Chevalier of the Legion of Honor, and possessor of the unique privilege, accorded by the French Government, of wearing male apparel'.[17]

Dieulafoy may have been eccentric, but she was able to provide a list of over 400 women who were willing auxiliaries to the French government in 1914.[18] Other French women also began volunteer organisations inspired by Britain's paramilitary organisations, and these groups wore uniforms and marched in Paris; one organiser insisted that her volunteers could wage real war, 'the members will be militarised, under the command of male officers . . . they will receive a khaki uniform and learn to use a gun'.[19] Another hopeful group of women even wrote to the Ministry of War that 'our dearest hope is to be able to offer France a part of our youth and thus to co-operate with our brothers in the national defense'.[20] The Patriotic Union of Aviatrices and the Women's Automobile Club both lobbied the government to provide their services, and neither was successful.[21]

American women were similarly enthusiastic about military participation, particularly around the idea of home defence. The attacks on Belgian civilians, especially women, by Germany in the opening phases of the war became a propaganda rallying cry around the world. When the US entered the war, women began to prepare for their own defence against the fate of the *femmes Belges*. Suffragists in Old Orchard, Maine, heeded the call to 'learn to shoot and shoot straight' in the Women's Defense Club, 'so that if American women are ever called upon to defend their homes, their children, and themselves, they will not be as helpless as were the Belgian women'. Demand for the club was so high that it was decided to extend the plan nationally.[22] One of the organisers, Mrs Lurana Sheldon Ferris, was at pains to point out in a later letter to the *New York Times* that

> we do not drill nor wear khaki; we are not studying military tactics or meeting in armories; we are not learning to drive artillery horses nor load cannon; we are not endeavouring to instil the militaristic spirit in the brains of either women or children.[23]

Mrs Ferris's letter was necessary because other women *were* drilling and engaged in military preparedness. The American Women's League of Self-Defence gave a public demonstration of their drills, wearing assorted military uniforms featuring khaki, 'trim skirt[s]' and one 'big military hat'. Field Secretary Ida Vera Simonton sported

> a more picturesque uniform she had worn in the French Congo when she headed a troop of Singalese soldiers . . . she wore a white silk

shirtwaist for comfort but the uniform was completed by a short, snug coat of the khaki and a campaign hat. To make sure she did not lose her femininity in uniform, she wore small high-heeled boots and big pearl earrings.[24]

The matter of uniform was vexed, with a debate deemed newsworthy enough to appear in the *New York Times* under the headline, 'May Wear either Skirts or Breeches: Uniforms for Women's Self-Defense League are finally decided upon'.[25]

The league sought to 'teach the women who are not too flighty the use of firearms. We are doing this because of the atrocities suffered by the women at the front in Belgium and Poland'.[26] Many of these women's defence organisations had another purpose: to encourage (if not shame) men into joining the war. As Ida Vera Simonton put it,

> it is the greatest thing in the world to waken the men slackers. Look at the women here who want to enlist. If a war comes we shall be able to defend our homes and the homes of the women who haven't learned how.[27]

Throughout Europe, state authorities had rarely or never considered the formal mobilisation of women until manpower demands made it inevitable. Governments were fortunate they could capitalise on women's voluntary organisations when it became apparent the war's manpower needs were insatiable. In Britain, it was necessary to conscript men in 1916, which opened a debate on the role of women. The plethora of women's voluntary organisations was deemed too scattered to effectively release men for the front, but the existence of women's organisations made mobilisation easier,[28] and indeed the authorities particularly relied on the Women's Legion.

In France, women were not formally mobilised, but the government took full advantage of the women's organisations. The 'private yet semi-official aid provided by women to military personnel spread quickly from nursing to many other services' and the organisations sought, and were given, official recognition.[29] Women were treated as civilian employees, reflecting the nation's strong tradition of linking citizenship to military service; the French 'denied any suggestion that women, like men, were being called to national service for which they should be recompensed with rights'.[30] In 1914, France's army was 'the most masculine France had ever deployed in Europe and likely the most masculine French army ever'.[31]

France mobilised the largest overall number of women in the First World War,[32] some 200,000,[33] but perhaps in the most resolutely traditional fashion, with women working as civilians in stereotypically female roles ranging from typists to cooks, orderlies to phone operators, secretaries to mail workers.[34] Even qualified female doctors were told they were better to enrol as nurses.[35] In the end, as one commentator wrote,

> women are proud enough to say that they can be good soldiers, not by seizing a rifle or a grenade but by tapping on a typewriter, stirring sauces, plying a needle, wielding brush and scouring powder, adding up columns of numbers . . . Feminine patience and application will be precious auxiliaries to the superhuman valor of our soldiers.[36]

German women were organised into the Etappenhelferinnen, the Women Army Auxiliaries, after a sharp rise in casualties in 1916 required serious discussion of male conscription and female mobilisation. As elsewhere in Europe, there had been little planning for a long war and no planning for women's participation.[37] By spring 1917 men could not satisfy all Germany's manpower needs, and so the coordinated use of women's auxiliaries to free further men for front-line combat began.[38] The organisation of the women's auxiliaries similarly relied on pre-war women's organisations, using their leaders to run women's departments in the War Office and using their expertise and networks to maximise the number of men available to be sent to the front.[39] The wartime slogan became 'the mobilisation of women by women'.[40]

German women assisting the military remained civilians. Twenty-eight thousand nurses and 20,000 auxiliaries served with the German military.[41] Germany attempted to establish a women's signal corps organised along the lines of the British organisations; this would have been a more military organisation requiring uniforms, but as it was proposed in July 1918 the plan never really got off the ground before the war ended.[42]

Women's auxiliaries were also created in Austria-Hungary, where between 36,000 and 50,000 women served.[43] The United States, with

its late entry into the war, mobilised only 12,000 women into clerical and recruiting roles across the services; but women remained
civilians and did not wear a uniform.[44]

British women were mobilised along military lines, but legally they
remained civilians, 'enrolling' rather than 'enlisting' for service. The
primary British auxiliary was the Women's Army Auxiliary Corps
(WAAC), which sent its first draft of fourteen women to the front
in March 1917. These women were all members of the Women's
Legion.[45] It was later named the Queen Mary's Women's Army
Auxiliary Corps after receiving the patronage of the queen. The
WAAC was subsequently joined by auxiliaries for the Navy (Women's
Royal Navy Service, WRNS) and air force (Women's Auxiliary Air
Force, WAAF). Between 80,000 and 90,000 women served across all
three with the majority in the WAAC, with nine fatalities.[46] While
the authorities occasionally struggled to get enough women to enrol,
female enrolment quickly outpaced male enlistment, and the number
of volunteers meant that mooted plans for female conscription in
1918 were unnecessary.[47] Women also served in the Commonwealth,
including Australia and Canada.[48]

As the auxiliaries were not military, they had to dream up their
own conventions for naming their members and devising a uniform.
What to call the women of the WAAC instead of military titles
posed a challenge. At one stage the term 'amazon' was mooted and
rejected; while Helen Gwynne-Vaughan, the WAAC's director, felt
this suggestion was 'mercifully disregarded', it certainly would have
been more colourful than 'worker', the ultimate decision.[49] British
authorities also worried about how to keep military women's appearance feminine without being sexy. While the WAAC's skirts may
have been a 'most daringly short' twelve inches from the ground,
their uniforms had the breast pockets removed so as not to emphasise a WAAC's bust.[50]

Even though women were deemed necessary for the war, in many
quarters they were still treated as clearly inferior to men. There was
a general view that women could replace men — but it would take
more than one woman to replace the work of a single man. In
Britain, this was referred to as the 'principle of dilution' — where
four women clerks would be necessary to do the work of three male

clerks.[51] Field Marshal Douglas Haig felt that even simple tasks at the front could not be performed by women – work as apparently basic as sorting the mail: 'The work of sorting as it is carried out in France is totally different to that in England and it is extremely doubtful women could undertake it'.[52] Haig also believed that women nurses 'could not have stood the enormous and incessant strain, both mental and physical' of the hospitals at the Somme[53] – despite the presence of women medics at many of the places of fiercest fighting away from the Western front (and the fairly recent history of British women withstanding the incessant strain of war throughout the nineteenth century).

The wartime auxiliaries, despite efforts to keep them as non-military as possible, clearly upset people's strongly held gender expectations. There were extensive rumours across all the auxiliaries about female sexual licentiousness. No doubt this stemmed in part from the belief that women associated with the military were like the camp followers of the previous centuries – in other words, whores.

In Germany, rumours about sexually louche women were rife; the 'dear Officers' treated the women as 'female creatures to amuse themselves with'.[54] In France, one general argued that women's 'inevitable promiscuity' would create an 'obligation for officers . . . to exercise surveillance like that of a parent and a vice cop'.[55]

By late 1917 rumours of sexual immorality were undermining the WAAC's recruitment efforts in Britain. The rumours were worse for women who were based in France, already 'perceived in the public imagination as a hotbed of vice and prostitution'.[56] Helen Gwynne-Vaughan noted that 'at one time we were actually stated to have produced more babies than there were women in the Corps in France'.[57] Investigations into the claims proved them to have little foundation,[58] and ultimately the sponsorship of Queen Mary was needed to restore the unit to respectability.[59]

Sexual innuendo was only one of the problems facing women in the First World War. As the war dragged on, women working with the military faced increasing resentment from the men they replaced. Being freed to go to the front was hardly a desirable proposition for many men, who would have preferred to stay behind enemy lines. French men resented women for this reason.[60] In Germany, a female

Women's Department official noted that the 'auxiliaries were sometimes greeted with outright threats, the statement that "the war would
be prolonged because of them"'.[61]

While the official auxiliaries kept women as far away from the
conflict as possible, this was not to say that women themselves were
always of the same mind. In fact, some were enthusiastic about
fighting. In 1909 a schoolgirl wrote to *Votes for Women*:

> Dear Sir:
>
> I am an average girl of the day. I have two cousins about my own
> age in the Territorials. In the case of one I am actually stronger than
> he, and though not stronger in muscle than the other, I am stronger
> in endurance and stamina, for when we return he is tired out and I am
> scarcely fatigued at all . . . My brother, a strong, healthy specimen,
> is certainly very much stronger than I . . . but, on the other hand, I
> am equal to him in physical and moral courage. I am sure I could
> fight as well as my boy or men friends if I had to – at any rate, I am
> quicker and have more presence of mind.
>
> Yours, etc. A Schoolgirl.[62]

Women were very keen to become involved, and in many cases
far more involved than the powers that be would allow. A Mrs Alec
Tweedie wrote to Lord Kitchener, offering to 'enlist one hundred
women, largely from her friends; they could muster at her house
. . . drill ourselves to get for *work of any kind*'.[63]

German girls were equally enthused. An eighteen-year-old called
Anna Sauter wrote to King Ludwig of Bavaria:

> my two brothers have volunteered and they have been gone since
> September, my father will still have to go and so I don't want to sit
> at home and be idle while so many men lay down their lives for the
> fatherland. I, too, have German blood running through my veins and
> I want to have a closer relation to the war.[64]

Some women did more than write letters. They actually went to
the front. In France, the exploits of Marie Marvingt, even before the
war, were so remarkable as to be almost ridiculous. Among other
things, Marvingt was accomplished in swimming, horse riding,
archery, automobile driving, riflery, billiards, tennis, golf, gymnastics,

athletics, canoe racing, martial arts, mountain climbing, skiing, luge and hot-air ballooning.[65] She was also an accomplished cyclist, usually astride her favourite bike, Zéphyrine, and in 1908 she decided to enter the Tour de France. Undeterred by her official rejection, she rode the 4,497-kilometre course behind the men, and while seventy-six of the initial male entrants failed to complete the course, Marie Marvingt and thirty-six men made it all the way to the end.[66]

In addition to her various sporting accomplishments, Marvingt was a famous *aviatrice*. She began her airborne career in a balloon, becoming the first woman to cross the Channel from Europe to Britain (apparently *impromptu* while blown by a gale). She then became the third woman in France to gain a pilot's licence, and set the first French aviation records for women.[67]

At the outbreak of war, Marie Marvingt was one of France's most experienced pilots. She volunteered her services as a pilot to the French authorities, expecting to be enthusiastically greeted – her plane was requisitioned, but Marie herself was not.[68] Undaunted (a term that seems to have applied to much of her life), she enrolled as a nurse, which provided the opportunity for her to become the first woman to fly in combat. In 1915 Marvingt discovered that a crucial mission was in jeopardy because one of the pilots was injured. She did what to her was obvious: standing in for the injured pilot, she flew a bomber to the German aerodrome of Frescaty, near Metz – an action for which she received the Croix de Guerre, the citation for which points to her two raids on this aerodrome.[69] This was likely the first flight of a woman in combat.

Having cracked aerial combat, Marvingt moved on to the battle-field itself. Disguising herself as Private Second Class Beaulieu, in the 42nd Batallion of the Chasseurs à Pied,[70] she made her way to the front. Exactly how she did so remains slightly opaque, although in 1965 she claimed that it was with the connivance of Marshal Foch himself.[71] Her sojourn at the front appears to have lasted three to six weeks, during which time she fired on the enemy and received another *palme* on her Croix de Guerre.[72] In the end an injury forced her to leave the front and reveal herself, to the surprise of her comrades. Marie remarked, 'You should have seen their love-starved faces when they realised they'd been sharing their quarters with a woman!'[73] Marvingt went next to the Dolomites to join the Italian Third Regiment of Alpine Troops, where no doubt her alpine sporting skills were put to good use, skiing in supplies and evacuating the injured.[74]

Marvingt was not only a skilled pilot, trained nurse and multi-talented athlete. She had the skill to spot opportunities to combine her various talents. As early as 1911, it occurred to her that a plane furnished with a telegraph would make an ideal vehicle for bringing medical help to the front and evacuating soldiers to hospital behind the lines; as she put it,

> It wouldn't be used at first so much to transport the wounded as to find them, notify physicians of their whereabouts, and bring medical supplies to the first-aid stations. I've been looking at a sort of flying stretcher, which could be adapted to my plane.[75]

Marie's friend Émile Friant made a painting featuring this idea, which was later sold as postcards and posters in order to raise money for a plane to be built to her specifications. Marvingt spent nearly forty years advocating for air ambulances.

Marvingt's exploits made her a heroine, but also made her no-torious. In 1916 she applied for a permit to go to Italy to report on the war as a journalist; to do so required reference from her local préfet, who did so grudgingly:

> Mlle Marvingt is very well known in sporting circles in our region . . . Masculine in appearance, Mlle Marvingt has very free morals, and although no precise facts have been established, her behaviour in her private life leaves much to be desired. Despite this her patriotism cannot be doubted.[76]

Officialdom was in general quiet about her exploits. Information about her successful bombing raid was only made public in 1932.[77]

The many fronts of the First World War saw many different armies – and on some of these fronts, it was simply more possible for women to join the fighting. British woman Flora Sandes, the daughter of a clergyman, had initially sought to support the war effort through nursing. She was rejected by the Voluntary Aid Detachment, and as a result set off for Serbia with a contingent of Red Cross nurses.

Conditions on the Serbian front were shocking, with few supplies and rampant typhus. Eventually, Sandes became the unit's unofficial surgeon, and her diary contains notes such as 'cut off a man's toes with a pair of scissors this afternoon'.[78]

Seeking a position closer to the front, Sandes became an ambulance driver, but the war was taking a dire turn against Serbia. In October 1915 Germany, Austria-Hungary and Bulgaria launched a major offensive which eventually encircled Serbian forces on the large plains surrounding Kosovo. Flora began her transition from medic to soldier. One commander lent her a horse, and she noted in her diary that

> he seems awfully bucked that I can ride, and declares they have a small cavalry detachment of 30 of the best riders . . . and that I'd better belong to that . . . they seem bent on turning me into a soldier, and I expect I'll find myself in the trenches next battle![79]

It was clear by November 1915 that the Serbian army, their king and thousands of civilians were thoroughly entrapped, and the only way out was to retreat through Albania, over the mountains to Scutari (Shkodër). Flora Sandes was perhaps the only ambulance driver remaining with the army. Serbian General Miloš Vasić enrolled her as a private in the army. She later became a corporal.

The retreat moved through the mountains in the middle of winter. It wasn't only the army. A long tail of civilians, thought to be in greater danger staying in Albania than fleeing, accompanied them. 'The soldiers were all retreating across the snow,' wrote Sandes, 'and I never saw such a depressing sight. The grey November twilight, the endless white expanse of snow, lit up every moment by the flashes of guns and the long column of men trailing away into the dusk wailing a sort of dismal dirge.'[80] The army traversed high mountain passes under Austrian bombing (one of the first recorded bombings of civilians). Conditions were frigid. Gordon Gordon-Smith, an English journalist accompanying the Serbs, wrote that conditions were so cold that

> every few hundred yards we would come on corpses of Serbian soldiers, sometimes singly, sometimes in groups. One man had evidently gone to sleep beside a wretched fire he had been able to light. The

heat of it had melted the snow, and the water had flowed over his feet. In the night during his sleep this had frozen and his feet were imprisoned in a solid block of ice. When I reached him he was still breathing. From time to time he moved feebly as if trying to free his feet from their icy covering. We were powerless to aid him, he was so far gone that nothing could have saved him.[81]

Four hundred thousand people began the journey; approximately 240,000 of them died, both civilians and soldiers.[82]

As they neared Scutari, Flora's Fourth Company became bogged down in mud:

It came right above the tops of my top boots, and one could hardly drag one's feet out of it. The road was full of rocks and pits, and every two or three yards there were dead or dying horses which had floundered down to rise no more; and it was pitch dark and very cold.[83]

Eventually the convoy made it to Scutari, where many were evacuated.

In 1916 the Serbs began to push back against their primarily Bulgarian adversaries, in what is now Macedonia. Sandes was with the Serbian army during its advance on Monastir (now Bitola). She was busy. 'Chased Bulgars all day over the most awful hills and stones, I don't know how many miles,' she reported in her diary, 'had a great shooting match at long range. I used up all my ammunition.'[84] The fighting in the hills required Flora and the men to huddle in small holes awaiting the order to attack. Sandes wrote that

if anyone in Croydon begins to ask me to describe the war I shall tell them to go to their back garden and dig a hole and sit there for anything from three days and nights to a month, in November, without anything to read or do, and they can judge for themselves, minus the chance of being killed, of course.[85]

During the final assault on Monastir, Sandes was wounded by a grenade. She relayed to the *New York Times* that

we had been crouching and shivering in our little shallow pits for hours, waiting impatiently for the order to attack. At 7 a.m., the order came. It was snowing, and snow lay on the ground. I was out of my pit in half a second and running as fast as my legs could carry me. I was always the first to leave cover; it was my duty as a petty officer. I had nearly reached the brink of the Bulgarian trench when a well-aimed grenade dropped near, and I fell wounded. A young officer crawled up toward me over the snow, and seizing my hands, pulled me over its smooth surface into the shelter of a rock. The torture of being dragged by the hand of my broken arm was acute, yet it was not very much greater than what I had already been suffering.[86]

Her immediate first aid was 'fully half a bottle of brandy' and a cigarette.[87] Sandes had ended up with, according to the newspaper, twenty-five wounds and one or two 'splinters' – in actuality the shrapnel wounds would require repeated surgical attention.[88] The worst of the damage was apparently blocked by her revolver, which had absorbed the impact.[89] The battle itself was brutal – 6,000 men launched the assault on Monastir, and only 1,800 survived unscathed.[90]

In hospital, Sandes was granted the highest Serbian military decoration, the Order of the Kara George Star – delivered at her bedside by the Prince Regent (the New York Times article that reported her wounds also blithely headlined the article 'Wounded English Girl Wins Serbian Cross' – she was forty).[91] The medal carried with it a promotion to sergeant major. Her citation read that one Flora Sandes 'has distinguished herself by her courage and by a rare spirit of self-sacrifice in all combats . . . she served as an example to her company by her bravery'.[92]

Sandes was not the only woman in the Serbian army. Her memoirs mention others, and scholars report a tradition of women in the Serbian army:[93] the desperate need for personnel made commanders more open to women.[94] One Serbian woman, Milunka Savić, was in the same regiment as Flora and was wounded at least five times.[95]

Flora Sandes went back and forth to her regiment in between treatments for her injuries, and she was back again in the last months of the war when the Serbian army made its final push against the Bulgarian army, marching forwards while the Bulgarians burned the grass and scrub to mask their retreat. The Serbs pursued them over steep and rocky territory. During this advance Flora was again honoured with a medal, the citation for which read:

She has stopped the enemies counter attack [*sic*] as head of the squadron
. . . opening rapid fire against them . . . she fought very courage-
ously . . . outstripping all the company, despite the open ground, and
leading by her example as usual the soldiers to accept with joy even
the roughest combat.[96]

All the other sergeant majors – men, of course – were promoted
en masse to second lieutenants at the end of the war. Flora was not.
She went to her commanding officer to complain – as there were
no regulations *against* women officers, he agreed to take it up the
chain of command. After positive references from all her commanders
and the personal investigation of Serbian Crown Prince Alexander,
she was promoted to second lieutenant – which required a special
Act of Parliament.[97] She was eventually demobilised in 1923.

Between the wars Flora married a Russian soldier who had joined
the Serbian army and the pair continued to live in Serbia. In 1941
she was again mobilised, alongside her husband, into the Serbian
army, but Serbia's quick capture led to their internment. Sandes'
husband died after their release later in 1941, and she returned to
England, where she lived until her death in 1956.

If a woman wanted to engage in combat in France or Britain, her
presence would be detected and she would be politely (or not so
politely) rebuffed. After all, Flora Sandes had to go to Serbia to fight,
and Marie Marvingt's persistent hassling of the authorities was persistently denied, her limited work in combat ultimately relying on luck.
The letters of patriotic women and girls begging to go to the front
in Britain, France and Germany did not succeed. Yet this was not
true everywhere in the First World War.

At the outbreak of war, young Russian women were keen to fight.
One girl wrote to the tsar:

I pray to Your Imperial Majesty to allow me to join the ranks of
the troops with the same kind of noble and radiant outburst for the
MOTHERLAND, with which the heart of Durova was filled and
with which my own soul, filled with courage and fearlessness and
unwomanly boldness, burns . . . When I hear soldiers' song or see
troops (the cavalry, I so, so, love horses) I am transformed, everything inside brightens and rejoices, and at the sight of dashing soldiers my

soul wants to leap out of my body, and I want to be among them and also be a defender of the Motherland.[98]

But unlike other European women, Russian women only started by writing letters. As many as a thousand women went to the front, and possibly more; the fact that they dressed as men may mask larger numbers.[99] By 1915 the Russian press was reporting that female soldiers were a common sight,[100] and they fought in the infantry and the cavalry, as military reconnaissance and as medics (a role reserved for men in the Russian army).[101] So many women sought to fight that the Russian authorities were forced to come up with a policy on the question, deciding that women could be allowed to fight only when the tsar approved their petitions. These petitions were duly archived, and while not all were successful, some women did make it to the front with the official imprimatur of the tsar.[102]

Russian women had a proud martial tradition. Nadezhda Durova, a noblewoman who disguised herself as a male cavalry officer, fought in the early part of the nineteenth century, fighting in her first battle in 1807. She experienced real danger, 'so close to me that it couldn't have been closer. A shell fell under my horse's belly, immediately exploded, and whistling splinters flew in all directions'.[103] She continued to serve with the blessing of Tsar Alexander I after she was discovered. Durova was a national heroine in Russia and the first woman to win the Cross of Saint George for valour.

Individual Russian women made it to the front, with or without official permission. In July 1914, only days after the First World War erupted, Zoya Smirnova and eleven of her friends from the same Moscow high school crept out of their homes early one morning, into hired carriages, without telling their families. 'We decided to run away to the war at all costs,' Zoya later recounted. 'It was a bit terrible at first; we were very sorry for our fathers and mothers, but the desire to see the war and ourselves kill Germans overcame all other sentiments.'[104] The girls, aged between fourteen and seventeen, joined a train filled with soldiers, who hid them from the authorities and provided them with military uniforms. The train was headed towards the Carpathian front, the mountain ranges dividing the Russian Empire from the Austro-Hungarian Empire (cutting between what is now Slovakia and Hungary in the west and Ukraine and Romania in the east). The Carpathian front was a brutal battlefield in the generally brutal eastern front.

Zoya and her friends were discovered on arrival at the front, but allowed to stay with their new regiment. They had arrived at one of the worst places to fight of the war. Not only did soldiers face the usual dangers of battle; they also faced the mountains and the snow, frostbite, exposure and hypothermia. Over a million Russians died, and Austria-Hungary lost a quarter of a million more. The average soldier on the Carpathian front survived 'between five and six weeks before he was killed, wounded, or captured. Suicides became a common occurrence'.[105]

Zoya's response to life on the front was unsurprising. 'Who wouldn't be afraid?' she asked. 'When for the first time they began to fire with their heavy guns, several of us couldn't stand it and began to cry out.' One of Zoya's friends, sixteen-year-old Zina Morozov, was killed by an artillery shell. The girls 'somehow collected her bones and laid them in a hastily dug grave. In the same grave we also laid all Zina's things, such as she had with her'. Zoya, like many of her friends, was wounded once, and then twice, after which she was taken to hospital and lost track of her regiment and her fellow runaways. She was left with nothing but her Cross of Saint George military honour and the documents proving she'd received it for bravery during reconnaissance. Having lost her regiment, she turned to nursing.[106]

Zoya was not alone. Other women also fought. Anna Krasnilkova, who was twenty and a miner's daughter, disguised herself as a man, fought in nineteen battles and was awarded the Saint George Cross, Fourth Class.[107] Martha Malko fought with her husband until he was killed. In total she fought in three battles and captured the German flag at a battle in Poland.[108] L. P. Tychninina, a student, disguised herself as a man and enrolled as an army medic in an infantry company despatched to the trenches, and was wounded six times trying to get her comrades out from behind enemy lines.[109] Vasia Federenko had written for permission to her regional governor saying that 'Thousands of women could be fighting in the ranks of the Russian army. Why don't they trust that we, like men, can also take up arms and go to the defense of our homeland with pride?'[110] Denied, Federenko and two friends sewed to make money for the journey to the front, where they were spotted and arrested.

Western observers were quick to take notice of Russia's women soldiers. Florence Farmborough, a British nurse on the Russian front, observed that

> a woman soldier, or boy soldier, was no unusual sight in the Russian Army. We had even come into contact with a couple of Amazon warriors; one, in her early twenties, who had had a nasty gash on her temple caused by a glancing bullet.[111]

The American journalist Rheta Childe Dorr interviewed one young woman soldier, fighting in a male regiment. The soldier was in hospital, 'a bullet in her side and a broken hand in a plaster cast'. She assured Dorr that 'fighting was the most congenial work she had ever done'.[112] She had been wounded in her first battle, where a thousand of her comrades had stormed enemy trenches, and she was one of only thirty-seven who had survived. Wounded, and 'bleeding pretty badly', she saw her captain: 'and he was badly wounded, almost unconscious in fact, and I had to get him to the rear on my back'. She collapsed when she reached the Red Cross.[113]

Russian women played a unique role in the First World War. One reason for their ability to join in combat was a generally higher level of official disorganisation in the Russian military. Women were able to evade military physicals by joining troops at the front rather than at recruiting stations,[114] which again was particularly Russian; any French or English woman who attempted the same thing would very likely be summarily dismissed. Class likely played a role, too.

Russia's lack of industrialisation also explains why the prevailing model of femininity, the domestic angel safely occupied at home, was less dominant and so created more space for unusual female activity. While the view that the ideal middle-class woman was delicately devoted to her family did spread to Russia,[115] the fact was that Russian peasantry constituted 86.9 per cent of the population in 1858, only falling to 79.3 per cent by 1913.[116] Russian society was entirely accustomed to seeing women carrying heavy loads, killing animals and living a life as rough at home as would have been the case on the battlefield. Maria Bochkareva, who was to play a crucial role in the First World War, was a butcher before the war. It was far less of a leap to imagine a female soldier when your village had a female butcher.

Russian women didn't just serve as plucky individuals. Like their Western European counterparts, they were able organisers, and with the support of the government organised entire battalions. The women's battalions clearly owed their creation to the desperate Russian military situation after the Provisional Government took power in the February Revolution. Morale was at rock bottom, and the combination of an unpopular war and revolutionary politics was potent. The Provisional Government swiftly acted to give women the political rights for which they had been agitating. Revolutionary fervour, an unpopular war with a manpower problem, and women fortified with a new political voice combined with the already existing tradition of women soldiers to open up the possibility of female military service in a much more organised fashion. As in the rest of Europe, agitation by women's groups led to the creation of a women's military organisation; the difference in Russia was that women were willing to fight and the government was willing to let them.

Women's groups began to organise various forms of military support. One group, the Women's National Military Union of Volunteers, published an advertisement that read:

> women citizens, all to whom the freedom and happiness of Russia is dear, hurry into our ranks – hurry while it is still not too late to stop the collapse of our dear motherland. By participating directly in military activity, we women citizens must raise the spirit of the army.[117]

The union's advertisement highlighted a key feature of Russian women's mobilisation: women could 'encourage morale' among the men at the front. In this context, encouraging morale was seasoned with a large dash of shaming men: if women could fight, it would show men that their dwindling support for and even cowardice in the face of the war was particularly pathetic.

Women's battalions were raised all over the Russian Empire, from Ekaterinodar to Odessa and Tashkent, both with and without official sanction. In July 1917 the Army General Staff noted that lately there have appeared . . . women's delegations from many cities in Russia, proposing their services for formation of military units made up of women volunteers, with the request that they be sent to the front as quickly as possible for direct participation in battle.[118]

This extensive military enthusiasm created significant headaches for the wobbly Provisional Government, which began to worry about the merits of having large groups of armed women who could potentially undermine it, and so tried to stamp out unofficial units.[119] In total, sixteen all-female units were created between May and October 1917,[120] in fifteen cities, including Harbin, Moscow, Kiev, Petrograd and Tashkent.[121] Smaller units, such as machine-gun detachments, also began to appear.[122]

The most famous women's unit of the war was the only one that saw combat: the Battalion of Death, led by Maria Bochkareva. Bochkareva, depressed following the collapse of her unfortunate marriage to a petty criminal, tried to enlist in 1914; when the commanding officer refused, she had him telegraph the tsar, who gave permission. Bochkareva prided herself on her manly soldiering skills, from smoking and drinking to visiting brothels (the latter supposedly to satisfy her curiosity). She fought with distinction and was one of the only enlisted women to be awarded the Saint George Cross as a *woman* soldier rather than as a disguised man or a medic. She had an outsized international reputation, the *Daily Telegraph* praising her as 'finely yet strongly built, with broad shoulder and healthy complexion, she can lift 200 pounds with the greatest of ease. She has never known what fear is'.[123]

When the idea of the women's battalions first began to circulate, Bochkareva was an obvious potential leader. By May 1917 there were posters of Bochkareva recruiting for the new all-women unit, and Bochkareva herself was touting for soldiers on the lecture circuit, where she exhorted,

I have decided to form a Women's Battalion of Death . . . to create real soldier-women and go with them to the front . . . it must serve to shame those male deserters, who, on the eve of final victory, avoid the enemy and run away from their civic duty.[124]

Bochkareva was an illiterate peasant, and she ran her unit on brutal lines: the women were required to get crew cuts, encouraged to smoke, swear and spit; and not allowed any personal hygiene items. They trained for hours in hand-to-hand combat and firearms before sleeping on bare-board beds with thin sheets.[125] Bochkareva said in her memoirs that 'giggling was strictly forbidden . . . some were expelled for too much laughing, others for frivolities'.[126] The women 'were outfitted and equipped exactly like the men soldiers. They wore the same kind of khaki trousers, loose-belted blouse and high peaked cap',[127] but also wore a capsule of cyanide around the neck in case of capture.[128] The women swore an oath: 'my death for the Motherland and for the freedom of Russia is happiness'.[129] Needless to say, Bochkareva's rules deterred many of her 2,000 initial recruits.[130]

On 9 July 1918 the Women's Battalion of Death saw its first engagement with the enemy. One of the many challenges facing the Provisional Government was the establishment of unions for soldiers, or Soldiers' Committees, after the overthrow of the tsar. These committees could and did decide not to fight, leading to desertions and even mass mutinies. On 9 July some of the male units refused to fight, and Bochkareva's battalion (subject entirely to their commander's will – Bochkareva did not hold with the notion of a soldier's committee and made her women sign a paper renouncing the idea) advanced. Afterwards, the commander of the 525th Regiment wrote that the women

> conducted themselves heroically in battle, consistently maintaining their position in the front lines, carrying out service on par with [male] soldiers . . . the battalion provided an example of courage, bravery, and composure, raised the spirits of the soldiers, and showed that each of these heroines deserve the name of warrior in the Russian army.[131]

The fighting was fierce. One of the battalion's women told an American journalist how she killed a German soldier whose helmet she had as a trophy: 'I stabbed him . . . it was his life or mine. I raised my rifle. I plunged with all my strength. The bayonet went deep into his body. At the same moment I pulled the trigger. He dropt [*sic*] dead'.[132] The battalion took casualties: at least thirty-six were wounded and two killed.[133] After the battle a memorial service for the dead was held in Kazan Cathedral where the priest said,

> this is a terrible, and yet a glorious hour for Russia. Sad it is, and terrible beyond expression that men have allowed women to die in their places for our unhappy country. But glorious it will ever be that Russian women have been ready and willing to do it.[134]

The American press was fascinated by the battalion's activities.[135] Bessie Beatty, an American journalist who visited Russia in 1917, went to the front to meet Bochkareva and her women, describing the young soldier women, with their badges on their sleeves 'red "for the Revolution that must not die," and black "for a death that is preferable to dishonor for Russia"'.[136] Maria Skridlova, Bochkareva's right-hand woman, saw Beatty after the battalion's first military engagement. 'There were wounded Germans in a hut,' she recounted, 'we were ordered to take them prisoners. They refused to be taken. We had to throw hand grenades in and destroy them. No; war is not easy for a woman.'[137] Beatty concluded that 'Women can fight. Women have the courage, the endurance, even the strength, for fighting.' For her, the question was not whether women could fight but whether they should. 'She is a potential soldier, and will continue to be until the muddled old world is remade upon a basis of human freedom and safety,' she reflected.[138]

All the women's units garnered attention. The Moscow battalion, before its eventual dissolution, received a visit from the British suffragette Emmeline Pankhurst, who inspected the troops. Mrs Pankhurst was very much on message about the potential impact of the Battalion of Death: she exhorted one fundraising rally, 'men of Russia, must the women fight? Are there men who will stay at home and let them fight alone?'[139] The British military attaché, Major General Sir Alfred Knox, also saw the women drilling:

> about 1,000 women marched past the Embassy this morning on their way to be inspected by Kerenskii on the Palace Square. They made the best show of any soldiers I have seen since the Revolution, but it gave me a lump in the throat to see them, and the utter swine of 'men' soldiers jeering at them.[140]

(The effort to shame Russian men into fighting by arming women certainly would have worked on Knox – he was outraged by the 'crowds of able-bodied men, lounging, chewing sunflower seeds every day, and watching women train to fight while they shirked their duty').[141]

By the autumn of 1918 Russian officials were no longer convinced that the women's units were accomplishing what it had set out for them to do. Morale had not increased, and thin resources were being stretched to accommodate them. The government decided to dissolve all the women's battalions except for Bochkareva's and the Petrograd unit, which was about to play a fateful role in the collapse of the Kerensky government.

The Petrograd Battalion was mobilised to help defend the Winter Palace in the final days of the Kerensky government.[142] Two hundred women were inside the palace, which the Bolsheviks took easily. The facts of what these women did have been tainted by the pro- and anti-Bolshevik sentiment that colours the record of the fall of the Winter Palace. John Reed, an American journalist and Bolshevik supporter, was an eyewitness to the events. After the fighting, he asked after the women soldiers; he was told 'they were huddled up in a back room. We had a terrible time deciding what to do with them – many were in hysterics'.[143] But there are other eyewitness accounts that the women were not hiding but among the last to give up the fight.[144] The women were incarcerated by the Bolsheviks after the revolution, and Sir Alfred Knox tried to secure their release, a request initially denied by the functionary in charge because he claimed that the women 'had resisted to their last at the Palace, fighting desperately with bombs and revolvers'. Knox also recounts that after their release the women came to see him:

> They asked if it were possible for them to be transferred to the British Army, as they could do nothing more to help Russia. I told them Englishwomen were not allowed to fight, and that they would be jealous if their Russian sisters were permitted to go to the front.

This latter statement was patronising tact; after the women left, Knox declared 'no nation except the Russian had allowed its women to fight, and certainly the British nation never would'.[145]

When the Winter Palace fell, and with it the Provisional Government, the Battalion of Death was still at the front, where they experienced huge animosity; indeed, the danger they faced from Russian soldiers exceeded the threat of the enemy.[146] The remaining women of the Petrograd Battalion, with their short hair, were easily identified and abused before the Bolsheviks dissolved the unit.[147] Maria Bocharnikova, who fought with the Petrograd Battalion, told of a volunteer who wrote of her treatment: 'I am not in a position to tell what was done to us . . . it would have been better had they shot us, than let us go after what we had been through'.[148]

Throughout Europe, at the end of the war (or following the Revolution) women returned to normal society. Despite their organisational skills, upon which nearly every country relied in order to assist the war effort, and despite noteworthy individual action, the line between the home front and the battlefield seemed to be more firmly drawn than ever, splitting the increasingly male military world from the more and more feminine domestic one.

The horrific experiences of ordinary men, not professional soldiers, at the front no doubt further sharpened this distinguishing line. Between 1914 and 1918 more than twice as many men were killed or died later of war wounds than had been killed in *all* major wars between 1790 and 1914.[149] If ordinary men, tested in the crucible of war, struggled to cope with the horrors, faced terrible injury and died in great numbers, then why would they subject their mothers, wives and sisters to the same fate? War was bad enough, but men had been encouraged to fight with propaganda that reminded them they were protecting the women in their lives. Any thought that lingered over whether women had a place on the battlefield could hardly stand against the lived experience of men who had suffered.

The particular nature of trench warfare also built up the myth of the bond created among a small band of men, fighting together under terrible circumstances. The historian George Mosse points out that in the trenches soldiers worked in small units of around twelve people, giving rise to intense bonds amid the omnipresence of death. Celebrating the bonds between men in the trenches was a way to pull positivity out of the despair and death of the war. The 'Myth of the War Experience . . . looked back upon the war as a meaningful and even sacred event'.[150] It was centred on masculinity and virility, and included women only in 'passive and supporting roles', as symbols of what was left behind at home.[151] The bond may have been intensified by the fact that some men enjoyed the war – as Joanna Bourke has persuasively argued, the intimacy of violence, the pleasure of combat, draws men towards each other.[152] A sacred bond among men was one way to rationalise the fighting, but the experience of war also suggested that women had no place at the front, and as time passed, its glorification extended to the belief that such a bond among men was essential to military success. The myth of the band of brothers was supported by the trenches of the First World War.

The end of the First World War marks the final shift that drew the lines that kept women at home while men went to war. The home front now existed, and was the only appropriate place for a woman. The women who did fight in the war were curiosities, like Flora Sandes, or exceptions, like Marie Marvingt. Flora Sandes undertook a very successful lecture tour of Australia in 1920, where the governor of New South Wales remarked, 'I have not heard of anything finer, brighter, more natural, braver, more skilful, or more modern than the work of Lieut. Flora Sandes'.[153] Even forgotten were the instances where women's combat skills had shown they could cross the line from home front to war zone. No consideration was given to whether other women would have been as capable as Flora. The experience of Russian women was easy to dismiss – even in Russia – as a crazy decision made by a desperate state with a chaotically organised military. It was certainly no model for the world.

The First World War was a final turning point: the bonds between citizenship, military service and masculinity that had been tightening since the nineteenth century were now complete. An American journalist noted that 'A stock argument against women having the vote has always been that women could not fight for their country. The Battalion of Death has answered that argument.'[154] Even their civilian contributions were carefully weighed against those of men; after all, if military service had earned men political rights, had women done 'enough' to get the vote?[155] In Britain and the US, it was enough of a factor to push the government to extending suffrage, but not enough to keep women in their wartime roles. By the start of the

Second World War women's organisations had to fight for mobilisation, even just to civilian roles, all over again.

Total social mobilisation in the First World War did not challenge the belief that women should not fight. In fact, it had a reinforcing effect, as the need to mobilise women for war in a world that now saw the presence of women on the battlefield as undesirable at best and insane at worst meant that strict lines had to be drawn. Women would be allowed to support the military, but strictly prevented from doing anything like fighting. Only in Russia, with its potent combination of women's political emancipation, revolution and a dire military situation, were circumstances any different. In the Second World War much remained the same: women were kept away from combat – often behind the thinnest of fig leaves – except in the Soviet Union.

7

The Soviet Union in the Second World War

IN 1930 A twenty-seven-year-old English pilot called Amy Johnson became the first woman to fly solo from England to Australia. She set off from London with sandwiches and chocolate, avoiding storms, a leaking petrol tank and sandstorms, flying for 11,000 miles to reach Australia in nineteen days.[1] Johnson would go on to set many other records: she was the first pilot to fly from London to Moscow in one day; she held time records for flights from Britain to Japan as well as from Britain to South Africa. She was the most famous British woman pilot of her generation, perhaps only eclipsed internationally by Amelia Earhart.

Eight years later a twenty-seven-year-old Soviet pilot called Marina Raskova and two other women were determined to set a women's record for the world's longest straight-line flight. They flew east from Moscow for thirty straight hours. As they were flying over Siberia, poor weather and dwindling fuel caused the trio to make a forced landing. As the plane descended, Raskova jumped out to lighten the plane's load and ensure a safer landing for her fellow pilots. She was lost in the wilds of the Russian Far East for ten days with no water and almost no food.[2] (The other two pilots apparently had to contend with marauding bears and a lynx in the cockpit.)[3] Even with their unscheduled landing, the three women had flown 4,010 miles, and succeeded in setting the record. Raskova and her comrades were the first women to be awarded medals as Heroes of the Soviet Union.

What happened to these women during the Second World War reveals a great deal about wartime roles for women in such different societies. Johnson became a pilot for the women's section of the Air Transport Auxiliary (ATA), a civilian agency that ferried aeroplanes for the Royal Air Force. She was briefly a candidate for the leadership of the ATA, but was rejected on the grounds that her celebrity status and working-class background would cause the RAF, already in a state of 'scarlet-faced apoplexy'[4] about the notion of any women in their aircraft, to reject the whole idea. As it happened, her career in the ATA was so short she never got to fly a fighter plane: she was tragically killed after taking off in bad weather in January 1941. And while other women in the ATA did fly almost every type of aircraft in the RAF, they were never allowed to do so in combat. Their job was just to reposition aircraft, moving them from airfield to airfield. They were not allowed to fight.

Raskova's story is completely different. In the chaotic year of 1941, when the Nazis invaded the USSR, people rushed to the defence of the motherland. The authorities scrambled to organise a military response. Raskova pitched an idea to Stalin and the Soviet high command: using her celebrity status to get attention, she made passionate speeches arguing for the creation of all-female air combat regiments: 'hundreds of thousands of drivers, tractor drivers, and pilots . . . are ready to get into a combat machine and to dash into combat with the bloodthirsty enemy'.[5] Raskova got her way. On 8 October 1941 Stalin authorised the creation of three women's air combat regiments, and the 122nd Aviation Corps, containing a fighter regiment and two bomber regiments, was born. By the end of the war members of the corps had destroyed thirty-eight enemy aircraft in the air. The second of the bomber regiments flew an astonishing 24,000 combat missions.

Raskova and her comrades were at the very tip of the spear, engaging the enemy and being rewarded for their military service. And they were not alone. By the end of the war the Soviet Union had mobilised more women fighters than any other nation. As many as a million[6] women took up roles in the Red Army, of which approximately 120,000[7] had direct combat positions such as gunners, snipers, artillery fighters, combat pilots and even junior commanding officers – about 3 per cent of army personnel.[8] To put this number in perspective, almost as many Soviet women saw combat as American men.[9] So many Soviet women served in the military that it created linguistic difficulties. Russian is a gendered language, and before the Second World War 'no feminine gender had existed . . . for the words "tank driver", "infantryman", "machine gunner", because women had never done that work. The feminine forms . . . were born in the war'.[10]

And of course, many of the non-combat personnel also engaged in fighting: once at the front, whether a person is a doctor or a rifleman becomes irrelevant when under enemy fire. This was particularly true for Soviet medical personnel, who were expected to fight when necessary. Vera Malakhova, who was a doctor in the Red Army, noted: 'I could shoot very well with a carbine'. She was wounded twice and much decorated for her courage under fire.[11] Valeria Gnarovskaia, an infantry private and medical orderly, became a Hero of the Soviet Union (the country's highest military honour) for saving forty-seven of her comrades – but also for killing twenty-eight Germans.[12] The possibility that non-combatants like medics would end up fighting was the precise reason British and German women were kept well back from the front. (We will see later how in Iraq and Afghanistan the distinction between combatant and non-combatant roles once again blurred, forcing the issue of opening up combat to women onto the agenda.)

While women in the rest of Europe responded to the dark clouds of oncoming war by knitting socks, rolling bandages and training as nurses, in the Soviet Union they had 'tank-driving circles'.[13] In the USSR women also trained as nurses, but 43 per cent of military surgeons and 41 per cent of front-line doctors were women.[14] So what made it possible for so many Soviet women to fight for the motherland when their British and German counterparts were not allowed to do so? How was it that Soviet women were decorated snipers, shooting in trenches and driving tanks, when British women working in anti-aircraft (AA) batteries were allowed to do everything associated with the battery except fire the gun? One answer may seem obvious. The Soviet Union was in such extreme danger in 1941 that its very existence was under threat. Bringing women into combat was radical, but radical solutions were necessary to make sure the country survived.

There is some truth to this argument. The strategic situation for the USSR was indeed dire. But, the Soviet authorities were surprisingly slow to mobilise women, even into civilian roles in military service. It was not until 1942 that Stalin decided to officially admit women into combat, and even then the decision occurred with little public fanfare, via a series of secret decrees.

If Soviet desperation explains the decision to allow women into combat, we would expect women to have been mobilised in civilian roles as well, and in greater numbers than in other states. In fact, the Soviets mobilised fewer women per capita than Britain or the United States.[15] What is striking about the Soviet mobilisation is not its size but the nature of the roles into which women were placed. If extreme danger was sufficient to cause states to abandon long-held scruples about women in combat, it had no such effect in any of the other wartime powers, none of whom came close to using women in the same way.

What is most striking about the Soviet Union is that women entered combat *before* they were officially allowed to do so, without official conscription and well before Soviet officials believed that the war constituted a dire emergency.[16] In 1941 appeals to and acts of patriotism were common. Stalin and other members of the Soviet high command gave stirring speeches about the necessity of patriotic defence against the Nazi onslaught, and people responded with enthusiasm, flocking in their thousands to recruiting posts. Hordes of women – between 20,000 and 40,000 – joined front-line units on a voluntary basis in the very first days of the invasion, constituting as many as 50 per cent of volunteers in the earliest days of the war,[17] carrying on the tradition of individual female enlistment set out in the First World War. This figure is just the ones who were accepted, only a proportion of those who 'besieged' recruiting posts, 'begging, demanding, and crying' to be sent to the front.[18] Sometimes women who were rejected simply showed up the next day, and the next.[19] The first Soviet women entered combat because they chose to do so, not because they were directed to. It was a spontaneous volunteer movement, not a policy response dictated by extreme danger. It also had resonance with the First World War, where individual women were given permission to fight by the tsar.

Nina Yakovlevna Visnevskaya was one such volunteer. She became a medical assistant in the 32nd Tank Brigade of the Fifth Army, and eventually served in one of the world's biggest ever tank battles.

Nina and her friends wanted to join up together: 'None of us understood then what war was; for us it was some sort of game, something from a book. We had been brought up on the romanticism of the revolution, on ideals'.[20] When she went to the recruiting office, the stronger, older girls were chosen. Nina, who was seventeen and only just over five feet tall, was sent home.

She managed to get to the front anyway. Nina's friends hid her in the back of the truck taking them to the heart of the fighting. Every time the commanders tried to send this small, under-age girl home, Nina would run away to the forest.

> And I did that for three days, until our battalion went into combat . . . everybody went to fight, and I was preparing dugouts for the wounded . . . and the dead . . . one of our girls was killed in that battle. And they all forgot that I was meant to be sent home.

Eventually she became a sergeant major and was awarded military honours for her service at the Battle of the Kursk Bulge, the Order of the Red Star and the Order of the Patriotic War, second degree. Nina enlisted with five friends. She was the only one who survived the war.[21]

It is simply impossible to imagine a British, French or German woman approaching a recruiting post with the intention of fighting in the first place, let alone actually being allowed to do so. The fact that Russian women had been allowed to fight in the First World War – albeit in smaller numbers – was an important contributing factor. But in order to understand how Soviet women came to fight in this way, we have to understand the entirely different way gender was treated within the Soviet Union.

Women were, as a matter of policy in the new Soviet state, to be emancipated and equal with men. The Bolsheviks argued that in a new social world, gender inequality would disappear; and in order to make that happen, the family was to wither away. Women could participate equally with men only if their domestic burden was lifted from them and given to society (no one seems to have suggested that perhaps men could share the burden). The state would provide domestic support such as childcare, laundry and food, so that women and men could participate equally in society.[22]

It is very easy to look at the Soviet Union of the 1920s and 1930s as a new frontier of gender equality. But a deeper examination reveals that, as with many revolutionary movements, there was a considerable gap between revolutionary dreams and mundane reality. The rapid entry of women into the workforce had created a situation that occasionally verged on chaos; for example, the provision of social services to support working women simply could not keep pace. Rather than being free of housework, working women faced a difficult 'double burden': they had to work outside the home and maintain domestic life in a society where housing was short and the promised laundries and childcare inadequate.[23]

The consequence of such rapid and unsupported change was that women stopped having babies. Abortions rose dramatically and the fertility rate plummeted. The situation was chaotic and required a firm hand.[24] Stalin's preferred approach to gender equality was innately more conservative. He returned Soviet society to a far more traditional position, in what historians call the Great Retreat. To sort out the fertility crisis, Stalin reversed or altered many of the radical gender reforms of the Lenin period, banning abortion in 1936.

So the Soviet Union was far from a paradise of gender equality, either in its early radical phase or after Stalin's reversals. But for women, even the short period of gender equality, albeit imperfectly applied, opened up opportunities that would have been unthinkable anywhere else in the world at the time. The generation of women in their twenties at the outbreak of war in 1941 were the 'First Soviet Generation': many were born after the Revolution, and those who were born before it were still very young children when the Soviets took over. These young women were the first to be raised Soviet, to be brought up in a society that was considerably more gender equal than just about anywhere else. During the Second World War this generation 'combined a sentimental, "feminine", passionate belief that they were "strong women" and equal partners in the heroic Soviet project with men'.[25]

Women were increasingly taking on traditionally male jobs. The Soviet Union was pursuing rapid industrialisation, and this created severe labour shortages. The obvious solution was to mobilise women.

Between 1929 and 1932 over a million women entered the industrial workforce, and another 2.5 million took other non-agricultural jobs.[26] This included nearly every area of heavy industry. In the first half of 1931 women constituted a half or more of all new workers in coal mining, engineering, electrical industries, chemicals and timber.[27]

It is hard to imagine any other society in the late 1920s that would have had similarly heated and extensive debates as to whether women should be allowed to drive large tractors;[28] the idea probably simply would not have occurred to anyone else. And of course, the industrial imperative defeated any latent concerns about gender. The 'woman tractor driver, arguably more than any other icon of the 1930s, came to personify both Soviet economic progress and the realization of sexual equality and social justice in a socialist state'. By 1935, 19,000 Soviet women were driving tractors.[29]

At the outbreak of war Soviet society was accustomed to seeing women doing all sorts of things they had previously been deemed incapable of doing; there was no sense that femininity excluded them. Women were entering worlds previously only occupied by men, and were even being put in charge of men. And society was entirely used to the idea that women could be physically capable, including with weapons. Throughout the pre-war years all young people, including women and girls, received military training via the Komsomol youth organisations to prepare for war with the capitalist West. They learned first aid but also rifle shooting, grenade throwing, parachute jumping and how to glide an aircraft.[30] Vera Danilovtseva, who became a sniper and a sergeant in the Red Army, explains:

> the heroes of the Civil War and those who fought in Spain often came to our school. Girls felt equal to boys; we weren't treated differently. On the contrary, we had heard since childhood and at school: 'Girls – at the wheel of tractors!', 'Girls – at the controls of a plane!'[31]

By the time war broke out young Soviet women had been brought up with an expectation that they would fight, and knew that they could fight. So when the call to arms went out, they saw no reason not to respond. The men who were responsible for running recruiting posts apparently saw no difficulty either. After all, these girls had trained alongside their sons and brothers; they were brave enough to turn up; and women had been doing all sorts of things women had never done before. Tens of thousands of women felt ready to fight, and managed to convince the authorities that they should be allowed to do so. The war revealed that, for all its uneven application, Soviet society had had a revolutionary impact on gender politics and opportunities for women.

Soviet women were involved in every aspect of the military defence of the Soviet Union. The most famous examples are the three women's air regiments set up by Marina Raskova: the 588th Night Bomber Regiment, later to be renamed the 46th Taman'sky Guards Night Bomber Aviation Regiment, and more famously known as the Night Witches; the 586th Fighter Aviation Regiment; and the 125th Bomber Regiment. These were the first officially organised mobilisations of Soviet women.

The 125th Bomber Regiment was commanded by Raskova until her death in a crash in 1943. While it began as an all-female regiment flying an outdated aircraft, it was subsequently provided with a more modern plane that required a crew of three. As there was no time to recruit sufficient female crew, men were brought into the regiment and it remained mixed until the end of the war. By that time five members of this regiment had received the honour of Hero of the Soviet Union.

The 586th Fighter Aviation Regiment is the least known of the three air regiments, perhaps because it has a complex history involving its first commander, Major Tamara Kazarinova. Kazarinova was apparently pushed out of the regiment by the pilots, who blamed her for an accident that killed one of their comrades. It appears that Kazarinova, after her departure, may have conspired against the regiment by ensuring that it did not receive any official honours and by directing it to hazardous missions.[32] The 586th was one of the regiments in which Lidya Litviak served. Litviak was the first woman to shoot down an enemy aircraft, and remains the world's top-scoring female fighter ace, despite the fact that she was only active for a year before she went missing in action.[33]

The most famous of the air regiments was unquestionably the Night Witches. This regiment flew an extraordinary 24,000 missions, and became the most highly decorated female unit, as well as the only one of the three regiments that remained all-female for the duration of the war. Twenty-three of its members were designated Heroes of the Soviet Union. The achievement of this honour was extraordinary. Normally, pilots who had flown 500 missions were eligible. The Night Witches were only eligible after 800 missions.[34] The change in their official name occurred to honour the regiment for its role in defeating the Germans in the Battle of the Taman Peninsula.[35]

The Night Witches used a wood and canvas biplane with an open cockpit, the Polikarpov U-2 (or Po-2). These planes had been used as crop dusters and training aircraft before the war and were not designed as bombers. According to one pilot, Alexandra Semyonova Popova, the planes were

> small, slow. They flew only at a low level. Hedge-hopping. Just over the ground! Before the war young people in flying clubs learned to fly in them, but no one could have imagined they would have any military use. The plane was constructed entirely of plywood, covered with aircraft fabric. In fact, with cheesecloth. One direct hit and it caught fire and burned up completely in the air, before reaching the ground. Like a match.[36]

The planes did not have parachutes or machine guns until later in the war. At first, the only weapons they carried were bombs, attached to bomb racks under the wings. They could carry only four at a time, so the pilots had to fly five or more missions a night, sometimes as many as eighteen, returning each time to gather more bombs.[37] The planes flew extremely low, between 1,200 and 1,300 metres – any lower, and they would have been destroyed by their own bombs.[38]

The Night Witches earned their name (Nachthexen in German) because of these old, wooden planes. To drop their bombs, pilots would deliberately stall the engine and bring the plane close to land. To the Germans below, the planes swooped down, virtually silently, before unleashing their payloads; the only noise they made was a soft whooshing, which sounded like a broomstick.[39]

From the plane, it did not sound as gentle as that. Pilot Alexandra

Popova discovered after the war that her heart was scarred, and attributed this to the stress of flying. 'You approach a target, and you're shaking all over. Your whole body is shaking, because below it's all gunfire: fighter planes are shooting, anti-aircraft guns are shooting . . . we flew mostly during the night.'[40] The multiple bombing raids were so tiring that the pilots had to be lifted out of their cabins at the end of their bombing run. The 'girl armorers'[41] who armed the planes had to lift four bombs weighing 110 pounds (50 kg) each, attaching them by hand; over the course of a night they hauled as much as three tons.[42]

The Germans were horrified by their brazen, female attackers. They taunted the Soviets for having to rely on women to save them from invasion, and called Soviet women fighters 'Bolshevik Beasts' and 'Amazons devoid of femininity'.[43] Field Marshal von Reichenau's order for 'The conduct of armed forces in the East' (10 October 1941) referred to women combatants as 'degenerates', criticised their treatment as legitimate POWs and called for them to be summarily executed. Few women ended up in POW camps for this reason.[44] Those that did were subjected to an order that made it clear they should be eliminated.[45]

While the exploits of Soviet airwomen are stunning, it is perhaps not surprising that they played such a significant role. After all, air forces have traditionally been the first place for women to enter combat, because many of the concerns about women's physical ability to fight do not apply to flying an aircraft. But Soviet women were also fighting on the ground, alongside and in command of men. One female soldier remembered it well: 'I remember crunching . . . once hand-to-hand combat begins, there's immediately this crunching noise: the breaking of cartilage, of human bones. Animal cries.'[46]

Soviet women were at the heart of the fighting. They drove tanks, worked as riflemen and performed every imaginable infantry task. As with men, their skills varied from poor to heroic. One male officer recalls with astonishment watching a tactically perfect machine-gun engagement: 'I believe no one in my company had seen such performance by the machine gun before'. Another male observer of the same incident marvelled: 'to let the enemy approach the trenches as close as possible, to fire point blank, to fire until the first lines are destroyed and the last lines turn around' – it was the 'combat signature' of twenty-year-old Nina Onilova.[47] Onilova was declared a Hero of the Soviet Union after her death in combat in March 1942.

The women themselves were often desperate to be in command, and to do it on the front line. Stanislava Petrovna Volkova was a sapper, an exceptionally dangerous role, and trained to be an officer. When she and her fellow female officers insisted that they were ready to take command at the front itself, their company commander said, 'Young ladies! Do you know how long the commander of a sapper platoon lives? The commander of a sapper platoon lives only two months . . .' They replied, 'We know. That's why we want to go.' Volkova was sent to the Fifth Shock Army, 'constantly on the front line'. Initially, the men under her command were unimpressed. But, as she remembers, 'a year later, when I was awarded the Order of the Red Star, these same boys, those who were still alive, carried me on high to my dugout. They were proud of me'.[48]

Women were extremely successful as snipers, building on the pre-war tradition of training in rifle skills and sharpshooting. They were not formally called upon to do so until the catastrophic military situation of 1942–3. Women were sent to co-ed sniper schools in order to perfect their skills. Some of the war's most decorated snipers were women. Lyudmila Pavilchenko, for example, was credited with 309 enemy kills, and was wounded four times, including in the head.

The training regime for the snipers, male and female, was demanding to the point of brutality. It involved (all in the outdoors, come rain, shine or freezing Russian temperatures) fifteen-hour days, training marches in full dress and camouflage techniques, in addition to learning to shoot.[49] As snipers were considered fully fledged infantry soldiers, they were also trained in the use of submachine, machine and tank guns; grenade throwing; and bayonet and fist fighting.[50]

By the time they went to the front, they were joining a Red Army that was effectively starving and in the midst of the most brutal combat. One Soviet sniper, Yulia Zhukova, wrote a memoir that provides a clear-eyed depiction of the eastern front. Zhukova was 'exhausted, starving, freezing'. She kept two bullets in her pocket for herself, because she and her fellow snipers 'feared capture more than death: more than once had we seen what the fascists did to prisoners'.[51] Zhukova was right to be afraid. She had come across the body of one of her female sniper comrades, 'monstrously tortured'.[52]

Women soldiers did face a terrible fate if captured: rape, torture and death. The fact that women might be vulnerable to these horrors remains one of the chief arguments against deploying women in combat. However, all these horrors and terrors apply equally to men. As Zhukova wrote in her memoir, 'war is by its very nature unnatural and brutal; it is not waged in kid gloves'.[53] War is horror. And Soviet women participated in it.

Women were sometimes complicit bystanders. One Soviet soldier, A. Ratkina, recalled witnessing the widespread rape of German women: 'Of course, it happened . . . not many write about it, but that's the law of war. The men spent so many years without women, and of course, there was hatred.'[54] For three days after a successful campaign, looting and rape were allowed – after that, you would end up in court. Ratkina remembered 'a German woman who had been raped. She was lying naked, with a grenade stuck between her legs. Now I feel ashamed, but then I didn't.' Later on, she felt more guilty. 'After several months . . . five German girls came to our battalion . . . they had wounds, jagged wounds. Their underwear was all bloody. They had been raped all night long. The soldiers stood in line.' This time Ratkina organised for the women to view a line of the men in the battalion so the rapists could be shot on the spot. The Germans

> sat there and wept. They didn't want to . . . they didn't want more blood. Then each one got a loaf of bread . . . You think it is easy to forgive? To see intact . . . white houses with tiled roofs. With roses. I myself wanted to hurt them . . . of course . . . I wanted to see their tears. It was impossible to become all good all at once.[55]

Women actively, and sometimes enthusiastically, participated in the violence. The sniper Yulia Zhukova recalled her first kill with exhilaration.

> Although I saw it with my own eyes, I could not believe I had killed
> a Fritz with my own hands. What a mood I was in when I returned!
> The girls came up to congratulate me. The company's commander
> sent his thanks.

Although Zhukova later felt regret, ultimately she decided that 'the
annihilation of the Germans ultimately became a chore, an obligation which I needed to do well. Otherwise they would kill you.'[56]

Some Soviet women were traumatised by their experiences, but
others were not. Bella Isaakovna Epstein, a sniper, remembers:

> In one German village we were billeted for the night in a castle.
> There were many rooms, whole big halls. Such halls! The wardrobes
> were filled with beautiful clothes. Each girl chose a dress for herself.
> There was a yellow one I liked, and also a house robe. I can't tell
> you what a beautiful house robe it was – long, light . . . like a fluff
> of down! We had to go to bed, because we were terribly tired. We
> put these dresses on, and went to bed, and fell asleep at once. I lay
> in that dress and the robe on top of it.[57]

The experience of Soviet women, then, is like the experience of
any other soldier. Some survive, and some do not. Some fight bravely,
and some run away from the fighting. For some, war is an endless
stretch of terror. For others, it is the greatest adventure of their lives.
Some return plagued by guilt or memories; others come home with
a part of them yearning for the war. What Soviet women fighters
demonstrate is that the experience of war does not differ much for
men and women.

The presence of so many men and women together didn't just
mean they experienced war the same way. It also meant that love
and sex were inevitably a part of military life. The extent to which
sex, love and sexuality mattered, and caused problems, seems to be
enormously variable. The Soviet military never established any policy
regarding sexual relationships at the front.[58] Perhaps as a result, the
experience of women soldiers ranged from proud celibacy to madly
in love, to exploited and assaulted.

Many women fighters insisted that romantic entanglements would
hinder the pursuit of their mission. Sofya Krigel, a sniper, explained:
'as we were leaving for the front, each of us gave an oath: there

will be no romances there. It would all happen, if we survived, after the war'.[59] Elena Viktorovna Klenovskaya, a partisan fighter, disapproved of people who fell in love while fighting, saying, 'I thought it wasn't the time to be concerned with love. Around us was evil. Hatred.'[60]

Some women entered into relationships of convenience at the front, living with their lovers. These women came to be called 'mobile field wives' or, in the Russian acronym, PPZhs. Mobile field wives occupy a complex place in the spectrum of love and sex in the Red Army. To modern eyes, these relationships are marked by inappropriate power relations. And they did often edge into recognisable sexual harassment. One commander, a Lieutenant Morisov, lived with four women sergeants in a row; he 'asked several sergeants to live with him and when they refused he demoted them or made their life a living hell'.[61] Women also paid the price for refusing to have sex with their superiors, including some who were deliberately sent to danger at the front.[62]

But other mobile field wives drew comfort, and even happiness, from their relationships. Sofiya, a medical assistant whose recollections were kept anonymous, explains: 'I'm not afraid of telling the truth . . . I was what's called a field campaign wife. A war wife. A second one. An unlawful one.' She lived with her commander.

> I didn't love him. He was a good man, but I didn't love him. But I went to his dugout after several months. What else could I do? There were only men around, so it's better to live with one than to be afraid of them all.

When he was killed, she fell in love with the next commander.

> I went into combat with him. I wanted to be near him. I loved him, and he had a beloved wife, two children. He showed me their photographs. And I knew that after the war, if he stayed alive, he would go back to them . . . so what? We had such happy moments! We lived such happiness![63]

Sofiya returned from the war pregnant with the commander's child. After the war she lived in a communal apartment. 'My neighbours were all married, and they insulted me. They taunted me:

"Ha-ha-ha . . . tell us how you whored around there with the men."
They used to put vinegar in my pot of boiled potatoes. Or add a
tablespoon of salt . . . Ha-ha-ha . . .'[64]

Other women were treated as sisters, or daughters, by the men
around them. Natalia Peshkova, who was a medic, insisted that

> I have a very high opinion of the men. They never cursed when I
> was near. They stopped swearing when I appeared. They were just
> privates, not intelligentsia. There were no romances, much less harass-
> ment. I escaped all this, nobody even tried to court me.[65]

Vera Malakhova, the doctor who prided herself on her skills with
her carbine rifle, recalls that the men she worked with looked after
her. Her unit only marched at night, and sometimes the women
were desperate to urinate.

> You'd march along emaciated and exhausted, and all of a sudden
> you'd need to . . . But how? To move off was dangerous, because
> the land was sometimes mined. So three of the [older men] would
> turn their backs in a circle and open their greatcoats and say, 'Little
> daughter, come here, don't be ashamed. We see that you can't walk
> away.' And we'd squat and pee.[66]

Another medic, Mariana Milyutina, remembers the rare treat of a
hot bath.

> My god, such happiness! Everybody undressed in there. There was
> a plywood partition between the male and female sections, and behind
> it they brought some soldiers to wash. Then it turned out that all
> the tubs were on our side, and there wasn't a single one on theirs.
> Suddenly this wall started shaking and collapsed, and these soldiers
> were running at us. We all got scared, we were naked after all, but
> they started snatching these tubs from our hands, they didn't give a
> damn about us.[67]

True romance also blossomed at the front. Anastasia Leonidovna
Zhardestskaya, a corporal and medical assistant, fell in love and married
at the front. She made her wedding dress out of bandages 'overnight.
By myself. My friends and I spent a month collecting bandages. Trophy
bandages . . . I had a real wedding dress! I still have a picture. I'm in
this dress and boots, only you can't see the boots'.[68]

One soldier, Nina Yakovlevna, later recalled the death of her friend, Tonya Bobkova. 'She shielded the man she loved from a mine fragment. The fragments take a fraction of a second to reach you . . . how did she have time? She saved Lieutenant Petya Boichevsky. She loved him. And he survived.' Many years after the war, Nina and Petya visited the place where Tonya died. 'He took some earth from her grave . . . carried it and kissed it'.[69]

Klavdia Grigoryevna Krokhina, a sniper, met her husband at the front.

> We were in the same regiment. He was wounded twice, had a concussion. He went through the whole war, from beginning to end, and was in the military all his life afterward. Was there any need for me to explain to him what war was? Where I had come back from? How I was? Whenever I raise my voice, he either pays no attention or holds his peace. And I forgive him, too.[70]

It is hard to imagine how anyone, looking at the Soviet example, would draw the lesson that women could not fight on an equal basis with men. And yet, perversely, the Soviet Union did just that. After the war the Soviets quietly and quickly removed women from all branches of the armed services. They disbanded all the female air regiments. Women pilots continued to serve in training schools, but by the early 1950s this role too was closed.[71] This reversal is made all the more extraordinary by the fact that the Soviet Union retained the largest military in the world, which it had to maintain in the face of an astonishing loss of male lives: by 1945 women outnumbered men by 16 million, a structural feature of Soviet demographics that persisted for four generations.[72]

But even so there was no serious consideration that the army could benefit through retaining women veterans. It appears it was not even necessary to make a specific decision to remove women. Everyone simply expected it to occur. While women were actively and successfully fighting at the front, in 1943 policies at home began to change. Women were excluded from a new system of military cadet schools, and schoolgirls were directed into domestic science while boys did further military training.[73] Co-education, which had been standard since 1918, was abolished in secondary schools in order to ensure that boys and girls were appropriately prepared for their differing future stations in life, particularly around leadership and military service.[74]

Women had assumed a range of leadership roles in Soviet wartime society, often to replace men away fighting. Twenty per cent of *kolkhoz* (collective farm) leaders were women during the war, dropping to 5 per cent by 1950 and 2 per cent by 1952. Women were pushed out of these positions, as well as many other positions of political and social authority, to make room for men.[75] The treatment of Soviet women at the end of the war is a robust reminder of the wafer-thin Soviet commitment to gender equality: women were simply a resource to be utilised for industrialisation, the war or Soviet glory.

The Soviet propaganda machine was heavily reliant on stories of wartime heroism during the Cold War, to inspire the Soviet people but also to remind the West that they were a force to be reckoned with. During the war Mikhail Kalinin, the chairman of the Presidium of the Supreme Soviet, had acknowledged that women had directly strengthened the army and also improved the behaviour of the men.[76] And yet the stories of women heroes were not just forgotten, they were actively suppressed. Despite their prominent service, women were scarcely noticeable in the victory parades of 1945.[77] Many were not allowed to participate, and demobilised female soldiers were required to sign a pledge of silence regarding their wartime service.[78]

A return to civilian life is difficult for any soldier. For the women soldiers of the Soviet Union, it was doubly difficult because their service was officially unrecognised and suppressed, but on top of that they also suffered social disapproval. The sniper Klavdia S—va remembers:

> How did the Motherland meet us? I can't speak without sobbing . . . it was forty years ago, but my cheeks still burn. The men said nothing, but the women . . . they shouted to us, 'they know what you did there! You lured our men with your young c—! Army whores . . . military bitches . . .' They insulted us in all possible ways . . . the Russian vocabulary is rich.[79]

Tamara Stepanovna Umnyagina was a medical officer during the war. When she returned home, she was constantly reminded that as a *frontovichki*, or front-line girl, her marital appeal was limited, and even the marriage prospects for her two sisters were reduced. The *frontovichki* were on their own. 'We'd had enough, we frontline girls. And after the war we got more. After the war we had another war. Also terrible. For some reason, men abandoned us. They didn't shield us. At the front it was different'.[80]

The front-line girls experienced all the trauma of the war and received very little benefits after peace. Vera Malakhova, the battle-field doctor, recalled later in her life:

> Now they spit on us, on all the veterans. And all the same I fought . . . especially women, it's unfair . . . because we women who served at the front don't deserve to be called whores, forgive me for saying that so directly, we don't deserve it, we weren't that way. There were very few PPZh and even those lived with just one man . . . We lived honourably, fought honourably, and I don't know, I consider that we had good girls . . . no one is interested now, absolutely no one, and we are dying out, most of us are gone, and we are the last. And that's that.[81]

Few opportunities accrued to women veterans. Even those who had excelled found there was no military profession open to them. They were punished by society. And they were not even allowed to speak of their wartime service. Yet in July 1945 Kalinin had made a speech to the front-line girls about what their post-war lives would be like. He was optimistic about their prospects because their physical fitness, discipline and ability to keep their nerve would stand them in good stead for future employment. Nonetheless he also warned them, saying 'do not give yourselves airs in your future practical work. Do not speak about the services you have rendered, let others do it for you. That will be better'.[82]

At bottom, Soviet gender roles remained extremely traditional, and the window of opportunity provided by a revolutionary state with radical gender politics was short. Under Stalin, the push to get women into the workforce was only motivated by the need to industrialise and compete with the rest of the world, not by any serious ideas about gender equality. The assumption that front-line girls must have been whores demonstrates that notions of gender equality never penetrated far on the home front. Women at the front were upsetting traditional social expectations. After the war the focus swerved sharply away from the wartime service of women officers, pilots and front-line service towards the cult of heroic motherhood, complete with medals for women with more than ten children.[83] Soviet women had been removed from the front line and firmly placed back in the domestic sphere.

The Soviet experience echoes nearly all wars where women fight, whether as soldiers, resistance fighters or revolutionaries. Once the war is over, no matter how bravely these women have fought, 'normal' life seems to require them to return to their peacetime roles. Allowing women into the military was an exception, allowed only by the extremes of war. In light of the military success of Soviet women, and the clear need to maintain a large army, the decision not to carry on using women seems wholly irrational. But powerful beliefs about gender inspire irrational behaviour, even among other militaries.

The example set by Soviet women was simply never seriously examined by other militaries, not even when they were conducting analyses of whether to place women into combat in the wake of the feminist movement. The Soviet example had been suppressed so successfully that in the late 1970s the leading academic journal in the field of international security confidently asserted that Soviet female pilots were an 'exercise in public relations' where women were 'shown off' prior to the war,[84] rather than an effective fighting force. Military inquiries into female combat readiness in the US repeatedly assessed all other types of data,[85] from average upper body strength to lung capacity to what happens to a woman's body during menstruation. But these studies never seriously looked at what had happened to the hundreds of thousands of women – in numbers, the equivalent of eighty rifle and tank divisions[86] – who had fought in the Great Patriotic War.

In 1992 a presidential commission explored the question of which roles women in the armed services should be allowed to pursue. The commission's report yet again dismissed the Soviet example of women in combat as an act of desperation by a state that had exhausted all other alternatives.[87] Its only comment on the many women soldiers who fought with distinction in ground combat was a note that while there were no documented problems with integration in mixed male and female units, 'women did have trouble with tasks involving upper body strength. For example, there were instances of women being killed because they were unable to throw grenades effectively'.[88]

Soviet women were indeed killed by grenades, but in circumstances that would have stunned the commissioners, had they bothered to investigate. Earlier, we encountered Valeria Gnarovskaia, the medical orderly who saved forty-seven of her comrades while killing twenty-eight Germans. She did so at the cost of her own life. German tanks were approaching her unit, so Valeria grabbed a bagful of grenades and threw herself underneath the leading tank, detonated the grenades and halted the attack.[89]

Two Soviet snipers, twenty-one-year-old Natalya Kovshova and her nineteen-year-old friend Mariya Polivanova, were also killed by grenades. Surrounded by the enemy at a battle in Novgorod in 1942, they killed 300 Germans before deliberately detonating their grenades to avoid being captured. Earlier in the war, Kovshova had written to her 'darling, beloved mummy' of her desire to kill the enemy. 'I will hit them point blank,' she wrote. 'I will pump bullet after bullet into their foul skulls, stuffed with insane thoughts about our beloved Moscow, of rule over us, a free, proud and bold people. I will fight them to the very end, until the full joy of victory.'[90]

In 1992 the very idea of female combat was still so taboo that the only way to explain Soviet women fighters was to dismiss them as the act of a 'desperate state' in the 'darkest days of World War II'.[91] The implication was that dire circumstances might allow the use of women, but serious militaries did not and should not allow women into combat. The presidential commission was concerned that allowing women into combat would upset the 'deep-seated cultural and family values millions of Americans hold and are still teaching their children. As one Commissioner put it, these values can be summed up in one simple phrase: good men respect and defend women.'[92] In other words, female combat is unimaginable because it overturns gender expectations. Placing women in combat puts them in danger. The commissioners took special note of the role of Night Witches and their inferior planes, their 'expendability', and the fact that they had a 75 per cent casualty rate. The implication was that the Soviet decision to put women in such danger was morally suspect. Only a deep-seated belief that women require protection and cannot fight can explain how anyone could draw this lesson from the evidence. During the Battle of Britain, the life expectancy of an RAF pilot was four weeks, and yet no one drew the conclusion that the death rate among these pilots was unacceptable given the stakes involved. In the United States in the Second World War, stress and fear among pilots was causing serious problems with morale, so pilots were restricted to a maximum tour of duty of twenty-five combat flights; some of the Night Witches flew more than 1,000 missions in combat. Surely the Night Witches demonstrate that women are capable of extraordinary bravery and physical capacity, and do not require the protection of men.

Once again, women's wartime service was dismissed and forgotten, and in the Soviet Union, deliberately suppressed. While the task of recovering the stories of Soviet women fighters began in the 1980s, it has not changed cultural perceptions. In the present war with Ukraine, Russia has stuck to an all-male military despite manpower problems and an adversary with no issues about deploying thousands of women in combat. This experience of at best deliberate forgetting and at worst active suppression was common around the world.

8

Britain in the Second World War

I N LONDON, WHEN war broke out, Violette Bushell joined the Women's Land Army. She was assigned to strawberry picking, which she found a bore, so she returned home and fell in love. When she married, and her husband went away to fight, Violette yearned for something more important to do. She signed up to work in an AA battery, shooting down enemy aircraft. This was the closest British women got to combat – at least officially. Violette's job was to predict the trajectory of German aircraft so the battery could shoot them down. She realised she was pregnant only a short time into her service and so she went home again.

In June 1944, only five days after the D-Day landings, a woman drove off from a small village near Limoges on a mission to help improve the organisation of French resistance efforts against the now retreating Nazis. She was no simple messenger. She was armed with a Sten gun and eight magazines of ammunition, and she was about to become one of the war's most famous and tragic women.

Violette Bushell was by then Violette Szabo, an agent of the Special Operations Executive, and had arrived by parachute in order to assist the French resistance. She was on her second mission in France when she set off with her Sten gun and a French driver code-named Anastasie. She and her companion spotted a Nazi roadblock and realised that they had no escape. As Philippe Liewer, the leader of her resistance group, later reported, 'with great coolness and gallantry she fought it out for 20 minutes with her Sten gun, covering *Anastasie* while he was retreating . . . she only surrendered being completely exhausted and short of ammunition, and she is believed to have killed one German'.[1] Violette was arrested and taken first to Ravensbrück, then to a labour camp, and then back to Ravensbrück, where she was executed in February 1945.

Violette Szabo most certainly engaged in combat, and was trained to do so. She and the other women of the SOE are perhaps the most recognisable and certainly the most romantic British military women of the war. But Violette Szabo and her SOE comrades, even with their demonstrated and extraordinary bravery, constituted a tiny minority of British servicewomen who were trained in combat and allowed to fight only under conditions of utmost secrecy. Working in an AA battery, as Violette did, may have appeared to be close to the fight. But actually, the military establishment bent over backwards, and bent the truth, to maintain the appearance that women who were engaged in shooting down enemy aircraft were not combatants – because they did not actually fire the gun. And the government and the military succeeded in ensuring that most British women's wartime experiences were far away from anything that resembled combat.

The story of British women in the Second World War is a story of skirting combat, of deliberate decisions to mobilise women but to keep them out of harm's way. The only circumstance where women could fight was as spies, where their work was totally unknown by the wider public. Otherwise, British women were allowed to undertake dangerous activity – as long as it did not cross the line of actual combat, even when that line was blurry in the extreme. Sometimes the effort to keep women out of combat created odd contradictions; sometimes it may have required more effort to draw these artificial distinctions between combat and non-combat than it would to allow women to fight.

Like the Soviet Union, Britain was under the most severe pressure during the Second World War, especially after the fall of France. It was only under the pressure of war that women could be mobilised, and only when that pressure increased that women could be formally conscripted and placed closer and closer to combat. If the Soviet Union demonstrates how the pressure of war, ideology and a history of women in unconventional military roles combined to open the doors of combat to women, then the British case demonstrates how a strong commitment to traditional gender roles could resist organisational efforts of women themselves and even the most dramatic pressure for survival.

When war finally came in 1939 it was not a surprise, but British society as a whole was not fully on a war footing. Preparations for war had been stymied by a number of factors, including a reluctant population with all too recent memories of the First World War and a general lack of agreement about how best to handle a resurgent Germany. A lack of clear policy about war preparations in general extended to what to do about women in particular.

A significant subset of British women, however, were in vociferous agreement that women were going to be vital to an inevitable war effort. They took it upon themselves to begin mobilising for war, and when it came, they were prepared. As no one was directing official policy, unofficial avenues for women's influence opened up. The 1930s showcased an abundant variety of ladies' military auxiliaries, some of which, like the Marchioness of Londonderry's Women's Legion, carried on from the first war to the second.[2]

New organisations sprang up. In 1922, Mary Allen advertised (through means of a letter to *The Times*) the creation of a Women's Reserve, to train women in first aid, fire drill and lorry driving.[3] Allen was an extraordinary character: a suffragette who had received a Hunger Strike Medal for valour from Emmeline Pankhurst, she had joined the Women Police Volunteers, after which she wore a police uniform in public for the rest of her life. Allen's policing adventures took her all over the place, and she continually irritated the authorities for, among other things, masquerading as a Metropolitan policewoman (for which she was arrested in 1921), meeting with Egyptian authorities in her uniform while purporting to be on an official visit and meeting Hitler to discuss women's policing in 1934. Allen's increasingly vocal support for fascism raised eyebrows. She wrote that 'if we want street fighting and mass murder in England, the surest way to attain it is to continue the hysterical anti-Hitler propaganda'.[4] The Marchioness of Londonderry had had enough and proposed that the Women's Legion subsume other voluntary organisations, in part to shut down the more distasteful variants like Allen's.[5]

This proposal faltered, and the legion turned to developing a women's officer training section, called the Emergency Service. It was led by Dame Helen Gwynne-Vaughan, who as well as being in charge of the WAAC in France in the First World War was a noted professor of botany, specialising in fungi. The Emergency Service began with training, including evening classes at a barracks in London and an annual camp in Hemel Hempstead which included exercise, military drilling and the preparation of meals from military cookbooks.[6] The camp also required ladies to bring 'country clothes, low-heeled shoes . . . a short skirt or shorts' and 'an afternoon dress for dinner in the evening'.[7]

The British class system undoubtedly played an important role in the creation of these amateur women's military auxiliaries. Well-connected upper-class women were able to directly petition brothers, husbands and other important men. The Marchioness of Londonderry's husband was secretary of state for air in Ramsay MacDonald's Cabinet; in addition to her military pursuits she ran a political club called the Ark where members had animal nicknames, including Winston the Warlock (Churchill), Arthur the Albatross (Balfour) and Hamish the Hart (MacDonald).[8] Dame Helen Gwynne-Vaughan's Emergency Service had the Duchess of Gloucester as its patron and was full of well-connected ladies, including the wife of the Chief of the Air Staff.[9]

The energetic creators of all these women's auxiliaries, from professors of botany to marchionesses to self-proclaimed police-women, continually pushed the government and all three branches of the British military into considering what role women would occupy during the war. Their attempts to propose the creation of women's auxiliaries that would be part of formal military structures were persistently knocked back; in 1935 the War Office argued that women would only be participating in war to replace soldiers as 'ambulance drivers, waitresses, cooks, domestic workers, wireless operators, telephone operators, clerks, and anti-gas personnel', and that this would not require military training.[10]

The women pressed on. Lady Londonderry and the Countess of Athlone, president of the First Aid Nursing Yeomanry (FANY), a front-line nursing organisation created in 1907, pestered Leslie Hore-Belisha, the secretary of state for war, to the point that he complained the two women were 'always at him about their shows'.[11] Other women applied pressure too. Dame Katharine Furse, who had commanded the WRNS during the First World War, sent repeated letters to naval and political authorities.[12]

By 1938 things had changed. War looked ever more certain. It was simply no longer possible to ignore the question of arming the nation – and, thanks to the women's voluntary auxiliaries, it was equally clear that women and their labour were part of the armament agenda.[13] 'Obviously,' an internal memo stated, 'we are going to employ women in some numbers in the next war.'[14] Only the finer details remained.

For the leaders of the women's auxiliaries, the finer details were crucially important. There were two sticking points: whether women would be civilians or incorporated into the military; and whether their service would be paid or voluntary. Gwynne-Vaughan won on the question of pay, pointing out that 'the supply of leisured girls' who would work as volunteers 'is smaller than it used to be'.[15] She lost on the question of military membership. The distinction was important, because as civilians the women would technically be 'camp followers', with all the baggage that entailed.[16] The military did not budge, and women entered the war as civilian adjuncts to men.

Without the persistent advocacy of women themselves, the government and military leadership may well have taken far longer to mobilise women and think about the most efficient way of doing so. On 9 September 1938 (a mere three weeks before the Munich Agreement) the Auxiliary Territorial Service (ATS) came into being, the fruit of more than twenty years of work, building on a previous war and through a fragile peace. Helen Gwynne-Vaughan left her fungi behind in order to take on the role of its first director. With the birth of the ATS came a push to formalise women's services in other areas; in November 1938 the Women's Royal Naval Service (WRNS), which had seen service in the First World War, was re-established, followed in June 1939 by the Women's Auxiliary Air Force (WAAF).

The formal outbreak of war saw the three military women's auxiliaries and all the other voluntary organisations kick into gear. The idea was that they would replace men in non-combatant roles and release them for the front. The government was operating under the prevailing belief that it was simply impossible to replace men with women on a one-to-one basis, a belief that had persisted since the First World War – the principle of 'dilution'. Manpower needs were dictated by assumptions about the 'replacement rate', or, how many men could be replaced by one woman. As Churchill was to point out later on in the war, a woman who volunteered 'not only renders a high service herself, but releases a man – actually four-fifths of a man – for the active troops'.[17] Even in 1945, 44 per cent of ATS personnel were deployed in roles that presumed that five women would replace four men, or three would replace two.[18]

The WAAF mobilised women to replace men in such roles as cooks, clerks, orderlies, equipment assistants, motor drivers and fabric workers for balloon squadrons.[19] Without the WAAF, the RAF would have required an additional 150,000 men.[20] While the women of the WAAF were not combatants, the work was dangerous. As air force bases were routine targets of German bombing raids, they took high casualties. One WAAF wrote in 1940 that 'there is hardly anyone now who has not lost a friend'.[21]

The WRNS – colloquially known as Wrens – was initially entirely civilian and intended to be under the ambit of the Civil Establishment department rather than the Second Sea Lord, the usual administrator for naval personnel.[22] Early naval estimates suggested it would need a small number of women, perhaps only 3,000,[23] and employed only in office roles, like clerical and shorthand work, or on domestic duties, like waitresses and cooks.[24] Both the estimated numbers and imagined roles were entirely too limited. By June 1944 the Wrens employed 74,620 women in 125 roles, including minewatchers, radio mechanics and intelligence officers.[25]

The Wrens were by far the most popular service – no doubt helped by the glamorous uniform. As one Wren said, 'Really, we'd only joined the Wrens on a whim. I think we both fancied the navy-blue uniforms – we Wrens did look marvellous whereas the other services, through no fault of their own, didn't.'[26] Becoming a Wren had such cachet that the authorities had to make joining as a volunteer deliberately difficult, adding special entry requirements as diverse as proficiency in German and practical experience of boats.[27]

The Wrens were popular and looked marvellous. The ATS did not look marvellous at all, and it was the least popular service. Their unflattering khaki uniforms were a particular turn-off. One woman complained to *The Times* that 'khaki is a colour detested by women and makes a well-developed girl look vulgar'.[28] An ATS recruit described the rest of the uniform: 'thick lisle stockings, which went a sickly yellow colour after repeated washings, balloon shaped khaki knickers, and the sort of vests which our Grannies wore'.[29] The ATS's persistent unpopularity was a significant problem because the service was the largest of the three auxiliaries and consistently fell short of its extensive recruitment targets. The government decided to get to the root of the unpopularity, commissioning a survey on the question in November 1941.

The snobbery which dogged the ATS was unquestionably linked to its high proportion of working-class women and presumptions about their sexual morality. One survey response indicated that in the ATS,

the rougher type seems to predominate . . . ready for a good time, drunk without much provocation, sexually promiscuous and in language as blue as the men . . . in appearance they incline to be a sloppy and frowsy lot, altogether a rather 'bitchy' crew.[30]

Some were even more blunt: 'Nothing but a league of amateur prostitutes'.[31] The report on the survey data concluded that 'a very powerful influence is being exerted to prevent several million women in this country from joining the ATS' because a very high proportion of men said they would not allow the women in their lives to join up.[32] One man said, when confronted with the prospect, 'Christ no! I can't stand that. I'd murder her.'[33] Men were worried that it might ruin femininity. One officer claimed: 'I think it is the horrible khaki and the inconsistency of a woman being a soldier . . . it takes away something that is particularly feminine, perhaps their capriciousness, perhaps their lack of hardness'.[34]

The survey revealed the deep-seated unpopularity of the ATS, and it was increasingly clear that volunteers alone would not provide enough women. The ATS had a target enrolment of 5,000 women a week and was only receiving 1,600.[35] Something more dramatic had to be done to ensure that the British military had enough women.

Conscription appeared inevitable, but it was not popular. The Soviet decision to mobilise women, despite its successes, reinforced the idea that military women were distasteful in the UK. The adjutant general of the army warned in July 1940 that 'once we take the step of enlisting women for Army Service there will no longer be any bar to the employment of women for definitely combatant duties . . . Apart from the Russians no civilised power has yet resorted to that practice'.[36] A parliamentary debate on a bill for female conscription ensued. The MP for Glasgow, Agnes Hardie, put it bluntly:

My point is that war is not a woman's job . . . I am as good a feminist as anyone – I say they have no right to conscript women for war. It has been a tradition for many generations that war is a man's job, that women have the bearing and rearing of children and should be exempt from war.[37]

Eleanor Rathbone, the member for the Combined English Universities, disagreed:

I am tremendously proud of the success women have already achieved in this difficult and more or less dangerous occupation. I hope they will be used even more in the combatant units. There ought to be no test of the kind of service that a woman should be called to but what kind of service she is able to perform.[38]

Churchill opposed the notion because he believed men in the forces would demonstrate 'vociferous opposition'; the leadership of the forces agreed that conscription might cause 'unrest and opposition'.[39]

Despite the debate the numbers game prevailed – there were just too few women recruits. In December 1941 National Service Act (no. 2) was passed, enabling all unmarried women between the ages of twenty and thirty to be called up. Tellingly, however, it avoided the word 'conscription', which was in line with the fact that women in the military at first remained civilians. By the spring of 1941, frustrated by the fact that women could simply walk away from their military roles without sanction, all three auxiliaries were deemed to be military organisations.[40]

Conscription created heightened anxiety around how women, particularly young, unmarried women, would cope with difficult wartime conditions, and forced the government to promise to look into the conditions for serving women and to address the question of sexual morality head-on. (It is simply impossible to imagine anyone caring about these questions in the pre-Crimean War British military – an astonishing degree of change in less than a hundred years.) The first attempt, an all-male committee, raised the eyebrows of women MPs, with one noting in Parliament would it be considered a poor idea to 'set up an all-women committee to inquire into conditions in the male Services?'[41] The problematic nature of all-male committees and 'mansplaining' were familiar to the women leaders of the Second World War. Jane Trefusis Forbes, the director of the WAAF, complained that her ideas were often only accepted if explained by male colleagues, and claimed to be 'dead sick of having my views explained by someone else'.[42]

Common sense prevailed and the leadership of the committee was given to Violet Markham, who had been the deputy director of the organisation responsible for women's recruitment in the First World War, where she had also conducted an inquiry into the morality of women serving in France.[43] The Markham Committee's report concluded that there were no grounds for concern over sexual morality, and that the facts available demonstrated 'on what slender foundations a superstructure of scandal has been reared'.[44] It is striking to note that the report did not examine the impact of men's sexual morality and behaviour.

While the Markham Committee had found that the ATS was not a hotbed of immorality, sexual relationships did occur. The authorities were aware that same-sex relationships might cause issues. In

1941 ATS officers were given a memorandum called 'A Special Problem', which provided officers with the skills to detect the differences between 'the adolescent "crush", normal friendships between women, unhealthy friendships and true promiscuity'.[45] Daphne Brock, a Wren, was checking the hem on her slip one evening, when

> this six-foot woman came in, chucked me over the bed and leapt on me. I was terrified. Although I was absolutely innocent in sexual matters I knew what she was after. I lost my cool and shouted and screamed . . . then she heard someone coming and got off.[46]

Daphne had bad luck, because she had another, more frightening run-in one night.

> It was a lovely bright moonlit night, so that I could see someone standing by my bed. It was a sailor, and he started trying to strangle me. Somehow I got him off . . . he must have hit me. I opened the door and went into my friend Anne's cabin opposite. She almost had hysterics when she saw me. I was streaming with blood.[47]

With sex came inevitable pregnancies. Lady Margaret Egerton was an ATS officer in an AA station in the Orkney Islands.

> One evening we heard a girl screaming in one of the huts. I asked what was wrong and was told: 'I think she's got constipation – chronic constipation'. She was taken to hospital, where all the doctors were drunk but not too drunk to say: 'Chronic constipation my foot, she's having a baby'. And she had it in five minutes flat.[48]

British women were now, mostly, mobilised the same way men were. But it was absolutely clear that they were not going to be mobilised for the same roles. The National Service Act made it clear that if women were going to be deployed to support lethal weapons, they had to formally give consent. Arranging it so that women were non-combatants required significant linguistic and practical contortions by both government and military officials, especially because there were at least three areas where women were skirting very close to combat, or would have benefitted from being allowed to engage in combat, or were, in fact, actually fighting. British women arguably should have been allowed to use weapons as pilots repositioning aircraft; they came very close to fighting in AA batteries, where they also should have been allowed weapons; and British women spies received combat training and used it in the field.

The pilots repositioning aircraft were not members of the WAAF. They were part of the Air Transport Auxiliary (ATA) set up by Gerard d'Erlanger, the director of the British Overseas Airways Corporation. D'Erlanger realised that the RAF would require civilian support to free up military air resources, particularly in ferrying aircraft from factories to airfields and positioning planes where they were needed. The ATA was composed of skilled pilots who were nonetheless unable to meet RAF selection criteria. The first eight women pilots were recruited in 1940 under the auspices of Pauline Gower, the world's third female commercial pilot, proprietoress of a joyriding flight business and alumna of two different air circuses.[49] These pilots were exceptionally well qualified, having flight hours well over the minimum requirements.[50] Diana Barnato Walker, later to become one of the ATA's distinguished pilots, described the auxiliary as a motley crew:

> We had two one-armed pilots . . . they collected millionaires, butchers and bakers, young girls and First World War pilots — all sorts of people of all shapes and sizes, and the only thing we all had in common was that at some time or other we'd learned to fly.[51]

The ATA also included the famous pilot Amy Johnson, who had flown solo to Australia. By the end of the war women composed 16 per cent of pilots in the ATA.[52]

The ATA's decision to use eight specially selected women immediately garnered negative attention. The editor of *Aeroplane* magazine wrote:

> We quite agree that there are millions of women in the country who could do useful jobs in the war. But the trouble is that so many of them insist on doing jobs which they are quite incapable of doing. The menace is the woman who thinks that she ought to be flying a high-speed bomber when she really has not the intelligence to scrub the floor of the hospital properly.[53]

At first, women were restricted to flying biplanes and training aircraft, but the pressure of the war pushed change. In August and September 1940 the RAF suffered astonishing losses. In just two weeks 103 pilots were killed and a further 128 wounded, and by mid-September a quarter of the pilots had been lost.[54] The losses were so significant they opened the door to Pauline Gower, who had been trying without much luck to persuade the RAF and ATA to allow the recruitment of more women.[55] By summer 1941 the RAF was under sufficient pressure that according to pilot Lettice Curtis 'they didn't mind if you were a man, a woman or a monkey'.[56] The original eight women had performed sufficiently well that all qualified women were eligible to join the ATA,[57] and they even began to recruit women who had never flown before and trained them to fly.[58]

The ATA women were certainly adventurous. Diana Barnato Walker, the daughter of financier Woolf 'Babe' Barnato, a former winner of the Le Mans twenty-four-hour car race and owner of the Bentley car company,[59] decided to learn to fly at the age of eighteen, to escape her protected life.

> You were guarded in those days. You had nannies and you had governesses; you couldn't go anywhere by yourself . . . even at eighteen you were clung to, and I wanted to get away. So I thought, 'Well, if I learned to fly, nannies and governesses won't come up in an airplane.' That was the basic underlying reason.[60]

The ATA pilot's uniform was very glamorous – and wholly impractical for flying, having a tight navy blue skirt under a smart jacket which made it hard to put on a parachute and manoeuvre in and out of the plane. It also made it very difficult to avoid flashing knickers at awkward moments. Diana Barnato was flying in her uniform (rather than dungarees) as she had not had time to change, when she was caught in thick cloud. The sensible thing to do would have been to bale out, but 'I couldn't bale out! My skirt would have ridden up with the parachute straps and anyone who happened to be below *would have seen my knickers!* No, it simply couldn't be done.' So instead she made a skilful and lucky landing, later learning that the cloud cover had caused the deaths of two other ATA pilots.[61]

The pilots of the ATA had to be skilful. They were flying brand new planes from the factory which could have defects. Part of their task was to record any 'snags' in each plane.[62] And the pilots also flew two or three different planes a day, and sometimes planes that they had never flown before. Their only guide was 'a little book of words, six inches by four, with every aircraft you might have flown on loose leaf', which they could use to double-check details.[63] The ATA women pilots enjoyed causing a stir with their skills. According to Diana Barnato, 'When you landed . . . they'd be looking behind you as you got out of the plane, to see who the pilot was. They couldn't believe such a tiny girl could handle such a big, heavy airplane'.[64]

ATA pilots flew without radio contact, flying 'by map and compass readings and dead reckoning – just looking at the ground' in order to keep the RAF communication channels free and in some cases because new planes had not yet had radios installed.[65] They flew constantly. Lettice Curtis flew for thirteen days, with two days off, for a shade over five straight years,[66] and under threat of attack from the Luftwaffe. Diana Barnato said:

> I don't think I was scared. You're not scared when you are young, anyhow. You don't know what you are in for. I'd be scared now, of course. You weren't scared until afterwards, because your training was so good that you did all the right things in sequence, and in my case got away with it.[67]

By 1943 women could fly virtually all the aircraft in the RAF with the exception of heavy flying boats, and as a result were granted equal pay with male pilots.[68] The big question that loomed for the ATA women pilots was this: if they could fly all the planes, and if the RAF constantly struggled to maintain pilot numbers, why weren't women pilots sent into combat? Diana Barnato said, 'I think we would have been perfectly decent fighter pilots. But it was assumed that war was men's business. We had a duty to back them up. We could hardly sit about looking pretty and doing nothing, could we?'[69]

The RAF did the fighting, and the ATA only did flying. But there were inconsistencies created by placing women so close to the front lines of the fighting. As Diana Barnato recalls, we were non-combatant in our classification, and that never changed. We sometimes flew aircraft with the guns loaded. The ammunition was in them, but the guns weren't cocked. We couldn't press a button to shoot anybody, and yet we were there to be shot at. It was a fine dividing line.[70]

Another pilot was tempted to turn combatant:

Sometimes when I was flying a loaded plane, I felt like turning it round towards Germany, and letting them have it. The war made me so angry. I would fly across the countryside and see it all blown up, things destroyed . . . but of course if I'd ever gone off and dropped a bomb myself I would have been kicked out.[71]

The pilots were occasionally shot at by Germans. On one occasion Diana Barnato was a passenger in a plane being ferried when 'tracer bullets' appeared and the pilot shouted '"Jeez, it's a Gerry!" . . . we hid in the cloud until the Messerschmitt went by underneath and I saw the swastika cross marking on it'.[72] The ATA did consider putting gunners (male, of course) in some planes for this reason, but it was never implemented.[73]

The ATA was a dangerous service. The combination of flight hours and unfamiliar and untested planes led to a high casualty rate. The female pilots died less often than the men; one in ten of ATA's women died compared with one in three men.[74] The objection to women's combat service elsewhere could not have been danger, because women were engaged in the riskiest of endeavours. The objection had to be more closely associated with combat – particularly with killing. The ATA women could die, but they could not kill. This dividing line was even more sharply – and somewhat bizarrely – drawn in AA batteries.

Defending against aerial attack was to become a crucial component of the war. In 1937, Sir Frederick Pile was placed in charge of Britain's air defences. Imaginative and unconventional – as an artilleryman during the First World War he had allowed exhausted soldiers to ride on his guns, shocking other officers[75] – he early on spotted the potential to use women in air defence. Even before the war began, he consulted with a leading female engineer, Caroline Haslett, to find out if women would be physically capable of working in the batteries. Her view was that they could do almost everything short of firing the guns. Pile later wrote

> I could see no logical reason why they should not fire the guns too . . . However I was not going to suggest going so far as employing them on lethal weapons. I was quite aware that there would be struggle enough to get their employment through in any operational form at all.[76]

He was right. An initial proposal to use women in October 1939 was rejected on the grounds that the ATS was a purely non-combatant force. It took the deepening of the war in 1941 to open governmental and military minds to the necessity of using women in AA batteries.

Pile was increasingly convinced that not only would women's deployment 'mean a great saving in men, but also . . . the women would actually perform their duties more efficiently than some of the low-category men who were being allotted to us'.[77] He brought the request back to Cabinet in March 1941, where, according to Pile, it was described as 'breathtaking and revolutionary' and greeted with 'outraged cries of horror'.[78] Churchill was one of the few who immediately saw the benefits of releasing men for front-line duty this way,[79] writing to the secretary of war that he wanted to get rid of the 'complex against women being connected with lethal work'.[80] Any remaining opposition was quelled by the compelling numbers: a report suggested that as many as 140,000 men could be released for service through the recruitment of women for the batteries.[81] As Pile put it, 'it was pure mathematics that forced everybody's hand'.[82] The compromise was, as Pile had predicted, that women could work in the batteries but they could not fire the guns, which ensured that women did not violate the terms of the Royal Warrant of Appointment of the ATS, which explicitly excluded combat.[83]

Pile had his pick of ATS recruits in terms of physical strength and capability, but by definition had only the weakest men, with the strongest sent abroad. This led to a strange disjuncture where women were not allowed to fire the battery but were often more capable than men; women who took the task of gun laying had to be A1 physically and above average IQ, a standard which not all the men met.[84]

Pile had fairly radical views about the deployment of women, including that women should be paid equally with men,[85] and that they should be treated the same in terms of discipline and even with the same ranks. Initially, female recruits were added to existing all-male batteries, which did not work well and caused resentment, so by 1942 men and women entered training as a mixed group and were deployed together. Sir Frederick Pile had already made a point of selecting commanders who had 'run civilian "shows" in which men and women had worked together',[86] and mixed games teams and recreational activities encouraged *esprit de corps*.

The first of the mixed batteries was deployed in Richmond Park in London in August 1941. The battery, Pile wrote, 'became one of the wonders of the world. Women marching, eating, drilling, working with men! . . . it was as good as a visit to the Zoo!'[87] The attention persisted. One woman in the ATS recalled that 'whenever a mixed battery took up site . . . its perimeter was haunted for the first few days by local people staring at the female curiosities and hoping, perhaps, to catch a glimpse of a pair of khaki bloomers dangling from the barrel of an ack-ack gun'.[88] By 1943 there were 56,000 women in AA batteries, mainly around London,[89] and their presence was widely praised. *The Times* noted that 'first evidence of one of the most far-reaching experiments ever made in the British Army is meeting with great success. They [the women] have shown that short of actually manning the heavy guns, they are the equal of men'.[90]

Anti-aircraft batteries required multiple people. Their job was to locate an enemy plane and shoot it down by identifying it, predicting its trajectory, targeting it and firing the gun. Joan Cowey, an ATS woman, described the work as

all firing from morning to night, learning the instruments to fire the guns, determining the height and distance. They had planes going back and forth with sleeves or tow-targets on the back of them. There would be two hundred guns going off at once. It was all

women and men all the way along the cliff. It was cold; I remember
my hands would always freeze to the metal.[91]

Praise for the ack-ack women was extensive – and often patronising. A male commander of a mixed battery wrote that basic
training 'and the issue of their clothing and necessities is their first
excitement – and what woman doesn't like new clothes and new
happenings?' He also noted that in the 'early stages' of training 'the
amount of chatteration that goes on . . . in a team! It takes quite
a long time to stop it and they just don't seem to realise that they
are doing it!'[92] Finally, in his view, women were less good at 'spot-
ting' aircraft because they were less interested in aeroplanes; however,
'womanlike, once they have mastered anything of this sort, the
thing sticks'.[93] But he had nothing but praise for the women in his
battery: 'The girls are nothing more or less than "women soldiers".
They work hard and expect to be treated as such . . . They are
tough and can stick hardships every bit as well as the men.' He
admitted,

> I loathed the idea of commanding this type of battery when I was
> named for the job . . . I tried hard to get out of the change, but
> now I have joined this battery, raised it, watched it grow up and
> shared in its sorrows and joys I can say I have never been happier
> than I am now . . . My men and girls are great.[94]

Without the ATS women, AA batteries would have required 28,000
men,[95] and by late 1944 women in AA command outnumbered
men.[96]

The women in the battery were aware that they were there to
attack the enemy, even if they were not officially combatants.
Violette Szabo confessed that 'the thing uppermost in my mind
. . . was having a go at the enemy',[97] and she was not alone. Many
ATS woman were keen on revenge and killing Germans.[98] Joan
Cowey claimed that 'to shoot down a plane was something else.
We loved it when we had a busy night, just loved it'.[99] She went
on:

> A lot of the boys I went to school with were killed at Dunkirk.
> Half of the village . . . didn't come back. You want to know what

that does to a small village? It made us mad, that's what. I was a bit too young but I remember I wanted to get into a uniform of some kind . . . after Dunkirk, you could say I wanted to do it even more.[100]

Joan was not afraid of fighting. 'The whole idea appealed to me. I would have loved to be a guerrilla fighter. I always read about them . . . I thought, "Aren't they lucky that they can fight."'[101]

The first female casualty in the ATS was eighteen-year-old Private Nora Caveney. She was operating the predictor machine on a gun site in Southampton when she was struck by a bomb splinter and collapsed. Private Gladys Keel, a spotter, immediately took her place and the battery carried on working. It was Nora's first engagement with the enemy, and the battery's second in command reported, 'every man and girl in the battery is out for revenge . . . the girls' discipline under fire is most praiseworthy. Seasoned soldiers could not have behaved better'.[102] By the end of the war, 717 members of the ATS had been killed.[103]

The strict adherence to keeping women 'non-combatants' not only ignored the reality of what the women in the ATS were doing but led to contortions in practice and perverse outcomes. As Pile put it, 'we were quite ready to let them fire light anti-aircraft guns, but there was a good deal of muddled thinking which was prepared to allow women to do anything to kill the enemy except actually pull the trigger' and on searchlight sites 'the same political issue prevented them from firing back at any bomber which engaged them with its machine guns'.[104] It also meant that a woman and a man doing exactly the same job in a battery were different − one was a combatant, and one was not.[105]

The blurred lines between combat and non-combat also had potential legal consequences for women: if women who were to all intents and purposes firing on the enemy were taken prisoner, in theory they could be shot because, under the Hague Convention, non-combatants who took up arms were not afforded POW protections. This conundrum was one of the factors leading to the decision to give women auxiliaries military rather than civilian status.[106]

The women in AA batteries were not only excluded from firing anti-aircraft guns. They were also, along with all other women serving, prohibited from using firearms. In the event of an attack, women were supposed to hide with the civilian population, or give first aid and communications assistance, and only in the very last resort use arms and defend the battery.[107]

ATS members were also required to perform sentry duty, which they did with a pickaxe handle and a whistle – their male counterparts had rifles.[108] This incongruity was especially peculiar given Pile's view that the women 'showed themselves far more effective, more horror-inspiring, and more bloodthirsty with their pick-helves than many a male sentry with his gun'.[109] It also meant that women were at much higher risk than the men, who could defend themselves.

Women also worked in anti-aircraft defence by directing searchlights at enemy aircraft. Searchlight duty was particularly challenging because German pilots used the beam as a guide in order to shoot at the light itself and extinguish it. One woman who served in a searchlight unit said that she and her comrades felt a 'bit like sitting ducks waiting for the enemy aircraft to come firing down the beam. When the men manned the sites there were Lewis guns there, when we took over the guns were removed'.[110]

Despite the contortions that kept women officially out of combat, Pile had little doubt about what his AA women were doing: 'the British girls were the first to take their place in a combatant role in any army in the world'.[111] While the Red Army might have disagreed on who was first, Pile clearly thought his women were fighting. He wondered

> why we were ever such fools as to doubt that the thing would work. And work it did. The girls lived like men, fought . . . like men, and alas, some of them died like men. Unarmed, they often showed great personal bravery. They earned decorations and they deserved more.[112]

There was another group of women who lived and fought like men. The women spies of the Special Operations Executive were allowed to engage in combat – but at the time, no one else was allowed to know they existed.

After the Nazis captured France in 1940, it became apparent that Germany would rule most of Europe. The only way to defeat the Germans was to push them out of Europe, a colossal military task that required covert action behind enemy lines while an invasion was readied. The SOE was born in order to make life as difficult as possible for the Germans. SOE agents, often chosen because they had language skills that would allow them to pass as locals, were smuggled behind enemy lines and provided military and financial support to local resistance groups. As the war rolled on these groups became more and more important, because resistance fighters could help ease the path of the D-Day invasions.

The SOE worked outside regular military and even intelligence channels. As a result, it was imaginative and willing to entertain unusual ideas – including the notion of female agents. While there was considerable debate about whether it was even 'legal to use women on warlike operations',[113] in April 1942 the War Cabinet agreed, and women were put to work as SOE agents.[114] It made sense. The Nazi war machine had put the young men of occupied Europe to work, and so there were few of them on the streets. A woman could move around more easily – especially because the innate sexism of Nazi policy meant that officials were not convinced women were particularly capable of action anyway. As SOE agent Nancy Wake put it, 'it was much easier for us, you know, to travel all over France . . . A woman could get out of a lot of trouble that a man could not'.[115] Women were primarily placed in the roles of courier and wireless operator.[116]

The women of the SOE were trained alongside the men. The first training course required running through the countryside, navigation and the use of both pistols and sub-machine guns; nearby villagers were told that commandos were being trained, but 'were left to wonder for themselves why women might be taking part in it'.[117] Those who passed were sent to Scotland for paramilitary training, including the use of firearms of all different types. Prospective agents were trained in combat shooting, the so-called double tap, more reliable than a single shot. They were also taught silent killing techniques stemming from unarmed combat.[118] Basic infantry techniques, including how to ambush houses, were on the curriculum, as were demolition techniques and the explosive types necessary for sabotage.[119] The final stage of training saw recruits move to a stately home called Beaulieu, where they were taught everything they needed to know to survive behind enemy lines, from identifying relevant police and security forces to surviving interrogation, as well as all the spycraft they needed to communicate with London in code and recruit teams of resistance fighters. Finally, recruits were taught how to parachute, one of the main means of bringing them to Europe.

Selwyn Jepson, the main recruiter for SOE, noted that in training

> what was noticeable was that the women were so much better than the men in all the kinds of skills that the work would ask for. They took up, funnily enough, they took up pistol shooting with great ability. I don't know what psychological drive there was there but there wasn't one of them who wasn't keen on it even when the pistol, which would be a .45 automatic, the recoil would sometimes be so shattering that they would fall on their backs . . . then they would get up and fire again . . . it was that sort of determination that was so impressive.[120]

The SOE's clandestine activities required significant organisation. Weapons needed to be dropped from British planes, which required safe landing fields; sabotage required explosives and training; plotting and planning required the ability to communicate, but also the necessity of absolute secrecy. As a result, the SOE required agents who could fight and conduct sabotage operations, but also couriers and, crucially, wireless radio operators. The radio operators were essential: they had to get messages back to London, requesting weapons and providing updates. But radio operation was dangerous as radio signals were easily traced, and even when radio operators frequently moved to avoid detection, they were often captured – their average life expectancy was six weeks.[121]

On the ground, many of the women exceeded expectations. Pearl Witherington was the daughter of a Northumbrian gentleman with a drinking problem and no money, who raised his family in Paris where life was cheaper. Pearl's fluent French made her a useful asset, first to the British embassy in Paris, and later, after she had escaped the occupying Germans, as a secretary in London. She was bored and volunteered for the SOE. While she passed her training course with flying colours – her final report said, 'this student, though a woman, has definitely got leader's qualities. Cool and resourceful and extremely determined. Particularly interested in and suited for active work'[122] – her first practice attempts at fieldwork yielded concerns. 'Loyal and reliable but has not the personality to act as a leader,' the report said, 'would be best employed as a subordinate under a strong leader in whom she has confidence'.[123] This second report, with its patronising tone, was about to be proved wrong.

Pearl arrived in France by parachute in September 1943. Her initial role was to be a courier, which she accomplished by disguising herself as a travelling cosmetics saleswoman.[124] The leader of her circuit was captured by the Germans, so Pearl began to run her own. By May 1944 she was leading a 3,000-strong army in the Sologne, armed with British weapons dropped by parachute. She was so effective that the Germans offered 1 million francs for her capture. After D-Day, Pearl and her *maquisards* managed to bring rail traffic in the region to an almost complete halt.[125] She later summarised her own achievement: 'German losses over five months 1,000; the wounded can be counted in thousands. We participated in the surrender of 18,000 Boches at Issoudons'.[126]

Pearl Witherington was not the only SOE woman to shatter expectations. Nancy Wake, an Australian who had lived in France before the war, also commanded a group of partisans. She trained a resistance force of 7,000 men prior to D-Day, successfully raiding a Gestapo garrison and an arms factory. 'The most exciting sortie I ever made,' she explained, involved throwing grenades into a house where German officers were lunching. Nancy 'ran like hell back to my car . . . the headquarters was completely wrecked . . . and several dozen Germans did not lunch that day nor any other day for that matter'.[127] Her group came under attack by 22,000 German troops in June 1944: the Germans lost 1,400 men and Nancy's partisans only 100.[128] Her successful military action brought her to the attention of the Germans and put a price on her head.[129] During one military engagement with the Germans, Nancy's group of fighters lost track of their radio operator; in order to re-establish communications with London Nancy cycled 500 kilometres in three days,[130] through towns and villages 'literally swarming with Germans'.[131]

Nancy did not enjoy violence, but nor was she afraid of it. She remembered her lessons in hand-to-hand combat well – 'They'd taught us this judo-chop stuff . . . at SOE' – and used it against a German guard – '[W]hack! And it killed him all right.'[132] After interrogating three captured women, one confessed to being a German spy. 'Reluctantly,' Nancy wrote, 'I informed her she would have to be shot as there was no alternative. At first the men refused to shoot the woman and agreed to form a firing squad only after I had announced I would undertake the task myself.'[133] One of her comrades said of her, 'she is the most feminine woman I know until the fighting starts – then she is like five men'.[134]

Any agent operating in occupied Europe needed the courage of five men. They were taking the most extraordinary risks. Spies are not considered to be combatants under the laws of war, which means that they are not entitled to any of the protections of a soldier, including the right to be treated as a prisoner of war. In December 1941 Hitler announced a policy that took full advantage of this rule. Spies and resistance fighters would be tortured and punished and would ultimately disappear. The policy was called *Nacht und Nebel*, or 'night and fog' – because after they had given up their secrets, prisoners would be made to disappear. Melting into the night and fog would have been preferable to the reality. Most prisoners were tortured and sent to various concentration camps, from where they would never return. A quarter of the 400 SOE agents sent to France died.[135]

The leaders of SOE had no illusions about the danger their agents faced; they presumed half would never return.[136] Female agents were sometimes enrolled in the WAAF, which gave them a cover story at home and, abroad, the slimmest chance that they might be given POW status rather than disappear in *Nacht und Nebel*.[137] Others were officially members of the First Aid Nursing Yeomanry, which had a different advantage: they were classed as civilians, allowing them to carry arms and travel overseas, avoiding bans on both in the women's services.[138]

In fact, women did not have much to rely on in the cover story department. Men could (and did) claim that they were Allied airmen and hope for the best. Once captured, women could only rely on their femininity. Sonja Butt, the youngest SOE agent to work in France, said that when in trouble,

> You just react to the moment and think 'I'll get by alright with a nice smile'. I just sort of smiled and waved to them. All the time. Women could get by with a smile and do things that men couldn't and no matter what you had hidden in your handbag or your bicycle bag, if you had a nice smile, you know, just give them a little wink . . . You did that [flirted] automatically.[139]

Getting caught had disastrous consequences. Of the fifty women sent to France, at least twenty were imprisoned and thirteen died during the course of the war.[140] Eileen Nearne was subjected to the *baignoire*, simulated drowning that we know today as waterboarding. Odette Sansom was burned with a red-hot poker and had all her toenails removed – but revealed nothing. She was one of the rare SOE women to survive deportation to a concentration camp. The majority were executed.

The remarkable stories of the women of the SOE have garnered considerable attention over the years. During the war their activities were kept entirely secret. After the war ended the women were not eligible for the same military awards as their male counterparts. In fact, Pearl Witherington, once described by her handlers as 'outstanding. Probably the best shot, male or female, we have yet had', was offered the civilian award of an MBE but turned it down, pointing out that she had 'done nothing remotely civil' during the war.[141]

But what the women of the SOE demonstrated was that women were indeed capable of considerable bravery; of inflicting and receiving the most terrible injuries; of organisation and coolness under fire; of working with men in the field without being 'a distraction'; of facing down assault, even sexual assault, without breaking. In other words, they showed that they were capable of doing all the things that in subsequent years women were supposed not to be able to do effectively enough to be allowed into combat. The debate about women in combat that started to simmer decades later, and to rage by the end of the twentieth century, never considered the women of the SOE – and the fact that these women were not recruited because they exhibited immense physical strength or unusual bravery; they were ordinary, hardly the type that anyone would assume would be successful fighters. One of their instructors wrote that 'the girls were not commando material. They didn't have the physique though some had tremendous mental stamina. You would not expect well brought up girls to go up behind someone and slit their throats'.[142]

Violette Szabo, after all, was just over five feet tall and began her training as the mother of a one-year-old. Prior to the war she had worked as a shop assistant selling perfume, not an occupation that would presage any combat ability. But when she and her fellow agent Anastasie came under fire, she was ready, taking up a position next to the car and shooting. Anastasie ordered her to retreat, and the two fell back, covering each other with gunfire.

> We had to continue our progress towards the wood crawling flat and cautiously on the ground, an exhausting and awfully slow process. Then we heard the infantry running up the road . . . so we had to resume firing in turn to cover the other's progress.

When they neared the woods, Violette, whose clothes were by then

> ripped to ribbons and [who] was bleeding from numerous scratches all over her legs, told me she was exhausted and could not go one inch further. She insisted she wanted me to try and get away . . . So I went on while she kept firing from time to time.

Eventually she was captured, and Anastasie, hiding nearby, heard her laugh as she told the Germans, 'You can run after him, he is far away by now'.[143] The leader of Violette's resistance group also reported that the gun battle had lasted for over half an hour.[144]

The women of the SOE were *ordinary* women who happened to speak a language fluently. And yet they showed that even the most ordinary women were capable of combat – and capable of the extraordinary. But these ordinary women were presented as the exception to the rule, an exception that was only facilitated by the most dire necessity. When the war ended, those women lucky enough to survive the war were returned to civilian life, alongside all the other women who had proved their capability across a range of fields.

The other women of the British military effort did not appear to pose much of a challenge to the conventional view that women shouldn't – and probably couldn't – engage in combat. But the women of the ATA and the women who worked in AA batteries showed the inconsistencies of this view. In the ATA, a very small group of women showed that they were pilots just as capable as the men around them, and could have fought in combat – or at the very least been allowed to fire back when they came under attack. In the AA batteries, only the very strictest interpretation of the rules allowed the government and the military to avoid the claim that women were fighting. And in all these cases women demonstrated that they were exceptional leaders. After all, it was women who established the interwar auxiliaries that formed the nucleus of women's wartime mobilisation. But at the end of the war, almost without exception, and no matter what skills they had demonstrated, women returned to a traditional existence that bore little resemblance to their wartime lives.

In Great Britain, despite the fact that female anti-aircraft batteries were an 'unqualified success',[145] the AA women who had made General Sir Frederick Pile so proud were, at the end of the war, given training in 'the arts and crafts essential to maintain the communal life, including the domestic arts with ancillary handicrafts . . . vegetable and flower gardening, music and plays'.[146] The ATS established a Home Training and Handicraft Centre to help women transition to post-war life.[147] One woman who had served in the AA batteries remarked that as the war was winding down, droves of 'silly (but dedicated) Women came round to teach us Handicrafts, Housewifery, Musical Appreciation, and other irksome and boring nonsense . . . and they addressed us most of the time as if we were delinquent three-year-olds!'[148]

Women pilots had no more chances than other military women.

Lettice Curtis, who could fly almost any plane in the RAF and ten different types of public transport aircraft,[149] applied for a job as a test pilot with the Aircraft and Armament Experimental Establishment in 1947. She arrived for a flight test (having been invited as E. L. Curtis Esq.), and was asked in the waiting room if she knew she was applying to be a test pilot; her affirmative answer caused 'a roar of laughter' to bubble out from the boardroom.[150] While the recruiting team were 'quite satisfied' with her flying and technical skills, they turned her down. 'I am bound to tell you that they may hedge at employing a woman,' the recruiter explained, 'for, as you yourself realise, Government Departments do not like to set a precedent.'[151] Despite her flying skills, including setting an international women's record in a Spitfire in 1948, Curtis could not get the government to set a precedent, and did not become a test pilot. She flew on her own until the 1990s, including pursuing qualification as a helicopter pilot in her seventies. Despite their evident skills, the ATA women struggled to get jobs as commercial pilots, and desperately missed flying. Jackie Moggridge, an ATA pilot, wrote that 'it was as frustrating for me not to fly constantly as it is for a woman yearning for a home and family to be a spinster'.[152] After repeated rejections for pilots' jobs, she wrote, 'So this is what I flew in the war for . . . to make the world free . . . if you're a man.'[153]

A post-war attempt to create an official women's pilot reserve as part of the RAF failed because it was unclear exactly what roles women were to occupy given the large number of male reservists. Although one female pilot, a member of the ATA, was the first woman to get RAF pilot wings, the programme was allowed to lapse, and women were not again allowed to fly in the RAF until the 1980s.[154]

Many of the women who served in the Second World War returned to being ordinary wives and mothers. Pauline Gower, who had recruited women for the ATA and was herself a talented pilot, married at the end of the war. She died in 1947, of a heart attack, just after giving birth to twin sons. A return to the ordinary life of a woman was not without danger either.

9

Germany and the United States in the Second World War

D URING THE SECOND World War in Germany one of the abiding preoccupations of both civilian and military authorities was the issue of morale on the home front, building on a deep-seated belief that a collapse in morale had led to Germany's defeat in the first war. As a result, authorities were finely tuned to the public mood, keeping a close eye on the social impact of women taking on war work. After the invasion of the Soviet Union the German internal security police found evidence that women being away from home was indeed having a detrimental impact on morale. There was 'widespread marital discord, because when the husband comes home from work evenings, he must wait for his meal, and what is more, has to pass the time in an uncleaned and uncomfortable apartment'.[1]

Small concerns like these were hardly holding back women from military service anywhere else; but Germany was different. It was protected from the need to mobilise women because first victory and then Nazi policies of slave labour provided the regime with the necessary manpower – for a time. As a result, women were mobilised to a much lesser degree than in nearly every country fighting in the war – except for one. The United States, as a result of its physical distance and its success in the war, also avoided manpower pressure and the need to mobilise women in large numbers. The creative thinking around women's roles demonstrated in the USSR and Britain, and the lack of female mobilisation in Germany and the US both demonstrate that the opposition to women in combat was deep-seated. Desperation was a crucial ingredient in the decision to abandon powerful social beliefs about women in combat, and neither Germany (for a long time) nor the

US experienced the sort of urgent need that could transform thinking about women's roles.

In Germany, even under the pressure of the most global war in history, the basic view that women should not fight was barely challenged. Nazi ideology strongly held that the appropriate place for women was in the home, a belief which continually hampered efforts to place women into military roles.[2] Adolf Hitler explained in 1934 that women's emancipation was an invention of Jewish intellectuals, and further that

> the man's world is the state, that the man's world is his struggle, and his readiness to devote his powers to the service of his community, then it may be said that the woman's is a smaller world. For her world is her husband, her family, her children, and her home.[3]

Joseph Goebbels agreed: 'things pertaining to men must be left to men: these include politics and the ability of a nation to defend itself'.[4]

Partially as a result of these ideological views, the Nazi regime struggled to conscript women for war service at all, both in industry and as military auxiliaries. Hitler's strong views about appropriate roles for women and the domestic sphere were, at first, easy to sustain. After all, the Nazis were victorious in the first years of the war – unlike the British, who entered the war and then watched the rest of Europe collapse against Hitler's onslaught.[5] Victory abroad meant there was no early need to disrupt the idea that women best served the Reich in the home, as wives and mothers.

Keeping German women in the home and maintaining a fantasy of Aryan motherhood relied on a cruel reality: forced labour of all kinds, from eastern European deportees to concentration camp inmates to prisoners of war, meant that Germany's manpower needs were not as great as those of Britain and the USSR.[6]

It wasn't just Nazi ideology that promoted the view that women should remain at home. It was strategic policy, based on the view that morale would collapse if too many women were mobilised. A demoralised Germany was open to Bolshevik agitation, the 'stab in the back' that Hitler viewed as critical to German capitulation in 1918.[7] German women were to stay home not only to fulfil their duties as mothers of the Reich but also to protect the German war effort.

Hitler consistently stuck to the view that women should not be fighting, anywhere near fighting, or even doing something slightly unwomanly, for as long as possible. After the tide of war began to turn, the irrationality of keeping women in the domestic sphere became more noticeable. Ideology is a powerful thing: only when German defeat looked certain did beliefs change over whether women could play a military role. It was a change born of desperation rather than a realisation of women's capacities.

Hitler only began to change his position on women's military work as the tide of war began to turn against Germany in 1943. In January 1943 fifteen- and sixteen-year-old boys were recruited to work in anti-aircraft batteries; by the summer women and teenage girls were also working there.[8] In August 1943 German women were deployed as anti-aircraft or Flak crews; in line with the British AA women, they were not allowed to fire the guns.[9] Had more women been mobilised, it might have prevented the use of very young teenage boys in AA batteries. In October 1943 a searchlight unit was hit by enemy fire and its entire crew – all boys younger than fourteen, under the officially sanctioned age of fifteen – were killed.[10] By March 1944, 111,000 women were involved in air defence, but their training included useful reminders that they could retain their 'womanly character' – by remembering that 'the wooden barracks must become a home. Where women live, there is no dark, dusty corner'.[11]

The deteriorating military situation throughout 1944 finally prompted a discussion about female conscription. In August Hitler demanded that male clerks and administrative workers in the Wehrmacht be released for front-line duties, prompting the first conversations about how to mobilise the 140,000 women who would be needed to replace them[12] without destroying morale. The regime proposed legislation to conscript young, single women to support the Wehrmacht. The law was abandoned because the Nazi leadership was convinced that female conscription would destroy morale at home and consequently undermine men fighting at the front.[13] The result was that even as Allied forces pushed closer and closer to Berlin, the regime had to rely on ineffective voluntary recruit-ment.[14] As one Nazi official noted, women were only signing up 'very sluggishly'.[15]

Women were assisting the Wehrmacht as volunteers under strict conditions. The military leadership was dubious that women had the capacity to replace men, commenting that 'no work is to be given to women that requires particular presence of mind, deter-mination and fast action'.[16] The guiding principle for Hitler, and the Wehrmacht, was that women should be deployed to assist the military as far from the front as possible, because the very notion of women near combat was 'not consistent with our National Socialist conception of womanliness'.[17]

Even as the war became more and more desperate, Germany strug-gled to mobilise women. In late 1944, when defeat began to look like a reality, Hitler and his inner circle devised a plan for the Volkssturm, a levée en masse of German people who would rise up to stop the Allied incursion. As Heinrich Himmler put it, 'every urban housing block, every village, every farmstead, every trench, every thicket and every wood will be defended by men, boys and pensioners, and if necessary, by women and girls'.[18] But Hitler personally prohib-ited women from enrolling in the Volkssturm.[19] Martin Bormann, who was head of the Nazi Party Chancellery, insisted that as long as there were any capable men, 'the employment of armed women must be rejected'.[20] Bormann took the view that the German people were wholly unprepared psychologically for the notion of armed women and would not support it without preparation.[21]

The final defence of Berlin – and the Reich – brought about the only serious attempts to place German women into combatant roles, but even then it was a last-ditch choice. As the Allies pushed their way through Nazi-controlled territory towards Berlin, the Germans mobilised sixteen-year-old boys to defend the Reich.[22] By 1945 they were using fourteen-year-olds.[23] An American com-mander reported fighting against an artillery unit manned by children younger than twelve: 'Rather than surrender,' he noted, 'the boys fought until killed.'[24] All this was more possible than mobilising adult women, who were still denied firearms training until the winter of 1945.[25]

As the Allies were grinding through to Berlin, women were creeping closer to the front lines. AA batteries were repurposed as ground artillery units, with fifty all-female units entering training. Only ten made it into service before the end of the war.[26] A female Flak battery defended Vienna against the oncoming Red Army in 1945.[27] By April 1945 teenage girls as young as fourteen and fifteen were trained with anti-tank guns considered 'girls' weapons' because they did not create a heavy recoil requiring significant body strength to absorb[28] – there were reports of boys as young as eleven firing these guns in 1944.[29]

Finally, in March 1945, only weeks before the collapse of Berlin, Hitler endorsed an experimental women's battalion as a model for potential future units, but his main goal was to humiliate men.[30] '[I]f we put them [women] into the second line,' he mused, 'the men won't run away at least.'[31] It was less that Hitler was convinced that women were capable fighters; more, he was despairing of what he saw as the cowardice of German men. He noted that 'so many women who want to shoot are volunteering now that I am of the opinion that we ought to take them immediately. They are braver anyway'.[32] The women's battalion was never raised or trained,[33] and records of it and other attempts to mobilise women for combat are scant, as the very idea was so taboo that few orders were written down.[34]

By the end of the war many German women were living a life of extreme danger. The conflict was all around them. A combination of Allied bombing raids and armies advancing on German cities from east and west meant there was no longer any distinction between the front lines of battle and the safety of home. In fact, homes were subject to immense danger: destruction by bombs or attacks by soldiers. German women experienced an astonishing level of sexual violence during the war, perpetrated by all the advancing militaries, not just Soviet soldiers. In late April 1945 French soldiers attacked a south German village where 'no female person between the ages of 12 and 80 was safe from rape. According to the local doctor . . . 152 women required medical attention because they had been raped'.[35] In total more than 2 million German women were raped during the course of the war.[36]

Finally, the catastrophe through which German women were living began to change the rhetoric of the collapsing Nazi regime. At the very end of the war the regime finally recognised that women would need to defend themselves against the onslaught of the Red Army, and women were exhorted to 'take up arms if they drop from the hands of wounded or killed soldiers . . . defend yourselves against the Soviet hordes'.[37] But the reminders of traditional femininity persisted. Women could defend themselves, but as women; in the words of a radio broadcast on 27 April 1945, 'if needs must, mother takes out her largest pair of scissors and becomes a freedom fighter too'.[38]

Germany experienced a far shorter duration of women's mobilisation than did the other combatant powers, and did so as part of a war that ended not only in abject defeat but in the reconstruction of society. Particularly profound was the desire to return to a normal world: a world that pre-dated Nazism, where women were safe and at home, and as far away from fighting as possible. The war's greatest victor was to draw the same conclusion, but on very different grounds.

The American experience differs sharply from that of all the other wartime protagonists. The United States never faced a significant military threat to the bulk of its territory, and so was resolute in its desire to keep women out of combat roles – or even in roles that would go beyond the traditional. The Americans did mobilise women. Between 1941 and 1943 all branches of the military, including the Marines and Coast Guard, had women's organisations attached, with about 275,000 women deployed.[39] But only in two of these branches did women come close to combat or take on non-traditional roles: in an experimental anti-aircraft battery associated with the Women's Army Corps (WAC) and in the WASP (Women's Airforce Service Pilots) programme.[40] As we have seen, in general, women in the Second World War came closest to combat in the AA batteries, and while only Soviet women fought as pilots, British women demonstrated that they had the capacity to do so through the Air Transport Auxiliary. In the United States, even in anti-aircraft batteries and as transport pilots, women's roles were strictly circumscribed, held back by prevailing beliefs about gender and protected by the United States' geographic safety.

While in Britain discussions about the practical role women could play in the war effort took place throughout the 1930s, in the US the decision to create women's military organisations took much longer. As late as 1941 a doctor mused while testifying before Congress that 'it is perfectly possible to utilise the patriotic spirit of the nation's young women, thousands of whom are anxious to do their part for the national defence, in order to recruit a splendid corps of volunteer hostesses'.[41]

Although America was slower to mobilise women, women themselves played a leading role in making sure it happened. As the clouds of war gathered over Europe, Congresswoman Edith Nourse Rogers seized the initiative. Rogers firmly believed that a women's army corps would be necessary, and that, further, it needed to be a formal part of the military, not a civilian auxiliary. When asked later about her motives for the plan, Rogers answered:

> MY motives? In the first World War I was there and *saw*. I saw the women in France and how they had no suitable quarters and no Army discipline. Many . . . who served then are still sick in the hospital and I was never able to get any veterans' compensation for them . . . I was resolved that our women would not again serve with the Army without the protection that men got.[42]

Rogers' pressure forced the War Department into action. A memo accompanying its initial planning complains that

> Congresswoman Edith Nourse Rogers has been determined for some time to introduce a bill to provide a women's organisation in the Army. We have succeeded in stopping her on the promise we are studying the same thing, and will permit her to introduce a bill which will meet with War Department approval. Mrs Roosevelt also seems to have a plan.

The War Department planners did not sound especially keen, going on to say:

> the sole purpose of this study is to permit the organisation of a women's force along lines which meet with War Department approval, so that when it is forced upon us, as it undoubtedly will be, we shall be able to run it our way.[43]

Congress would have to approve the notion of a women's military organisation, and everyone knew that that would not be straightforward. The first debate was over whether the women's corps should be an auxiliary corps, and therefore remain civilian, or come under military control. The argument in favour of militarisation was that it would be legally easier to manage (which proved to be true, and the reason the resulting corps gained military status in 1943).[44] The argument against was that men everywhere – in the military, in Congress, in general – hated the idea. Congresswoman Rogers backed down and accepted auxiliary status, noting that although she wanted women to be in the army to give them access to pensions and allowances, 'I . . . realized that I could not secure that. The War Department was very unwilling to have these women as part of the Army'.[45]

So was Congress. The War Department could not come up with a bill that was going to satisfy the many criticisms that would lie in the way – not even with General George C. Marshall, who had come around to the likely practical necessity of requiring women, shaking his finger at his underlings and shouting, 'I want a women's corps right away and I don't want any excuses!' It took Pearl Harbor to sweep away the remaining objections.[46] But even then, these were only objections that stood in the way of bringing the bill to Congress – Congress still had to agree, and that was not going to be straightforward.

Colonel John Hilldring was the military planner in charge of shepherding the bill through Congress and into reality. Hilldring later recalled, 'It was a battle. In my time I have got some one hundred bills through Congress, but this was more difficult than the rest of the hundred combined.'[47] The objections came thick and fast, and took a form that would still sound familiar fifty years (and more) later, with the usual appeals to the need to protect femininity. Congressman Clare Hoffman of Michigan noted that unlike men, 'women, thank God, are not killers', and that men would be distracted from the war by the need to rescue women accompanying them. 'Where is the man,' he asked, 'fighting in a foreign land with these women in the camps or behind the battle line, who will not shudder and hesitate if the tide turns against him and he knows that the women in the armed force are to become the prisoners, the slaves, or worse, of the Nazis?'[48] The congressman was also worried about what would happen on the home front should women be enrolled. 'Who will do the cooking, the washing, the mending, the humble, homey tasks to which every woman has devoted herself; who will rear and nurture the children?'[49] Congressman Somers of New York asserted,

> this is the silliest piece of legislation that has ever come before my notice. A woman's army to defend the United States of America. Think of the humiliation. What has become of the manhood of America that we have to call on our women to do what has ever been the duty of men?[50]

Eventually, the bill made it. Congress was generally reassured by the fact that women would do traditionally female jobs, as stenographers, telephone operators, stewardesses and clerks – even, as one early planning document suggested, as 'waitresses, chauffeurs, messengers and strolling minstrels'.[51] Crucially, none of these jobs would be done anywhere near the actual battle (one imagines that there was a particularly low demand for strolling minstrels at the front). One congressman wondered why women were not also being utilised as cooks, and was given the answer that cooks had to travel to the combat zone, and therefore cooks needed to be male.[52]

Once created, it did not take long for the WAAC to become the centre of controversy. The WAAC was plagued by rumours that any woman serving in a military capacity must only be in it for the sex: either with other women or with military men.[53] Like the ATS women before them, the women of the WAAC were targeted by a slander campaign. According to gossip, WAAC women were sexually promiscuous and immoral; they drank too much and had al fresco sex just about everywhere, resulting in alarming rates of pregnancy and disease. One exotic rumour claimed that they were roaming the streets to capture and rape sailors.[54] Investigations into the slander campaign revealed that the rumours were likely started by disgruntled military men and had no basis in fact.[55]

It is hardly surprising, in the context of the controversy around creating women's military organisations and the war's lack of physical impact on American soil, that American women did not come close to experiencing the war in the same way as did their European sisters. Far smaller numbers of women served. Only 2 per cent of American women participated in the armed forces, compared with 9 per cent of British women and 5 per cent of Soviet women.[56] No women in the WAAC were killed in service, not even overseas.[57] Only in two cases did American women's wartime work resemble that across the Atlantic, and both were initially characterised as experimental. Neither was long-lived.

The first experiment with placing women outside traditional roles came in anti-aircraft defence. The Americans were closely watching the British experiment with ATS women – even from within the White House. Eleanor Roosevelt had made an early suggestion that American women take on anti-aircraft roles, following their British counterparts.[58] In 1942 General Dwight Eisenhower was asked to investigate the British experiment, and he reported back positively. General George C. Marshall decided that the US would build a secret all-female AA battery experiment. The secrecy was necessary because the military's legal advice indicated that women working in AA batteries would be assigned to combat roles, rendering the whole enterprise illegal – but the experiment proceeded anyway.[59] The secrecy was such a success that the programme's existence only became known in the 1950s.[60]

Colonel Edward Timberlake was put in charge of the experiment, and in his view the women passed with flying colours. They exhibited 'an outstanding devotion to duty, willingness and ability to absorb and grasp technical information concerning . . . all types of equipment'.[61] In fact, the women were faster learners than the men, most of whom had been designated 'limited duty service'. Timberlake was so enthused he suggested that women could replace men in 60 per cent of all AA positions.[62] The leaders of the experiment were ready to increase the number of women – and this caused the women's AA battery programme to come to an abrupt halt.

The problem was that the creation of the WAAC had been pretty controversial in the first place – it had only been accepted because of promises that traditional gender roles would be preserved. The legislation had banned women from combat, and this would have to change in order to make the experiment bigger. Marshall's military lawyers helpfully drafted an amendment: 'nothing in this act shall prevent any member of the Women's Army Auxiliary Corps from service with any combatant organisation with her own consent'.[63] The draft made it clear: if the anti-aircraft experiment became permanent, the WAAC would be serving in combat. Marshall knew that this would be politically impossible, and was advised that women could be more usefully used elsewhere, especially 'under present circumstances'.[64] As the director of the Military Personnel Division put it, neither national policy nor 'public opinion is yet ready to accept the use of women in field force units'.[65]

The 'present circumstances' were that the US was not experiencing a military assault on its own soil, and did not have major manpower issues. America's military might and geographic position meant that it did not have to challenge prevailing expectations about women's capabilities. There was no real need to place women in combat roles. AA batteries were not really required on the home front.[66] Unlike in Britain and the USSR where the immediate prospect of national destruction had made the broad social mobilisation of women possible, in America the soil of home was safe. In Germany, it took *months* of long, grinding defeat to persuade Hitler to even consider the notion of women fighters. The US was under no such pressure, and the secret women's AA battery was abandoned and remained a secret until the mid-1950s.

The second experimental use of women outside traditional roles placed women in the sky: as in Britain and the USSR, women pilots were mobilised to support the war effort. By 1942 two different air transport units, both of which had women members, amalgamated to form the WASP. Once again, Mrs Roosevelt was a key proponent. Writing in her national newspaper column 'My Day' in September 1942, she rubbished the idea that 'women are psychologically not fitted to be pilots' as

> I see pictures every now and then of women who are teaching men to fly. We know that in England, where the need is great, women are ferrying planes and freeing innumerable men for combat service . . . I believe . . . if the war goes on long enough, and women are

patient, opportunity will come knocking at their doors. However, there is just a chance that this is not a time when women should be patient. We are in a war and we need to fight it with all our ability and every weapon possible. Women pilots, in this particular case, are a weapon waiting to be used.[67]

The WASP was led by Jacqueline Cochran, a glamorous and successful racing pilot with a millionaire husband. Her wartime glitz belied her humble origins: she had grown up poor in Florida, married for the first time at fourteen and had had a baby at the age of fifteen.[68] Jackie was a record-setting pilot – in fact, she set more records than any of her contemporaries, male or female.[69] She was the first woman to fly a military plane over the Atlantic, ferrying a bomber in 1941. Early in the war she again flew to England escorting twenty-five American women to serve with the ATA,[70] and was asked shortly after her return to set up a similar organisation in the US. This organisation, combined with another led by pilot Nancy Harkness Love, became the WASP in June 1943. WASP pilots ferried aircraft, but they also towed targets for firing practice, simulated bombing attacks and worked on daytime and night-time tracking missions;[71] they worked as administrative pilots, flying personnel, and instrument instructors.[72]

The United States needed the WASPs because early in the war it did not have enough pilots. General Henry 'Hap' Arnold, chief of the Air Corps, was initially unconvinced that 'a slip of a young girl could fight the controls of a B-17 in the heavy weather they would naturally encounter',[73] but the WASPs proved him wrong. WASP women were soon able to fly all America's military planes, and approximately 1,000 women eventually joined the service. They even had an insignia designed by Walt Disney: Fifinella, a girl gremlin riding a bomb.[74]

The WASP was a civilian organisation, and its members even had to pay their own transport costs to the organisation's main base in Texas. The very existence of the WASP was kept as quiet as possible.[75] In fact, some pilots were approached by one woman who declared, '"That is the first time I have ever seen a uniform of the Mexican Army. How do you like it here?" The women quickly replied "no comprende"' and turned away'.[76] No one could believe a woman was a military pilot, which resulted in WASP pilots even being detained on suspicion of impersonating military personnel or trying to steal aircraft.[77] Suspicion occasionally extended to outright hostility on the airfields. One WASP pilot was killed in a crash landing, and later investigation revealed sugar in the gasoline tank had stopped the engine.[78]

Eventually, the push came to make the WASP, the only remaining civilian women's organisation, officially military. Doing so brought it to Congress for approval and into the public spotlight. This process eventually caused the WASP to disband after only two years and before the end of the war.

Cochran had begun to place laudatory articles about the WASP in the press in order to give impetus to the militarisation efforts[79] – but in the end circumstances conspired to have the opposite effect. Making the WASP part of the regular military coincided with a significant change in the war. By 1944 American air superiority was assured, and conservative war planning resulted in surplus American aircraft and pilots. Manpower needs were no longer in the air – they were going to be on the ground, specifically in the Pacific war against Japan. Needless to say, trained pilots were not keen on going to fight in a bloody infantry war when 2,500 women pilots were on far safer domestic duties.

Any sober military efforts, including those of General Arnold, to explain that an expanded WASP could actually assist the war effort by freeing up men for what they were most needed – actual combat – were silenced by a well-orchestrated campaign that tried to claim that less qualified WASPs were stealing (safer) jobs from experienced male combat pilots.[80] The headlines said it all. 'Army Passes up Jobless Pilots to Train WASPs: Prefers Women to Older, Experienced Flyers' shouted one, while another put it more colourfully: 'Lay That Airplane Down, Babe, Cry Grounded He-Man Pilots'.[81]

Jacqueline Cochran's glamour proved to be a particular liability. Rumours abounded that she had used her feminine wiles to turn General Arnold's head, and so his support for the WASPs was tainted. One article even said: 'in the last week the shapely pilot has seen her coveted commission come closer and closer . . . one of the highest placed generals, it seems, gazed into her eyes, and since then has taken her *cause celebre* very much "to heart".[82] Another rumour included a less seductive form of feminine scheming. Apparently Eleanor Roosevelt had pushed the WASP scheme for her own feminist ends.[83]

The WASPs could not withstand a sustained negative public campaign in a Congress already lukewarm on women's military service.[84] The bill militarising the WASPs failed. It was the only piece of legislation supported by the air force to be turned down since the start of the war.[85] General Arnold announced in October 1944 that by the end of the year the WASP would be closed down. In his last address to a graduating class of WASPs, he said:

> I want to stress how valuable I believe this whole WASP program has been for the country. If another national emergency arises – let us hope it does not . . . if it does, we will not again look on a women's flying organization as an experiment. We will know that they can handle our fastest fighters, our heaviest bombers.[86]

The WASP remained a civilian organisation. Its members were not eligible for military funerals, military pensions or other veterans' benefits. During the war, WASP pilots clubbed together to pay to ship home the bodies of pilots killed in action.[87] In fact, they were so forgotten that in 1976 the US Air Force announced that women would be allowed to fly military planes for the first time ever – never mind that the WASPs had done it thirty years previously.[88] Their contributions were utterly forgotten.

At first glance, the wartime experiences of the United States and Germany could not be more different. One was a victor, and with that victory became the world's pre-eminent military power. One was defeated, its pretensions to power crushed. But a comparison of the two reveals a surprising amount about the factors that have made it so difficult to place women in combat, and why and how women came to be formally excluded from combat.

The stories of women in the Second World War from around the world reveal that desperation was the vital ingredient enabling leaders to allow women to do unexpected things, including fight. For a considerable period of the war a victorious Nazi Germany supported by foreign and slave labour experienced no real need to mobilise women. Only when the tide of war turned was the idea even entertained – and even then, Nazi ideology prevented a wholesale mobilisation of women. The United States' military power and geographic position combined to prevent any real need for women to be mobilised. Ongoing victory meant that very few American women serving with the military were ever in harm's way, and there was no real need to challenge the prevailing belief about the capacity and desirability of women's military service.

Victory for America and defeat for Germany, even though they appear contrasting, also reinforced the dominant idea that women could not and should not serve in the military. In the US, the so-called band of brothers myth[89] became dominant: that men fight wars and women do not; that this band of brothers has a special bond that would be entirely disrupted by the presence of women.

The band of brothers story became so powerful because, for Americans, it wasn't a myth. It was true. American men fought overseas with very few women. In fact, only 20,000 American women served overseas during the war, and all of them were away from the front line.[90] The story of the greatest American military victory is a story of a war that was won on the battlefield by men, supported by women at home – and those women at home, even when mobilised, were in resolutely traditional roles.

The most powerful military in the world is almost always the military that all contenders want to emulate. The American military machine was the envy of the world, and it won without women doing the sorts of things that upset conventional notions of femininity. In fact, American women (having been given very few opportunities to be 'extraordinary', unlike Russian and British women) stayed in their ordinary roles. The model of military excellence that won the war and dominated the Cold War was an all-male military.

The German defeat likewise reinforced prevailing beliefs that women cannot and should not participate in war. Victory ultimately protected American women from danger as much as it denied them unconventional opportunities. Defeat left German women horribly exposed to the realities of a vicious war. The substantial impact on German women, from death to rape, led to a belief that women must be excluded from the military in order to keep them safe.

The lesson of the Second World War was the same for its greatest victor and its most abject loser: women have no place in war. If you are genuinely a military power, and you are winning, you should have no need of women at all. And if you are losing, your women will be in the gravest of danger and should be kept out of harm's way. The American military machine was not only the most successful in the world; it continued to be so for the next fifty years and arguably remains so today. The dominance of all-male American military might simply crowded out other stories of military success that included women. And of course, in both Britain and the Soviet Union, women were swiftly returned to the domestic sphere. Women's wartime contributions were minimised, even forgotten, and leaders shifted their focus to the US military machine: how to be like it; how to beat it; or both. The all-male military became the norm.

10

Post-war Transitions

IF THE FIRST World War demonstrated to the world that war was entirely the province of men, and solidified the view that women had no place on the battlefield, then it might appear that the Second World War proved the opposite. After all, millions of women had served their countries with distinction, from Soviet snipers and Night Witches to the British women of the ATS and SOE agents. And ordinarily, military history tells us that successful military innovations – such as the ability to usefully draw from a hitherto unused half of your population to build a military – generally get widely adopted, as nations seek to capitalise on the military advantages that will keep them safe in the dangerous world of international politics. And of course the Second World War transitioned into the Cold War, where large militaries remained crucially important. So we would expect that the story would be that women, having proved their mettle, would continue on in militaries around the world.

But they didn't. They didn't even do so in the Soviet Union and United Kingdom, despite their recognised successes. And neither the defeated power of Germany nor the victorious United States had significantly mobilised women in the first place. All around the world the lesson drawn was simple: women, where they had been allowed to fight, had only been allowed to do so as an aberration from the norm created by the extreme pressures of war. In the absence of those pressures the world could be put back on its axis, and women removed from the military as thoroughly as could be imagined.

A glance at official war memorials reveals how quickly women's wartime military service was neglected. All over the world memorials have one thing in common: the absence of military women.[1]

Women have been memorialised as mothers or widows, but not as members of the military. It took until 1997 for the US to create a women's memorial at Arlington National Cemetery, and a Canadian memorial the same year, and until 2005 for the British monument to women in the Second World War to be established near the Cenotaph.[2] And even the creation of these memorials has not been without controversy. In Britain, there was extensive debate about whether the women's memorial should commemorate female service members or all British women who had lived during the war; it ended up doing both. Initial designs featuring a female air raid warden shielding children atop a plinth were simplified into a plinth only, which features a variety of clothing (civilian and military) that women wore during the war.[3] In other words, it is a memorial that does not lionise women's *military* contribution to the war but rather their total social contribution. Of course, there are merits to recognising the social service of women's war efforts. But it is impossible to imagine a memorial to men's military service taking the same form.

After the war, states were faced with a challenge. The fact that women during the war had prised open the door to combat, and had been present in wartime militaries in such large numbers, meant that for the first time governments had to specifically legislate against the idea of women in combat. Ironically, the success of women in the military in general, and in combat or near-combat roles in particular, meant that militaries needed to be very clear about what women were and were not allowed to do. The answer was this: women should be allowed to do very little indeed.

All around the world, a post-war reckoning made sure that women's military roles were kept strictly traditional. Because women had come so close to fighting, and actually fought, for the first time governments had to make sure that legislation specifically banned them from fighting. In the United States, the Women's Armed Services Integration Act (1948) excluded women from combat and also tightly limited their numbers in military service. In 1948 Eisenhower argued in front of Congress that women in the military wouldn't require retirement benefits: 'I believe after an enlistment or two enlistments they will ordinarily – and thank God – they will get married'.[4] People were reassured by the view, as one congressman explained, that women would generally fill 'a so-called housekeeping nature such as your excellent secretaries in many of your offices'.[5] In 1949 further restrictions prevented mothers from enrolling and discharged mothers with children under eighteen.[6] After the war women's participation was fixed at 2 per cent of the total military and they were barred from command positions until 1967.[7] American women weren't even trained in weapons use until 1975.[8]

In Britain, women in the military were prevented from using weapons and totally excluded from combat.[9] The Women's Royal Army Corps, the successor to the ATS, placed women only in defensive roles since the 'the arming of women in any circumstances is distasteful to the British people. There are many soldiers who would find it incongruous to say the least that women officers should take part in a battle'.[10]

In West Germany, the new constitution specifically banned women from military service with weapons as a direct response to the disasters experienced by women in the latter stages of the war.[11] Debate on the new constitution in 1956 reinforced the idea, in the words of Christian Democrat Elisabeth Schwarzhaupt, that 'our conception of the nature and destination of women prohibits women to serve with arms'.[12]

In Canada after the war, women were not even allowed back into the military until 1950, and by 1965 their numbers were capped at 1.5 per cent of the armed services (1,500 women, despite the fact 5,000 women had supported the Korean War and 50,000 women had enlisted during the Second World War).[13] In Australia, until 1969 a married woman had to leave the defence force unless they had their husband's written consent and the military required their 'special talents'.[14] Women worldwide were also generally segregated into separate women's auxiliaries rather than integrated into the armed forces, restricted to traditional 'helping' roles, and with their numbers capped almost universally at 2 per cent.[15]

Women were not just physically removed from the forces they had once served in larger numbers and in more militarily significant roles. Women's wartime service was also culturally transformed and recast into a more socially palatable form. Women were erased in official memorials, but also, in cultural terms, there was a sharp shift in how women's military service was remembered. In the Soviet Union, where women were left out of official remembrances of the war, even the narrative of their wartime service shifted. The women who had fought valiantly alongside men, whose exploits had been lauded in the wartime press, were replaced in news stories and literature by a different type of woman: the tragic victim of wartime circumstance. The historian Anna Krylova has traced this phenomenon in depth, pointing out how the stories of the women who were decorated as Heroes of the Soviet Union were gradually replaced by the iconic story of Zoia Kosmodemianskaia, a young woman who joined the partisans and was executed horribly after enduring torture and humiliation. Zoia's story exemplified sacrificial girlhood, not heroic womanhood, but depictions of young women and girls joining the fight only to be martyred by the Germans began to push out the stories of women's combat heroism.[16]

Keeping women out of the armed forces except in small numbers and deliberately suppressing or ignoring their less 'feminine' military service made the combat exclusion extremely robust. The post-war military looked more and more 'normal' in Western countries, and it was supported by changes in the nature of war. The Cold War's division of the world into two armed camps led by superpowers, under the threat of mutually assured nuclear destruction, meant that major power war largely disappeared. When the US and the USSR did fight, they did so at a distance, in countries far away; or by proxy, funding ideologically sympathetic allies in wars equally far away. This type of war meant two things. First, there were no large-scale expeditionary wars that placed militaries under the sort of manpower pressure that had forced change during the Second World War. And second, it was very easy to keep the very few women in the military safely behind enemy lines when wars were rarely fought and fought far away from home. It was all too easy to forget that wars had not looked this way in the past, and would not look this way in the future – and that outside the superpower conflict there were plenty of wars that looked completely different.

Njinga Mbandi negotiating a peace settlement with the Portuguese governor in Luanda, Ndongo, in 1622. When he failed to offer her a chair, she demanded her servant make a seat for her.

Madame de Saint-Balmon's dashing trousers are clearly visible in this seventeenth-century equestrian portrait, typically a genre featuring male military leaders.

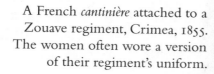

A French *cantinière* attached to a Zouave regiment, Crimea, 1855. The women often wore a version of their regiment's uniform.

Gesche Meiburg and several other women defended the Braunschweig city walls during a three-month siege in 1615.

This undated photograph believed to be Lakshmi Bai, depicts the Rani of Jhansi in her royal finery. She was killed while fleeing the British in 1858.

The French press was fascinated by the Mino regiments fighting against the French Foreign Legion in Dahomey. This image from March 1890 reflects the racialised and sexualised views of nineteenth-century European observers when confronted with women combatants.

Hannah Snell served with the marines in India. Despite being wounded several times, she only revealed her sex on her return to Britain in 1750.

The exhumed skeleton of cavalry specialist General Casimir Pulaski was found to be either female or intersex; the facial hair and male-pattern baldness suggest that intersex is more likely.

Albert Cashier was barely five feet tall. His fellow soldiers were astonished when they heard of his female identity after an accident in 1911.

Sergeant Major Flora Sandes, from Yorkshire, talks with a Serbian officer in Salonica, Greece, 1917. Sandes, the daughter of a vicar, went to Serbia as a nurse before becoming a soldier and receiving the highest decoration of the Serbian military.

Maria Bochkareva, leader of the Women's Battalion of Death, with British suffragette Emmeline Pankhurst when she visited Russia in 1917. Pankhurst greatly admired the battalion.

The young women of Bochkareva's battalion submitted to her strict rules, including shaving their heads.

A pre-war flying heroine, Marina Raskova was instrumental in efforts to recruit women for the Red Army's air forces and founded the 46th Taman'sky Guards Night Bomber Aviation Regiment.

Women were highly effective snipers in the Russian forces. Here members of the Red Army are on their way to the front, 1943.

This Nazi propaganda poster, 'You Too Can Help!', depicts the traditional approach to female mobilisation in Germany.

Violette Szabo with husband Etienne, 1940. She operated as an armed spy behind enemy lines. Captured during a gunfight with German soldiers, Violette died, aged twenty-three, in a concentration camp.

ATS officers operating a searchlight, 1944. Women were neither allowed to fire anti-aircraft guns nor to guard installations with firearms, resorting to shovel handles instead.

Dorothy Kocher Olsen of the Women's Airforce Service Pilots (WASP) wears an A-2 WASP jacket with a Fifinella logo patch designed by Walt Disney.

THERE ARE BUT TWO
SIDES IN A WAR - SHE
FIGHTS ON THE SIDE OF
AFRICAN FREEDOM
- GULF FINANCES
THE OTHER.

BOYCOTT Gulf

Pan-African Liberation Committee, P.O. Box 514, Brookline, Mass. 02147

This poster created by the
Pan-African Liberation Committee
shows a common feature of rebel
group propaganda: a woman fighter
with a gun and a baby, Angola, 1972.

Kurdish political and military organisations operate with strong rules of
gender equality, as seen in this propaganda photo of women
fighters released by the Kurdish PKK in August 2014.

Major Rhonda Cornum with Colonel Richard Williams after her release, 1991.
She was captured by Iraqi forces when her helicopter was shot down
during the Gulf War.

A marine deployed with the Female Engagement Team in Helmand province, 2011.
The pressures of counter-insurgency warfare caused the US to deploy women closer
to combat in Iraq and Afghanistan, ultimately ending the combat exclusion.

PART III

Fighting for the Future

II

Women Rebels

IN THE 1960s and early 1970s, bogged down in Vietnam, the
United States was facing the classic problem of the counter-
insurgent force. Despite superior firepower and greater economic
resources, the Americans could not make progress. As the war dragged
on, General William Westmoreland's main strategy relied on attrition:
once enough Communists were killed, the Vietnamese would have
to give up the fight. But Westmoreland's assessment of the number
of enemy troops *excluded* the number of women involved in fighting
and other essential roles[1] – there were far more fighters and a much
bigger army than Westmoreland realised.

The Vietnamese were using a supply route that skirted out into
Laos and Cambodia and which became known as the Ho Chi Minh
Trail. It provided those fighting against the Americans with thousands
of tons of supplies and thousands of men. For the Americans to
win, the trail would need to be severed. It took seven years for the
Americans to destroy a key bridge and railroad along the Trail.
Military planners were baffled. They knew how many men were in
the area, and holding out for so long should not have been possible.
They didn't know that Vietnamese men weren't the only people
keeping the trail moving – there were also huge numbers of women.[2]
As Vietnamese female fighter Nguyen Thi Hoa put it, 'one woman's
sacrifice is nothing – only like a grain of sand. But many women,
many grains, can contribute a lot, and those contributions can help
the country'.[3] Ignoring women caused the US to miscalculate the
true strength of the Vietnamese forces.[4]

The removal of women from combat in major militaries after the
Second World War was thorough and complete. But banning women
from combat in state militaries only removed them from one type of

war: major power war. And wars involving major powers were the *least* common form of war in the international system after 1945; wars where one major power directly fought another were non-existent.[5] Civil wars were the most common type of warfare post 1945 – and civil wars have seen plenty of women combatants. When the US military fought in Vietnam, it fought against a Vietnamese army that included women in combat roles. In fact, women have fought in rebel and resistance movements in Latin America, Europe, Africa and Asia. The military experience of these women has often been discounted because it occurred on a civil war battlefield, not in a war between major powers. It could be written off as another exception.

If so many women have fought in civil wars, why were governments so quick to claim that there was simply no evidence that women could make successful combatants? Sometimes this has been wilful blindness. The military historian Martin van Creveld could not even admit that women fought in civil wars: 'one only has to look at the TV pictures . . . to realise that, a few viragoes apart, in *none* of them do women fight in the open'.[6] As we will see, this claim simply cannot be supported by the facts.

Civil wars, rebellions and resistance movements have always made greater room for women. Revolutionary movements are less fussy about social rules, which they often want to overturn. One of the chief plotters in Tsar Alexander II's assassination was the aristocratic Sofia Perovskaia, the first woman to be executed for a political crime in Russia.[7] Women fought in resistance movements throughout occupied Europe. In 1943, during the Warsaw Ghetto uprising, women took up arms; the SS officer in charge of quashing the uprising wrote of the women,

> agile as acrobats, shooting with a pistol in each hand . . . dangerous in hand-to-hand contact . . . when a woman like this was caught, she appeared scared as a rabbit, thoroughly despairing, and suddenly, when a group of our men was nearby, she pulled out a grenade hidden in her skirt or pants and threw it at them with a string of curses on her lips.[8]

It's also been easy to dismiss women's fighting in civil wars because, to the military superpowers, these wars aren't always 'real' wars – there's no sophisticated military kit, and they are often fought with basic weaponry. (In other words, they entail a lot of the close combat women aren't supposed to be very good at.) Of course, sophisticated militaries have often struggled against low-tech adversaries – the wars in Vietnam and Afghanistan demonstrate the pitfalls of underestimating a supposedly less disciplined and organised opposition.

These wars were almost never fought on Western soil. When Western powers were involved, it was at a distance, as intervenors: for them, the war had an obvious front line. More often, the West was involved by proxy, paying warring groups in treasure and weapons to continue the fight against shared enemies – usually the fight against Communism, and later the fight against militant Islam. As a result, the sort of war that was entirely normal in the vast majority of the world could still be treated as an aberration by the West, a disruption from the ordinary way of things. And in turn this meant that the presence of women in many of these wars could be easily dismissed as the sort of aberrant behaviour that occurs in aberrant war.

Another reason rebel women have been ignored is the same reason many of the female fighters in this book have been ignored – they have not been taken seriously. When Nguyen Thi Dinh, the first female general of the Vietnam People's Army, was asked by an American interviewer if she resented being left out of American accounts of the conflict, she said, 'Oh, I understand. Men do not like to talk about women generals. Even Vietnamese men, and we have a history of famous women generals'.[9]

But if we closely examine women in combat in rebel movements, we can tap a rich vein of data about how and when women fight, and the circumstances that allow successful participation of women in combat. If we assume that the most common type of war since 1945 is the 'normal' frame for war, it allows us to see combat from a different angle.

Compared with their sisters in conventional militaries, women in rebel movements and insurgencies are much more common: they began to participate in combat much earlier, and they fought in much larger numbers and in a wider range of militaries. For example, some NATO members allowed women in combatant roles from the 1980s, and now NATO militaries have an average of 12 per cent female membership, with seven countries exceeding 16 per cent of women in *all* roles, not just combat. Many rebel organisations have had more than this number of women in combat roles alone, and allowed women into combat as early as the 1940s.

The vast majority of militaries that allow women in combat are in the Western world, but women fight in rebel movements worldwide. Women fought in the Israeli War of Independence (1947–9), with the Mau Mau in Kenya (1952–60), in the National Liberation Front in Algeria (1954–62) and in Vietnam in the war against the French in the 1950s and against the Americans in the 1960s and 1970s.[10] By the 1970s women were engaging more and more in political violence, and played prominent roles in left-wing terrorist groups such as the Red Brigades, the Weather Underground and the Red Army Faction.[11] Since the end of the Cold War women have fought in armed rebellions in sixty countries,[12] on every populated continent that has experienced rebellion. Around a third of all rebel movements use women in combat,[13] compared with about 10 per cent of states.[14]

Women rebel fighters have been most common in Latin America – one study indicates that *no* Latin American rebel movements excluded women completely.[15] Three Central and South American rebel movements saw women fighters compose at least 30 per cent of their overall strength: the Revolutionary Armed Forces of Colombia (FARC), Nicaragua's Sandinista National Liberation Front (FSLN or Sandinistas), and El Salvador's Farabundo Martí National Liberation Front (FMLN). The Contras, who fought against the FSLN, had between 7 and 15 per cent women.[16]

Outside Latin America, women fighters composed a quarter of the total strength of several other rebel movements: the Liberation Tigers of Tamil Eelam (LTTE) in Sri Lanka, the Communist Party of Nepal (CPN-M; Maoist), the Revolutionary United Front (RUF) in Sierra Leone and the Eritrean People's Liberation Front (EPLF).[17] The Kurdistan Workers' Party (PKK) has maintained a force with one-third female combatants since 1993.[18] In general, organisations with high numbers of women fighters are ideologically left wing.[19]

Women in rebel movements choose to fight for a variety of

reasons, most of which parallel the reasons men want to fight. A FARC *guerillera*, Claudia, loved fighting. She explained,

> I went into (my first combat) with the machine-gun detachment, because there was no discrimination, armed only with a pistol. But if I had to go empty handed, I would have gone. I'm not afraid to fight, because the smell of powder excites me. I've fought in Antioquia, in Choco, Uraba [provinces], and never been scared . . . for me, it's like going to a fiesta. I sing, skip and jump because it makes me happy, fighting.[20]

Women fighters see no conflict between womanhood and their combat role. As Tamil fighter Kalaivily put it,

> women are full of mercy and kind hearted . . . in our day-to-day normal life we are still treated like this. Also qualities such as love, affection, caring are all quite natural to us. But in the war front we never think that we are women and we are soft by nature. These disappear from our mind. In the war front we have only our aim in our mind, our aim to get an independent nation. We never think that we are killing someone. We think that we are doing our duty . . . to get an independent nation.[21]

Civil wars, unlike the major power wars of the twentieth century, generally occur on the sort of battlefield that has few discernible front lines, and often no clear distinction between the military zone and the home. This permeability between home front and battlefield has historically accounted for women fighters and also explains why rebel women have been more readily accepted into combat – they are often fighting to protect their homes, and there is no real rearguard area where they might be kept safe. Another argument is that a woman defending her home and children, even with violence, poses only a small threat to gender expectations. We expect a mother to fight to the death for her child, or, in a common depiction of rebel women, a lioness to defend her cubs.[22] Also, unlike regular militaries, insurgent groups have far less specialised roles – an individual fighter is expected to do many things, ranging from first aid to logistical support to fighting – it may be easier to accept women soldiers if combat is only part of what they do.[23]

Armed groups and rebel movements are often rule breakers: the reason they fight is to bring about social change. If you are interested in changing the world, you are more willing to abandon the old ways – and therefore the taboo against women fighting is less of an issue. Unsurprisingly, violent political organisations seeking to overthrow a government are more likely to have women combatants than groups seeking independence[24] – revolutionaries find it easier to defy convention and employ women. They do so in a context where women are often strategically useful.

Using women fighters makes sound strategic sense because the simple fact that women are less often involved in political violence means they are suspected of committing it less often. Any role that requires subterfuge, such as smuggling, assassination, suicide bombing or simply evading checkpoints and carrying messages, can very usefully be done by a woman. The Sandinistas in Nicaragua took female subterfuge to its obvious conclusion. They realised that

> maybe the only part of the woman that they [the National Guard] would not search was the vagina . . . we made the messages in the form of a tampon. Then the task was to explain to a peasant woman who had never used a sanitary napkin what a tampon was, teach her how it was introduced and how it should be taken out, and how to make this tampon safe so it would not be destroyed.[25]

Nora Astorga, who was a lawyer in Nicaragua, used her femininity to entrap a general, Perez Vega.

> The plan was for me [Nora] to get him over to my house . . . I was to disarm him without arousing his suspicion, get him in a defenseless [sic] position, then grab him and give the signal – a code word – for the comrades to spring into action . . . Things went exactly as planned. I disarmed him, then got him undressed. At just the right moment I gave the signal and the armed comrades burst in. Vega put up a good deal of resistance. He was a very strong man.

Her comrades killed Vega while she went to the car to distract his bodyguard. Nora later became a political leader of four squadrons on the war's Southern Front.[26]

Even the most conservative armed groups can be persuaded to

use women if it gains them a strategic advantage. The use of women suicide bombers (who are more likely to evade detection before deploying their explosives) is a special case, as women perform this role for rebel movements that do not allow them in combat as well as for those that do. This tendency is particularly marked in Islamist groups, which rarely deploy women (only 28 per cent do) and when they do, it is as suicide bombers.[27] Women here are simply strategic cannon fodder, less likely to be detected than men, and able to contribute to the cause through the sacrifice of their own lives. A lack of enthusiasm for allowing women to kill apparently does not extend to fears over them killing themselves.

Not every reason to deploy women is purely instrumental. Rebel movements often seek legitimacy and the recognition of the inter-national community, and women fighters reap enormous international attention.[28] For example, Kurdish female fighters were the subject of nearly 400 English-language news stories in 2010–17 alone, including profiles in *Elle*, *Marie Claire* and *Vogue* magazines.[29] The YPJ, the women's wing of the Kurdish group fighting in Syria against Islamic State, has even had a story of dubious authenticity go viral. In 2014 the so-called Angel of Kobane, a blonde woman allegedly responsible for killing a hundred ISIS fighters, was apparently killed. Although there is no evidence the Angel ever existed,[30] she raised the profile of female fighters in Kurdistan and drew the world's eyes to the conflict.

Rebel groups seeking to take over as a potential successor state need the international community to believe they are legitimate, to support the development of a new government or to gain money from diaspora communities. Women fighters make rebel groups look better under the international spotlight as they can claim that they represent the whole of society.[31] In a twist on hundreds of years of gender stereotyping, an all-male rebel group can be written off as stereotypically male, fighting for no other reason than that fighting is what men do. If women are fighting, this reasoning runs, it suggests that they must have deeply considered the question, and been inspired to abandon their traditionally peaceful position.[32]

Sometimes deploying women fighters solves a practical problem. But there is also little doubt that women fighters have been deployed because they are extremely effective. One Colombian fighter, Lucia, boasted that 'there were many women who were very stud (*berracas*), really stud when they fight with the army, more than the guys'.[33] A former Colombian colonel, when asked what the women fighters were like, said 'Ay, terrible. Bloodthirsty. Very bloodthirsty. They have an impressive composure but they are more cold-blooded than the men'.[34] According to Karina, one of the FARC's highest-ranking commanders,

> the things that men are capable of doing can also be done by women . . . if a man was sent to combat, so was a woman. If a man had to carry 50 pounds on his shoulders, so did a woman.[35]

Karina lost sight in her right eye and her hearing in a grenade attack. She managed to get treated in a hospital in Medellín without her identity being uncovered – 'I said I was a housewife and my pressure cooker had exploded in the kitchen.'[36]

Women rebels demonstrate a usual soldier's bravado about danger. One eighteen-year-old Kurdish fighter, Mahabad Kobani, was killed in an IS ambush. Before her death, she said, 'I am not worried about dying, I will jump in the way of bullets if my friends are in danger'.[37] A female Tamil Tiger, Thevaki, said, 'I was especially trained to be a sniper. One day we will all die so why be scared?'[38] In Eritrea, women fighters were initially viewed as too fragile to fight, but

> when they saw how actively we participated in the struggle, they came to realize how wrong they had been. Fighters in the front line have had to take the guns out of the hands of their dead woman comrades before burying them. They realize that women too are making Eritrean history.[39]

Nepalese politician and former revolutionary commander, Hisila Yami, has noted that women make fierce insurgent fighters *because* of their gender. They cannot return to normal life easily:

> Sons will be welcomed back with open arms, but for the daughters, can there be a return? When they become guerrillas, the women set themselves free from patriarchal bonds. How can they go back? This is why the women are more committed.[40]

Women fighters in rebel movements and armed groups demonstrate, once again, that women need not be 'exceptional' in order to fight. Perfectly ordinary women are capable of bearing arms, and they are effective enough that countless rebel movements have been keen to have them fight – even in extremely conservative cultures.

But all this does not mean that rebel groups have opened the doors to women with ease. Often, these very conservative cultures have required a shove to allow women to fight in significant numbers. Sometimes history paves the way. Women fighters in rebel movements pop up in contexts where there is a history of strong women leaders and combatants. In Vietnam, there is a history of female martial heroism. The Trung sisters led a revolt against China in 40 CE. Lady Trieu Thi Trinh, who is portrayed 'riding high on her war elephant, three foot long breasts cast aside to better handle her sword',[41] rode to war with rebels behind her in around 240 CE.[42] Vietnamese women were involved from the beginning of Vietnam's twentieth-century conflicts with international occupiers and attackers, beginning with the French in the 1940s and 1950s and carrying on throughout the war with America in the 1960s and 1970s. This participation was not a function of gender equality. Duc Hoan, who later became a famous actress, joined in the resistance to French occupation in the late 1940s. She was only ten, but fought because her father did not care about her and her sisters. As she put it, 'as the old saying goes, a hundred girls aren't worth a single testicle'.[43] Duc Hoan went on to fight as an artillery woman in the siege against French-occupied Dien Bien Phu.

Kurdish history also contains examples of woman warriors. Khanzad, a seventeenth-century Kurdish woman leader, was known as a courageous swordswoman and led an army of some 40,000 men. During the Crimean War in the mid-nineteenth century a woman tribal chief, Farma the Black, led a contingent of tribesmen to prove her loyalty to the Ottoman Empire.[44]

Rebel groups often need more than historical examples to take the plunge and recruit women: defeat clarifies the mind and enhances focus on the strategic picture. There is abundant evidence that women often enter into combat roles when there are not enough men to fight – exactly the same pressures that created opportunities for women during the Second World War. For example, the LTTE's supply of male fighters was drying up in the mid-1980s, as government crackdowns displaced populations and placed young male Tamils under arrest.[45] The LTTE first started using women in 1985, with significant expansions in the late 1980s and again in 1990: all three points correspond to a significant increase in the intensity of the conflict and therefore the need for more fighters.[46] Even in the Kurdish movement, which is characterised by an ideology of gender equality, higher levels of women's participation were driven by military needs. By 1992 the PKK in Turkey was fighting on a larger scale and therefore made more women's participation essential.[47] A study of rebel movements worldwide concludes that the longer a war persists, the more likely we are to find women combatants, as the pool of men diminishes.[48]

Just because an armed group needs more fighters, it does not mean that group will recruit women; in fact, many groups still refuse to do so, no matter the strategic pressure. It's not surprising to discover that female rebel fighters are much more likely in societies that have higher measures of gender equality – a society's peacetime treatment of women provides an indicator of how they will be used in war.[49] Desperation may be one ingredient that pushes a conservative society to allow female fighters, but a political or ideological commitment to gender equality is also important. The LTTE was not an explicitly left-wing group, but it was committed to radical social change, pursuing the end of the caste system and changes to sexist policies on dowries and marriage, as well as supporting and protecting women who had been subjected to domestic violence.[50] These policies allowed the LTTE, when it faced a significant manpower challenge, to pivot to recruiting women, a notion that would have likely been unthinkable in other similarly conservative societies.

The Kurdish PKK and its affiliated groups represent perhaps the sharpest contrast between a movement committed to gender egalitarianism and a deeply conservative local culture. Often called the largest nation without a state, the Kurdish population straddles Iran, Turkey, Iraq and Syria. Wider Kurdistan remains a highly patriarchal society where arranged marriages are common and girls have limited educational opportunities,[51] and yet women fight in all areas. The PKK operates inside Turkey and has affiliates in Syria and Iraq, and both the Turkish and Syrian branches have seen extensive combat. In Syria, the YPJ has fought against ISIS.

Kurdish women have been able to break through the gender constraints of a patriarchal society because the PKK and its affiliated movements are famously gender-equal. Abdullah Öcalan, the movement's leader, has promoted women from the very beginning. In a typical statement, he wrote that

> the female and male gender identities that we know today are constructs that were formed much later than the biological female and male. Woman has been exploited for thousands of years according to this constructed identity; never acknowledged for her labour. Man has to overcome always seeing woman as wife, sister, or lover – stereotypes forged by tradition and modernity.[52]

The PKK's explicit gender ideology goes further than that of many Western societies. It has established quotas to encourage female leadership. All leadership positions are held jointly by a man and a woman, even in mayoral positions in Turkey won by legal Kurdish parties.[53] The PKK and its affiliates have imposed laws banning polygamy, unilateral divorce and child marriage, as well as insisting on equal inheritance for sons and daughters,[54] both in Turkey and in areas controlled by Kurds in Syria.[55]

The PKK's promotion of gender equality has shifted women's experiences on the ground. One father of a Kurdish fighter explained that he had tried to prevent his daughter from going to war.

> I tried to stop Ameena by all means but I couldn't. Her decision was final. We are born in a liberated society that respects women and their decision[s]. I never imagined my daughter's decision would be to be a fighter, but I have become very proud of her. She is braver than I am and stronger than her brothers.[56]

It's not easy for an armed group in a patriarchal society to shift to recruiting female fighters. The group's leaders must make all kinds of accommodations, from the ideological to the practical, to allow women to fight. In deeply conservative Tamil society, the LTTE carefully managed women's recruitment. Female and male fighters were to be kept separate, and the movement focused on chastity and modest dress.[57] As fighter Thamilvily said,

> men and women train and live separately because the movement is very conscious of discipline. Society is not quite happy to have women join the movement, so to have men and women train together would raise eyebrows . . . Also because the LTTE is so strong on discipline they want to avoid questionable behaviour.[58]

In the Kurdish world, the first question a woman militant could expect from her mother was 'whether she slept with a man in the ranks'.[59] In fact, accepting women as fighters in many contexts has been easier than accepting them as sexually free.

Several organisations developed strict rules on relationships and sex in order to assuage concerns about sexual relationships between male and female rebels. The LTTE and the Kurdish movement used formal bans on any type of sexual relationship – within the Kurdish movement it was an infraction punishable by death until 1994.[60] The LTTE also ran sex-segregated combat units and at first prohibited marriage between fighters (eventually this policy relaxed to allow those with five years' service to marry). The movement still encouraged the chastest possible gender relations, encouraging fighters to address each other as brother and sister.[61] The PKK also relies on similar imagery, deliberately painting women as gender-neutral beings, and fighting alongside men as brothers.[62]

These chaste relations didn't necessarily derive from feminist policies on sex. In 1994 the LTTE executed three women for having sex with men who were not in the movement, prompting the comment: 'the LTTE makes women look and act like men without giving them the rights of men'.[63] While Colombia's FARC recognised female fighters as having the same rights as men in 1985,[64] it was not always a beacon of gender equality. It had a policy of executing women deemed to be *relajada* – relaxed, or promiscuous.[65] Female fighters in the FARC were allegedly banned from having babies. Karina, the senior FARC commander, explained that 'Abortions for female guerrillas are FARC policy. Even if the guerrilla does not want to abort, she is forced to do it.'[66] The FARC officially deny forced abortion, but do maintain that all women knew when they enlisted that pregnancy was forbidden, in part to protect children,[67] and claim that the accusations of sexual misconduct and forced abortion are an effort by government forces to discredit the movement.[68]

While rebel movements deploying women have overcome conservative social and political mores, it is not surprising that accepting female leaders has been harder. Worldwide, only 26.4 per cent of rebel movements have female leaders, and they are dramatically more likely in the Western hemisphere, where over 80 per cent of movements have female leaders. In sub-Saharan Africa, just over 11 per cent of movements have female leaders.[69]

In the FMLN in El Salvador, where women comprised as much as 30 per cent of the total combatants, and 40 per cent of the movement, it was still difficult for women to take on leadership roles. One woman noted,

> during the war, we, the women, were always thought of as a supporting force. Even when we assumed military command positions, it was difficult for us to get the top command. In my case, for a long time, I interpreted this as being my problem or a problem with me, and not a problem that happened to all women. I continued to feel this way when I did the work and others reaped the rewards. I saw it in my case but also in the case of other women.[70]

In Nicaragua, while men and women were treated equally in terms of military training, and expected to split traditional tasks like food preparation equally, there was also a gulf between rhetoric and reality. Gladys Báez, the first full-time female combatant in the FSLN, remembers that the men

> thought that when a woman joined, they had their meals and laundry taken care off [sic]. I said that if this was what I had to do, I would prefer to stay in my house and take care of my children's meals and laundry. I didn't join for this.[71]

However, women did become leaders in the FSLN and a woman leader was in command when the FSLN had a major victory in the liberation of the provincial capital of Léon.[72]

In the PKK, achieving a level of comfort with female military leadership took time, even though the organisation had a strong tradition of female political leadership and official policies to ensure gender equality. One PKK leader, 'Deniz', describes how he and other male guerrillas initially found the presence of women in the ranks challenging since women were either given easier tasks because of their inability to withstand hardship, or they took excessive risks to demonstrate their courage to the men.[73] Despite this bumpy reception, the senior leaders of the PKK simply insisted that men would have to get used to it; if men complained or behaved badly with their female comrades and leaders, they were punished.[74]

Focusing on why rebel groups would want to use women fighters only looks at half of the equation. A lot of academic scrutiny has gone into why women themselves want to fight – far more than the scrutiny of male rebels, whose motivations are far more rarely examined. As Professor Swati Parashar argues, 'After all we never ask why a man took up arms or his motivations for committing suicide bombing – whether he was raped, humiliated, a social pariah or was thinking about the grandeur of an afterlife. We assume he had political issues to settle.'[75] What the scrutiny has revealed, however, is that women want to fight for much the same reasons as men do – and for many of the same reasons we have seen women taking up arms in earlier historical periods. Women fighters are ordinary women with ordinary motivations for combat, and these motivations are not gender-specific.

Women, like men, are drawn to rebel movements as a way to exact revenge for the oppression and violence inflicted on their families and communities. LTTE fighter Nirmala explains the thirst for revenge well:

> The options were few. When you see so much blood and wound [sic] and family members killed, what can you do? Fighting is not a choice, it is about survival. When the army killed my cousin, I knew that I had to fight.[76]

Nirmala was not alone. From the early 1980s onwards many Tamil women were inspired to join the LTTE in response to government repression, in particular the brutal anti-Tamil riots in 1983, which displaced nearly a million people and killed between 400 and 2,000

Tamils. The Sri Lankan government did not respond,[77] and women (and men) were inspired to join a movement that promised change.

In Vietnam, women often joined the fight against the Americans to push back against the violence that they saw. One woman said, 'when my two brothers were killed by American bombs, I wanted to avenge my family. When my workplace called for volunteers, I was ready to go. I thought if men could fight, so could I.'[78] Another Vietnamese woman commented, 'life was hard. In the jungle . . . at first I was homesick and afraid. But I wanted to avenge my family, to kill Americans for what they did.'[79] A woman called Doña Felicita joined the FMLN in El Salvador for similar reasons, because 'there was so much suffering and because they had killed my two brothers in cold blood – they hanged them'.[80] Of course, the fact that *women* fight in these conflicts means that it is not only wives, sisters and mothers who fight for revenge. In Nepal, there have been reports of bereaved men seeking to join the fight after their wives were killed.[81]

Rebel movements can also be attractive for their very rebelliousness: they seek to overturn the existing order, which can be appealing for young people seeking adventure or a different kind of life. Many of the women who donned trousers and went to war prior to the nineteenth century sought a different, freer life, to escape a home that was unhappy or dangerous or both, and women rebels have similar motivations. It is not surprising that rebellious young women often became rebels. Sonia, an FSLN fighter in Nicaragua, explained, 'I think I went off with the FSLN because of rebelliousness . . . the FSLN was like the possibility of changing my life. And yes, I changed it definitively'.[82] Chasing freedom is also a goal of women joining other Latin American movements, including Colombia's FARC.[83] In Vietnam, Nguyen Thi Hoa knew that she had to figure out how to escape the oppression of patriarchal society – 'And the only way to do it was to follow the revolution. The war did change the position of women in society.'[84]

Women also join rebel movements because they afford a degree of relative safety, just as earlier battlefields did. Avoiding sexual violence was a motivator for joining the rebels in El Salvador.[85] In Colombia, one in seven of the FARC women interviewed in one study claimed they had joined because of domestic problems, including family and sexual violence.[86]

Rebel movements can also provide basic necessities that are otherwise hard to find. Thangachi, an LTTE fighter, said: 'I was a child . . . I thought that if I join LTTE I would lead a better life. We were struggling even to get food. If I join the LTTE, at least these basic needs of mine would be taking care of [sic].'[87] In El Salvador, women joined for similar reasons. One woman, identified as Doña Reyna, explained, '[W]hy should I lie to you? I joined because I was pure illness. I was only bones. I joined, and I cured myself.'[88] The women of previous centuries who found themselves safer travelling with the military as camp followers or disguised as men in order to fight would see an echo of their experiences in these reasons.

Other women join insurgent movements because they yearn for freedom, a longing that is especially powerful in an otherwise deeply patriarchal context, such as in Kurdistan. Young women joining the Kurdish movement have used fighting as a way to escape arranged marriages or domestic violence at home. Zin, the oldest of twelve children in a peasant family, was captivated when she encountered some visiting female militants in the village. Later, Zin's family moved to the city, where she was charged with looking after her siblings and making embroidery. She told her parents, '[W]hatever I do at home, I am not satisfied. I do embroidery not to get married but just to spend time.' Zin ran away to join the PKK and fought for twelve years before being killed. Her other path was an arranged marriage.[89] Another twelve-year-old joined the insurgency because in her area girls of her age got married, which she wanted to avoid; she was also not allowed to go to school. When her family tried to force her to marry she ran away and joined the PKK.[90] Joining the PKK was also a route to advancement. One of the first PKK commanders joined as an illiterate fourteen-year-old in 1990 and went on to take up a commander role in 1993.[91]

Gyanu, a Maoist fighter in Nepal, also saw joining the insurgency as a route to greater freedom: 'I didn't want to get married so soon and close all doors of opportunity in my life . . . my life would be limited to household chores and child rearing. So I escaped the trap'.[92] Nepalese teenagers also recognised that women who fought could free themselves from lives as peasants. The Nepali writer Manjushree Thapa quotes a teenage girl as explaining that she joined the Maoists because 'you see, there used to be only sickles and grass in the hands of girls like us. And now there are automatic rifles'.[93]

Sadly, not every female (or indeed every male) fighter in an armed group has chosen to be there. Forced conscription of both adults and children is a common feature in civil wars. Women and girls have been abducted and forced to fight in conflicts in Colombia, the Democratic Republic of Congo, Liberia, Mozambique, Nepal, Rwanda, Sierra Leone and Somalia.[94] Girls have been identified in the armed forces of thirty-two countries between 1990 and 2000.[95] These women are forced into fighting and providing other services in the support train, including sexual services.

Whatever the reason for a woman's decision to join a rebel movement, the presence of large numbers of women in an armed group allows us to consider all kinds of interesting questions about the wider impact of women in combat. One of the debates about incorporating women into the military is whether the presence of women on its own can create change in the institution of the military, and change in society in general. What does the significant history of women in rebel movements reveal about the impact of women fighters on gender equality? The record is mixed, especially because after the war rebel movements have often returned women firmly to the domestic sphere.

The FMLN had a strong culture of gender equality, but it still experienced problems with increasingly politically conscious women and a baked-in culture of male machismo. One fighter remarked,

> We would talk about things. There was one leader in the FMLN who would use his military status to seduce young women. And we discovered that he did this to all the women of the FMLN . . . he even put his troops at risk so that he could see one of his girl-friends who lived in the village. We decided to go to the leaders of the FMLN and to denounce him publicly and it was quite something . . . That was like setting off a bomb in the FMLN because they had had other things in mind when they set up the women's movements.[96]

Some rebel movements have built a strong sense of comradeship among male and female fighters without significant problems of sexual harassment. A common statement among women in the LTTE was 'we were treated as equals and we did not have any difference between us. We were like brothers and sisters'.[97] Nonetheless the LTTE was not immune from sexual misconduct, and investigating how organisations can build comradeship rather than exploitative sexual relations is important. There have been few studies on sexual violence within rebel groups, but an intriguing study on restraints on violence in rebel groups generally offers some clues. Amelia Hoover Green wonders why some rebel groups use sexual violence or commit widespread atrocities against civilians and some do not. She argues persuasively that rebel groups that have a high level of political education and training are considerably less likely to use unrestrained violence against civilians or have high levels of sexual violence – even though the political education is very often general and about the group's aims rather than specifically designed to induce restraint.[98]

An examination of rebel movements suggests that something similar may be at work within a movement itself. The LTTE, the Kurdish-affiliated groups and the FMLN all report high degrees of comradeship among fighters, and all notably used political education for their fighters, particularly in the Kurdish case.[99] The PKK's female combatants are called Lions, reflecting a Kurdish saying 'A lion is a lion, be it a male or a female.'[100]

Ideological commitment to gender equality, commitment to altering sexist social rules (as was the goal of the LTTE and the practice of the PKK and its affiliates) and strict rules of appropriate conduct seem to be common in the movements that resulted in a high degree of comradeship and smaller amounts of sexual problems between men and women. The gradual inclusion of women over an extended period also seems to have made a difference, because it gives the organisation time to work out how to manage the process.[101] But perhaps the most important factor of all is actually winning the war.

The record has shown, however, that a post-war return to 'normal' is compelling. Rebel women, like women in the Second World

War, have been thrust back into domesticity after the end of hostilities. In the FSLN, Dorotea Wilson, one of the three women on the National Directorate and an early member, noted a shift in equality over time:

> We shared what we had. We shared the cooking duties, the gun cleaning, the responsibilities in their cadre . . . there wasn't gender consciousness in the guerrilla forces, what there was was incredible solidarity. At any time men as much as women could be killed. Later a machista life began, which is Nicaraguan culture. They returned to what they considered a normal life.[102]

In many societies, female combatants shattered expectations about the right way for women to behave, so much so that women soldiers could become trapped, unable to leave because their combatant status marked them out as different. For Tamil women, long hair is culturally important; female fighters cut their hair short, but this made it hard to go home. A visit from a short-haired woman would put her whole family at risk, because she would so easily be identified as a fighter.[103] In Central America, life was very difficult for returning combatants. Men were treated like heroes for their military careers, but families believed their women fighters had simply abandoned them for the revolutionary struggle.[104]

Many women veterans returned to normal life, and their military background melted away. One male veteran of the war in Vietnam remarked, 'Out there in the villages so many women who served with courage put down their guns and were never heard from again.'[105] In some areas, Vietnamese women were offered lessons that would not have surprised authorities assisting the women of the Second World War.

> Classes are regularly held for the brigade members, at which they acquire a general education and learning sewing and embroidery. Brigade 609's idea of a good woman is one who worked diligently, fights courageously, shows good morals and is likely to become a good wife and mother.[106]

Not only were women expected to return to normal life, but there was often no care given to the fact that normal life was not always ready to receive them – and that they may have carried scars that made such a return impossible. In Vietnam, women militia members often found that they were unwanted. Nguyen Thi Mau got sick during the war:

> I got malaria so bad I couldn't speak or hear. I was sent back to the rear. But there was no place for me. My boyfriend had married someone else and I was too sick to find another man, and I didn't want one anyway. My family didn't want to give my dowry land back to me and so I went to live for a while in an old female collective farm with other women veterans with no place to go.[107]

Many Vietnamese women had received physical injuries during the war that prevented them from starting a family, particularly the pressure waves from high-explosive bombs;[108] others feared the impact of having children after having been exposed to chemicals like Agent Orange or having suffered from chronic malaria.[109] Other women were childless and unmarried because of a lack of available men or the deterrent factor of their own history as fighters. But Vietnamese society had reverted to peacetime traditionalism and did not know how to place childless, unmarried women or single mothers who had chosen to have babies in a culture that placed a premium on child-raising.[110]

A Nepalese fighter, Amrita, was in a bomb explosion that injured her eyes. After the war she returned to normal life, but with damaged sight. She lamented,

> What did we get? I am confused. Yesterday we were fighting in the forests with guns and bombs, and suddenly today we are back in our homes, cooking, cleaning and looking after children. We were back to where we started, but this time with a disability.[111]

In some cases, the return to the private world of the home was dramatic. A 1993 study of FMLN women in El Salvador found that even more women fighters worked in the home than they had before the war; 57 per cent of the fighters interviewed had worked primarily at home prior to the conflict, but 93 per cent of the same women did so afterwards.[112] The only silver lining in this otherwise bleak picture seems to be that once returned to domesticity, women have more power in the home. Dora Maria, a commander in the FMLN, told an interviewer in 1979 that fighting gave women 'tremendous moral authority, so that any man – even in intimate relationships – had to respect them. A man would be hard put to lift a hand to hit or mistreat a woman combatant.'[113] It's hard to know if Dora Maria was right – and it seems that the sharp shift in El Salvador back to the domestic realm exacted a high price from female fighters. It is also worth noting that the Nicaraguan and Vietnamese wars were many years ago; the social climate of the late 1970s and 1980s was different. Whether the same reversals would occur today is hard to say.

Are there any movements where female combat has led to political and social gains? Of course, whether a rebel movement wins or loses has a real impact on whether women's participation is valued. A defeated rebel movement with female fighters and a platform of equality can be defeated both militarily and ideologically. Tamil women have been pushed out of Sri Lankan politics following the conflict; only one Tamil woman was elected to parliament in 2010 elections.[114] Because the LTTE had promoted women's equality, the decision to repress women is a potent reminder to the defeated of their loss.[115]

Rebel movements that show a deep and genuine commitment to gender equality can create change. The PKK and its related organisations and their strong commitment to gender equality have resulted in significant change in Kurdish communities in both Syria and Turkey, from sharing political leadership to changing laws that discriminate against women. This strong commitment to gender equality likely provides a robust scaffolding on which to build a military with female fighters and a strong sense of comradeship rather than sexual harassment. The LTTE was similar, and it is impossible to say what the societal impact on gender would have been had the LTTE been victorious. But these commitments are rare. Only four rebel movements have openly adopted a platform of gender equality,[116] and gender justice appears equally rare as a motivation for fighting. In a study of Latin American rebel movements, only 1 of 200 women interviewed about their experiences said that gender justice was the reason they had chosen to fight.[117]

The position of women post conflict in other rebel movements makes for depressing reading. From Nicaragua, where *more* women were in the home than prior to the war, to Vietnam, where women could not find husbands, even the unarticulated promise that proving themselves on the battlefield would mean the breakdown of gender inequality has not generally been fulfilled. The Eritrean fighter Sara Ogbagergis-Dubarwa said,

> we are showing by our power that we can do the same things as men . . . we can go back into society and society will understand, 'Okay, women should not just do house work'. In this way we will be able to participate in every aspect of life.[118]

But in Eritrea, despite composing 30 per cent of the fighting force over a thirty-year civil war, women found it hard to find husbands and were rejected by their families.[119] The result of the Eritrean civil war was the victory of a repressive dictatorship that exposes women to great harm, including through a system of compulsory conscription that has become a form of gender-based violence – one report calls military service in Eritrea 'a limitless period of physical exploitation'.[120]

The history of women in rebel movements is another reminder of how closely gender norms and military service are entwined. Even when women widely participate in combat, their service is easily ignored. The world at large ignores the extensive examples of women in combat in armed groups, paying attention only when they are particularly curious, such as the spectacle of women fighting against the extreme patriarchy of ISIS; it has ignored them even when trying to establish if women were capable of fighting. Perhaps sadder still, even the countries where rebel women have fought ignore them. Their combat is forgotten, and they are returned to a domestic world for which they may no longer be suited.

What does all of this have to tell us about the prospects for women in combat in state militaries? Rebel women serve as a powerful reminder that women can participate in combat, in a variety of conflicts and a variety of ways. On one hand, rebel women can emerge from the most conservative societies. Some rebel organisations seem to be able to create a situation where men and women are comrades, and where women's social position materially changes.

On the other hand, gender norms seem to be so deep-seated that desperation is necessary to inspire rebel movements to challenge them, and once the pressure of war is over, the gender norms simply flow back. The root of the change that will really allow women into combat isn't their demonstrated capacity to fight; it's the capacity of the society for which they fight to accept them.

12

Gender Equality and the Combat Exclusion

In 1978, Brenda Berkman wanted in. She'd been barred from a job in a male-dominated world. Brenda launched a lawsuit, won, and started her job – but she and the other women for whom she had opened the door were met with vicious levels of harassment, from porn stuck to their lockers to men urinating and defecating in their boots and even death threats.[1] Berkman knew she didn't look like her colleagues, 'white, male, 6 foot six inches, handlebar mustache, blond, you know, carrying an ax, bare-chested'.[2] A few years later, as the lawsuit and its appeals wended their way through the courts, thousands of male colleagues thronged the streets in protest.[3] A bumper sticker that read 'Don't send a girl to do a man's job' became popular.[4] The tests for women's participation were tweaked so that they included physical challenges that had very little to do with the job: 'in many cases, they were just put in there because a bunch of guys sitting around a table thought, "Hm, you know, my daughter can run a mile in eight minutes, therefore we have to make the pass mark for the mile run seven minutes"'.[5] One of the officers pointed out that 'an outstanding woman can do the job, but an average man can do it better'.[6]

Brenda Berkman was a firefighter. She challenged New York City's restrictions on women in the service. What followed was years of pushback, of the sort that would sound only too familiar to women pushing their way into restricted branches of the military. But in 1978 it was finally possible for women like Brenda Berkman to enter professions that had previously been entirely closed, even if they had to fight to get there.

For women in the West, the 1960s and 1970s were a whirlwind of change: with the power of the feminist movement behind them, women began to overturn expectations not just about whether they should work but about the kinds of jobs they could have. One by one, jobs that had previously been closed – officially or unofficially – were opened to women. By the early 1970s the pace of change was rapid: women became coal miners,[7] firefighters,[8] police detectives, and by 1978 America had enrolled its first female astronauts (they were a long way behind the Soviets, who had sent cosmonaut Valentina Tereshkova on a three-day solo mission to space in 1963). Women were quickly showing that when given the chance, they could do any job they liked. But one area remained totally closed: combat.

It is hard to imagine that in a liberal democracy after the 1950s there were any professions from which women were officially banned – there were jobs where women were discouraged and jobs where there were very few women, but not many where women were not even allowed to participate. Militaries were well aware that the wave of support for gender equality was eventually going to crash into the combat exclusion, and they did not sit still. Many militaries in Western countries otherwise thoroughly committed to gender equality turned their strategic capabilities towards carefully and deliberately drawing lines around combat to prevent the incursion of women into the all-male space of the battlefield.

Keeping combat closed to women also ensured that a military's higher echelons stayed relatively all-male. If combat remained closed then the path to promotion remained closed too – most senior leadership roles required combat service, creating a 'brass ceiling' impenetrable to women. Seventy-five per cent of jobs in the US military were closed to women.[9] In the British military, promotion past one-star rank was effectively impossible without combat service.[10] Australia faced similar strictures, as 40 per cent of star-ranked officers came from armoured and infantry corps, from which women were excluded.[11] In the US, combat wasn't just important for military advancement; twenty-six presidents were military veterans, and between Franklin Delano Roosevelt and Bill Clinton every single president had served in the military. The combat exclusion had a profound impact on closing down women's advancement in society. The fact that all these other formerly closed professions managed to open – even with difficulty – while the military remained closed demonstrates the degree to which militaries actively worked to keep women out of combat. The rules were set to make sure that women stayed out; women themselves pushed against and tested the rules, only to find that the rules changed again and again.

The famous US military academies (West Point, Annapolis and the Air Force Academy) were the route to command and success in the US military. They had never enrolled women before. By the early 1970s, when arguments for equal opportunity were increasingly dominating public discourse, these institutions were under heightened pressure to admit women.[12] The military establishment was unimpressed with the suggestion that the great academies could train women. One memo on the subject read,

> my feeling is that we should come out with an 'over my dead body' approach to girls at West Point . . . The more we act like we can do it the more likely we are to be told to do it. I believe we should hang our hat on 'this society is not prepared to accept women as combat leaders yet'.[13]

The debate hinged on whether it made sense to allow women into academies designed to train elite combat officers when they could never become combat officers; the establishment argued that admission was thus pointless, whereas proponents argued that women were disadvantaged by losing access to the leadership training provided by the academies. But the argument hinged on the fact that basic equality required women's admission, and it was impossible to argue that these educational establishments could ban women entirely. The proponents won and the academies were opened to women – despite fears that this decision was, as one politician argued, 'really a foot in the door of putting women in combat'.[14]

Individual women were occasionally attempting to put their own feet in the door of combat, and once there, demonstrating that they were perfectly capable of fighting. In 1980 an intelligence officer called Kathleen (Kate) Wilder signed up for the US Army's Special Forces School – the training ground for the Special Forces known as Green Berets. Wilder was keen to get her Special Forces qualification because she thought it would help her do her job. One day, she was providing a pre-deployment intelligence briefing to the Green Berets when she was interrupted by one of the men:

> at one point, the leader of that group, a young captain, raised his hand and goes, 'Excuse me, ma'am, but you're talking about night-time going over rough terrain with 80 pounds in our rucksack – I don't think we can make it back to our exfill point in time . . . do you know what it's like to carry an 80-pound rucksack over this terrain at nighttime?'[15]

Wilder realised she didn't know. 'How would I know?' she queried – because, unlike male intelligence officers, she'd not had the experience that would allow her to know.

Wilder decided to take the Green Beret course herself, checking the rules to see if a woman could enrol. She found out there were no rules: presumably no one had considered the possibility. So she signed up. She later explained,

> At the time the combat-exclusion policy was in place barring service-women from any unit or job that was going to war. I told them in my paperwork that the policy did not apply in this case. I wasn't asking for a job in a combat unit, I was just looking for a slot in an Army school, and I didn't think anyone in a school was being shot at by an enemy.[16]

Even so, it took over a year for her to persuade the Army there was nothing preventing her from taking the course.

Wilder completed the course despite the hostility of those controlling it. She assumed she'd passed the course alongside her classmates, but then was suddenly informed by the head of the school that she hadn't. Wilder was kicked out for doing something in the course's concluding segment that many of the men had done without punishment. She said at the time, 'The Special Forces course itself was not that difficult for me . . . the difficult part was all the stumbling blocks thrown in my path by the Special Forces school'.[17] Wilder knew she had finished the course and done so on the same basis as the men: 'I was the real McCoy. I was not the Ladies Auxiliary Special Forces'.[18] She filed a sexual discrimination complaint, and the Army investigation agreed, declaring her a graduate of the Special Forces Officer course and granting her the right to wear her Green

Beret full-flash emblem. Kate Wilder had graduated, but the Army made sure it could never happen again. They changed the rules to prevent women from taking the Special Forces course again – and the next woman only graduated in 2020, after combat restrictions finally disappeared.

Kate Wilder's story encapsulates exactly what the militaries of many Western societies were up to in the 1970s and 1980s. The US Army had to contend with the reality that women were in the military in growing numbers, and keeping them out of combat was harder and harder. The solution in many militaries was simple: change the rules to ensure that women stayed out of combat.

All militaries in Western democracies, whether they liked it or not, were forced by changing social circumstances to confront the question of how to integrate women. Any reluctance they may have felt on the issue was likely swept away by the decreasing numbers of available male soldiers.[19] Militaries now had to explain, just as every other type of employer did, why women should be prevented from participating on an equal basis with men.

Some nations had little difficulty – at least on paper – adapting their militaries to the new world of gender equality in the 1970s. They just assumed that the military, like every other workplace, had to admit women in every role. The development of international legal instruments, for example the Convention for the Elimination of All Forms of Discrimination Against Women (CEDAW) of 1979, caused some states to throw open the doors of their militaries. A series of European countries opened combat roles to women begin-ning in the late 1970s. Belgium, for example, opened its military to women in general roles in 1978, because of the country's ratification of the Convention on the Political Rights of Women (1952), and as of 1981 military implementation of this treaty opened all roles including combat to women.[20] By the mid 1970s Sweden's interna-tional reputation as a leader in gender equality clashed with barring women from military roles.[21] Sweden opened combat roles to women in 1983, after a three-phase reform programme that opened most, but not all, combat roles to women, who were still unable to serve as fighter pilots, submariners and in a number of ground close-combat roles. In 1989 these roles were opened to women and the Swedish government refused a request from the armed forces to maintain these roles as all-male.[22] In 1978 Denmark passed equal opportunity legislation and conducted trials of women in the military. By 1988 it had opened all military roles to women; the Netherlands did so in 1982 (with the exception of submarines and the Marine Corps); and Norway completed the process through a parliamentary decision in 1985. Canada (1989) and Germany (2000) both opened combat roles to women after successful lawsuits that challenged military restrictions on women's service – not just in combat – on grounds of gender discrimination.

These countries have a lot in common: all are northern European with the exception of Canada; all rank very highly on indices of gender equality; and all had small militaries that at the time of these decisions were very unlikely to see combat. The Cold War was at its height, and the spectre of nuclear annihilation blotted out the prospect of a land war in Europe, especially among countries planted very firmly underneath the American nuclear umbrella. Commentators noted at the time that it was far easier to make the decision to place women in combat when warfare was a distant prospect and women soldiers were not much more at risk than women civilians.[23] In the German case, women were admitted after a legal challenge a bit later on, but the German military itself was constitutionally focused on the defence of Germany (later including NATO), placing the German decision to mobilise women in combat roles in a similar context.

If some countries opened their militaries easily, and others took a bit of legal persuasion, in many places around the world, even in Western liberal democracies, the prospect was firmly off the table. In the United States, UK, Israel and Australia there were limited prospects for women's military combat service. And there was no guarantee women seeking to change the status quo would get much support.

If a woman wanted to break into a previously closed or limited profession in the 1970s, it was a reasonable guess that she would have the growing power of the feminist movement behind her. However, the feminist movement was not much interested in challenging the combat exclusion. The feminism of the time was closely entwined with pacifism, a connection which developed further during the Vietnam War in the United States and elsewhere.[24] Some feminists were (and remain) convinced that the military is an inherently patriarchal institution which cannot be altered by simply placing women inside its ranks. As the great feminist analyst of militarism, Cynthia Enloe, puts it:

> the use of women in militaries has rarely been the product of an assertive women's movement. Being hunted down by a helicopter gunship in a dry riverbed does not usually constitute liberation from patriarchy. Nor is gaining enough public trust so that one is aiming airborne machine guns at desperate figures darting from bush to bush along the riverbed the typical goal of feminist political activism.[25]

So unlike in other areas of endeavour, where the broad feminist movement stood firmly behind women pushing down barriers, women were often left to act alone, just as Kate Wilder did. In the US, women were assisted in pushing against the military by an organisation called the Defense Advisory Committee on Women in the Services (DACOWITS), which started out in the 1950s providing fairly conventional advice on traditional questions about women in the military. By the 1970s DACOWITS was taking an increasingly robust role in pursuing the combat exclusion and putting pressure on the government and military to change,[26] but its powers were small compared with those of the wider feminist movement.

The degree to which the wider feminist movement stood aside in many societies is especially interesting, given that gender segregation in the military was deeply entwined with gender equality and debates about how to improve it. This was particularly true in the United States, where the debate about women in the military and women in combat was caught up in a much wider debate about equal rights, even if the combat exclusion itself received surprisingly little feminist attention. While pioneering lawsuits helped women gain greater equality in many fields, the law didn't seem to help with the combat exclusion. The only lawsuit that sought to change the rules on combat was, at first, only indirectly about gender, and it was brought by a man.

The unpopularity of the Vietnam War and the growing peace movement had put America's military selective service system – or the draft – under scrutiny. A group of young men brought a case against the draft, fortifying it with as many potential challenges as possible; one of these was that the draft was a form of gender discrimination. In its early stages, the case was thrown out – except for the ground of gender discrimination. The original plaintiffs gave up, but a new plaintiff, medical student Robert Goldberg, was found. Goldberg was of the view that if he could be conscripted as a military doctor then the women he studied with should also be.[27]

The lawsuit stalled with the suspension of the draft after the Vietnam War, but changing circumstances breathed new life into the case. In 1980 President Jimmy Carter proposed to re-establish conscription in the form of the Military Selective Service System. In the United States, women had never been conscripted, even for civilian war work, but Carter recommended that they be included in the re-established system. While he made it clear he did not intend to challenge the combat exemption for women, he argued that

> my decision to register women is a recognition of the reality that both men and women are working members of our society. It confirms what is already obvious . . . that women are now providing all types of skills in all professions. The military should be no exception.[28]

The debate went to Congress, which determined that only men should be registered for conscription. After all, there was no point in registering women for the draft because 'training would be needlessly burdened by women recruits who could not be used in combat'.[29]

With the draft back in play, the question of gender discrimination and Goldberg's lawsuit were back in play too. At the district court, Goldberg won. The decision was appealed to the US Supreme Court, where it was overturned. The majority on the Supreme Court felt the same as Congress: the purpose of the draft was to raise troops for combat, and women were not eligible for combat, so therefore drafting women was pointless. The majority also took the opportunity to reinforce the idea that women should not be allowed to enter combat. Justice Rehnquist, writing for the majority, even quoted from the Senate Report on the question in his judgment: 'the principle that women should not intentionally and routinely engage in combat is fundamental, and enjoys wide support among our people. It is universally supported by military leaders'. Rehnquist took the view that the appeal must be considered with 'these combat restrictions firmly in mind'. He determined that men and women are not equal in relation to their suitability for drafting. An all-male draft was not the same as an 'all-black or all-white, or an all-Catholic or all-Lutheran registration . . . Men and women, because of the combat restrictions on women, are simply not similarly situated for purposes of a draft or registration for a draft'.[30] The issue was closed, and further lawsuits to bring US women into the military on truly equal terms were deterred – in fact, no other serious attempts were made until the 2000s.[31]

Goldberg's lawsuit, and its ultimate fate, was interwoven with a far broader debate about women's rights in America. The Equal Rights Amendment (ERA), which sought to guarantee equal legal rights for all Americans regardless of sex, had been introduced in the 1920s but was dormant until the 1970s, when it was passed by both houses of Congress in 1972. The American process for constitutional change then required the amendment to be ratified by thirty-eight of the fifty states, by a deadline of 1979 (later extended to 1982).

During this period a robust conservative campaign worked to prevent the ERA's ratification. The campaign was closely associated with the activist Phyllis Schlafly, and one of its most effective tactics was to claim that the ERA would force women into combat. Schlafly noted in her eponymous report that

> This Amendment will absolutely and positively make women subject to the draft. Why any woman would support such a ridiculous and un-American proposal as this is beyond comprehension. Why any Congressman who had any regard for his wife, sister or daughter would support such a proposition is just as hard to understand. Foxholes are bad enough for men, but they certainly are not the place for women – and we should reject any proposal which would put them there in the name of 'equal rights'.[32]

Schlafly was even more scathing in her testimony before the House Armed Services Committee, arguing that the push to repeal the laws which exempt women from military combat duty must be the strangest of all aberrations indulged in by what has become known as the women's liberation . . . movement. The very idea of women serving in military combat is so unnatural, so ugly, that it almost sounds like a death wish for our species.[33]

As conservative Democrat Representative Larry McDonald argued before the House Committee on Armed Services,

the game with regards to the equal rights amendment has been to push through this amendment while there is no military draft. Should this gambit succeed, then when the draft is resumed and women must be drafted on an equal basis with men, the perpetrators of this outrage will hide behind the skirts of the Constitution.[34]

The Equal Rights Amendment was defeated, in no small part because of the successful campaign to persuade the public that the amendment would mean that women had to take on military combat roles on an equal basis with men. In fact, political scientist Jayne Mansbridge argues that the amendment would have passed if people had not been so worried about the possibility of female combat. Rather than arguing that women were perfectly capable of combat, the ERA's supporters ought to have argued that the US Constitution and legal precedent established in *Rostker v Goldberg* (1981) both indicated that the military would decide what roles women would have in the military – explicitly closing off the combat question.[35] The links between female combat and gender equality were clear to see.

In the United States, the decision of Congress that kept women out of the selective service system and the *Rostker* decision created a virtually insurmountable legal obstacle between women and any possibility of combat service, providing crucial reinforcement to the military's other strategies to keep women out of combat. The UK's experience was similar: a legal case called *Sirdar*, heard in the European Court of Justice, established that the Royal Marines could ban women on the grounds that it was an entirely combat-oriented service. As the ban on female combat was a matter of UK national security, it overrode the European Union's gender equality directives.[36] Like the *Rostker* decision, the *Sirdar* (1999) decision gave the military legal ballast in its continued efforts to keep women out of combat.

It turned out, however, that even an explicit ban on combat wasn't enough to prevent women from fighting. As more and more women flowed into Western militaries, those keen on maintaining the fences that kept combat male only had to work harder and harder, because the reality was that once women were in the military in large numbers and with fewer restrictions on their roles, they could well end up fighting — even if it wasn't intended that they should. So the fences around combat had to be built out of the sturdiest material, and this required militaries and advocates of the combat exclusion to search for the most compelling arguments to keep women out of combat, ideally for good. These fences weren't built by accident. They were deliberately created.

Militaries tried a variety of strategies to keep women out of combat. These strategies are easy to find because in several countries women sued the military on the grounds that their exclusion clearly constituted gender discrimination. The militaries had to explain why they should be granted an exception to the ordinary rules about gender discrimination. To do so, militaries had to come up with their most convincing arguments as to why women should be banned from fighting. Some worked, and some didn't, and as time went on militaries were able to determine which argument was most successful. Tracing military responses to lawsuits reveals the degree to which they carefully planned the arguments most likely to keep women out of combat.

In several cases, the military responded to lawsuits by arguing that women couldn't be allowed in all military roles for practical reasons. In Canada, four plaintiffs sued the Canadian Armed Forces (CAF) in 1986 on the grounds that restricting women's roles in the military constituted gender discrimination in a case called *Gauthier*. The military attempted to argue that women in combat roles would create difficult problems around toilets and the preservation of female privacy; the Human Rights Tribunal, which heard the case, was totally unpersuaded. After all, at the time of the tribunal decision, in 1989, co-ed living was a normal feature of Canadian life, even around toilets, which were often unisex in workplaces.[37]

In Israel in 1994 the Israeli Defense Force (IDF) was sued by Alice Miller, a civilian pilot, who was denied entry to the pilot training programme when she was called up for compulsory military service. As she put it, 'I didn't get an invitation because of my chromosomes . . . I started asking, but no one had a good explanation'.[38] The IDF response was to argue that it was simply impractical to train female pilots because it would be too expensive. Training pilots was a significant financial investment, and accordingly pilots should serve for long periods; as Israeli women had shorter compulsory service periods, had limits on reserve duty and were able to take leave for pregnancy, marriage and childbirth, the Air Force deemed it impossible (and too expensive) for women to serve in an air crew.[39] The Court didn't buy it, ruling that the decision to ban Alice Miller from aviation training denied her equality under the law, and noted that 'the argument that the training of women for jobs as pilots is not cost-effective, notwithstanding their having suitable qualifications for this, is an outrageous argument' and that the Israeli Defense Force must make a contribution to 'strengthening the recognition of the importance of basic rights'.[40]

Opponents of expanding military roles for women had long stated their concerns over placing women in physical danger, and especially worried over the prospect of a woman prisoner in the hands of the enemy. The fear of a captured woman loomed large in the imagination of those opposed to increasing women's military roles. Colonel John Ripley, a Marine war hero from Vietnam, told a presidential commission in his testimony in 1992 that

> if we see women as equals on the battlefield, you can be absolutely certain that the enemy do not see them as equals. They see them as victims. The minute a woman is captured, she is no longer a POW; she is a victim and an easy prey.

Ripley went on to provide another variation of this argument: war is hell, and we should protect women from this hell – 'This is what happens on the battlefield. This is reality. The picture of a man's privates cut off and stuffed in his mouth, or his fingers cut off so they can pull his rings off, and other unspeakable atrocities'.[41] It was acceptable for men to suffer these atrocities, but not for women.

The risk of castration does not keep men from the battlefield, but the fear of what would happen to a woman fighter on the battlefield was commonly articulated: the spectre of rape apparently loomed far larger than the fear of castration.

Militaries continued to argue that keeping women out of combat was necessary because women should be kept from physical danger. In the Alice Miller case, the Israelis argued that women soldiers required particular protection from capture and rape, a concern amplified by the tense political situation in the Middle East.[42] Miller herself did not mince words about the nature of the concern, pointing out that sexual assault was a risk for women regardless of whether they were in front-line roles: 'I don't think the public pays attention to rapes reported every single day in the newspapers. But the feeling is that if Arabs do this to our women, that's terrible. It's a protective reaction.'[43] Miller won her case, but the IDF dragged its feet on the general admission of women to combat roles, as we will shortly explore.

The German military, the Bundeswehr, also faced a lawsuit on the grounds of its almost total exclusion of women. The only exceptions were the 4,000 or so women in medical roles, and sixty female musicians.[44] The constitutional ban on women carrying arms in military service was 'designed to ensure that women are *on no account* exposed to enemy fire as combatants'.[45] The German combat exclusion came under threat when Tanja Kreil, an electrician, applied to join the Bundeswehr as a technician specialising in the maintenance of weapons electronics and was denied on the grounds of her gender. Kreil was appalled, telling a German newspaper, 'It made me feel like I was living in the Middle Ages'.[46]

The Bundeswehr responded to the lawsuit by arguing that Germany's Second World War experience justified the protection of women 'to the greatest possible extent from the dangers soldiers faced in war'.[47] The Advocate General in the *Kreil* (2000) case noted that it was simply impractical to assume that there was much distinction, in terms of risk, between supposedly 'rear' and 'forward' positions. As the German government's case rested on the protection of women, this eroding distinction made no sense.[48] The Bundeswehr lost, and the German government acted almost immediately to open up all military roles to women. The argument that women were more likely to face physical danger wasn't legally convincing.

Militaries also turned to what might seem to be the most obvious argument against placing women in combat: on average, women are weaker, slower and less robust than men. If women were physically incapable of fighting as effectively as men, this might be an insurmountable argument against deploying women in combat roles. After all, militaries would clearly want the strongest, fastest and most physically capable soldiers in the field.

Arguments that women are not strong enough to fight are surprisingly easy to dismiss. It is not discrimination to exclude people from the military on the grounds that they cannot meet its physical standards. But it is absolutely discrimination to prevent people from attempting to meet them. This was the argument the Canadian tribunal used to dismiss the CAF's arguments in the *Gauthier* case. The tribunal believed that 'qualified women' would have no impact on the military's capability.[49] Women would either meet the physical standards or they wouldn't – but they had to be given the opportunity to try.

Even the most ardent opponent of female military combat would have to accept the fact that there might be some women strong enough to pass the physical fitness tests. Besides, there are a whole range of other responses to the idea that women are not strong enough to fight, including arguments that modern war-fighting relies on technology and so physical strength is less of an issue, and that it is simply not clear that battlefield performance is linked to upper body strength and running speed. Relying on physical strength as the determining argument is and was not a surefire way to keep women from military combat – and militaries and their supporters in the fight against women in combat, increasingly, knew it.

As it happened, militaries had a better argument available – almost the perfect argument. Women could not be allowed in combat roles because fighting units relied on something called organisational cohesion, the bond created by a group of men living, fighting and dying together. Organisational or unit cohesion is simply a more technical way to express the idea that a band of brothers on the battlefield develop an almost magical *esprit de corps*.

The argument about organisational cohesion in the military is emphatically an argument about gender. Those espousing this argument believe that other factors, such as leadership, training and the crucible of combat itself, are far less important than an all-male environment in creating organisational cohesion – they must be less important, because if they mattered then women could be incorporated. Placing women into this all-male environment threatens organisational cohesion and consequently threatens national security: without organisational cohesion, militaries might fail.

It is compelling: as we will see, it was to become the centre of the arguments against placing women in combat. But it wasn't always convincing. The Canadian Armed Forces failed to convince the tribunal in the *Gauthier* case that women disrupted organisational cohesion. In 1986 the argument of the Canadian chief of defence was that 'effectiveness in battle is vitally dependent on a strong bonding between the members, which is essential to units' cohesion and morale', and that 'human stresses' are 'compounded by mix-gender groups'.[50] The tribunal agreed that operational effectiveness was obviously important, and that it relied on unit cohesion, which was more than 'sticking together' or 'being united'. It was 'an essential ingredient of the drive to reach a goal, to perform well, and to die for one another, if necessary'.[51] The tribunal concluded that it was difficult to tell how important an all-male force was for operational effectiveness since it could only be judged by 'the "final product"' or 'how the system will work in war', and Canada had not recently been at war.[52] Without recent Canadian experience, the tribunal turned to other types of combat experience in different contexts and the historical record to understand the impact women might have on operational effectiveness. They did so with a lot of imagination, examining the experience of Soviet women in combat, and the roles women played during the war in general, including as spies, saboteurs and partisan fighters.[53]

There was another useful analogy open to the tribunal: other cases of military integration where people in the past had claimed that different types of soldier couldn't possibly work together. The tribunal examined racial integration in the US military after units formerly segregated on racial lines were opened up, and Canada's own experience with combining traditionally separate French and

English units. It concluded that integration in both cases was a success, with no impact on cohesion, and that the actual experience of women combatants in the Second World War demonstrated that women fighters were 'armed, suffered loss of life and injury, inflicted death and injury on others. In short, women were indistinguishable from men in terms of performance'.[54] The tribunal decided that excluding women from combat was discrimination, and there was no exception to be made on the grounds that women couldn't fight alongside men, or that mixed gender groups would fail – because the historical record showed that they worked.

It turns out Canada's examination of the historical record was unique. In other countries keen to keep women out of combat, the argument about organisational cohesion worked especially well because it was explicitly tied to an argument about national security. If women had never fought alongside men, then introducing women into all-male units during a war would be to conduct an experiment with potentially disastrous consequences. You can't mess with organisational cohesion if it messes with national security. The argument that introducing women into combat units was dangerous experimentation relied on a failure to examine the history of women in combat. Militaries and political leaders opposed to women in combat benefitted from the fact that in the past, women's combat contributions had been diminished, denied (as in the case of women in the American Civil War) or even actively suppressed, as in the Soviet Union. All this combined to cause an extraordinarily convenient amnesia about the history of women in combat.

In 1979 General William Westmoreland (the general who failed to note the presence of Vietnamese women fighters on the Ho Chi Minh Trail) testified before the House Committee on Armed Services saying: 'we have no experience for women under those types of pressures and we are taking in my opinion an unnecessary risk in putting them in that position . . . no man of gumption wants a woman to fight his battles'.[55] He was joined by Congressman Larry McDonald, who claimed 'the notion of sexually integrated combat has never commended itself to military leaders anywhere on Earth at any time in history'.[56]

If anyone pointed out that in fact there were historical examples of women fighting, they were quickly written off as exceptions best not emulated. The 1992 presidential commission report argued that nations like the Soviet Union and Israel only used women under extreme threat, and sensibly returned them to traditional roles once that threat had passed.[57] There was no need to investigate whether such a thing could be allowed in ordinary circumstances. Women in rebel movements, including those fighting at the same time as many of these debates, appear to have been largely ignored.

If women didn't fight in the past, or did so only under the sort of circumstances that ought never to be replicated, then it was crazy to consider deploying a mixed force on the battlefield. In the words of the Senate Armed Services Committee considering the question of whether women could be drafted prior to the *Rostker* decision,

> registering women for assignment to combat or assigning women to combat positions in peacetime . . . would leave the actual performance of sexually mixed units as an experiment to be conducted in war with unknown risk − a risk that the committee finds militarily unwarranted and dangerous. Moreover, the committee feels that any attempt to assign women to combat positions could affect the national resolve at the time of mobilization, a time of great strain on all aspects of the Nation's resources.[58]

In the UK and the US, as well as in many other states that persisted in banning women from combat, the organisational cohesion argument was the ultimate trump card: disrupting the band of brothers was, allegedly, an untested innovation that would cause armies to fail while in combat. The presence of women might cause this to happen because men would react especially poorly to an injured female comrade; or because a woman might disrupt the bonding rituals of the men around her; or because her presence might form a sexual distraction. Proponents believe that a highly masculine, cohesive military culture has historically been possible because of its powerful differentiation from women. Men who come from different classes, ethnicities, regions − who are different − can bond under the umbrella of the shared characteristics of masculinity – but only when that masculinity contrasts with the femininity of women who are kept out of the club.[59]

Many of these arguments are simply inherently flawed. For example, the idea that men might be especially upset by the injury of a woman in their unit ignores the huge cultural significance placed on 'leaving no man behind'[60] – apparently only an indicator of heroism when men rescue each other. Unit cohesion arguments also shift over time, with different outliers allegedly disrupting the crucial bond. Similar arguments were raised about the unit cohesion impact of Black soldiers when the US Army desegregated, and about gay soldiers prior to the 2000s.[61]

In fact, the whole idea of unit cohesion is a pretty modern invention. Prior to the Second World War, the term was virtually unknown, and is used sparingly in the 1950s and 1960s. It wasn't something that seemed to be a major preoccupation. But after 1970 its use explodes, in part because of the impact of the Vietnam War. Failure in Vietnam was perceived to be a failure of morale, and so the military was particularly interested in unit cohesion as a way to frame improving performance – and as a useful way to distract from any errors at the strategic level.[62] Of course, one other trend began in the 1970s and dramatically challenged organisational cohesion – the integration of women.[63]

The connections between unit cohesion and women in combat are obvious. Every time women made advances into the military, the military fretted about the impact it might have on unit cohesion. It is not too cynical to point out that militaries were particularly interested in unit cohesion because it set a bar that would be next to impossible for women to clear. Once physical standards are set, women can meet them – perhaps not many women, and perhaps not easily, but they can be met. A mythical bond, on the other hand, is pretty hard to beat.

Retired US Marine Corps General Gregory Newbold explains how organisational cohesion is more important than physical standards. Conceding that some women might meet the physical standards, he asks, rhetorically: 'even if it is only the top 5 per cent of women who can replace the bottom 5 per cent of men, why not allow the 5 per cent to integrate and thereby improve the combat efficiency of the unit?' He has the answer, although admits that others must simply take it on faith:

the falsity of this debate is found in its restriction to the physical context . . . practitioners of infantry warfare have great difficulty describing the alchemy that produces an effective infantry unit, much as it is difficult for those of faith to explain their conviction to an atheist.

The magic of an all-male bond 'tempers the steel of an infantry unit and therefore serves as the basis of its combat power'. In direct combat, he argues,

you do not fight for an ideal, a just cause, America, or Mom and apple pie. You endure the inhumanity and sacrifices of direct ground combat because, 'Greater love hath no man than this, that a man lay down his life for his friends.' This selflessness is derived from bonding, and bonding from shared events and the unquestioning subordination of self for the good of the team.[64]

Unfortunately for women, this alchemical bond (as Newbold himself recognises) is impossible to measure; we just have to take his word for it. But if it can't be measured then neither can it be proved that women would disrupt the bonds of organisational cohesion. As the British military put it,

we have no way of knowing whether mixed gender teams can develop the bonds of unconditional trust, loyalty and mutual support that must be strong enough to survive the test of close combat. Nor can we tell what will be the impact on the other members of a team if a member of the opposite sex is killed or maimed. Moreover, there is no way of testing to find out, since no conceivable trial could simulate the full effects of close combat.[65]

This was despite an assessment that women's

capability in almost all areas is not in doubt, they win the highest decorations for valour, and demonstrate that they are capable of acting independently and with great initiative. But these situations are not those typical of the small tactical teams in the combat arms which are required deliberately to close with and kill the enemy.[66]

Women had to be kept out of combat lest they ruin organisational cohesion, a standard essentially designed to be impossible for women to meet.

Even in the societies working hard to keep women out of combat, the unstoppable force of gender equality was increasingly confronting the formerly immovable object of military views about combat. More and more women were joining the military, and keeping them out of combat required careful and deliberate maintenance of the combat exclusion.

In the United States, women's enlistment increased throughout the 1970s and 1980s. Women formed 1.4 per cent of the American military in 1970 and 8.4 per cent in 1980, rising to 11.1 per cent by 1991.[67] This pattern was repeated in the UK and Australia, both of which were equally opposed to women in combat. Arguments about physical strength and organisational cohesion were important reminders to political leaders and the general public about why women should be kept out of combat. But the military had to contend with how to make sure that women entering the armed forces in ever-increasing numbers didn't end up in combat by accident. The only way to do this was to build the fences keeping women out of combat with ever-greater specificity, carefully defining combat and non-combat roles, to make sure that women could do the latter but not the former. The military deliberately worked to make sure that women could not participate in combat (even by accident) by manipulating the definition of combat. Doing so created some nonsensical positions.

Jobs that are officially non-combat can still be very dangerous – just think of the poor women manning AA batteries in wartime England, armed only with a pickaxe handle to guard the perimeter of the unit and not allowed to fire the gun. They weren't fighting, but they were in danger. And then some positions that were obviously non-combatant, such as carpenters, had to be classified as combatant so that front-line units had the necessary support. As the need to define combat became more and more important in keeping the combat exclusion going, so the definition itself became more detached from reality, with some non-fighting roles classified as combatant and other roles in which fighting was quite likely classed as non-combatant. In the US Army, this meant closing specialities like interior electrician, carpenter, mason and plumber if deployed in combat zones.[68] As Major-General Jeanne Holm put it in 1982, 'If all the women were discharged tomorrow, most of the distinctions [between combat and non-combat jobs] would be abandoned the day after'.[69]

Keeping women out of combat required regular attention to exactly who in the military was allowed to do what job, and making these decisions required tweaking the definition of 'combat' so that whatever jobs a woman did didn't count as actual fighting. It's no coincidence that combat roles are the highest-status roles in the military – and that women were not allowed to do them. In fact, when women are integrated into militaries, they are usually relegated to the lowest-status jobs in the hierarchy.[70] So the definition of combat doesn't just keep women out of fighting; it makes sure that they cannot achieve the same status as men – and not just because promotional pathways are barred, but because some lesser jobs automatically get seen as jobs for women.

Lack of agreement about what did and did not constitute combat also created significant confusion on the ground. The British ensured that women would be kept out of combat by preventing them from serving overseas, which created some odd scenarios. An Australian woman officer explains:

> I was in England, on exchange, a female officer in the British Army was commanding a troop of 120 men when the Falklands Islands war was declared. Her squadron deployed and she was on the aircraft ready to go and someone came and said 'ma'am government has said no women are going'. She had led these men for two years, she knew every single one of them, she had been the one planning all the exercises, and she had been their leader. And she was removed from the aircraft and a cadet that had just graduated was put in her place. He didn't know anything about them, he hadn't even done his basic signals course, nothing, and it was just based on gender that she didn't go on operational service.[71]

In 1983, when the US invaded and then occupied Grenada, it was entirely unclear whether women were allowed to (or should be allowed to) go too. United Press International reported that 'the question of whether to allow women soldiers in Grenada was the object of a bitter dispute at the upper levels of the military hierarchy', with women military police officers initially deployed, then sent back to Fort Bragg because the commander on the ground thought that that would be breaking the rules on combat. The commander at Fort Bragg (an 'avid supporter of the women troops') disagreed and sent the women back to Grenada.[72] The women involved were not happy. Major Ann Wright, the highest-ranked woman deployed in Grenada, said that women denied service on the island 'kicked up an incredible fuss and I don't blame them . . . if you're going to train women to do a job, then dammit, let them do it'.[73] The four sent back to Fort Bragg were not the only women left unable to perform their roles. Wright also noted that 'we had instances of unit leaders being left behind simply because they were women and weren't allowed in combat, which is not only unfair but hurts a unit's morale, its *esprit de corps*'.[74]

After the kerfuffle about women in Grenada, attention circled back to definitions. To say these definitions were complex would be an understatement. The army 'uses a demand methodology based on a direct combat probability coding system that identifies those positions . . . with various probabilities of routinely engaging in direct combat'.[75] Positions also popped in and out of the combat classification. In 1982 the US Army raised the number of positions from which women were prohibited from thirty-eight to sixty-one, and a review the following year apparently disagreed, settling on the number forty-nine.[76] In short, combat was largely what the Army determined it was — and the determination had the impact of limiting women's military careers.

In 1988 the US military established a new rule which recognised another hole in the fence blocking off combat to women: even in non-combat units women could face considerable risks. So, the Department of Defense established the Risk Rule, which stated that roles could justifiably be closed to women if they occurred in a context where the risks faced were the same or greater than a combat unit in the same theatre of operation. The Risk Rule was another variation in the endless redefinition of combat that served to keep women out.

Military leaders keen to exclude women from combat had a secret weapon in their arsenal, one that perpetuated the uneasy compromise created by the presence of lots of women in the military kept from combat by apparently tidy definitions: the Cold War. From the late 1970s onwards, when Western states fought in wars, they were overseas and short. In fact, they had a second weapon: they were rich, militarily powerful Western states fighting wars of choice; they were not contending with foreign invasion or fighting a civil war against an oppressor. They fought far away, when they fought at all; and this type of war made it possible to keep women only in the positions where the military wanted them. Combat definitions were elastic enough to keep up with where and how war was being fought.

Those countries keen to keep women out of the military also had another argument that was hard to refute: all those states that had opened combat roles to women early on had done so in the shadow of the US nuclear umbrella, at the height of the Cold War. The militaries of the countries who opened combat roles to women in the 1980s were small. The prospect of a war where women would actually have to fight was slim, and the prospect of mutually assured destruction may not have prevented war, but it certainly made fighting a land war less likely than thermonuclear destruction. So the decision was basically meaningless – these women might have the right to enter combat, but the likelihood of them actually fighting was low.

The militaries that remained resolute in their opposition to keeping women out of combat, particularly in ground combat positions, most notably the UK, the US and Australia, were all large, both in raw terms and in terms of their relative size and expenditure.[77] They all had a high degree of military readiness and recent experience of combat, the US and Australia in Vietnam, the UK in the Falklands. For them, the memory of ground combat was recent, and if they opened combat roles to women, the women would certainly fight. However, the kind of combat these nations experienced during the Cold War was one that allowed for relatively easy distinctions to be made between front-line, combat positions and other military roles. The nature of war meant that women in the military could be kept safe at home, and the combat exclusion was protected by this happy circumstance.

By the late 1980s arguments about physical strength and organisational cohesion were successfully preventing meddling politicians or public activism from placing women into combat, and constant attention to the very definition of combat itself meant that the military could make sure its ever-increasing number of women didn't end up in combat by accident. All of this was underpinned by a geopolitical context in which significant Western militaries were rarely fighting, and when they did, were fighting in places where women could be left behind. It is easy to pretend that cooks are fighting soldiers and a woman driving a truck is not – when there are few wars and the women can be left safely at home. However, major expeditionary war was looming over the horizon, and all these compromises, redefinitions and rules were about to get blown away. Carefully constructed fictions have a hard time standing up to reality.

13

The Gulf War, Iraq, Afghanistan and the End of the Combat Exclusion

IN 1987 A young US navy pilot submitted an article to *Proceedings*, a US Naval Institute magazine. When considering if women could take on combat roles, the question, according to Niel Golightly, was not 'whether women can fire M-60s, dogfight MiGs, or drive tanks' but whether or not 'introducing women into combat would destroy the exclusively male intangibles of war-fighting and the feminine images of what men fight for – peace, home and family.' Golightly worried for 'the young man under fire and neck deep in the mud of a jungle foxhole, sustained in that purgatory by a vision of home . . . he is here . . . so that all the higher ideal of home embodied in mother, sister, and girlfriend do not have to be here'. He concluded: 'there is no advantage that women bring to the front line that is worth the expense and encumbrance of providing private facilities, creating "milspec" tampons, and keeping ships' stores stocked with feminine hygiene needs'.[1]

Even in 1987, in a military magazine, society had changed enough that Golightly's article did not go unchallenged. While one letter said the arguments were 'too outrageous to go unanswered', the writer acknowledged that such views were 'widespread' in the navy.[2] No one suggested that these ideas were so offensive they ought never to have been uttered, because they were pretty common – and not just in 1987. In fact, they were more polite than a lot of official testimony to Congress on the question of female combatants. As late as 2011, in response to Australia's announcement that all combat roles would be opened for women, Greg Sheridan, the *Australian* newspaper's long-term defence and strategic studies columnist, wrote that the decision was 'a kind of derangement of nature contrived by ideology against reason, common sense, military professionalism and all human experience'.[3] (Once again human experience apparently had no women fighters.)

By 2020 the world was a very different place. Golightly, now a senior executive at Boeing, was forced to resign after the discovery of his comments caused a furore. The former navy pilot wrote that he disowned his views shortly after writing them, and that the article made painful reading: 'painful because it is wrong. Painful because it is offensive to women'.[4] Once, it was entirely usual to make sweeping sexist statements about women in the context of their military service. But just short of ten years after the process began to allow American women into combat, these views were sufficiently out of step with broader society to be deemed so offensive that it was untenable for an executive of a major company to have expressed them.

The response to Niel Golightly at Boeing is a symbol of dramatic and rapid change. In 1987 women were not allowed in combat in the United States military and there was no realistic prospect that they would be. The moves to admit women into combat roles in Canada and some European countries that we examined in the last chapter were regarded as experimental decisions by militaries that had not recently experienced and were unlikely to experience major war-fighting. As the *Australian*'s Sheridan was still arguing in 2011, 'some media reports yesterday said only Canada and New Zealand operated similar policies, but it may be there are one or two other militaries that do so as well. They do so because they are not militarily serious nations'.[5]

In 1987 combat remained a distant prospect for women in the US, UK, Israel and Australia. These militaries had done everything they could to keep it that way. The legal avenues to change were tightly closed. Military professions had been designed and reclassified (and designed and reclassified again and again) to make sure that combat roles were firmly kept away from women. These militaries had no intention of allowing women into combat. They had survived the integration of increasing numbers of women and still managed to keep the fences around combat thoroughly secure.

Israel managed to maintain the fences around combat despite

successful legal challenges. Contrary to popular perception, the existence of female conscription in the IDF does not mean that Israeli women were allowed to fight. As Alice Miller, who won her gender discrimination case against the IDF, succinctly explains, 'there's this myth of the Israeli woman soldier fighting at the front and doing exactly what men do. But if you take a deeper look, you see that most women in the army serve tea to their commanders'.[6]

In fact, Israel successfully and enthusiastically resisted the whole idea of women in combat. Israeli women were mobilised to fight in the 1948 War of Independence, but firmly returned to traditional roles afterwards, mimicking the patterns of insurgent movements around the world. After the war, men and women were both conscripted, but women were conscripted for a shorter period, with a greater range of exceptions from service, and never for combat – this was not a specific legal ban but a military policy.[7] Even though Israeli women served in the military, they did not do the same work as men, and they were not treated equally.

From the beginning, Israeli authorities emphasised the difference between men's and women's soldiering. The head of the Women's Corps in 1950 reassured society that the army 'had no intention of destroying the "woman" in the woman soldier and turning her into a gloomy barracks creature'.[8] Israeli women soldiers were involved in a large range of non-military activities, including teaching, nursing, social work and supporting immigrants,[9] as part of a deliberate strategy in which women were the humanitarian face of Israel, and men the courageous and military vanguard.[10] Women conscripts served formally in the Women's Corps (the acronym for which, CHEN, means 'charm'),[11] which was fully responsible for all women until 1997.

Israel scrupulously maintained its gendered division of military roles despite the pressure of constant military readiness and frequent war. The head of the Women's Corps made it clear to the public that during the wars of the late 1960s and early 1970s women were not at the front.[12] During the 1982 war with Lebanon, Israeli women soldiers were initially required to stay in Israel and forbidden from crossing the border. When the war became protracted, some women were sent to Lebanon with their units, but were not allowed to carry ammunition or leave the base without two armed escorts (males, of course).[13]

By the late 1990s the Israeli military had both formal and informal constraints on women's service. In 1999 women served in 330 of the 551 jobs that were officially open to them, and a further 187 jobs were closed to women either because they entailed combat or there were prohibiting religious reasons.[14] There were further reports that hundreds of women had completed basic training in 1996 without firing any bullets.[15] The closest women came to combat was as instructors in tank, artillery and target-shooting units, which they did in small but growing numbers.[16]

Even while women were gaining new roles in the IDF, they still faced setbacks. In the mid-1990s the conflicted approach was in the spotlight. At the same time newspaper articles were noting a tradition of generals hiring the most attractive IDF women as secretaries,[17] women members of the Israeli parliament were pushing the IDF towards gender-neutral recruitment based on the Canadian, American and Dutch militaries. The personal opposition of then Prime Minister Yitzhak Rabin to the idea of women in combat meant that the push for greater inclusion went nowhere.[18]

Even successful legal cases could not dent the commitment to keeping women out of combat. After Miller won her lawsuit in 1997, the IDF refused to act on opening up roles for women until the Knesset instructed it to do so.[19] Alice Miller was mocked by Israeli President Ezer Weizman, a former air force commander, who remarked: 'Sweetie, did you ever see a man knit socks? . . . a woman conduct an orchestra? . . . a woman surgeon?'[20] Weizman's views should not have come as a surprise, given he was also famous for apparently originating the saying 'the best men to the air force . . . and the best women to the pilots'.[21] Miller was rejected from the air force after an army psychologist determined she suffered from 'overmotivation'; her interview with the psychologist had lasted six hours whereas for male recruits the experience took only minutes.[22] After Miller's case, the Israeli navy lost a similar case, but also dragged its feet on integrating women.[23]

In 2000 the Knesset passed a law that theoretically opened all military roles to women, including combat, but, in part because

gender restrictions in the Israeli military also have a religious component (very religious men do not have to serve with women), the
road to integration has been slow and many combat roles remain
closed to women. The pace of change relies, not surprisingly, on
very effective demarcations between combat and non-combat. Israel
remains one of the few places in the world that can draw a distinction between home defence and 'vanguard' units designed to attack
outside state boundaries, and Israel has managed to confine those
women allowed in combat into the former.[24] In 2018 the head of
the IDF insisted that he would not allow the integration of women
into the IDF's vanguard combatant units,[25] and Israeli women do
not serve in combat roles outside Israel.[26] As of 2020, 15 per cent
of combat roles remained closed to women, particularly those in
close combat with a high possibility of encountering the enemy,
such as armoured cavalry and elite infantry units. Israel's military and
political position has allowed the combat exclusion to survive.

Elsewhere, the fences around combat, which had been propped
up by the absence of expeditionary wars that might test them, were
about to be challenged for the first time thanks to deeper changes
in the international system.

The end of the Cold War gave rise to the first possibility for
major international enforcement action against an aggressor state. In
August 1990 Iraq invaded the neighbouring state of Kuwait, taking
only forty-eight hours to occupy it completely. By January 1991 an
international coalition of some thirty-five states, led by the United
States, began an assault to drive the Iraqis from Kuwait. It was the
largest American deployment since Vietnam, and the largest British
deployment since the Second World War. Of course, these deploy-
ments were not just marked as different by their size – they were
also, for the first time, drawn from militaries that had a significant
number of women.

The US military, now containing many women personnel,
deployed on a vast scale. Of the approximately 697,000 troops that
served in the war,[27] 41,000 were women,[28] including thirteen commanding officers.[29] Thirteen American servicewomen were killed
during the Gulf War, and two were taken as POWs.[30]

The complicated web of rules around which military positions constituted combat roles and which did not, caused some confusion on the ground, especially where units were left to interpret the rules on their own. One report observed that 'some people were not sure what the restriction rules were and the unit's changing, and seemingly contradictory, policies seemed to highlight that uncertainty'.[31] Confusion came from the fact that, as a report to the US Navy put it, there were differences between 'enforcing the written law regarding women in combat and using them because they were among the best persons needed to maximize the success of the mission'.[32]

Like most of the countries still banning women from combat, an obsession with women's physical safety permeated debate prior to the Persian Gulf War. All the worries came true during the battle: women were killed, captured and assaulted. The women themselves were less worried about it than might be expected. Major Marie Rossi, an army helicopter pilot, was killed in a crash the day after a ceasefire was declared. She'd been interviewed earlier in the conflict, pointing out that 'what I am doing is no greater or less than the man who is flying next to me'[33] and that 'personally, as an aviator and a soldier, this is the moment that everybody trains for – that I've trained for – so I feel ready to meet a challenge'.[34]

Military flight surgeon Rhonda Cornum was in Iraq, flying in a Black Hawk helicopter. Her job was to fly behind attack helicopters during their missions, so that in the event of an accident or engagement she could provide immediate medical care. In an evaluation report covering the period from 13 August 1990 to 27 February 1991, her commanding officer wrote:

> Outstanding performance in combat. Rhonda Cornum is the finest aviation medical officer in the Army. She is a tough, no-nonsense officer who demonstrated magnificent technical skill combined with outstanding leadership. Rhonda has had the most profound impact on the combat effectiveness of my battalion . . . People follow her anywhere . . . a true ultimate warrior. [35]

Although Cornum wasn't technically fighting, her commanding officers had little doubt that she was a warrior.

On the same day her commander wrote that evaluation, 27 February 1991, Cornum was sent on an emergency combat search and rescue mission where her helicopter came under heavy enemy fire and crashed. Cornum survived, alongside two others; she had to dig her way out of the helicopter's wreckage despite two broken arms and a gunshot wound. She was taken prisoner by Iraqi soldiers and sexually assaulted. Cornum's attitude was not what the men who worried about women's sexual safety would expect. She was unfazed by her sexual assault: 'you're supposed to look at this as a fate worse than death. Having faced both, I can tell you it's not'. She went on to say, 'Every 15 seconds in America, some woman is assaulted. Why are they worried about a woman getting assaulted once every 10 years in a war overseas? It's ridiculous . . . it's an emotional argument'. Cornum suggests that the emotional arguments about keeping women out of combat are necessary because people 'can't think of a rational one'.[36]

The Pentagon 'found it had overestimated the angst with which the public would react to women POWs and women killed in war'.[37] Assistant Secretary of Defense for Public Affairs Pete Williams pointed out that 'one of the lessons we've learned from Operation Desert Storm is the extent to which the nation accepted the significant role of women . . . until then there had always been a concern that having women involved in combat would be traumatic for the country'.[38] The basic arguments behind the combat exclusion were not surviving an encounter with reality.

The Gulf War demonstrated that once many women were in the military, and the military was fighting a large war overseas, separating roles on the basis that they were combat or non-combat made little sense. Half of the 375 American troops who were killed in the conflict were in *support* roles, not combat roles – so the combat exclusion was hardly protection from danger.[39] And sometimes the military situation on the ground simply meant that women had to be sent to the front. Maria Villescas, a Marine sergeant tractor trailer driver, was told that she would be driving her large truck into Kuwait and the heart of the fighting, despite the rules about female deployment. She knew this meant she would be taking her truck into the combat zone, and insisted that her commanding officer recognise the implications. Maria was worried that one of her truck drivers, her 'girls', might die in Kuwait only to have the military pretend she was never at the front, just to preserve the fiction that women weren't fighting.[40] If Maria's truck had come under enemy fire, and she had defended it, then surely there would have been no question that she was in combat. In fact, four Marine women received the Combat Action Ribbon, awarded for fighting with the enemy, and 71 per cent of women reported being exposed to combat at least once (in comparison to 70 per cent of men).[41] It was getting harder and harder for the military to pretend that the combat exclusion was working in practice.

As a result of women's experiences in the Persian Gulf War, the question of whether women should engage in combat came back on the table for the first time since the early 1980s. It may have been on the table, but the answer remained the same: no. In 1991 the Senate Armed Services Committee investigated whether women could become air force pilots. One senator asked Air Force General Merrill McPeak if he would allow a woman to fly in combat if she was 'of superior intelligence, great physical conditioning, in every way superior to a male counterpart vying for the same squadron position'. McPeak answered: 'No, I would not. I admit it doesn't make much sense, but that's the way I feel about it.'[42] (There was a lot about policy in regard to female pilots that didn't make much sense – women in the US Navy could train men to become the combat pilots they were not allowed to be,[43] and Danish female fighter pilots were trained in the United States.)[44]

Even if General McPeak was willing to stick to a combat exclusion for pilots that made no sense, Congress wasn't. Congress recognised the inconsistencies in the fighter pilot legislation, and voted to repeal the law banning women from combat aviation in 1991. In fact, in the Senate, the vote in favour of the repeal was far larger than had been expected, causing opponents of the bill to push for the creation of a commission to consider the broader question of women in combat roles.[45]

In 1992 the resulting Presidential Commission on the Assignment of Women in the Armed Forces considered whether women could be allowed into ground combat roles. It concluded that they could not, and that the historical evidence backed this view:

several countries have placed women in ground combat units with little success. Historically, those nations that have permitted women in close combat situations . . . have done so only because of grave threats to their national survival. After the crisis passed, each nation adopted policies which excluded the employment of women in combat . . . countries that have tested integrating women in ground combat units have found those tests unsuccessful.[46]

This dismissal of women's combat experience allowed the commission to decide that women should be excluded from combat and that this exclusion should be codified. The commission turned to that most successful of reasons for the combat exclusion: organisational cohesion, or 'effectiveness of ground units'.[47] Of course, this determination was not born of actual experience during the Persian Gulf War. Two years after its conclusion, a Government Accounting Office published a report that had an entire chapter in its analysis of the war entitled 'Gender Homogeneity was Not a Prerequisite for Unit Cohesion', where interviewees from ten different mixed-gender units that had deployed to the Gulf noted that not only was gender not really important for cohesion but that cohesion was often better in the mixed gender units.[48] Once again, the reality of women's performance in combat roles was dismissed or not investigated when making choices about whether or not to lift the combat exclusion. Women were still not allowed to fight in land warfare.

Entirely restricting women from combat was proving more difficult. Jeannie Flynn graduated at the top of her pilot training class in 1993 – an achievement usually rewarded by the first choice of the aircraft the pilot wanted to fly. Flynn, of course, couldn't choose from all available aircraft because she wasn't allowed to fly fighters. That didn't stop her. She announced her choice of the F-15E fighter plane, but was assigned to a refuelling aircraft instead. That same year President Bill Clinton allowed women to be fighter pilots and to serve on combat ships (which in turn required repealing the specific legal instruments that banned women from these roles).[49] Jeannie Flynn became the first woman pilot of the F-15E.[50] The decision to open combat aircraft to female pilots felt like a potentially far-reaching one. One senior army officer told the *Washington Post*, 'it's going to be hard to defend not doing a total repeal of the combat-exclusion law . . . you've taken the heart and soul out of the law'.[51]

But no total repeal was forthcoming. At the same time women were allowed to take to the air and fight, they were banned from more than 300,000 direct ground combat positions.[52] The policy excluded women from

> assignment to units below the brigade level whose primary mission is to engage in direct combat . . . direct ground combat is engaging an enemy on the ground with individual or crew served weapons, while being exposed to hostile fire and to a high probability of direct physical contact with the hostile force's personnel. Direct ground combat takes place well forward on the battlefield while locating and closing with the enemy to defeat them by fire, maneuver, or shock effect.[53]

The battlefield in the Gulf War had put paid to the idea that women could be protected from risk. Women themselves had demonstrated that they would not crumble under pressure of capture, and that society would not get the vapours if a woman was killed or injured. But it didn't matter. The combat exclusion stayed in place for the most conventional type of soldiering: face-to-face combat on land. Opening this door would take a long, protracted war that thoroughly erased the distinction between rearguard and front line, and in so doing made a mockery of the division between combat and non-combat roles.

The Gulf War did not have a noticeable impact on the combat exclusion in the UK and Australia. While there were more women in the British military by the 1990s, and more deployed to the Persian Gulf (1,000 women in a total force of about 35,000),[54] they were very firmly kept away from combat, specifically by preventing women's service in any forward positions, consistent with British policy. Before 1989, women serving with the British Army in Europe were not allowed anywhere near what were deemed to be forward positions; instead, they were kept to the rearmost boundary, the ports on the Channel.[55] Between 1991 and 1993, including during the Gulf War, women were also kept from serving too close to the front; in the Gulf, they were allowed no further than rear divisional headquarters.[56] As a result, the combat exclusion did not confront any serious tests. Women remained outside of combat.

In 1990 Australia opened many posts to women, including 94 per cent of roles in the Royal Australian Air Force, all ships in the Royal Australian Navy bar submarines and 19 per cent more roles in the army – but all combat, including aviation combat, was still excluded.[57] By 2000 the Act was amended to open 90 per cent of the Australian Defence Force's roles to women – except for combat, which remained banned. The British military made changes only in 1997. Recognising the need to have a military that reflected society, Secretary of Defence George Robertson opened all non-combat jobs in the military to women, an increase from 47 per cent to 70 per cent.[58] Combat remained closed, as the legal implications of the *Sirdar* decision meant that the exclusion from combat was accepted on the grounds it was 'proportionate, appropriate and necessary for the purpose of guaranteeing public security'; however, the UK was required to review the positions closed to women every eight years to decide whether continued exclusion was justified.[59]

The combat exclusion had survived its first post-Cold War test. In the US, only the margins had come under successful attack: pilot and naval roles were open to women. Interestingly, nearly every country opening combat to women begins with the air force and the navy. In 1993 the first American woman became a fighter pilot; in 1989 Britain announced plans to recruit female pilots and navigators, but the first fighter pilot did not qualify until 1994. Australia did not open fighter pilot roles to women until 1995, and did not have its first female combat pilots until 2017.[60] It is no coincidence that opening pilot roles to women came first: the physical strength and organisational cohesion arguments discussed in the last chapter were simply less applicable to pilots, where women have a generally equal physical capacity and where the band of brothers argument is harder to attach to a pilot flying alone or with a small crew.

The UK was certainly not moved to open up ground combat roles to women, even as late as 2000. General Sir Charles Guthrie was Chief of the Defence Staff from 1997 until his retirement in 2001. The focus of his final public speaking engagement was to argue against the 'perils in going slavishly down the route of political correctness for its own sake' and to say that while individual rights were important, 'there are times in the military when those rights must be subordinated for the collective good. Military life is different . . . when life becomes difficult, in the chaos and confusion of combat we need people who will work together as a team'. He went on to say that while women played an important role in the British military, in relation to combat, 'we must ensure that nothing, I repeat nothing, damages the combat effectiveness of the British Armed Forces'. He urged future chiefs of staff to protect combat effectiveness over everything else, and if this advice 'upsets those who seek equality as an end in itself then so be it'.[61]

Guthrie knew further resistance was necessary. The military had been under pressure from Defence Secretary Geoff Hoon and Employment Minister Margaret Hodge to allow women into combat since at least October 2000;[62] and it turned out the military had been keeping trials of women in combat secret throughout the last quarter of that year. The trials were revealed by the *Observer* in December 2000. They had shown women to be capable of combat, even in close environments involving tanks, bunkers and heavy fire, but the findings were considered so secret that only a tiny number of senior officers and those involved in the trials knew about them. A military source told the newspaper that 'they are so worried about it they have kept it hermetically sealed'. In its exposé the *Observer* noted that 'the army is almost unanimously against any further change', and quoted one former commander of an elite infantry unit as saying, 'there is no way that I would want anything other than a single-sex combat command' and that women in the military 'would be immensely destabilising and possibly demoralising. And my wife would go completely mad'. Those in the know about the trials trotted out the old argument that trials were experiments that didn't resemble combat; the commander said, 'it's camping with fireworks . . . it's got sod-all to do with fighting'.[63] The core principle that ground combat must be closed to women remained intact. It would take wars that were longer, bigger and deadlier to blow the combat exclusion open for good. Not one, but two such wars were about to engulf many Western militaries.

The wars in Afghanistan and Iraq constituted the largest military engagements that Western militaries had undertaken since the Second World War. At the moment the United States first took action in Afghanistan in 2001, even given that country's clichéd status as the graveyard of empires, there was little anticipation that the West would soon face casualties on a scale not seen for at least a generation. That quickly changed.

Many countries fighting in Afghanistan – including Canada – were taking their first combat casualties in an overseas war since Korea. When Canada admitted women to combat in 1989, cynics pointed out that it was an easy decision, given the remote possibility that Canadian soldiers would see combat, and that people might sing a different tune if a woman were to be killed. In 2006 Captain Nichola Goddard was killed in Afghanistan during a two-day joint Afghan–Canadian operation to secure the outskirts of Kandahar. While her death was caught up in a controversy over whether pictures of the coffins of Canadian soldiers should be transmitted,[64] the Canadian public did not respond with alarm to Goddard's gender.[65] Goddard's death, while a first, was not the shock the authorities feared it might be. In fact, it raised awareness of the contributions of Canadian servicewomen.[66]

In September 2001 it did not look like Afghanistan would become the 'Forever War', and that it would cause the US and UK militaries in particular to rewrite their playbooks on how to fight an insurgency. Politicians and military planners failed to predict a great deal about the war in Afghanistan: they didn't foresee the intensity of the fighting and the number of casualties, in part because they didn't understand the nature of the conflict and anticipate its duration. The 2003 war in Iraq was subject to many of the same misconceptions, with the Bush administration significantly underestimating the duration of the conflict and the nature of the Iraqi resistance. While Iraq and Afghanistan were distinct conflicts, both degenerated into protracted insurgent warfare.

Fighting an insurgency creates difficulties for large, wealthy and technologically advanced militaries. Committed insurgents will do almost anything to push out foreign troops, and this dynamic took hold in both Afghanistan and Iraq. The sustained counter-insurgency in both countries forced the US to adapt its counter-insurgency doctrine, emphasising that counter-insurgencies are long-term commitments and focusing on the importance of securing the support of local populations.[67] Insurgents in Iraq and Afghanistan overcame their technological disadvantage against the US and its allies through a combination of devastating patience and asymmetric tactics. The classic tactics of insurgent warfare are the quick, low-technology attack (such as an ambush), after which insurgents melt back into the local population. Rather than a battlefield with forward and rear positions, Iraq and Afghanistan were 360-degree war zones where the threat could come from any direction at any time. All these elements – the duration of the conflict, the nature of insurgent warfare, the doctrinal change to focusing on populations – combined to reveal the inconsistencies in the combat exclusion, by removing even the fiction that any member of the military could be kept safe or out of the fighting. But ultimately, the combat exclusion was destroyed by women themselves, because once they were caught in combat, even if it hadn't been intended, they showed that they were perfectly capable of being there.

The intensity of combat, particularly in Afghanistan, 'as difficult and dangerous a theatre as any in which British troops have ever fought or are ever likely to fight',[68] meant that even women in officially non-combat positions ended up having to fight. One Royal Marine noted that in his company in Afghanistan, only two people had never fired at the enemy – himself and his male radio operator. All the women had fired upon the enemy.[69] An American army major who served in Iraq noted that the women serving in military police units came under ferocious enemy fire.

> That is where I encountered female soldiers that were in the same firefights as us, facing the same horrible stuff, even if they weren't technically in combat units. They could fight just as well as I could, and some of those women were tremendous leaders. It gave me such respect.[70]

Admiral Mike Mullen told CNN,

> I know what the law says, and I know what it requires . . . in a war where there is no longer a clear delineation between the front lines . . . and the sidelines . . . where the war can grab you anywhere, this will be the first generation of veterans where large segments of women returning will have been exposed to some form of combat.[71]

Rob Garnett, a US Navy SEAL, recalled an incident in Baghdad in 2003, when he and a guard spotted a vehicle failing to stop at a checkpoint and opened fire together. 'The vehicle slowly came to a stop after the driver was killed,' he wrote,

> As the soldiers moved to inspect the vehicle, they found the trunk was full of 155 rounds made into an IED. When I walked over to the soldier who had first engaged the vehicle to say 'great job', I realized this person was not a soldier but an airman, as well as a female. I remember joking with her and saying, 'No females in combat, right?' She just smiled and said, 'Fuck off.'[72]

The pressure of insurgent attack made a mockery of carefully drawn up combat distinctions. After all, it's hard to insist that your women soldiers are not engaging in combat when they are decorated with the Silver Star for their heroic actions. In Iraq in 2005, Sergeant Leigh Ann Hester, a member of the military police, was ambushed while accompanying a truck convoy. The attacking insurgents fired on the convoy with machine guns and rocket-propelled grenades. Hester directed her team to fire at the enemy before she and her squad leader attacked a trench line with grenades and machine-gun fire. Hester cleared two further trenches and killed three insurgents, saving the lives of the many people involved in the convoy.[73]

Monica Lin Brown was also awarded the Silver Star. Brown was a combat medic attached to the 82nd Airborne Division. In April 2007 she was part of a convoy that came under attack in a complicated ambush involving improvised explosive devices and mortar strikes. Under significant fire, Brown rescued her fellow soldiers from a burning Humvee. When mortars began hailing down on Brown and the injured, she threw her body over one of the soldiers. Then the Humvee, loaded with explosive ammunition, blew up, raining down more debris. Her platoon leader was astonished Brown survived. 'There were small arms coming in from two different machine-gun positions, mortars falling . . . a burning Humvee with 16 mortar rounds in it, chunks of aluminium the size of softballs flying all around . . . it was about as hairy as it gets,' explained Lieutenant Martin Robbins.[74]

Robbins also admitted that Brown wasn't supposed to be there at all. He conceded: 'we weren't supposed to take her out' on missions, 'but we had to because there was no other medic . . . by regulations you're not supposed to [but Brown] was one of the guys, mixing it up, clearing rooms, doing everything that anybody else was doing'.[75] Despite her Silver Star, Brown was removed from her unit a few days later because of the rules against women in combat.[76] 'I didn't want to leave,' she said. Her gunner from the day of the attack was sorry to see her go: 'I've seen a lot of grown men who didn't have the courage and weren't able to handle themselves under fire like she did . . . she never missed a beat'.[77]

The pressure of fighting an insurgency didn't just mean that women ended up fighting; governments realised that there were strategic advantages to deploying women very close to the front lines. If the way to win a war against insurgents was to work with the local population, how was it possible to do so in a cultural context where foreign men interacting with women is extremely problematic? This cultural problem had strategic implications. In Iraq, insurgents knew full well that foreign troops would be careful about searching women so recruited women couriers, smugglers and suicide bombers. The solution was to employ female teams – soon dubbed the Lionesses – to search Iraqi women and homes. The first Lioness group was created by an engineering battalion commander using the women in the battalion. The women volunteered to accompany first Army and later Marine units in Ramadi in 2003–4.[78]

Because danger was everywhere in Iraq, even though they were officially non-combat, the Lionesses had to fight. Staff Sergeant Ranie Ruthig pointed out the blurring of the lines:

> We'd been downtown searching houses, and fighting would break out . . . we've had grenades thrown at us, shooting at us with AK-47's. It's a fight-or-flight thing. When someone is shooting at you, you don't say, 'Stop the war, I'm a girl.'[79]

By 2009, after eight years of warfare in Afghanistan and three years implementing a counter-insurgency strategy with a famous focus on hearts and minds, the US and its allies were still fighting and the insurgency was showing little sign of ending. A focus on hearts and minds was, at this point, a focus on *male* hearts and minds. Military planners only belatedly realised women could be a key part of the strategy – but male soldiers working with Afghan women in a deeply patriarchal society was impossible. Mobilising women could create a significant strategic advantage. As Principal Deputy Assistant Secretary of Defense for Special Operations/Low-intensity Conflict Michael Lumpkin explained, 'when 71% of the population are women and children, you have to have buy-in from a greater number of people in the villages to really connect with them, and to understand what's really going on'.[80]

Building on the success of the Lioness programme in Iraq, the US began to deploy women in Marine infantry units in Afghanistan during 2009.[81] The earliest groups were ad hoc creations of women Marines drawn from other roles such as cooks and engineers.[82] They were dubbed Female Engagement Teams (FETs). In March 2010 the programme had been formalised and forty Marines were training in Camp Pendleton for deployment.[83] The FETs would deploy women in groups of two or three, to patrol with a regular Marine unit. By 2012 the programme was operating in ten districts and eighty-five villages in Helmand province,[84] and in the Army as well as the Marines. FETs also faced a conflict where the line between combat and non-combat was blurry. A FET in Marja province had 'shot back in firefights and ambushes, been hit by homemade bombs and lived on bases hit by mortar attacks'.[85] The Australian women who participated in FET teams were not allowed to go 'outside the wire' because of the likelihood of direct confrontation with the enemy.[86]

The FETs sought to build connections with local women through educational programmes and facilitating basic medical services.[87] Even better for military purposes was the potential intelligence value. By talking to women, FET teams could gain important information about a district's social life and politics – crucial data for a complex counter-insurgency. As one instructor training the first official FET deployment explained, 'if the population has told you that their biggest problem is irrigation and your unit does something about it, that's a huge success'.[88] And it wasn't just women who opened up to the FET teams. Marine Captain Brandon Turner says Afghan men did too: 'You put a lady in front of them, they'll start blabbing at the mouth'.[89]

For all the press they generated, the impact of FETs is hotly contested. The FETs were not resourced in a way that might be expected for a unit that was supposedly strategically important. They were staffed by junior enlisted soldiers, because women of higher ranks were deemed too important in their current roles to participate in an activity that was 'not a priority'.[90] One long-time observer of Afghan society and a NATO military adviser, Sippi Azarbaijani-Moghaddam, was particularly sceptical about their successes, which she argued were dramatic overstatements of routine extensions of Afghan hospitality. She observed that the young women soldiers assigned to the teams were far too junior. The whole experiment, she declared, 'was the sociological equivalent of sending troops out with malfunctioning weaponry'.[91]

There was also a disconnect between what the FETs could most usefully accomplish – gathering intelligence – and their roles as quasi-aid-workers dispensing educational and medical support, often without appropriate training. The journalist Ann Jones recounts the story of a young Afghan wife from Nangarhar province who encountered a FET team. This gave her the confidence to leave her abusive husband, a member of the Taliban, and come to the army base to tell her story. At first, the authorities listened to her story – but then it was dismissed and the woman was jailed for several months. 'After that,' Jones noted wryly, 'it's hard to imagine any woman in Nangarhar turning up to meet American women again or offering information to the Army.'[92]

The FET teams nicely demonstrate a central claim of feminist scholarship on war. Women are usually deployed in the military, this argument runs, when there is a job that only women can do – and that these jobs are often treated as far less important than the traditional male business of war.[93] The FET teams fit this description almost exactly: they were not equal in status to the male forces they assisted, but they were doing something that men could not do.

One Marine told a journalist that female Marines could clearly build a rapport with local children by handing out stuffed animals; if a male Marine did the same, 'it's just a bunch of guys with rockets and machine guns trying to hand out a bear to a kid, and he starts to cry'.[94]

The women of the FET and Lioness teams, as well as all the other women who found themselves in combat despite not being officially allowed to do it, were treated as second-class soldiers in one particular way their predecessors in the two world wars would recognise: they were paid less. The FET and Lioness teams in particular were not given combat-related pay (because, according to one report, their tasks were not 'combat enough'), and they were not considered for promotions that required combat experience.[95]

FET teams were stymied by the combat exclusion, which caused the American military to jump through a series of hoops of its own creation in order to make them possible. Because women were prevented from undertaking non-combat roles in combat units, they had to be 'assigned' rather than 'attached' to these forward-deployed units. Women were also banned from 'co-location' with combat units, which technically would have required them to live apart from the combat units. To get around this restriction, women were even sent to rear areas overnight.[96] All the rules made Marine commanders reluctant to send women on patrols. Lieutenant Natalie Kronschnabel, a FET team leader, had to persuade a Marine captain to allow her team to go on patrol – they were not allowed to leave the base without a male escort, despite the fact that they were trained in combat in the same way as their male counterparts, and even carried the same weapons.[97]

It did not take long for these complicated manoeuvres around the combat exclusion to get noticed back in the United States. In July 2010 FETs were pulled from the sixteen outposts where they were working, and sent back to a secure base while their legal status was reviewed. Major General Richard Mills, Marine commander in Helmand, had been contacted by an unnamed congressman with concerns over what the women were up to.[98] Did they comply with the rules about women in combat?[99] Lawyers and Marine commanders had to determine whether the women complied with the non-combat rule. It was pretty clear that they were skirting around the rules, and it took about three weeks to set out a new variation that would protect the combat exclusion:[100] the FETs could not accompany units on patrols primarily focused on hunting and killing the enemy, and they could only be deployed to the combat bases on 'temporary stays'. General Mills determined that 'temporary' meant forty-five days – and the women simply travelled back to a larger military base for a one-night, rule-enforcing sojourn before returning.[101] Once again, supporters of the combat exclusion made changes that kept women out of combat, even when it created unnecessary roadblocks for a programme with strategic utility. The continued pretence that the FET teams, like the Lionesses, were not in combat when they clearly were was a way to belittle women's contributions and make them out to be different from the male soldiers around them. It meant that the military was prepared to mobilise women and place them in combat, but deny they were fighting at all.

The wars in Iraq and Afghanistan demonstrated that the combat exclusion both limited the strategic utility of the military and also ignored the reality of what women were doing on the ground. By 2013 over 284,000 American women had served in Iraq and Afghanistan; 881 were wounded and 144 killed.[102] By 2012 women had earned multiple awards for valour, including two Silver Stars, three Distinguished Flying Crosses, thirty-one Air Medals and sixteen Bronze Stars.[103] Of the 8,718 British women deployed in Iraq and Afghanistan, six were killed in Iraq while three were killed in Afghanistan.[104] Four British women from across the two conflicts were awarded the Military Cross. The Australian contingent was much smaller, and while an Australian woman was wounded by a rocket on her base in Baghdad in 2006,[105] they were still not officially allowed to fight in combat.

By the 2010s women soldiers themselves – if they ever had been – were no longer willing to pretend they weren't fighting. In the US, the first legal challenges to the combat exclusion since the *Rostker* case in the 1980s put the government under pressure to change the rules. Sergeant Major Jane P. Baldwin worked with the University of Virginia Law School to develop a class action against the United States military in an attempt to overturn the combat exclusion. The group called itself the Molly Pitcher Project, after the prototypical American Revolution heroine. It argued that the combat exclusion violated the Constitution's equal protection clause, and filed a lawsuit in May 2012. The grounds were that women's constitutional rights were infringed by exclusion from ground combat units and other positions on the basis of gender, and that the exclusion harmed their career progression. But before the suit was heard the US Secretary of Defense and the Pentagon announced that the combat exclusion was to be lifted. In January 2012 a memo was leaked to the *Washington Times* ahead of its formal announcement. General Martin Dempsey, the chairman of the Joint Chiefs of Staff, wrote that

> The time has come to rescind the direct combat exclusion rule for women and to eliminate all unnecessary gender-based barriers to service . . . the Joint Chiefs of Staff unanimously join me in proposing we move forward with the full intent to integrate women into occupational fields to the maximum extent possible.[106]

Australia's experience with women in Afghanistan played a role in shifting attitudes towards allowing women in combat. But another driver was also important: scandal. In fact, some argue that the decision to open combat roles to women in Australia in 2011 was an effort to distract from the major issues for equality created by a pervasive military culture of sexual harassment.[107] Multiple sexual scandals within the Australian Defence Force, in almost every branch as well as in the Australian Defence Force Academy (ADFA), triggered thirteen inquiries into military culture between 1995 and 2014 – demonstrating some of the more toxic elements of the band of brothers culture.

In 2011 a perfect storm of events occurred: there was a particularly shocking military scandal; Australian women were serving at great personal risk and effectively in Afghanistan; and a left-leaning Labor minister of defence, Stephen Smith, had had enough of military scandals when the so-called Skype Affair hit the news. A male cadet at ADFA had become 'friends with benefits' with a female colleague. As he put it to buddies in a text message, 'I have a f-k–in sick idea pop into my head, f— her n film it'. He did so, on Skype, while his buddies watched in another room.[108]

The scandal blew up because the woman in question went straight to the press with the story; this enabled military commanders to criticise her, and some leading figures showed an alarmingly obtuse inability to understand the problem. The Australia Defence Association's Neil James dismissed the female cadet as 'a troubled lass', as such misbehaviour was inevitable in an institution filled with young men 'as fit as Mallee bulls'.[109] Defence Minister Smith announced almost a week later that every role in the Australian military would be opened to women, and the chief of defence announced a series of inquiries into military culture.

The UK was the last major Western military power (and last NATO member) to lift the combat exclusion, in July 2016. Given that the *Observer*'s reporting on the military's secret trials on women in combat in 2000 was confidently asserting that the combat ban was 'set to be lifted after trials clouded in secrecy', and confirmed that the trials found no reason women 'should not fight alongside men',[110] how did it possibly take sixteen years for combat roles to be opened for women? The first answer is that banning women from combat was well protected by law in the UK, because the decision in the *Sirdar* case had affirmed the existence of a narrow exception from gender equality rules for combat soldiers on grounds of national security. In turn, this allowed the UK to rely on arguments that bringing women into combat would lower operational cohesiveness and potentially cause national security issues.

But the rest of the answer can only lie in intransigence on the part of the British military itself, as nowhere other than in the UK was the question of women in combat so thoroughly reviewed. Some of these reviews were required by *Sirdar*, which required the decision to exclude women to be reviewed at regular intervals. Others were called by successive Labour and Conservative governments, beginning with the successful secret trials in 2000. Further trials were conducted in 2002, and these were also successful:[111] they concluded that even though some women might meet the standards set for physical combat, the majority would not, so there was no point in allowing women to try. A third study in 2009/10 changed the goalposts entirely, abandoning the question of physical standards in favour of considering the impact of women on unit cohesion,[112] making the classic switch from an objective standard that can be meet to a subjective standard that is impossible to quantify.

The Ministry of Defence's 2009/10 study on unit cohesion determined that men in mixed-gender teams reported the same level of cohesion as in a single sex team while women reported lower cohesion; this was backed up by interview data, where men and women who had served together in Afghanistan reported high cohesion (in fact, the 'overwhelming message was that cohesion is fundamentally about trust and confidence in other team members to do their jobs, and that this builds over time').[113] The actual experiences of British troops in Afghanistan now suggested unit cohesion was not a problem. That didn't mean that the military was finally ready to accept women in combat roles. The Secretary of State for Defence determined that there was a 'lack of direct evidence, either from field exercises or from the experience of other countries', for the impact of women on unit cohesion, and so the military must make the decision. The military decided that it was too risky to admit women to 'high-intensity, close-quarter' battle where group cohesion was important and failure could have 'far-reaching and grave consequences'.[114]

Apparently men were concerned about allowing women to take the final step of being officially allowed to kill. Despite

having positive experiences of women in the roles they currently fill, a significant number of men felt that they would not want women in the Infantry; they would not feel comfortable asking a woman to close with and kill the enemy at very close range, and were concerned about the woman's and others' response to this situation should it arise. This final step is felt to be different, and a step too far.[115]

But British women were in the thick of the fighting (and killing). Chantelle Taylor, a sergeant in the Royal Army Medical Corps, was reported to be the first British woman to kill an enemy in combat, in July 2008 (Pearl Witherington and Nancy Wake and the other SOE women of the Second World War would disagree). Taylor's unit came under fire and she shot back.[116] Another combat medic, nineteen-year-old Private Michelle Norris, received the Military Cross for gallantry in combat when her company was attacked by 200 insurgents in 2006. She climbed to the top of an armoured vehicle to treat her commander, who had been shot in the face, and continued to treat him while under sniper fire and fire from heavy small arms and rocket-propelled grenades. Her citation described her actions as 'extremely courageous and outstandingly brave' – perhaps especially so because this was the first time she had ever treated a battle casualty.[117]

Women like Chantelle Taylor and Michelle Norris were clearly demonstrating that women could participate in close-quarters combat and survive it. Their contributions to their units could only have enhanced cohesion. But the British military establishment, particularly the army, remained determined to keep women out.

As late as 2014 the British military establishment still could not commit to opening combat roles to women without commissioning yet another study. Not only were the previous studies apparently not conclusive, neither were the Australian and American decisions to open combat roles to women. The 2014 review (finally) took a very different view of cohesion, arguing that 'competence, leadership and collective training' are the most important ingredients of cohesion, and that 'negative issues are likely to be fleeting and can be offset by collective experience and strong leadership'. The review concluded that 'the issue of cohesion should not be considered in future research' but called for research into the physiological demands of combat.[118] But this positive review *still* did not trigger change, and in December 2014 Secretary of State for Defence Michael Fallon explained that while the ban would eventually be lifted, another review was necessary.[119] Finally, in 2016 Prime Minister David Cameron opened combat roles to women,[120] but it took until 2018 for all military roles to open, including special forces and the Royal Marines.[121]

The US decision to open combat roles to women in 2013 gave branches of the military until January 2016 to open all roles to women, or to apply for an exemption. Again, not all branches of the military responded with alacrity to a request to allow women to fight. The US Marine Corps was the only service to request an exemption for opening combat roles to women.[122] They were denied. In 2013 the Marines, the most combat-oriented branch of the American services, still had 38 per cent of its positions closed to women.[123] Even when directed to open combat roles, it both openly and covertly resisted integrating women. For example, the Marines deliberately changed entry standards for their infantry course, which required a combat endurance test on the first day. Previously, when the course was all-male, recruits who failed the course on the first attempt were allowed to retake the test; the Marines changed the requirement so that the test had to be passed on the first day or not at all. Men were allowed to retake the Infantry Officer Course at Quantico, while women were not, until an article in the *Washington Post* exposed the discrepancy.[124] The upshot was that in 2014, of the twenty-nine women who attempted the course, only four passed on the first day — and all four were subsequently eliminated for other reasons.[125]

Despite the reticence of the Marine Corps, the pace of women's progression in the rest of the military, in infantry and even in elite units, has been remarkable, especially considering that these were the roles generally assumed to be impossible for women to perform. In 2015 the first two women, Kirsten Griest and Shaye Haver, passed the US Army Rangers course; the Army emphasised that they did not get any special treatment. Indeed, their male colleagues were impressed. Second Lieutenant Michael V. Janowski noted that Haver helped him get to graduation: 'No matter how bad she was hurting, she was always the first to volunteer to grab more weight . . . I wrote about how I would trust her with my life'.[126] Shortly after the two women graduated, the US military opened all remaining roles to women — women were still banned from entering infantry, armour and special forces occupations until 2016. Secretary of Defense Ash Carter said,

> There will be no exceptions . . . They'll be allowed to drive tanks, fire mortars and lead infantry soldiers into combat. They'll be able to serve as Army Rangers and Green Berets, Navy SEALs, Marine Corps infantry, Air Force parajumpers and everything else that was previously open only to men.[127]

After this announcement, the pace of change, particularly in the Army, increased. Griest became the first woman to lead an infantry unit in 2016.[128] In 2019 Captain Shaina Coss led a Ranger platoon into combat in Afghanistan.[129]

Women began to do better and better in training. The third woman to graduate from Ranger School was Lisa Jaster, a thirty-seven-year-old reservist and mother of two (as well as a Brazilian jiujitsu enthusiast).[130] March 2020 saw the first woman come top of the Ranger School training course, and by April 2020 fifty had graduated.[131] Women are continuing to break through into formerly closed units, even in the special forces, where they were never supposed to be able to meet the exacting physical standards designed to create elite teams of warriors. In 2020 a woman passed the Green Beret course (and unlike Kate Wilder actually got to join the Green Berets);[132] and in 2021 the first female sailor completed the US Navy's special warfare training, qualifying her as one of the crewmen who transport Navy SEALs.[133]

Women have entered combat roles in the US military; they have been placed in command of men, and have completed the most demanding military training courses in the world. The sky has not fallen in. Military performance has not collapsed. It remains true that far fewer women than men are attempting and completing infantry officer training and special forces training. But this doesn't matter, because arguably having women in these combat roles will provide multiple benefits to the military, and not just in the expected ways, the demonstrated ways in which diversity improves performance in just about every other collective endeavour we undertake. Keeping women out of combat requires reducing military capacity. The basic principle that 'every Marine is a rifleman' – that every member of the military can cope with the rigours of a war zone, and every member can fight when they need to fight – means that across the board a military ought to be more militarily capable.

Keeping women away from fighting also created an artificial focus on combat, especially on the sort of brutal combat that occurs at the very tip of the spear. Justifying a male-only combat arm required valorising all the things that men could do that women apparently couldn't. But in turn this means diminishing a range of other skills that might have military value. In a counter-insurgency, for example, empathy and intelligence might yield a better result than brute force. Some of the greatest military leaders of the past may not have been physical giants capable of hand-to-hand combat – their brains compensated for any lack of brawn. Would they have risen to the top just by being the strongest people on the battlefield? Opening up fighting to men *and* women may shift the perception that brute force is all militaries need, and open the pool of future military leaders whose intellect and strategic judgement ultimately win wars.

All this is not to say that opening combat roles to women is a silver bullet that can cure all military ills. There is little doubt that one of the main problems facing Western militaries is sex, on a scale ranging from how to handle relationships at one end to shockingly high rates of assault and harassment on the other. Integrating an organisation that has relied for its very identity on the exclusion of women for well over a hundred years at a minimum requires significant effort.

There are still very small numbers of women in the military across all roles. The state with the highest percentage of women in the armed forces is Israel, which maintains a uniquely high rate of conscription of both men and women; its forces are 40 per cent female. Australia and the United States are 17 per cent women, Canada 16 per cent.[134] Interestingly, the Chinese military is only 5 per cent female, has male-only conscription and still restricts roles by gender.[135] It will take time to raise these numbers, and they may never be large. But signalling to women, and to society, that women are capable of combat will gradually send an important social message.

There may be some who fantasise about an all-male military, and see it as the gold standard. In this fantasy the band of brothers would fight undistracted by women, and there would be no scandal. But this type of military cohesion often only exists because of hazing and bullying. Western militaries have a long tradition of scandals caused by hazing rituals that were part and parcel of the band of brothers, long before women were there as a distraction. The United States' West Point and Australia's Duntroon military academies both had major scandals attracting press interest in 1908 and 1913 respectively.[136] Even *without* women, scandals, harassment and bullying have been part of military life.

There is little doubt that bad sexual behaviour, including the most serious assaults, has been an issue in most Western militaries since women joined in large numbers. The Tailhook scandal in 1991 was a factor in opening pilot and combat ship roles to women in the

US. A 2003 study recorded that 30 per cent of American female veterans from Vietnam to the first Gulf War had been raped in the military.[137] Since 1995 there have been thirteen substantial inquiries into sexual abuse in the defence forces in Australia.[138] In Canada, a government inquiry found in 2015 that more than a quarter of women in the military reported they had been sexually assaulted during their careers, and were twice as likely as the general population to have been assaulted in the previous year.[139] Since 2019 the Canadian forces have been engulfed in scandal, as senior officers have been accused of sexual misconduct combined with cover-ups of the misconduct, often at the highest levels. As a result, eleven military leaders have 'been removed, investigated, or forced to retire in relation to the scandal',[140] including two chiefs of the Defence Staff, as well as multiple generals and admirals.

Sexual assault in the military is a serious problem. But it is not directly related to the question of women *in combat* – the presence of women in the military *at all* seems to be the problem, as sexual assault and harassment pre-date the admission of women to combat roles. Men also experience sexual assault in the military: in a 2014 study 2.1 per cent of men reported an assault since joining (in contrast to 14.69 per cent of women). However, because men outnumber women in the military, in raw numbers, this means that more men than women were assaulted (10,600 to 9,600). Men were four times more likely than women to describe the assault as 'hazing'.[141]

The sexual objectification of women is part of the band of brothers culture that allegedly creates unit cohesion.[142] In rebel groups, the political scientist Dara Kay Cohen has found, when fighters are involuntarily conscripted, the rebel group is likely to commit sexual assaults, because sexual assault is the sort of norm-breaking behaviour that acts as a terrible and effective way to build unit cohesion. It may be that sexual assault is part of the cocktail creating the unit cohesion that militaries have argued is so desirable. It is also ironic that for many years protecting women from sexual assault at the hands of the enemy was a leading argument against placing women on the front lines – even if we now know that the risk is just as likely to come from their own side.

Sexual assault and sexual harassment are considerably more

common in the military than they are in wider society.[143] Feminist scholars have long argued that, again, the band of brothers culture goes a long way towards explaining why.[144] It seems obvious that disrupting it may go some way towards improving conditions for women in the military. But it's not as simple as 'add women and stir'. New research demonstrates that removing the combat exclusion has not destroyed the 'brass ceiling' and has thus far led only to incremental change.[145]

Real change will involve a massive overhaul of military culture, and it will take a long time. And without adding women to all parts of the military, such change is probably impossible. After all, reversing the combat exclusion is undoing more than a hundred years of explicit state policy, and an even longer military tradition.

Feminist scholarship notes that wholesale institutional transformation is likely to be necessary for military culture to change. The difficulty here is that, as we have seen, much feminist scholarship is sceptical about the military as an institution per se – either because of a commitment to pacifism or a belief that it is probably impossible to create a military that does not perpetuate patriarchy. But somewhere between the extremes of a retrograde desire to keep women out and a fervent belief that the military cannot change lies the reality that change is possible; that it will require leadership commitment, and it is likely to be slow.

In 2013 Lieutenant General David Morrison was chief of the Australian Army, which was experiencing another scandal of sexual abuse and harassment of its women. He made a video that went viral, reminding all members of the Army that

> those who think that it is OK to behave in a way that demeans or exploits their colleagues have no place in this army. Our service has been engaged in continuous operations since 1999, and in its longest ever war in Afghanistan. On all operations, female soldiers and officers have proven themselves worthy of the best traditions of the Australian army. They are vital to us maintaining our capability now, and into the future. If that does not suit you . . . then get out! . . . If we are a great national institution, if we care about the legacy left to us by those who have served before us, if we care about the legacy we leave to those who in turn will protect and secure Australia, then it

is up to us to make a difference. If you're not up to it, find something else to do with your life. There is no place for you amongst this band of brothers and sisters.[146]

There may be some hope for optimism over the long term. After all, the link between masculinity and combat has taken generations to form; undoing it will not be an easy task, but when the most powerful militaries in the world begin to break the link, it provides a sharp demonstration of a changed reality. Maybe 'add women and stir' won't immediately change the military. But it may change society. After all, one of the unintended consequences of allowing women to attend elite military academies like West Point was that it demonstrated that women were capable in ways few had believed possible. Imagine the impact of seeing women's capabilities in the world's most elite military forces.

Conclusion: Buried History

THE GRAVE OF the Viking warrior woman at Birka is not the only example of the grave of a woman soldier. The graves of women buried with weapons or indeed as warriors have been found all over the Viking world, women buried with shields, axes, swords, spears and arrows, and Viking iconography and texts indicate that the 'idea of the armed woman was not at all foreign to the population'.[1]

Female warrior graves have also been found all over the Near East. The inhabitants of as many as 37 per cent of tombs on the Eurasian steppe are armed females, and there are women warriors' graves in noticeable numbers in the area between the Don River and the Caspian Sea, in the northern Black Sea and in south-western Siberia.[2] It is entirely possible that the women buried as warriors around the world played multiple roles: as priestesses or as wives or noblewomen. Just as the women of the campaign community performed many roles that could not just be reduced to whore, or even laundress or wife, so may have the women buried alongside weapons. But recognising that warrior was one of these roles extends to women of the past a recognition of the rich complexity of their lives, a courtesy that has been automatically extended to men simply by virtue of their gender.

There may be even more women buried as warriors than we know about. One of the challenges of researching Viking burial sites is the nature of the soil in northern Europe, which means that skeletons are not often preserved well enough to allow analysis for gender. Archaeologists got round this problem by simply assuming that if a grave was full of weapons and the accoutrements of a warrior's life, then the body inside was male.[3] They also assumed that a male skeleton with injuries from axes or spears must therefore have been a combatant; if a woman's skeleton had similar marks, it was assumed she was a victim of domestic violence rather than a fighter.[4] How many warriors' graves are there around the world that contain female remains but which no one has ever thought about checking? The discovery of Casimir Pulaski's gender was an accident: the body was tested to solve the mystery of the burial site, not to determine its gender. If there had been no such mystery, Pulaski's story would have continued down through the ages as that of every other Revolutionary War hero: brave, heroic and resolutely male.

If we look back at history with the belief that women were capable of fighting, and did fight, then we can find archaeological evidence that they did. Understanding that women are capable fighters may also allow us to interpret other aspects of the historical record in the same way. We can take the blinkers off, the blinkers that tell us military history is masculine and the profession of combat is exclusively male. Evidence of women's military capability is everywhere throughout history; it's a matter of knowing where and how to look, because this history has been so obscured by the monolithic belief that war is quintessentially men's business. The belief that women didn't fight anywhere, at any time, has been moderated by careful historical research into many wars in many places. Not many military historians would be bold enough to say today, as John Keegan did, that women did not fight anywhere. But there are still startling after-effects of this belief. The fact is, we simply will never know how many women warriors there were, because the way we look at history itself presumes that when we see a person on a battlefield, chances are that the person in question was male.

It is worth questioning how we came to wear the blinkers in the first place, and what it means that we have done so. Women fighters are part of the history of war. Sometimes they fought, and sometimes they helped men fight, but in either case they were exposed to danger, they were wounded and killed; they saved the men around them from being wounded and killed. But if you asked just about any person involved in military matters at the highest level in the twentieth century if this history existed, they would say you were crazy. If you provided evidence, they would tell you that women who fought were myths, like the Amazons or Joan of Arc; or exceptions, barbarian fighters from 'uncivilised' cultures that had simply not learned that women were delicate, insubstantial creatures at unique risk from violence. Or they might say that those fighting women you mentioned weren't fighting in proper wars – they were defending their towns from a siege, or were part of a rabble of rebels. They certainly weren't doing the sort of soldiering necessary in modern warfare.

Even when governments deliberately probed the question of whether women were capable of fighting, through legal proceedings or government inquiries, they rarely looked at the historical evidence, often assuming (or pretending) there wasn't any. On the odd occasion where historical examples were taken into consideration, the guiding assumption seems to have been that they occurred in contexts so different that they were simply useless for comparison purposes. A guerrilla movement or a nation facing certain military defeat might employ women to fight, but as soon as they had a choice they would stop doing so. But within those desperate nations, those movements fighting for revolution, there were plenty of examples that demonstrated that women were capable, if only anyone had looked. Looking at the past with the assumption that only men can fight, and only men have fought, means that women fighters are seen as an aberration rather than as evidence that women are capable of combat.

The history of women in combat after the Second World War should also leave us in no doubt about something else: that the combat exclusion provides us with the clearest imaginable illustration of how the patriarchy works. Militaries in the US, the UK and elsewhere deliberately made choices that kept women out of combat, choices cloaked in the guises of protection and chivalry that kept them disempowered. Make no mistake: telling women they were incapable of combat did not just disqualify them from military advancement. It told society that *all* women simply didn't have what it took: certainly not the strength, but consequently not the courage, the leadership, the fortitude – all the virtues that we associate with success in society, in politics and in just about every field of human endeavour. The women the feminist movement raised up to realise that they were capable, they were equal, they could do anything – the military sharply reminded these women that, in fact, they weren't and couldn't – they weren't good enough to fight. And not only were women not capable of fighting, they needed men to do the fighting for them.

Changing this narrative has the potential to be one of the most profound changes in gender equality we can imagine. Infiltrating the last preserve of masculine privilege can transform how women view themselves, but also how we look at battlefields and even what constitutes combat itself. The history of women warriors demonstrates that battlefields are far broader than those the conventional military tells us about: women have fought defending their homes or worked to defend a city. The definition of combat has all too often been what senior military leaders have wanted it to be – and throughout the twentieth century it has been tweaked to make sure that whatever combat is, women aren't doing it.

Militaries have not just manipulated the definition of combat to keep women out. The myth of the band of brothers, the vaunted magic of organisational cohesion, has been touted as the foundational reason why women cannot fight. The harder it was to keep women out of combat, the more militaries relied on the mystique of an all-male team. If you have to keep women out, you have to sharply differentiate the special magic of male bonding to underline why women couldn't possibly be accommodated. Artificially inflating the significance of a masculine band of brothers isn't healthy. The culture of warrior masculinity makes it difficult for men to speak openly about wartime trauma, and if a more diverse military opens this culture up then it will help with franker discussions. Encouraging a highly masculine organisational culture, sharply differentiated from a more gender-equal society, can encourage shocking behaviour on the part of military men, including sexual harassment and assault and even the commission of war crimes. The band of brothers has relied all too often on hazing to develop its essential bond. Since 2017 Australia has been rocked by revelations regarding war crimes committed by its Special Air Service Regiment, its most elite army unit, in Afghanistan. A government inquiry uncovered extensive war crimes, including 'blooding', where junior officers were encouraged to get their 'first kill' by executing prisoners, a crime that was then covered up by the unit.[5] The band of brothers has no special magic, and indeed any powers it has may be far more dangerous than they're worth.

The fact that women's combat and battlefield roles in the past were routinely dismissed, denied and even deliberately suppressed was an essential component of a strategy to keep women out. If there was no evidence that women had ever fought – or if you could persuasively dismiss any errant example that might pop up – then it became easier to sustain the argument that women could not fight in the modern military either.

Military change and social change are clearly linked. The change in military organisation that excluded women from the battlefield accompanied a social shift that emphasised women's delicate femininity and propaganda that reminded soldiers they were fighting for an idealised form of womanhood. After the Second World War the dominant view of femininity focused again on women's proper place in the home, and the military became ever more resolutely male.

Telling the history of women in combat also reveals that the history of war is far more complex than it might at first appear to be. We have long known that war is remarkably gendered, and that the culture of military masculinity has posed challenges for decades. Probing the history of women in combat reveals the specific power of gendered beliefs about war, particularly those that reinforce military masculinity in contrast to a weak and incapable femininity. Even when fighting the Second World War, the quintessential war of national survival, nations could not conceive of the ways women could assist them until they were desperate. This cuts against the view that states make military decisions according to the best strategic analysis of costs and benefits. If they did then we ought to have seen German women fight before teenage boys, and British women allowed to take a more active role without any camouflage of whether what they were doing constituted combat.

In fact, the formal exclusion of women from combat, once established first by practice around the First World War, and then by law after the Second World War, was a device that required constant maintenance. Once women were no longer on the battlefield, a process which concluded in the late nineteenth century, keeping them off it was hard work. The era of total war required states to find a balance between mobilising women to support the war effort but preventing them from fighting – even in situations where, as we have seen, this was strategically costly. After the 1970s, social changes forced the military to accept women in increasingly large numbers. If a military wanted to keep women out of combat then its leaders had to create elaborate rules.

The baroque distinctions about combat and non-combat roles were hardly militarily efficient. They existed because of the need to keep up the pretence that women were not fighting. Changes on the battlefield blew apart these rules. After Iraq and Afghanistan, where women who defended truck convoys, stormed houses of insurgents with the military police or protected their units from enemy fire were 'not in combat', it was impossible to argue that the combat exclusion could persist. And this is all to the good. In the next war, far less time will be spent worrying about how the military can best deploy its man- and woman-power – soldiers can be directed to any job that they are capable of doing. In turn, this might reduce some of the mystique around combat. Combat is just part of a soldier's job, if it can be done by men and women.

In fact, there are interesting questions to ask about which way round the relationship between military and social change actually runs. On the one hand, we have seen plenty of evidence that the social change of gender equality has gradually eroded the military stance on the position of women. But on the other, we've seen evidence that change in the military has altered people's perceptions about what women are capable of doing in society at large. Admitting women into the US military academies in the 1970s created a generation of women leaders not just in the military but, after they left the military, in wider society too. As more women like Captain Shaina Coss, the first woman to command an Army Ranger battalion in combat, appear on the scene, it will be a visual demonstration that women are capable of the most apparently masculine of tasks – and that may be good for gender equality in society. Imagine how different the course on military history might have been if the military exploits of Njinga were taken as evidence of what all women were capable of doing, if given the chance; or if the ways in which women led during sieges were taken as examples of how women can plan, strategise and lead.

All this is not to ignore the many problems faced by women in the military. There is an appalling culture in many Western militaries of sexual harassment and assault. Many militaries with the longest records of allowing women into combat struggle to recruit women into these roles. And of course there is the question of whether the horrors of war are good for anyone, male or female – that expanding the warrior culture to include women, for pacifists, is not a 'win' at all. Examining the history of women in combat goes some way to illuminating these problems.

The history of women in combat is, at the most important level, a history of *capability*. Conventional military history assumes that women were incapable of fighting, because they were not on the battlefield in large numbers. My goal has been to prove that there were women on the battlefield in larger numbers than is often assumed, but more importantly, to point out that the numbers of women on the battlefield do not say anything specific about the capability of those women. For so long, women have been told that they cannot fight, that they lack the requisite skills, and that this is the one area where they simply cannot compete with men. And yes, it's true that only a small number of women will qualify to fight as part of modern volunteer armies with stringent physical tests. But the history of women in combat shows that even though women may not have the same physical strength as men, they have equal courage, equal ability to endure discomfort, equal ability to make a difference fighting for ideals or grasping for survival, and even, when given the chance, equal ability to lead.

Combat remains an unfortunate constant in our modern world, as Russia's invasion of Ukraine in 2022 showed. There is nothing about women that makes them intrinsically unable to manage the toll of the battlefield, a fact that is borne out by the women who fought prior to the twentieth century, as well as by their sisters in the campaign community, who bore all the discomfort and danger even if they did not actually fight.

We are at the crest of a major change, where generations will move through the military with no ceiling on their progression and no rules telling them what they cannot do. The consequences of this change are already visible in places like Ukraine. The first Russian invasion in 2014 caused Ukraine to reassess its use of women in the military, because the reality of a war made the distinctions between combat and non-combat roles useless, and in 2018 all positions were opened to women.[6] By 2021 there were 57,000 women in the Ukrainian military, about 22.8 per cent of the force (vastly exceeding most other countries).[7] Ukrainian women were ready to fight when the war came, and there has not been much fuss about it. They have taken on all roles, including leadership positions. They are fighting an enemy that has resolutely kept women out of their military, despite significant recruitment issues (and a long, if now ignored, history of female combat). Ukraine is far from a perfect place for gender equality in wider society. But as it becomes normal for women to fight, and as they become heroes of the war, so things may change.

The conflict between Ukraine and Russia also underlines the argument that authoritarian governments, while diverse in their geography, ethnic make-up and even the reasons for the success of authoritarian leaders, have one thing in common: they suppress women's rights.[8] The authoritarian regime of Vladimir Putin follows this playbook. Putin is of course famous for pursuing hyper-masculine politics, basing his authority and strength on his masculinity.[9] He has begun to push more traditional views about gender, including financially rewarding women for having more than one child. In 2021 he explained, 'I uphold the traditional approach that a woman is a woman, a man is a man, a mother is a mother, and a father is a father'.[10] Domestic violence was decriminalised in Russia in 2017, and now is only punishable as a crime when the abuse is so severe it requires hospitalisation.[11] Russian women are still barred from a list of 100 professions.[12] Unsurprisingly, the Russian military facing off against Ukraine has no women combatants in it – even when Putin had to forcibly conscript men to fight in 2022, he did not mobilise women. The list of states that admit women into combat roles remains almost exclusively a list of democracies with high levels of gender equality.[13] Allowing women in combat roles is a key measure of gender equality.

This book has demonstrated that the combat exclusion was a deliberate strategy requiring careful maintenance; in Western democracies, the strategy was preserved for decades *despite* a powerful feminist movement pushing for equality in every other sphere. Understanding what the military and its supporters did to keep women out will prevent the same thing from occurring again. If the suppression of gender rights is a hallmark of a shift towards authoritarianism, understanding a bit more about how women recently gained this right is essential to prevent it from disappearing. Allowing women into combat, to fight and to lead, will provide powerful reinforcement to the idea that women and men are truly equal.

While authoritarian regimes look to the past, and persist in treating women as second-class citizens, it appears that when we imagine the future we have little difficulty seeing gender equality. Our imaginings of militaries of the future include women soldiering alongside men in unexceptional ways. In movies from *Star Wars* to *The Edge of Tomorrow* to *Dune* and *Alien*, women are fierce fighters who are equal to their male counterparts; the same goes with TV series like *Battlestar Galactica* and *Star Trek* (and its movie incarnations too). We have no apparent difficulty in accepting that the women of the future will fight. This book has demonstrated that we should have no difficulty accepting that the women of the past fought too.

The history of women in combat is a history that, while rarely recorded, exists almost entirely because of the acts of women themselves. Prior to the First World War, women were rarely officially organised for military purposes. The women of the campaign community were largely on the battlefield under their own steam. The cross-dressed warriors of the world were women determined enough to join the military that they did so in disguise. The mobilisation of women during the First World War was possible only because women had themselves used their social and political organising skills to develop organisations that the state could then use to fight the war. Many of the Soviet women who fought in the Second World War enlisted on their own, before any official call to arms. And Second World War conscription efforts in Britain and the

United States again relied on women's initiatives in setting up auxiliary organisations and preparing for war.

During the post-1945 era, when women were removed from the military and banned from fighting, the history of combat remains a story of female determination. Outside the major militaries, women in rebel movements were inspired to take up arms alongside men, and often for the same reasons. Inside the militaries that persisted in banning women from combat, women had to learn to push around the rules to develop their careers and get what they wanted.

The women on the battlefields in this book have fought: they have fought as generals, as commanders of sieges. Women were on the battlefield, sharing all the danger and discomfort, to make sure that men could fight; they were accompanied by women dressed as men who were actually fighting. Women have been prevented from fighting when they wanted to, and they have been restricted from fighting by complex rules. But throughout, women have been fighting, and in ways that do matter for military history and matter for the way we organise society. Their stories form an historical narrative that shows that an all-male military history is a construct that obscures a more interesting reality, one where neither combat nor the battlefield are as straightforward as we might think. It is hard to see how, without women, militaries could have functioned: from campaign communities to regimental wives to formal volunteer organisations that were then taken on by the state in the twentieth century. The history of women in combat is a powerful reminder that women have always found a way around the rules that were made to keep them down. When they were told they could not fight, they did it anyway. They ignored the rules. The history of warrior women reminds us that when women were told they were not capable, they found a thousand ways, small and large, to show that they were.

There are very few monuments to the women warriors of the past. Even their tombs have gone unmarked, and are often unrecognised. The memorials that mark women's combat contributions have often come many years after the war, as the Second World War memorials around the world show, and are almost never specifically devoted to women warriors. The monumental act of forgetting women's contributions, an amnesia that helped keep women out of combat roles for years after life became more gender equal in other fields, perhaps erased the chances for formal recognition. Without a memorial, how can we remember history's forgotten women warriors? Perhaps the answer lies in the fact that we now know that every tomb of the unknown soldier, every battlefield, every grave, may include a woman. The most appropriate memorial is a corrected vision of the past, one that allows us to see clearly the band of brothers and sisters marching to battle together.

Acknowledgements

W HEN I FIRST sat down to write this book, it was going to be a conventional academic book, designed for a very particular market. But as I delved deeper into the research, I discovered so many astonishing women, situations and political and historical developments that I wanted to make sure that as many people as possible could hear about this history, and really engage with the idea that women's military history is different from the expectations of most people. So I took a new direction and wrote the book you are reading today. Its nature, building as it does on the brilliant scholarship from feminist history and politics in particular, leaves me with a great many debts to acknowledge.

There is a group of people who encouraged me to take a new direction and write the book for a general audience. My colleagues David Duriesmith and Stephen Bell were particularly enthusiastic about the idea. When I was writing up the proposal, I turned to my old friend and great source of advice, Christine Whelan, who started the ball rolling by persuading me that this was the obvious choice and started me thinking about agents. While I was working on the proposal, I was also making my first radio series with my friend and podcastière sidekick Edwina Stott, who has given strength to my storytelling voice. (Ed, I can hear you every time I write, saying 'the story doesn't need that – it's boring!') Theo Farrell also gave me terrific advice and introduced me to my agent, Bill Hamilton. A special word here about Bill: it has been the greatest pleasure and greatest education working with him on the book from the very beginning. He is so knowledgeable and patient, and has such a sharp eye – it was like having the very best PhD supervisor you can imagine, only, of course, a supervisor in every aspect of publishing a book commercially.

ACKNOWLEDGEMENTS

The subject matter of the book clearly relies on the great strides made by feminist scholars in history, politics and international relations. Without their determination to uncover women's untold stories and their resolve to consider the wider implications of gender in the military and in society, it would have been impossible. Their work has provided the foundations on which I have told my stories.

My family, near and far, have been amazing. First of all, thank you to my husband, James Edelman, and my kids, Tatiana and Jonah. Thank you for having dinner time conversations about women's suffrage, war, fun facts and even cannibalism. Thank you for letting me disappear when I needed to write and, particularly, while I was in the final stages of finishing the book. Jamie, you have always believed that I can do anything, even when I occasionally doubt it, and you have never let me take my eyes off the finishing line. Tatiana and Jonah, your curiosity about what I do and your enthusiasm have been a great joy. Alfie and Joey the whippets: thank you for your wise furry counsel.

Also thank you to my parents, David and Tikker Percy, who brought me up to be a proud feminist. As I have grown older and raised my own family, I have come to appreciate the extraordinary gifts you gave me: an interest in the wider world, in politics and in the past; and, most importantly, the foundation of totally secure love no matter what I did or where I went. Matthew and I were the luckiest kids to have you as parents. Mom, writing this book has reinforced to me the height of the barriers you had to navigate as a young woman, a mother and a person trying to build an education and a career in a new country: whether or not you knew it, you were modelling the importance of women's equality with everything you did.

When you live far away from your family, like we do, and if you're very lucky, you get to build your own second family. My Brisbane family: thank you for everything. Cindy Davies, Sarah Holland and Sarah O'Sullivan talked to me about the book from when it was just an idea right through to the very end, along with exercise, coffee, support, occasional tears and general laughter. Amanda Niehaus took me on my first DIY writing retreat, thereby teaching me a great way to write while balancing family life. Linny

Sampson and Damian Amato, thanks for the dinners, jokes, trips, child exercise, and stepping in when we've needed a hand. Alex and Ben Ward, thank you too for the friendship, advice and fun. Nick McKenna and Tadzia Grandpre were great sounding boards for ideas about the book, much missed since they left Brisbane.

In a busy family with two working parents, we've had the most wonderful women help raise our children. Lisa Baldwin, Erin Spark, Sarah Goodenough, Elizabeth Somervaille, Madeleine Campbell and Hannah Somervaille – you have made it possible for me to have the time and space to think and write, and you've taught our family so much. My particular thanks go to Katie Paterson who survived living with us for three years during the pandemic and who has been there almost every step of the way with this project and with the family.

My colleagues at the University of Queensland are the best bunch I've ever worked with. POLSIS, thank you. Special thanks to Nicole George, another writing retreat/book production buddy for all your help; Kath Gelber, for your support in work and life; Andrew Phillips, Chris Reus-Smit, Shahar Hameiri and Ryan Walter for talking about the book and everything else, lunches, reading, coffee and snacks. Debbie Martin in the UQ Library is a gem – she was always (and swiftly) able to help me. Thanks to Alastair Blanshard for his classics expertise.

Thank you to my research assistants, who have been not only great help but also great fun: Hannah Mercieca; Jessica Creevey, for assisting with lots of detailed tasks that helped me get the book finalised; and to Max Broad and Anna Whip, a special thank-you for the length of time you've committed to working on the project and your deep engagement with the material.

The team at John Murray and Basic Books have been a joy, guiding a first-timer like me through a new way to write and publish. Thanks Georgina Laycock for being a champion of the book from the beginning, and your incisive editorial advice throughout; Marissa Koors and Emma Berry from Basic Books for their editorial insight; Jasmine Marsh for your enthusiasm and publicity guidance; Caroline Westmore, Katharine Morris and Juliet Brightmore; and Hilary Hammond for painstaking and excellent copy-editing.

Picture Credits

Alamy Stock Photo: 1 below left/Album/detail from equestrian portrait by Claude Deruet/Musée Carnavalet, Paris, 2 centre right/ CPA Media Pte Ltd, 3 above right/Science History Images, 3 centre left/agephotostock, 3 below right/Granger Historical Picture Archive, 4 centre right/Chronicle, 4 below left/Trinity Mirror/Mirrorpix, 5 below left/Archivart, 5 above left/History and Art Collection, 5 centre right and 6 above right/Pictorial Press Ltd, 6 centre left/ CBW, 7 below/Kurdishstruggle/PKK, 8 above/Everett Historical Collection. Bibliothèque nationale de France/Public Domain: 2 below left. Giovanni Antonio Cavazzi: 1 above/engraving from *Istorica Descrizione De' Tre' Regni Congo, Matamba et Angola*, 1687. Getty Images: 1 below right/SSPL, 4 above left/Popperfoto, 7 above/David Pollack/Corbis, 8 below/Adek Berry/AFP. Herzog August Bibliothek Wolfenbüttel: 2 above left/Cod. Guelf. 36.13 Aug. 2°, folio 885 (CC BY-SA). US Air Force photo/Public Domain: 6 below right.

Notes

Introduction: The Tomb of the Unknown Warrior

1. Charlotte Hedenstierna-Jonson et al., 'A Female Viking Warrior Confirmed by Genomics', *American Journal of Physical Anthropology* 164, no. 4 (2017), p. 116.

2. Neil Price et al., 'Viking Warrior Women? Reassessing Birka Chamber Grave Bj.581', *Antiquity* 93, no. 367 (2019), p. 184.

3. Ibid.

4. Hedenstierna-Jonson et al., 'Female Viking', p. 192.

5. Price et al., 'Reassessing Birka', p. 191.

6. Ibid.

7. Nara Schoenberg, '"It's a Woman. It's Not Pulaski": New Documentary Argues That Revolutionary War Hero Was Intersex', *Chicago Tribune*, 3 April 2019, https://www.chicagotribune.com/lifestyles/ct-life-casimir-pulaski-intersex-040319-story.html

8. John Keegan, *A History of Warfare* (London: Pimlico, 1993), p. 76.

9. Martin van Creveld, *The Changing Face of War: Combat from the Marne to Iraq* (New York: Presidio Press, 2008), p. 266.

10. Robert T. Herres and Members of the Commission, *Presidential Commission on the Assignment of Women in the Armed Forces* (Washington, DC: US Government Printing Office, 1992), p. 114.

11. Joshua Goldstein, *War and Gender* (Cambridge: Cambridge University Press, 2001), p. 10.

12. Erica Chenoweth and Zoe Marks, 'Revenge of the Patriarchs: Why Autocrats Fear Women', *Foreign Affairs* (March/April 2022), https://www.foreignaffairs.com/articles/china/2022-02-08/women-rights-revenge-patriarchs

13. Paul Szoldra, 'Trump Could Kick Women out of Military Combat Jobs, Reversing a Historic 2013 Policy Change', Business Insider, 16 November

2016, https://www.businessinsider.com.au/trump-women-combat-jobs-2016-11?r=DE&IR=T

14. Jacquelyn Schneider and Julia Macdonald, 'Trump Voters Don't like Women in Military Combat Roles. That May Have Consequences for the Use of Force', *Washington Post*, 3 November 2016, https://www.washingtonpost.com/news/monkey-cage/wp/2016/11/03/trump-voters-dont-like-women-in-military-combat-roles-that-may-have-consequences-for-the-use-of-force/

15. Cynthia Enloe, 'Combat and "Combat": A Feminist Reflection', *Critical Studies on Security* 1, no. 2 (2013), p. 261.

16. Dianne Dugaw, *Warrior Women and Popular Balladry 1650–1850* (Cambridge: Cambridge University Press, 1989), pp. 140–1.

17. Jean Bethke Elshtain, *Women and War* (Chicago: University of Chicago Press, 1987).

Chapter 1: Women Generals

1. Dio Cassius, *Roman History, Volume VIII: Books 61–70*, trans. Earnest Cary and Herbert B. Foster, Loeb Classical Library 176 (Cambridge, MA: Harvard University Press, 1925), p. 85.

2. Tacitus, *Annals: Books 13–16*. trans. John Jackson, Loeb Classical Library 322 (Cambridge, MA: Harvard University Press, 1937), p. 157.

3. Antonia Fraser, *Warrior Queens: Boadicea's Chariot* (Salisbury: Phoenix, 1988), loc. 1501; Marguerite Johnson, *Boudicca* (London: Bloomsbury, 2012), p. 15.

4. Fraser, *Queens*, loc. 1591.

5. Cornelius Tacitus, 'Annals', in Arthur Murphy, ed. and trans., *The Works of Cornelius Tacitus with an Essay on His Life and Genius* (Philadelphia: Thomas Wardle, 1844), p. 259.

6. Peter Marsden, *Roman London* (London: Thames & Hudson, 1980), p. 31.

7. Dio Cassius, *Roman History*, p. 95.

8. Tacitus, *Annals*, p. 163.

9. Tacitus, 'Annals', p. 259.

10. Ibid.

11. Tacitus, *Annals*, p. 155.

12. Ibid.

13. Dio Cassius, *Roman*, p. 83.

14. Tacitus, 'Annals', p. 259.

15. Ibid.

16. Ibid.
17. Ibid.
18. Adrian Goldsworthy, *Pax Romana: War, Peace and Conquest in the Roman World* (London: Weidenfeld & Nicolson, 2016), p. 194.
19. Tacitus, 'Annals', p. 83.
20. Jane Crawford, 'Cartimandua, Boudicca, and Rebellion: British Queens and Roman Colonial Views', in Tamara L. Hunt and Micheline R. Lessard, eds, *Women and the Colonial Gaze* (London: Palgrave Macmillan, 2002), pp. 25–6.
21. Michael Roberts, 'The Revolt of Boudicca (Tacitus, *Annals* 14.29–39) and the Assertion of Libertas in Neronian Rome', *American Journal of Philology* 109, no. 1 (1988), p. 122.
22. Tacitus, *Annals*, p. 155.
23. William Monter, *The Rise of Female Kings in Europe, 1300–1800* (New Haven: Yale University Press, 2012), p. ix.
24. Tryntje Helfferich, *The Iron Princess: Amalia Elisabeth and the Thirty Years War* (Cambridge, MA: Harvard University Press, 2013), pp. 1–2.
25. Mary Elizabeth Ailes, *Courage and Grief: Women and Sweden's Thirty Years' War* (Lincoln: University of Nebraska Press, 2018), p. 160.
26. Monter, *Female Kings*, p. 50.
27. Ailes, *Courage and Grief*, pp. 149–51, 159.
28. Quoted in Helfferich, *Iron Princess*, p. 12.
29. Joseph F. O'Callaghan, *The Last Crusade in the West: Castile and the Conquest of Granada* (Philadelphia: University of Pennsylvania Press, 2014), p. 132.
30. Elizabeth A. Lehfeldt, 'The Queen at War: Shared Sovereignty and Gender in Representations of the Granada Campaign', in Barbara F. Weissberger, ed., *Queen Isabel I of Castile: Power, Patronage, Persona* (Woodbridge: Boydell & Brewer, 2008), p. 111.
31. William H. Prescott, *History of the Reign of Ferdinand and Isabella the Catholic*, ed. C. Harvey Gardiner (London: Allen & Unwin, 1962), p. 129; Lehfeldt, 'Queen', p. 112.
32. William Thomas Walsh, *Isabella of Spain* (London: Sheed & Ward, 1931), pp. 114, 38.
33. Christopher Duffy, *The Army of Maria Theresa: 1740–1780* (New York: Hippocrene Books, 1977), p. 18.
34. Ibid.
35. Hajo Holborn, *A History of Modern Germany: 1648–1840* (Princeton: Princeton University Press, 1964), vol. 2, p. 218.

36. Quoted in Edward Crankshaw, *Maria Theresa* (London and Harlow: Longmans, Green, 1969), p. 193.

37. Quoted in Duffy, *Maria Theresa*, p. 18.

38. Crankshaw, *Maria Theresa*, p. 193.

39. Monter, *Female Kings*, p. 148.

40. Quoted in Ailes, *Courage and Grief*, p. 147.

41. Ibid., p. 148.

42. Ibid.

43. Quoted in Helfferich, *Iron Princess*, p. 10.

44. Duffy, *Maria Theresa*, p. 15.

45. Christopher Duffy, *The Army of Frederick the Great* (New York: Hippocrene Books, 1974), p. 21.

46. Kelly DeVries, *Joan of Arc: A Military Leader* (Stroud: Alan Sutton, 1999), p. 29.

47. Larissa Juliet Taylor, *The Virgin Warrior: The Life and Death of Joan of Arc* (New Haven and London: Yale University Press, 2009), p. 68.

48. Quoted in DeVries, *Joan of Arc*, p. 94.

49. Taylor, *Virgin Warrior*, p. 58.

50. David Green, *The Hundred Years War: A People's History* (New Haven: Yale University Press, 2014), p. 203.

51. Quoted in DeVries, *Joan of Arc*, p. 69.

52. DeVries, *Joan of Arc*, p. 81.

53. Taylor, *Virgin Warrior*, p. 71.

54. Ibid.

55. Alain Chartier, *Les oeuvres latines*, ed. P. Bourgain-Hemeryck (Paris: 1977), pp. 326–9, as contained in Craig Taylor, *Joan of Arc: La Pucelle* (Manchester: Manchester University Press, 2013), p. 111.

56. Taylor, *Virgin Warrior*, p. 100.

57. DeVries, *Joan of Arc*, p. 156.

58. Taylor, *Virgin Warrior*, p. 117.

59. Ibid., p. 118.

60. Wilfred Phillips Barrett, *The Trial of Jeanne d'Arc* (1931; London: Routledge, 2014), p. 31.

61. Taylor, *Virgin Warrior*, p. 161.

62. Marina Warner, *Joan of Arc* (London: Vintage, 1981), p. 141.

63. Joan's date of birth is unknown but estimated to be 1412.

64. Taylor, *Virgin Warrior*, p. 52.

65. Quoted ibid., pp. 49–50.

66. DeVries, *Joan of Arc*, p. 56.

67. Ibid.

68. Kelly DeVries, 'The Use of Gunpowder Weaponry by and Against Joan of Arc during the Hundred Years War', *War & Society* 14, no. 1 (1996), p. 8.

69. Stephen W. Richey, *Joan of Arc: The Warrior Saint* (Westport: Praeger, 2003), p. 92; DeVries, *Joan of Arc*, p. 56.

70. DeVries, *Joan of Arc*, p. 35.

71. Quoted in Taylor, *La Pucelle*, p. 37.

72. Quoted in DeVries, *Joan of Arc*, p. 95.

73. Warner, *Joan of Arc*, p. 14.

74. Quoted ibid., p. 143.

75. Noël Valois, 'Un nouveau temoignage sur Jeanne d'Arc: La réponse d'un clerc Parisien à l'apologie de la pucelle par Jean Gerson (1429)', *Annuaire-Bulletin de la Société de l'Histoire de France* 43 (1906), reproduced in Taylor, *La Pucelle*, p. 127.

76. Her name has multiple spellings, including Djinga, Jinga and Nzinga. The term 'queen' does not translate literally into the context of seventeenth-century central west Africa, but was intelligible to those Western outsiders interacting with Njinga. Daniel Silva, '(Anti-)Colonial Assemblages: The History and Reformulations of Njinga Mbande', in Janell Hobson, ed., *The Routledge Companion to Black Women's Cultural Histories* (London: Routledge), p. 75.

77. Linda M. Heywood, *Njinga of Angola* (Cambridge, MA: Harvard University Press, 2017), p. 162.

78. More modern historians have a nuanced debate about the heart-eating, but it would have been widely understood to be true at the time. Fraser, *Queens*, loc. 4620.

79. Heywood, *Njinga*, p. 1.

80. John K. Thornton, *A History of West Central Africa to 1850* (Cambridge: Cambridge University Press, 2020), p. 162.

81. Heywood, *Njinga*, p. 57.

82. Ibid., p. 58.

83. John Ogilby, *Africa Being an Accurate Description of the Regions of Ægypt, Barbary, Lybia, and Billedulgerid, the Land of Negroes, Guinee, Æthiopia and the Abyssines . . . Illustrated with Notes and Adorn'd with Peculiar Maps and Proper Sculptures* (London: Tho. Johnson, 1670), p. 564.

84. Heywood, *Njinga*, pp. 50, 45.

85. Ibid., p. 40.

86. Ibid., pp. 7, 13.

87. Jared Staller, *Converging on Cannibals: Terrors of Slaving in Atlantic Africa 1509–1670* (Athens, OH: Ohio University Press, 2019), p. 122.
88. Heywood, *Njinga*, p. 51.
89. Silva, 'Njinga Mbande', p. 77.
90. Heywood, *Njinga*, p. 62.
91. Ibid., p. 61.
92. On poison, see James Duffy, *Portuguese Africa*, 3rd edn (Cambridge, MA: Harvard University Press, 2013), p. 64.
93. Thornton, *West Central Africa*, p. 151.
94. Heywood, *Njinga*, p. 65; Staller, *Cannibals*, p. 106.
95. John K. Thornton, 'The Art of War in Angola 1575–1680', *Comparative Studies in Society and History* 30, no. 2 (1988), p. 365.
96. Heywood, *Njinga*, p. 107; Thornton, *West Central Africa*, p. 154.
97. Heywood, *Njinga*, p. 197.
98. Thornton, 'Art of War', p. 364.
99. Heywood, *Njinga*, p. 59.
100. Ibid., p. 60.
101. Ibid., p. 69.
102. Thornton, 'Art of War', p. 366.
103. Heywood, *Njinga*, pp. 155, 161.
104. Ibid., p. 81.
105. Ibid., p. 115.
106. Ibid., p. 129.
107. Portuguese governor Francesco de Sotomaior, quoted ibid., p. 144. Ethiopia was the common European term for sub-Saharan Africa at this point.
108. Ibid., p. 151.
109. Joseph C. Miller, 'Nzinga of Matamba in a New Perspective', *Journal of African History* 16, no. 2 (1975), p. 211.
110. Heywood, *Njinga*, p. 143.
111. Ibid., p. 153.
112. Ibid., p. 146.
113. Ibid., p. 147.
114. Ibid., p. 165.
115. Silva, 'Njinga Mbande', p. 78.
116. Heywood, *Njinga*, p. 170.
117. Duffy, *Portuguese Africa*, p. 64.
118. Heywood, *Njinga*, pp. 75–7; Staller, *Cannibals*, p. 132.
119. Heywood, *Njinga*, p. 192.

120. Quoted in Thornton, *West Central Africa*, p. 180.

121. Heywood, *Njinga*, p. 242.

122. Ibid., p. 241.

123. John K. Thornton, 'Legitimacy and Political Power: Queen Njinga, 1624–1663', *Journal of African History* 32, no. 1 (1991), p. 40. Njinga is not well known in the wider world; her ultimate descendent, Queen Veronica, who is even less known, ruled and commanded for forty years.

124. Thornton, 'Legitimacy and Political Power', p. 38.

125. Ogilby, *Africa*, p. 565. See also Heywood, *Njinga*, p. 127; Thornton, 'Legitimacy and Political Power', p. 38.

126. Giovanni Antonio Cavazzi, *Missione evangelica nel Regno de Congo (c.1668)*, trans. John K. Thornton, Maria Luisa Martini and Carolyn Beckingham. Available at John Thornton's website, https://www.bu.edu/afam/people/faculty/john-thornton/john-thorntons-african-texts/, book 2, p. 16.

127. Heywood, *Njinga*, p. 59.

128. John T. Alexander, *Catherine the Great: Life and Legend* (New York: Oxford University Press, 1989), p. 140.

129. Ogilby, *Africa*, p. 564.

130. Ibid.

131. Staller, *Cannibals*, p. 127.

132. Ibid., p. 112; Cavazzi, *Missione evangelica*, p. 22.

133. Ibid., p. 124.

134. Heywood, *Njinga*, p. 249. Marquis de Sade, *Justine, Philosophy in the Bedroom, and Other Writings*, trans. Richard Seaver and Austryn Wainhouse (New York: Grove Weidenfeld, 1965).

135. G. W. F. Hegel, *Lectures on the Philosophy of History*, trans. J. Sibree (London: Henry G. Bohn, 1857), p. 101.

Chapter 2: Camp Followers

1. 'Annette Drevon', *Droit des Femmes: Revue Internationale du Mouvement Feminin* 14, no. 208 (1882), pp. 41–2.

2. Annette's exploits were widely reported in the English-speaking press beginning in 1880, appearing in numerous newspapers; see e.g. 'A Brave Woman', *The Englishwoman's Review of Social and Industrial Questions* (1882), pp. 141–2 (rpt. London and New York: Garland, 1985); 'Brave Woman', *New Zealand Herald*, 4 December 1880; 'A Celebrity of the Paris Market', *Manchester Courier and Lancashire General Advertiser*, 10 August 1880.

3. Thomas Cardoza, *Intrepid Women: Cantinières and Vivandières of the French Army* (Bloomington: Indiana University Press, 2010), p. 154.

4. 'Brave Woman'; Cardoza, *Intrepid Women*, p. 154; 'Annette Drevon', p. 42.

5. Margaret R. Hunt, *Women in Eighteenth-Century Europe* (London: Pearson Education, 2010), p. 308.

6. Geoffrey Parker, *The Military Revolution: Military Innovation and the Rise of the West, 1500–1800* (Cambridge: Cambridge University Press, 1996), p. 1. There were less than ten years of peace in the sixteenth century and in the seventeenth, only four.

7. Brian Crim, 'Silent Partners: Women and Warfare in Early Modern Europe', in Gerard J. De Groot and C. Peniston-Bird, eds, *A Soldier and a Woman: Sexual Integration in the Military* (London: Routledge, 2000), p. 27.

8. John Lynn, *Women, Armies, and Warfare in Early Modern Europe* (New York: Cambridge University Press, 2008), p. 36.

9. J. R. Hale, *War and Society in Renaissance Europe* (Leicester: Leicester University Press, 1985), pp. 158–9.

10. Fergus Robson, 'Siege Warfare in Comparative Early Modern Contexts: Norms, Nuances, Myth and Massacre During the Revolutionary Wars', in Alex Dowdall and John Horne, eds, *Civilians Under Siege from Sarajevo to Troy* (New York: Springer, 2018), p. 85.

11. Frank Tallett, *War and Society in Early Modern Europe* (London: Routledge, 2010), p. 55.

12. Hale, *War and Society*, p. 159.

13. Quoted in Parker, *Military Revolution*, p. 77.

14. James Turner, *Pallas Armata: Military Essayes of the Ancient Grecian, Roman and Modern Art of War Written in the Years 1670 and 1671* (London: Richard Chiswell, 1683), p. 274.

15. Lynn, *Women, Armies*, p. 18; Mary Elizabeth Ailes, 'Camp Followers, Sutlers, and Soldiers' Wives: Women in Early Modern Armies (*c.*1450–*c.*1650)', in Barton C. Hacker and Margaret Vining, eds, *A Companion to Women's Military History* (Leiden: Brill, 2012), p. 113.

16. Turner, *Pallas Armata*, p. 277.

17. Tallett, *War and Society*, p. 134.

18. Geoffrey Parker, *The Army of Flanders and the Spanish Road, 1567–1659: The Logistics of Spanish Victory and Defeat in the Low Countries' Wars* (Cambridge: Cambridge University Press, 1972), p. 175.

19. Scott N. Hendrix, 'In the Army: Women, Camp Followers, and Gender Roles in the British Army in the French and Indian Wars, 1755–1765', in De Groot and Peniston-Bird, eds, *Soldier and Woman*, p. 34.

20. Lynn (*Women, Armies*, p. 68) makes a similar argument.

21. Hendrix, 'In the Army', p. 36.

22. Lynn, *Women, Armies*, p. 77.

23. Robert Monro, *Monro, His Expedition with the Worthy Scots Regiment Called Mac-Keys* (London: William James, 1637), vol. 1, p. 29.

24. Turner, *Pallas Armata*, p. 77.

25. Quoted in Cardoza, *Intrepid Women*, p. 65.

26. Holly A. Mayer, *Belonging to the Army: Camp Followers and Community During the American Revolution* (Columbia: University of South Carolina Press, 1996), p. 9 (emphasis original).

27. Carol Berkin, *Revolutionary Mothers: Women in the Struggle for America's Independence* (New York: Knopf, 2006), p. 80.

28. Linda Grant DePauw, *Battle Cries and Lullabies: Women in War from Prehistory to the Present* (Norman: University of Oklahoma Press, 1998), p. 130.

29. DePauw, 'Women in Combat: The Revolutionary War Experience', *Armed Forces & Society* 7, no. 2 (Winter 1981), p. 219.

30. Hendrix, 'In the Army', p. 40.

31. Ailes, *Courage and Grief*, p. 54.

32. Barton C. Hacker, 'Women and Military Institutions in Early Modern Europe: A Reconnaissance', *Signs: Journal of Women in Culture and Society* 6, no. 4 (1981), p. 654.

33. Cardoza, *Intrepid Women*, p. 105.

34. *The Times*, 5 October 1854, p. 7.

35. Noel T. St John Williams, *Judy O'Grady and the Colonel's Lady: The Army Wife and Camp Follower Since 1660* (London: Brassey's, 1988), p. 11.

36. Lynn, *Women, Armies*, p. 120.

37. Mayer, *Belonging to the Army*, p. 46.

38. Ibid., p. 10.

39. Ibid., p. 15.

40. Duffy, *Frederick the Great*, p. 137.

41. Ibid.

42. Ibid., pp. 59–60.

43. DePauw, 'Women in Combat', p. 216.

44. Cardoza, *Intrepid Women*, p. 43.

45. Mayer, *Belonging to the Army*, p. 13.

46. Cardoza, *Intrepid Women*, p. 8.

47. Ibid., p. 122.

48. Andrew Orr, *Women and the French Army: During the World Wars, 1914–40* (Bloomington: Indiana University Press, 2017), p. 5.

49. Geoff Mortimer, *Eyewitness Accounts of the Thirty Years War 1618–1648* (London: Routledge, 2002), p. 30.

50. Ibid., p. 36.

51. Lynn, *Women, Armies*, p. 149.

52. Cardoza, *Intrepid Women*, p. 42.

53. George Bell, *Rough Notes by an Old Soldier: During Fifty Years' Service* (London: Day & Son, 1867), pp. 75, 183.

54. Ibid., p. 124.

55. Crim, 'Silent Partners', p. 28.

56. Cardoza, *Intrepid Women*, p. 51.

57. Jennine Hurl-Eamon, ed., *Women, Families and the British Army 1700–1880*, vol. 1, *From Marlborough's Reforms to the Outbreak of War with Revolutionary France* (London: Routledge, 2020), p. 91.

58. St John Williams, *O'Grady*, p. 14.

59. Sarah Fatherly, 'Tending the Army: Women and the British General Hospital in North America, 1754–1763', *Early American Studies* 10, no. 3 (2012), p. 573.

60. St John Williams, *O'Grady*, p. 15.

61. Wilhelm Haberling, 'Army Prostitution and Its Control', in Victor Robinson, ed., *Morals in Wartime* (New York: Publishers' Foundation, 1943), p. 56.

62. Mayer, *Belonging to the Army*, p. 126.

63. Philip G. Dwyer, '"It Still Makes Me Shudder" Memories of Massacres and Atrocities During the Revolutionary and Napoleonic Wars', *War in History* 16, no. 4 (2009), p. 394.

64. In Hurl-Eamon, *Marlborough's Reforms*, p. 96.

65. Julie Wheelwright, '"Amazons and Military Maids": An Examination of Female Military Heroines in British Literature and the Changing Construction of Gender', *Women's Studies International Forum* 10, no. 5 (1987), p. 489.

66. Lynn, *Women, Armies*, p. 67.

67. Alison Plowden, *Women All on Fire: The Women of the English Civil War* (Stroud: Alan Sutton, 1998), p. 95.

68. Ibid., p. 96.

69. Ibid.

70. Tallett, *War and Society*, p. 133.

71. Cardoza, *Intrepid Women*, p. 1.

72. Ibid., p. 123.

73. Christine Kelly, *Mrs Duberly's War: Journal and Letters from the Crimea, 1854–6* (Oxford: Oxford University Pres, 2007), p. 75.

74. Ibid., p. 273.

75. St John Williams, *O'Grady*, p. 9.

76. Maria Sjöberg, 'Women in Campaigns 1550–1850: Household and Homosociality in the Swedish Army', *History of the Family* 16, no. 3 (2011), p. 212.

77. St John Williams, *O'Grady*, p. 13.

78. Jennine Hurl-Eamon, *Marriage and the British Army in the Long Eighteenth Century: 'The Girl I Left Behind Me'* (Oxford: Oxford University Press, 2014), p. 25.

79. St John Williams, *O'Grady*, p. 13.

80. Ibid., p. 44.

81. Ibid., p. 13.

82. Fatherly, 'Tending the Army', p. 572.

83. Lynn, *Women, Armies*, p. 14.

84. St John Williams, *O'Grady*, p. 17.

85. Ibid., p. 19.

86. Quoted in Barton C. Hacker, 'Reformers, Nurses, and Ladies in Uniform: The Changing Status of Military Women (*c.*1815–*c.*1914)', in Hacker and Vining, *Companion*, p. 143.

87. St John Williams, *O'Grady*, p. 101.

88. Ibid., p. 104.

89. Ibid.

90. Hacker, 'Reformers', p. 155.

91. Thomas Cardoza, '"Habits Appropriate to Her Sex": The Female Military Experience in France during the Age of Revolution', in Karen Hagemann, Gisela Mettele and Jane Rendall, eds, *Gender, War and Politics: Transatlantic Perspectives, 1775–1830* (London: Palgrave Macmillan, 2010), p. 11.

92. Orr, *French Army*, pp. 7–8.

Chapter 3: Under Siege

1. Sometimes she is called Fouquet.

2. Ellen C. Clayton, *Female Warriors: Memorials of Female Valour and Heroism, from the Mythological Ages to the Present Era* (London: Tinsley Brothers, 1879), p. 87.

3. Ruth Putnam, *Charles the Bold: Last Duke of Burgundy 1433–1466* (New York and London: G. P. Putnam's Sons, 1908), p. 313.

4. Hale, *War and Society*, p. 192; Diane Gervais and Serge Lusignan, 'De

Jeanne d'Arc à Madelaine de Verchères: La femme guerrière dans la société d'ancien régime', *Revue d'Histoire de l'Amérique Française* 53, no. 2 (1999), p. 194.

5. Tallett, *War and Society*, p. 66.

6. Jane Finucane, 'Before the Storm: Civilians under Siege During the Thirty Years' War', in Dowdall and Horne, eds, *Civilians under Siege*, p. 138; John Childs, 'Surrender and the Laws of War in Western Europe *c.*1650–1783', in Hew Strachan and Holger Afferbach, eds, *How Fighting Ends: A History of Surrender* (Oxford: Oxford University Press, 2012), p. 158.

7. Tallett, *War and Society*, p. 53.

8. Ibid., p. 106.

9. Robson, 'Siege Warfare', p. 85.

10. Ailes, *Courage and Grief*, p. 28.

11. S. Annette Finley-Croswhite, 'Engendering the Wars of Religion: Female Agency During the Catholic League in Dijon', *French Historical Studies* vol. 20, no. 2 (1999), p. 129.

12. Quoted in Lynn, *Women, Armies*, p. 151.

13. Tryntje Helfferich, *Thirty Years War: A Documentary History* (Indianapolis: Hackett, 2009), p. 57.

14. Herodotus, *The History of Herodotus*, trans. G. C. Macaulay (London: Macmillan, 1890), p. 102.

15. Plowden, *Women All on Fire*, p. 65.

16. Ulinka Rublack, 'Wench and Maiden: Women, War and the Pictorial Function of the Feminine in German Cities in the Early Modern Period', *History Workshop Journal* 44 (Autumn 1997), p. 3.

17. Tallett, *War and Society*, p. 152.

18. Quoted in Brian Sandberg, '"Generous Amazons Came to the Breach": Besieged Women, Agency and Subjectivity During the French Wars of Religion', *Gender & History* 16, no. 3 (2004), p. 672.

19. Ibid.

20. Plowden, *Women All on Fire*, p. 64.

21. Ibid., p. 66.

22. Quoted in John Barratt, *Sieges of the English Civil Wars* (Barnsley: Pen & Sword, 2008), ch. 7.

23. Deborah Simonton, 'Surviving the Siege: Catastrophe, Gender and Memory in La Rochelle', in Deborah Simonton and Hannu Salmi, eds, *Catastrophe, Gender and the Urban Experience, 1648–1920* (New York: Routledge, 2017), pp. 23–5.

24. Quoted in Hale, *War and Society*, p. 193.

25. Sandberg, 'Amazons', p. 675.

26. Ibid.

27. Ibid., p. 676.

28. Quoted in Plowden, *Women All on Fire*, p. xii.

29. Christine de Pisan, *The Treasure of the City of Ladies*, trans. Sarah Lawson (Harmondsworth: Penguin, 1985), p. 129.

30. Kristen B. Neuschel, 'Noblewomen and War in Sixteenth-Century France', in Michael Wolfe, ed., *Changing Identities in Early Modern France* (Durham: University of North Carolina Press, 1997), p. 126.

31. Antonia Fraser, *The Weaker Vessel: Woman's Lot in Seventeenth-Century England* (London: Weidenfeld & Nicolson, 1984), p. 165.

32. John Burke, *A Genealogical and Heraldic History of the Commoners of Great Britain and Ireland* (London: Henry Colburn, 1837), vol. 3, p. 308.

33. Ibid.

34. Quoted in Plowden, *Women All on Fire*, p. 60.

35. Sandy Riley, *Charlotte de la Trémoïlle* (Newcastle upon Tyne: Cambridge Scholars, 2017), p. 1.

36. Described by a contemporary observer in Henriette Elizabeth Guizot de Witt, *The Lady of Latham: Being the Life and Original Letters of Charlotte de La Trémoille, Countess of Derby* (London: Smith, Elder, 1869), p. 76.

37. Edward Halsall, *A Journal of the Siege of Lathom House* (1644; London: Harding, Mavor & Lepard, 1823), p. 23.

38. Ibid., p. 47.

39. Ibid., p. 27.

40. Ibid., p. 53.

41. Ibid., p. 64.

42. Riley, *Charlotte de La Trémoille*, p. 114.

43. Quoted ibid., p. 104.

44. *The Scottish Dove*, 3–10 December 1645, p. 887.

45. Brilliana Harley and Thomas Taylor Lewis, *Letters of the Lady Brilliana Harvey: Wife of Sir Robert Harley, of Brampton Bryan, Knight of the Bath* (London: Printed for the Camden Society, 1854), pp. 178, 81.

46. *Calendar of the Manuscripts of the Marquis of Bath Preserved at Longleat, Wiltshire* (London: Mackie & Co. for HM Stationery Office, 1904), vol. 1, p. 40.

47. Ibid., vol. 1, p. 26.

48. Ibid., vol. 1, p. 4.

49. Ibid., vol. 1, p. 25.

50. Ibid., vol. 1, p. 27.

51. Letter of Lady Brilliana Harley to her son, Edward Harley, 9 October 1643, Harley and Taylor Lewis, *Letters*, p. 209.

52. *Marquis of Bath*, vol. 1, p. 27.

53. Ibid., vol. 1, p. 33.

54. Ibid.

55. Adrienne E. Zuerner, 'Disorderly Wives, Loyal Subjects: Marriage and War in Early Modern France', *Dalhousie French Studies* 56, (Fall 2001), p. 57.

56. Carmeta Abbott, 'Madame de Saint-Balmon (Alberte-Barbe d'Ernecourt)', in Anne R. Larsen and Colette H. Winn, eds, *Writings by Pre-Revolutionary French Women* (New York and London: Routledge, 2017), p. 259.

57. Quoted in Hubert Carrier, 'Women's Political and Military Action During the Fronde', in Christine Fauré, ed., *Political and Historical Encylopedia of Women* (London: Routledge, 2003), p. 51.

58. Jean Marie de Vernon, *L'Amazone chrétienne, ou Les aventure de Madame Saint-Balmon* (1678; Paris: Éditions de Soye, 1873), p. 147.

59. Abbott, 'Saint-Balmon', p. 258.

60. Carmeta Abbott, 'The Portrait as Text: Two Depictions of Madame de Saint-Balmon (1607–1660)', *Atlantis: Critical Studies in Gender, Culture & Social Justice* 19, no. 1 (1993), p. 131.

61. Zuerner, 'Disorderly Wives', p. 58.

62. Joan DeJean, 'Violent Women and Violence against Women: Representing the "Strong" Woman in Early Modern France', *Signs: Journal of Women in Culture and Society* 29, no. 1 (2003), p. 132.

63. Carrier, 'Fronde', p. 50.

64. Ibid.

65. See Duchesse de Montpensier, Anne-Marie-Louise d'Orléans, *Against Marriage: The Correspondence of La Grande Mademoiselle*, trans. Joan DeJean (Chicago: University of Chicago Press, 2002), p. 4.

66. Elise Goodman, 'Minerva Revivified: Mademoiselle de Montpensier', *Mediterranean Studies* 15 (2006), p. 80.

67. Mademoiselle de Montpensier, *Memoirs of Mademoiselle de Montpensier (La Grande Mademoiselle)*, trans. P. J. Yarrow and William Brooks (Cambridge, MA: Modern History Research Association, 2010), p. 47.

68. Quoted in Vita Sackville-West, *Daughter of France: The Life of Anne Marie Louise d'Orléans, Duchesse de Montpensier, La Grande Mademoiselle* (London: Michael Joseph, 1950), p. 110.

69. Goodman, 'Minerva', p. 100.

70. Stephen A. Shapiro, 'The Romance of the Fronde: The Siege of Orleans in the Mémoires of Mademoiselle de Montpensier', *Romance Studies* 28, no. 1 (2010), p. 20.

71. D'Orléans, *Against Marriage*, p. 7.

72. Montpensier, *Memoirs*, p. 76.

73. Ibid.

74. D'Orléans, *Against Marriage*, p. 7.

75. Quoted in Carrier, 'Fronde', p. 51.

76. Her date of birth is much disputed.

77. Lord Dalhousie, a chief proponent of this policy and the official who was to implement it in the case of Jhansi, was apparently expelled from Harrow for bullying, a remarkable accomplishment for a period of time in which the bounds of 'acceptable' bullying were loosely drawn indeed. Christopher Tyerman, *A History of Harrow School, 1324–1991* (Oxford: Oxford University Press, 2000), p. 202.

78. On the doctrine of lapse, see Joyce Lebra-Chapman, *The Rani of Jhansi: A Study of Female Heroism* (Honolulu: University of Hawai'i Press, 1986), p. 25.

79. Ibid.

80. Harleen Singh, *The Rani of Jhansi: Gender, History and Fable in India* (Cambridge: Cambridge University Press, 1986), p. 9.

81. John Lang, *Wanderings in India, And Other Sketches of Life in Hindostan* (London: Routledge, 1861), pp. 93–4.

82. Lebra-Chapman, *Rani of Jhansi*, p. 55.

83. Ibid.

84. Letter from Lakshmi Bai to Major Erskine (Allen Copsey), 12 June 1857, http://www.copsey-family.org/~allenc/lakshmibai/june-12-1857.html [accessed 30 January 2023]

85. Richard Hilton, *The Indian Mutiny: A Centenary History* (London: Hollis & Carter, 1957), p. 12.

86. Thomas Lowe, *Central India During the Rebellion of 1857 and 1858* (London: Longman, Green, Longman & Roberts, 1860), p. 236.

87. Fraser, *Queens*, loc. 5269.

88. Lebra-Chapman, *Rani of Jhansi*, p. 32.

89. Fraser, *Queens*, loc. 5525.

90. Vishnubhat Godse, *Adventures of a Brahmin Priest: My Travels in the 1857 Rebellion*, ed. Krishnan Mini, trans. Priya Adarkar and Shanta Gokhale (Oxford: Oxford University Press, 2014), p. 92; Lebra-Chapman, *Rani of Jhansi*, p. 73.

91. Lebra-Chapman, *Rani of Jhansi*, p. 83.

92. Lowe, *Central India*, p. 242.

93. Lebra-Chapman, *Rani of Jhansi*, pp. 87–8.

94. Ibid.

95. Sir John Kaye and George Bruce Malleson, 'Sir Hugh Rose in Central India', in George Bruce Malleson, ed., *Kaye's and Malleson's History of the Indian Mutiny of 1857–8* (1897; Cambridge: Cambridge University Press, 2010), p. 111.

96. Godaśe, *Travels*, p. 98.

97. John Henry Sylvester, *Recollections of the Campaign in Malwa and Central India under Major General Sir Hugh Rose G.C.B.* (Bombay: Smith, Taylor, 1860), p. 87.

98. Kaye and Malleson, 'Rose', p. 117.

99. Lowe, *Central India*, p. 257.

100. Kaye and Malleson, 'Rose', p. 118.

101. Lowe, *Central India*, p. 261.

102. Message from E. A. Reade, Agra, 11 June 1858, quoted in S. A. A. Rizvi and M. L. Bhargava, eds, *Freedom Struggle in Uttar Pradesh: Source-Material* (Uttar Pradesh: Publications Bureau, Information Department, 1959), vol. 3, p. 428.

103. Quoted in Lebra-Chapman, *Rani of Jhansi*, p. 114.

104. Letter from Major-General Hugh Rose, Commanding F.D.A. and Field Forces, to Major-General W. M. Mansfield, Chief of Staff of the Army in India, Gwalior, 22 June 1858, quoted in Rizvi and Bhargava, *Freedom*, vol. 3, p. 388.

105. Lebra-Chapman, *Rani of Jhansi*, p. 19.

106. Joyce C. Lebra, *Women Against the Raj: The Rani of Jhansi Regiment* (Singapore: Institute of Southeast Asian Studies, 2008), p. 90.

107. Singh, *Rani*, p. 164.

108. Ibid., p. 167.

109. Rublack, 'Wench', p. 7.

Chapter 4: Women Regiments

1. The speech is excerpted in 'Pauline Léon', in Lisa L. Moore, Joanna Brooks and Carol Wigginton, eds, *Transatlantic Feminisms in the Age of Revolutions* (Oxford: Oxford University Press, 2012), pp. 242–4.

2. 'Gardons-nous d'intervertir l'ordre de la nature. Elle n'a point destine les femmes à donner la mort; leurs mains delicates ne furent point faites pour manier le fer, ni pour agiter des piques'. Quoted in Gretchen van Slyke, 'Women at War: Skirting the Issue in the French Revolution', *L'Esprit Créateur* 37, no. 1 (1997), p. 38 (my translation).

3. Elisabeth Roudinesco, *Madness and Revolution: The Lives and Legends of Théroigne de Méricourt* trans. Martin Thom (London and New York: Verso, 1991), p. 96.

4. Olwen H. Hufton, *Women and the Limits of Citizenship in the French Revolution* (Toronto: University of Toronto Press, 1992), p. 30.

5. Harriet B. Applewhite and Darline G. Levy, 'Women and Militant Citizenship in Revolutionary Paris', in Sara E. Melzer and Leslie W. Kabine, eds, *Rebel Daughters: Women and the French Revolution* (New York: Oxford University Press, 1992), p. 93.

6. Quoted ibid.

7. Thomas Cardoza and Karen Hagemann, 'History and Memory of Army Women and Female Soldiers', in Karen Hagemann, Stefan Dudink and Sonya O. Rose, eds, *The Oxford Handbook of Gender, War and the Western World since 1600* (Oxford: Oxford University Press, 2020), pp. 182–3.

8. Quoted in Applewhite and Levy, 'Militant Citizenship', p. 95.

9. Quoted ibid., p. 96.

10. Cardoza and Hagemann, 'History and Memory', p. 182.

11. Karen Hagemann, '"Heroic Virgins" and "Bellicose Amazons": Armed Women, the Gender Order and the German Public during and after the Anti-Napoleonic Wars', *European History Quarterly* 37, no. 4 (2007), pp. 520–1.

12. DePauw, *Battle Cries*, p. 116.

13. DeAnne Blanton and Lauren Cook Wike, *They Fought like Demons: Women Soldiers in the American Civil War* (Baton Rouge: Lousiana State University Press, 2002), p. 26.

14. The name was coined by Burton and highlighted in Alpern's book of the same name. Richard F. Burton, *Mission* (London: Tinsley Brothers, 1864), vol. 2, p. 155 ; Stanley B. Alpern, *Amazons of Black Sparta: The Women Warriors of Dahomey* (London: Hurst, 1998), p. 12.

15. Goldstein, *War and Gender*, p. 11.

16. Alpern, *Black Sparta*, p. 6.

17. Goldstein, *War and Gender*, p. 13; Adrienne Mayor, *The Amazons: Lives and Legends of Warrior Women across the Ancient World* (Princeton: Princeton University Press, 2016), p. 72.

18. Frederick E. Forbes, *Dahomey and the Dahomans* (London: Longman, Brown, Green & Longmans, 1851), vol. 1, p. ix.

19. Mary S. Lovell, *A Rage to Live: A Biography of Richard and Isabel Burton* (London: Abacus, 2012), p. 419.

20. Ibid.

21. Robert B. Edgerton, *Warrior Women: The Amazons of Dahomey and the Nature of War* (Boulder: Westview Press, 2000), p. 40.

22. Ibid., p. 32.

23. Alpern, *Black Sparta*, pp. 74–5.

24. *Despatches from Commodore Wilmot Respecting His Visit to the King of Dahomey in December 1862 and January 1863*, presented to UK House of Commons, London, 16 June 1863, p. 5.

25. Ibid.

26. Frederic Martyn, *Life in the Legion, from a Soldier's Point of View* (New York: Scribner's, 1911), p. 207. He qualifies his opinion with a racial slur.

27. Edgerton, *Warrior Women*, p. 18.

28. Edna Bay, *Wives of the Leopard: Gender, Politics and Culture in the Kingdom of Dahomey* (Charlottesville: University of Virginia Press, 1998), p. 201.

29. Robin Law, 'The "Amazons" of Dahomey', *Paideuma* 39 (1993), p. 247. Gaddafi's all-female guard were subject to sexual and physical abuse. On the assassination attempt, see Elizabeth Flock, 'Gaddafi's Female Bodyguards Say They Were Raped, Abused by the Libyan Leader', *Washington Post*, 29 August 2011, https://www.washingtonpost.com/blogs/blogpost/post/gaddafis-female-bodyguards-say-they-were-raped-abused-by-the-libyan-leader/2011/08/29/gIQA8TOKnJ_blog.html; on the sexual abuse see also Martin Chulov, 'Gaddafi's "Amazonian" Bodyguards' Barracks Quashes Myth of Glamour', *Guardian*, 7 September 2011, https://www.theguardian.com/world/2011/sep/07/gaddafis-amazonian-bodyguards-barracks

30. *Despatches from Wilmot*, p. 14.

31. Ibid.

32. Edgerton, *Warrior Women*, p. 21.

33. Law, 'Amazons', p. 253.

34. Edgerton, *Warrior Women*, p. 17.

35. Burton, *Mission*, vol. 1, p. 268.

36. Edgerton, *Warrior Women*, p. 48.

37. Ibid., p. 52.

38. John Duncan, *Travels in Western Africa, in 1845 & 1846*, 2nd edn (London: Richard Bentley, 1847), vol. 1, pp. 232–3.

39. Quoted in Alpern, *Black Sparta*, p. 93.
40. Quoted ibid., p. 92.
41. Duncan, *Travels*, vol. 1, p. 233.
42. Auguste Bouët, as collected by Jean-Claude Nardin, 'La reprise de relations franco-dahoméennes au XIXe siècle: La mission d'Auguste Bouët à la cour d'Abomey (1851)', *Cahiers d'Études Africaines* 7, no. 25 (1967), pp. 59–126.
43. Forbes, *Dahomey*, vol. 2, p. 27.
44. Quoted in Edgerton, *Warrior Women*, p. 26.
45. Ibid., p. 24.
46. Burton, *Mission*, vol. 1, p. 169.
47. Quoted in Alpern, *Black Sparta*, p. 36. We are perhaps lucky that Burton's observations did not include measuring the penises of the men to assess their masculinity, one of his usual practices when travelling (Jeremy Paxman, 'Richard Burton, Victorian Explorer', *Financial Times*, 1 May 2015, https://www.ft.com/content/357140e4-eeaf-11e4-a5cd-00144feab7de).
48. Burton, quoted in Law, 'Amazons', p. 253.
49. Forbes, *Dahomey*, vol. 1, p. 132.
50. Quoted in Edgerton, *Warrior Women*, p. 106.
51. Law, 'Amazons', p. 258.
52. *Despatches from Wilmot*, p. 14.
53. Martyn, *Legion*, p. 233.
54. Ibid., p. 234.
55. Edgerton, *Warrior Women*, p. 24.
56. Martyn, *Legion*, p. 207.
57. Edgerton and Alpern both detail the range of weapons in the Amazon arsenal, and Alpern explains the razor in detail. Edgerton, *Warrior Women*, p. 20, and Alpern, *Black Sparta*, pp. 66–71.
58. Forbes, *Dahomey*, vol. 1, p. 23.
59. Bay, *Wives*, p. 202.
60. Law, 'Amazons', p. 253.
61. Edgerton, *Warrior Women*, p. 96.
62. Ibid., p. 101.
63. Forbes, *Dahomey*, vol. 2, p. 115.
64. Edgerton, *Warrior Women*, p. 100.
65. Ibid., p. 101.
66. Ibid., p. 102.
67. Ibid., pp. 1–5.
68. Ibid., pp. 32, 105.

69. Martyn, *Legion*, p. 233.

70. Ibid., p. 206.

71. Ibid., p. 207.

72. Edgerton, *Warrior Women*, p. 105.

73. Martyn, *Legion*, p. 208.

74. Edgerton, *Warrior Women*, p. 118.

75. Quoted in Alpern, *Black Sparta*, p. 94.

76. Lynne Ellsworth Larsen, 'Wives and Warriors: The Royal Women of Dahomey as Representatives of the Kingdom', in Janell Hobson, ed., *The Routledge Companion to Black Women's Cultural Histories* (London: Routledge, 2021), pp. 227–8.

77. Edgerton, *Warrior Women*, p. 18.

78. Alpern, *Black Sparta*, p. 104.

79. E. Chaudoin, *Trois mois de captivité au Dahomey* (Paris: Hachette, 1891), p. 352.

80. Kirsten M. Keller et al., *Hazing in the U.S. Armed Forces: Recommendations for Hazing Prevention Policy and Practice* (Santa Monica: RAND Corporation, 2015), p. 34.

81. Quoted in Edgerton, *Warrior Women*, p. 104.

82. Ibid.

83. Larsen, 'Wives and Warriors', p. 230.

84. Quoted in Bay, *Wives*, p. 279.

85. Charles E. Mercer, *Legion of Strangers: The Vivid History of a Unique Military Tradition* (New York: Holt, Rinehart & Winston, 1964), p. 168.

Chapter 5: Cross-dressing Soldiers

1. Lynn, *Women, Armies*, p. 165; Peter H. Wilson, 'German Women and War, 1500–1800', *War in History* 3, no. 2 (1996), p. 152.

2. Dugaw, *Balladry*, p. 65.

3. Rudolf M. Dekker and Lotte C. van de Pol, 'Republican Heroines: Cross-dressing Women in the French Revolutionary Armies', *History of European Ideas* 10, no. 3 (1989), p. 358.

4. Hagemann, 'Heroic Virgins', p. 510.

5. Wilson, 'German Women', p. 152; and Slyke, 'Women at War', p. 36.

6. Hagemann, 'Heroic Virgins', p. 514.

7. Fraser Easton, 'Gender's Two Bodies: Women Warriors, Female Husbands and Plebeian Life', *Past & Present* 180, no. 1 (2003), pp. 142–3.

8. Wilson, 'German Women', p. 107.

9. Jane Humphries and Carmen Sarasúa, 'Off the Record: Reconstructing Women's Labor Force Participation in the European Past', *Feminist Economics* 18, no. 4 (2012), p. 46.

10. William W. Gordon, 'Count Casimir Pulaski', *Georgia Historical Society Quarterly* 13, no. 3 (1929), p. 169.

11. Ibid., p. 170.

12. Ibid., p. 178.

13. Ibid., p. 176.

14. Sarah Mervosh, 'Casimir Pulaski, Polish Hero of the Revolutionary War, Was Most Likely Intersex, Researches Say', *New York Times*, 7 April 2019, https://www.nytimes.com/2019/04/07/science/casimir-pulaski-intersex.html

15. Gordon, 'Pulaski', p. 198.

16. John Frederick Lewis, 'Casimir Pulaski', *Pennsylvania Magazine of History and Biography* 55, no. 1 (1931), p. 17.

17. Gordon, 'Pulaski', p. 196.

18. Ibid., p. 222.

19. Angela Pienkos, 'A Bicentennial Look at Casimir Pulaski: Polish, American and Ethnic Folk Hero', *Polish American Studies* 33, no. 1 (1976), p. 10.

20. James S. Pula, 'Whose Bones Are Those?: The Casimir Pulaski Burial Controversy', *Georgia Historical Quarterly* 100, no. 1 (2016), p. 72.

21. Ibid.

22. Dekker and van de Pol, 'Republican Heroines', p. 359.

23. Van Slyke, 'Women at War', p. 36. The decree can be found in Gretchen van Slyke, 'The Sexual and Textual Politics of Dress: Rosa Bonheur and Her Cross-Dressing Permits', *Nineteenth-Century French Studies* 26, no. 3/4 (1998), pp. 321–5 (translation mine). While the idea that banning women from wearing trousers would be a successful way of controlling their movements may seem ridiculous, in fact the French trouser legislation was used later on to restrict the activities of French feminists. Women had to apply for special permission to wear trousers, and this permission was rarely granted. See also Gretchen van Slyke, 'Who Wears the Pants Here? The Policing of Women's Dress in Nineteenth-Century England, Germany and France', *Nineteenth-Century Contexts* 17, no. 1 (1993), pp. 17–33.

24. Dugaw, *Balladry*, p. 3.

25. Ibid., p. 38.

26. Hannah Snell, Christian Davies and Mary Ann Talbot all wrote memoirs.

27. Easton, 'Two Bodies', p. 144.

28. Wheelwright, 'Amazons', p. 129.

29. Hagemann, 'Heroic Virgins', p. 516.

30. Louise Françoise de Houssay, 'A Narrative of the Sufferings of Louise Francoise de Houssay, de Bannes', in Dianne Dugaw, ed., *Memoirs of Scandalous Women* (London: Routledge, 2011), p. 431.

31. Ibid., p. 437.

32. Ibid., p. 438.

33. Dugaw, *Balladry*, p. 127.

34. Thomas W. Laqueur, 'Sex in the Flesh', *Isis* 94, no. 2 (2003), pp. 300–6.

35. Isaac Land, *War, Nationalism, and the British Sailor, 1750–1850* (New York: Springer, 2009), p. 57.

36. Eric Richards, 'Women in the British Economy since about 1700: An Interpretation', *History* 59, no. 197 (1974), p. 339.

37. Peter Earle, 'The Female Labour Market in London in the Late Seventeenth and Early Eighteenth Centuries', *Economic History Review* vol. 42, no. 3 (1989), p. 346.

38. Dugaw, *Balladry*, p. 140.

39. Ibid., p. 123.

40. Hannah Snell, 'The Female Soldier', in Dugaw, ed., *Memoirs of Scandalous Women*, p. 265.

41. Christian Davies, 'The Life and Adventures of Mrs Christian Davies', in Dugaw, ed., *Memoirs of Scandalous Women*, p. 56.

42. Ibid., pp. 93–4.

43. Dugaw, *Balladry*, pp. 125–6.

44. DePauw, 'Women in Combat', pp. 212–13.

45. Berkin, *Revolutionary*, p. 80.

46. Quoted in DePauw, 'Women in Combat', p. 218.

47. DePauw, *Battle Cries*, p. 126.

48. Cardoza and Hagemann, 'History and Memory', p. 193.

49. Ibid.

50. DePauw, *Battle Cries*, p. 147.

51. Quoted in Blanton and Wike, *Demons*, pp. 19–20.

52. Cardoza and Hagemann, 'History and Memory', p. 193.

53. DeAnne Blanton, 'Women Soldiers of the Civil War', *Prologue Magazine* 25, no. 1 (1993), pp. 19–20.

54. Quoted in DePauw, *Battle Cries*, p. 149.

55. Brigid Schulte, 'Women Soldiers Fought, Bled and Died in the Civil War, then Were Forgotten', *Washington Post*, 29 April 2013, https://www.

washingtonpost.com/local/women-soldiers-fought-bled-and-died-in-the-civil-war-then-were-forgotten/2013/04/26/fa722dba-a1a2-11e2-82bc-511538ae90a4_story.html; Blanton and Wike, *Demons*, p. 14.

56. Blanton and Wike, *Demons*, p. 16.

57. Earl J. Hess, *Pickett's Charge: The Last Attack at Gettysburg* (Chapel Hill: University of North Carolina Press, 2001), p. 335.

58. Quoted in James R. Hedtke, *American Civil War: Facts and Fictions* (Santa Barbara: ABC-CLIO, 2018), p. 74. Hedtke notes that there was actually no rule against pregnancy, given that soldiers were supposed to be men.

59. DePauw, *Battle Cries*, p. 150.

60. Ibid.

61. Schulte, 'Women Soldiers'.

62. Hedtke, *Civil War*, p. 63.

63. Blanton and Wike, *Demons*, p. 199.

64. Ibid., p. 18.

65. Gerhard P. Clausius, 'The Little Soldier of the 95th: Albert D. J. Cashier', *Journal of the Illinois State Historical Society* 51, no. 4 (1958), p. 380.

66. Blanton and Wike, *Demons*, p. 17.

67. Rodney O. Davis, 'Private Albert Cashier as Regarded by His/Her Comrades', *Illinois Historical Journal* 82, no. 2 (1989), p. 110.

68. Blanton, 'Women Soldiers'.

69. Davis, 'Cashier', p. 112.

70. Blanton, 'Women Soldiers'.

71. Ibid.

72. Blanton and Wike, *Demons*, p. 169.

73. United States House Committee on Invalid Pensions, 'Sarah E. E. Seelye, Alias Franklin Thompson', H.R. Rep. No. 48, at (1884).

74. Blanton, 'Women Soldiers'.

75. Easton, 'Two Bodies', p. 138.

76. Blanton and Wike, *Demons*, pp. 31–2.

77. Easton, 'Two Bodies', p. 148.

78. Matthew Stephens, *Hannah Snell: The Secret Life of a Female Marine, 1723–1792* (Sutton: Ship Street Press, 1997), loc. 347.

79. Stephens, *Snell*, discusses the evidence for Hannah's wounds, which is equivocal, but her career in the marines is well documented.

80. De Houssay, 'Narrative', p. 423.

81. Easton, 'Two Bodies', p. 148.

82. Dugaw, *Balladry*, p. 107.

83. Blanton and Wike, *Demons*, p. 50.

84. Hacker, 'Reconaissance', p. 659.

85. Wheelwright, 'Amazons', p. 492.

86. Davies, 'Adventures', p. 47.

87. De Houssay, 'Narrative', p. 429.

88. Easton, 'Two Bodies', p. 135.

89. Blanton and Wike, *Demons*, p. 39.

90. Ibid.

91. Ibid., p. 176.

92. Anne-Simone Parent et al., 'The Timing of Normal Puberty and the Age Limits of Sexual Precocity: Variations around the World, Secular Trends, and Changes after Migration', *Endocrine Reviews* 24, no. 5 (2003), p. 673.

93. Blanton and Wike, *Demons*, p. 46.

94. David Hopkin, 'The World Turned Upside Down: Female Soldiers in the French Armies of the Revolutionary and Napoleonic Wars', in Alan Forrest, Karen Hagemann and Jane Rendall, eds, *Soldiers, Citizens and Civilians: Experiences and Perceptions of the Revolutionary and Napoleonic Wars, 1790–1820* (London: Palgrave Macmillan, 2009), p. 83.

95. Blanton and Wike, *Demons*, p. 46.

96. Quoted in Lynn, *Women, Armies*, p. 194.

97. Brigitte Eriksson, 'A Lesbian Execution in Germany, 1721: The Trial Records', *Journal of Homosexuality* 6, no. 1–2 (1981), pp. 31, 33.

98. Ibid., p. 33.

99. Dugaw, *Balladry*, p. 71.

100. Ibid., p. 83.

101. Hopkin, 'Upside Down', p. 81.

102. Ludwig Reiners, *Frederick the Great: A Biography* (New York: Putnam, 1960), p. 17.

103. 'From 1860–1916 the British Army Required Every Soldier to Have a Mustache', *Business Insider*, 22 October 2015, http://www.businessinsider.com/from-1860-1916-the-british-army-required-every-soldier-to-have-a-mustache-2015-10?IR=T

104. Blanton and Wike, *Demons*, p. 195.

105. Ibid., p. 202.

106. Mary Elizabeth Massey, *Women in the Civil War* (Lincoln: University of Nebraska Press, 1994), pp. 78–9, 84. Massey's book was first published in 1966 under the title *Bonnet Brigades, American Women and the Civil War*.

107. Hagemann, 'Heroic Virgins', p. 519.

108. Diana Greene, 'Mid-Nineteenth-Century Domestic Ideology in Russia', in Rosalind J. Marsh, ed., *Women and Russian Culture: Projections and Self-Perceptions* (New York: Bergahn Books, 1998), p. 79.

109. Deborah M. Valenze, *The First Industrial Woman* (New York: Oxford University Press, 1995), pp. 11–12.

Chapter 6: The First World War

1. Dianne Dugaw, 'Female Sailors Bold: Transvestite Heroines and the Markers of Gender and Class', in Margaret Creighton and Lisa Norling, eds, *Iron Men, Wooden Women: Gender and Seafaring in the Atlantic World, 1700–1920* (Baltimore: Johns Hopkins University Press, 1996), p. 53.

2. Thomas Kuhne, 'States, Military Masculinities, and Combat in the Age of World Wars', in Hagemann, Dudink and Rose, eds, *Gender, War and the Western World*, p. 498.

3. Karen Hagemann and Sonya O. Rose, 'War and Gender: The Age of World Wars and its Aftermath – an Overview,', in Hagemann, Dudnik and Rose, eds, *Gender, War and the Western World*, p. 369. The same term appears in German propaganda. Karen Hagemann, 'Home/Front: The Military, Violence and Gender Relations in the Age of the World Wars', in Karen Hagemann and Stefanie Schüler-Springorum, eds, *Home/Front: The Military, War and Gender in Twentieth-Century Germany* (Oxford: Berg, 2002), p. 8.

4. Margaret H. Darrow, 'French Volunteer Nursing and the Myth of War Experience in World War I', *American Historical Review* 101, no. 1 (1996), p. 81.

5. See Karen Hagemann, 'History and Memory of Female Military Service in the Age of World Wars', in Hagemann, Dudnik and Rose, eds, *Gender, War and the Western World*, pp. 470–97.

6. Orr, *French Army*, p. xii.

7. See Kimberly Jensen, *Mobilizing Minerva: American Women in the First World War* (Urbana, OH: University of Illinois Press, 2008), p. 19.

8. Tammy M. Proctor, *Civilians in a World at War, 1914–1918* (New York: New York University Press, 2010), pp. 3–4.

9. Quoted in Lucy Noakes, *Women in the British Army: War and the Gentle Sex, 1907–1948* (London and New York: Routledge, 2006), p. 58.

10. Quoted in Susan R. Grayzel, *Women and the First World War* (London: Routledge, 2002), p. 54.

11. Noakes, *British Army*, p. 58.

12. Marchioness of Londonderry [Edith Vane-Tempest-Stewart], *Retrospect* (London: Frederick Muller, 1938), pp. 112–13.

13. Diane Urquhart, 'Stewart, Edith Helen Vane-Tempest [Née Edith Helen Chaplin], Marchioness of Londonderry (1878–1959), Political Hostess and Writer', in *Oxford Dictionary of National Biography* [online edn], 3 January 2008, https://doi.org/10.1093/ref:odnb/45461

14. Orr, *French Army*, p. 8.

15. Margot Irvine, 'Imagining Women at War: Jane Dieulafoy's 1913 Campaign', *Women in French Studies* 27, no. 1 (2019), p. 119.

16. 'Mme. Jane Dieulafoy Dead', Obituary, *New York Times*, 28 May 1916, https://www.nytimes.com/1916/05/28/archives/mme-jane-dieulafoy-dead-explorer-and-author-fought-francoprussian.html

17. Ibid.

18. Irvine, 'Imagining Women', p. 127.

19. Quoted in Margaret H. Darrow, *French Women and the First World War: War Stories of the Home Front* (Oxford: Berg, 2000), p. 242.

20. Darrow, 'Nursing', p. 85.

21. Darrow, *French Women*, pp. 240–1.

22. 'Women in a Defense Club: Suffragists of Old Orchard, Me., to Learn to Shoot Straight', *New York Times*, 17 February 1916.

23. Lurana Sheldon Ferris, 'The Women's Defense Club', Letter to the Editor, *New York Times*, 31 March 1916.

24. '200 Women Soldiers Give a Public Drill', *New York Times*, 25 March 1916, https://www.nytimes.com/1916/03/25/archives/200-women-soldiers-give-a-public-drill-gen-mrs-millbank-in-stunning.html

25. 'May Wear either Skirts or Breeches: Uniforms for Women's Self-Defense League Are Finally Decided Upon', *New York Times*, 2 May 1916.

26. '200 Women Soldiers'.

27. Ibid.

28. Krisztina Robert, 'Gender, Class, and Patriotism: Women's Paramilitary Units in First World War Britain', *International History Review* 19, no. 1 (1997), p. 53.

29. Darrow, *French Women*, p. 231.

30. Ibid., p. 234.

31. Orr, *French Army*, p. 9. See also Jensen, *Minerva*, p. 212. It should be remembered that the *cantinières* had only very recently been removed from the French army.

32. Hagemann, 'History and Memory', p. 473.

33. Orr, *French Army*, p. 2. Jensen puts this number at 120,000. Kimberley Jensen, 'Volunteers, Auxiliaries, and Women's Mobilization: The First World War and Beyond (1914-1939), in Hacker and Vining, eds, *Companion*, p. 212.

34. Orr, *French Army*, pp. 14–15.

35. Darrow, *French Women*, p. 240.

36. Ibid., p. 248.

37. Helen Boak, *Women in the Weimar Republic* (Manchester: Manchester University Press, 2013), p. 15.

38. Bianca Schönberger, 'Motherly Heroines and Adventurous Girls: Red Cross Nurses and Women Auxiliaries in the First World War', in Hagemann and Schüler-Springorum, eds, *Home/Front*, p. 90.

39. Ibid., pp. 90, 95.

40. Boak, *Weimar Republic*, p. 18.

41. Hagemann, 'History and Memory', p. 476–8

42. Ibid.

43. Proctor, *Civilians*, p. 70.

44. Hagemann, 'History and Memory', p. 476. Proctor (*Civilians*, p. 68) places the number at 16,000.

45. Noakes, *British Army*, p. 68.

46. Ibid., p. 81.

47. Robert, 'Patriotism', 54.

48. Marilyn Lake and Joy Damousi, *Gender and War: Australians at War in the Twentieth Century* (Cambridge: Cambridge University Press, 1995), p. 32; on service in Canada generally see Linda J. Quiney, *This Small Army of Women: Canadian Volunteer Nurses and the First World War* (Vancouver: UBC Press, 2017).

49. Helen Gwynne-Vaughan, *Service with the Army* (London: Hutchinson, 1941), p. 16.

50. Ibid., p. 17; Nancy Loring Goldman and Richard Stites, 'Great Britain and the World Wars', in Nancy Loring Goldman, ed., *Female Soldiers – Combatants or Noncombatants?: Historical and Contemporary Perspectives* (Westport: Greenwood Press, 1982), p. 27.

51. Noakes, *British Army*, p. 69.

52. Quoted ibid., p. 65.

53. Ibid.

54. Quoted in Schönberger, 'Motherly Heroines', p. 97.

55. Quoted in Orr, *French Army*, p. 18.

56. Noakes, *British Army*, p. 77. The French, needless to say, perceived the English as sources of vice and licentiousness; a famous phrasebook for

English soldiers that included phrases such as 'Permettez moi de vous baiser la main – de vous embrasser' (allow me to kiss you on the hand – kiss you) created a furore in France. Susan R. Grayzel, 'Mothers, Marraines, and Prostitutes: Morale and Morality in First World War France', *International History Review* 19, no. 1 (1997), p. 77.

57. Gwynne-Vaughan, *Service with the Army*, p. 50.
58. Noakes, *British Army*, p. 80.
59. Goldman and Stites, 'Great Britain', p. 27.
60. Hagemann, 'History and Memory', p. 473.
61. Schönberger, 'Motherly Heroines', p. 97.
62. 'The "Physical Force" Fallacy', *Votes for Women*, 12 March 1909, p. 425
63. Quoted in Noakes, *British Army*, p. 41.
64. Quoted in Schönberger, 'Motherly Heroines', p. 87.
65. See Rosalie Maggio, *Marie Marvingt, Fiancée of Danger: First Female Bomber Pilot, World-Class Athlete and Inventor of the Air Ambulance* (Jefferson: McFarland, 2019).
66. Ibid., p. 16.
67. Ibid.
68. Darrow, *French Women*, p. 240.
69. Maggio, *Marvingt*, p. 78.
70. Alison S. Fell, *Women as Veterans in Britain and France after the First World War* (Cambridge: Cambridge University Press, 2018), p. 86.
71. Ibid.; Maggio, *Marvingt*, p. 79.
72. Maggio, *Marvingt*, p. 80; Elisabeth Shipton, *Female Tommies: The Frontline Women of the First World War* (Cheltenham: The History Press, 2014), p. 66.
73. Maggio, *Marvingt*, p. 80.
74. Ibid., p. 81.
75. Ibid., pp. 89–90.
76. Fell, *Women as Veterans*, p. 87.
77. Maggio, *Marvingt*, p. 78.
78. Quoted in Janet Lee, 'A Nurse and a Soldier: Gender, Class and National Identity in the First World War Adventures of Grace Mcdougall and Flora Sandes', *Women's History Review* 15, no. 1 (2006), p. 94.
79. Quoted in Louise Miller, *A Fine Brother: The Life of Captain Flora Sandes* (Richmond, Surrey: Alma Books, 2012), p. 94.
80. Flora Sandes, *An English Woman-Sergeant in the Serbian Army* (London: Hodder & Stoughton, 1916), p. 70.
81. G. Gordon-Smith, 'The Retreat of the Serbian Army', *Current History* 11, no. 1 (March 1920), pp. 472–81.

82. A. Tomić, 'Past Imperfect Continuous: Remembering Serbia's 1915 Retreat 100 Years Later', doctoral thesis, University of Leiden, 2021.

83. Miller, *Fine Brother*, p. 115.

84. Quoted ibid., p. 146.

85. Flora Sandes, *The Autobiography of a Woman Soldier: A Brief Record of Adventure with the Serbian Army, 1916–1919* (London: H. R. & G. Witherby, 1927), p. 29.

86. 'Wounded English Girl Wins Serbian Cross', *New York Times*, 31 December 1916, p. 3.

87. Sandes, *Autobiography*, p. 65.

88. Shipton, *Female Tommies*, p. 129–32.

89. Sandes, *Autobiography*, p. 65.

90. Miller, *Fine Brother*, p. 165.

91. 'Wounded English Girl', p. 3.

92. Miller, *Fine Brother*, p. 168.

93. See Lee, 'Nurse and a Soldier', 96; Angela Smith, *British Women of the Eastern Front: War, Writing and Experience in Serbia and Russia, 1914–20* (Manchester: Manchester University Press, 2016), p. 96.

94. Miller, *Fine Brother*, p. 110.

95. Sandes, *Autobiography*, p. 76.

96. Quoted in Miller, *Fine Brother*, p. 214.

97. Sandes, *Autobiography*, pp. 195–6.

98. Quoted in Joshua Alexander Sanborn, 'Drafting the Nation: Military Conscription and the Formation of a Modern Polity in Tsarist and Soviet Russia, 1905–1925', PhD thesis, University of Chicago, 1998, pp. 412–13.

99. Laurie Stoff, 'They Fought for the Homeland: Russia's Women Soldiers of the First World War', PhD thesis, University of Kansas, 2002, p. 43; Melissa Stockdale ('"My Death for the Motherland Is Happiness": Women, Patriotism, and Soldiering in Russia's Great War, 1914–1917', *American Historical Review* 109, no. 1 (2004), p. 85) puts the number of approved women as at least 49, with as many as 400 actually fighting.

100. Stoff, 'Homeland', p. 44.

101. Ibid., p. 48.

102. Stockdale, 'Motherland', p. 86.

103. Nadezhda Durova, *The Cavalry Maid: The Memoirs of a Woman Soldier of 1812*, trans. John Mersereau Jr and David Lapeza (Ann Arbor: Ardis, 1988), p. 52.

104. 'Young Girls Fighting on the Russian Front', *Current History* 4, no. 2 (1916), pp. 365–7.

105. Graydon Tunstall, *Blood on the Snow: The Carpathian Winter War of 1915* (Lawrence: University Press of Kansas, 2010), p. 12.

106. 'Young Girls Fighting', pp. 365–7.

107. Richard Stites, *The Women's Liberation Movement in Russia: Feminism, Nihilism, and Bolshevism, 1860–1930* (Princeton: Princeton University Press, 1991), p. 280; Stockdale, 'Motherland', p. 85.

108. Stoff, 'Homeland', p. 55.

109. Ibid., p. 60.

110. Ibid., p. 54.

111. Quoted in Grayzel, *First World War*, p. 136.

112. Rheta Childe Dorr, *Inside the Russian Revolution* (New York: Macmillan, 1917), p. 78.

113. Ibid., pp. 80–1.

114. Stoff, 'Homeland', p. 43.

115. Greene, 'Domestic Ideology', p. 66.

116. Peter H. Lindert and Steven Nafziger, 'Russian Inequality on the Eve of Revolution', *Journal of Economic History* 74, no. 3 (2014), p. 774.

117. Stoff, 'Homeland', p. 89.

118. Quoted in Stockdale, 'Motherland', p. 93.

119. Stoff, 'Homeland', p. 145.

120. Ibid., p. 167.

121. Ibid., p. 212.

122. Stites, *Women's Liberation*, p. 298.

123. *Daily Telegraph* quoted in 'Those Russian Women', *Literary Digest*, 29 September 1917, p. 53.

124. Stoff, 'Homeland', pp. 107–8.

125. Ibid., p. 114.

126. Maria Bochkareva, *Yashka: My Life as Peasant, Exile and Soldier* (London: Constable & Co., 1919), p. 163.

127. Dorr, *Russian Revolution*, p. 58.

128. Stoff, 'Homeland', p. 58.

129. Stockdale, 'Motherland', p. 92.

130. Grayzel, *First World War*, p. 55.

131. Stoff, 'Homeland', p. 160.

132. W. G. Shepherd, 'Russian Girls Pledged to Kill Themselves if Captured', *UPI*, 30 July 1917.

133. Stockdale, 'Motherland', p. 107.

134. Dorr, *Russian Revolution*, p. 76.

135. Jensen, *Minerva*, ch. 4.

136. Bessie Beatty, 'Classic Dispatches: The Battalion of Death', *Quarterly Journal of Military History* 32, no. 2 (2020), p. 78.

137. Ibid., p. 81.

138. Ibid.

139. Stites, *Women's Liberation*, p. 297.

140. Alfred William Fortescue Knox, *With the Russian Army, 1914–1917: Being Chiefly Extracts from the Diary of a Military Attaché* (London: Hutchinson & Co., 1921), vol. 2, p. 704.

141. Ibid., p. 319.

142. On the defense in general, see Stockdale, 'Motherland', pp. 109–10. Various online sources assume that it was the Battalion of Death at the Winter Palace, but it was in fact the Petrograd Battalion, a confusion possibly created by the memoir left by Maria Bocharnikova, whose name was similar to Bochkareva's. See Stoff, 'Homeland', pp. 169–71, 229.

143. Quoted in Richard Abraham, 'Mariia L. Bochkareva and the Russian Amazons of 1917', in Linda Edmondson, ed., *Women and Society in Russia and the Soviet Union* (Cambridge: Cambridge University Press, 1992), p. 124.

144. Ibid., p. 131; Stockdale, 'Motherland', p. 109.

145. Knox, *Russian Army*, vol. 2, p. 712.

146. Stoff, 'Homeland', p. 243.

147. Ibid., p. 242.

148. Quoted in Abraham, 'Bochkareva', p. 140.

149. George L. Mosse, *Fallen Soldiers: Reshaping the Memory of the World Wars* (New York: Oxford University Press, 1990), p. 3.

150. Ibid., p. 7.

151. Ibid., p. 61.

152. Joanna Bourke, *An Intimate History of Killing: Face-to-Face Violence in Twentieth-Century Warfare* (London: Granta Books, 1999).

153. 'Lieut. Flora Sandes', *Queensland Times* (Ipswich), 20 September 1920, p. 4.

154. Jensen, *Minerva*, p. 19.

155. Noakes, *British Army*, p. 59.

Chapter 7: The Soviet Union in the Second World War

1. 'Amy Johnson's Great Feat', *Sydney Morning Herald*, 26 May 1930.

2. Reina Pennington, 'Raskova, Marina Mikhailovna Malinina', in Reina Pennington and Robin Higham, eds, *Amazons to Fighter Pilots: A*

Biographical Dictionary of Military Women (Westport: Greenwood Press, 2003), vol. 2, p. 352.

3. 'Valentina S. Grizodubova, 83, a Pioneer Aviator for the Soviets', *New York Times*, 1 May 1993, https://www.nytimes.com/1993/05/01/obituaries/valentina-s-grizodubova-83-a-pioneer-aviator-for-the-soviets.html

4. Giles Whittell, *Spitfire Women of World War II* (London: Harper Perennial, 2008), p. 44.

5. Anna Krylova, *Soviet Women in Combat: A History of Violence on the Eastern Front* (Cambridge: Cambridge University Press, 2011), p. 11.

6. Beate Fieseler, M. Michaela Hampf and Jutta Schwarzkopf, 'Gendering Combat: Military Women's Status in Britain, the United States, and the Soviet Union During the Second World War', *Women's Studies International Forum* 47 (2014), p. 116.

7. The exact numbers are a matter of dispute between historians, ranging from between 500,000 and 1 million. Krylova (*Soviet Women*, p. 3) puts the number at 520,000; Roger D. Markwick and Euridice Charon Cardona (*Soviet Women on the Frontline in the Second World War* (London: Palgrave Macmillan, 2012, p. 1)) at 1 million; and Kazimiera Cottam (*Women in War and Resistance: Selected Biographies of Soviet Women Soldiers* (Nepean, Ont.: New Military Publishers, 1998, p. xx) at 800,000. Reina Pennington ('Offensive Women: Women in Combat in the Red Army in the Second World War', *Journal of Military History* 74, no. 3 (2010), p. 782) asserts that most Soviet sources put the number at 800,000, and that the reason for the discrepancy in numbers is because the Soviets did not keep a separate track of women.

8. Fieseler, Hampf and Schwarzkopf, 'Gendering Combat', p. 116.

9. Krylova, *Soviet Women*, p. 10.

10. Svetlana Alexievich, *The Unwomanly Face of War*, trans. Richard Pevear and Larissa Volokhonsky (London: Penguin, 2017), p. xii.

11. Barbara Alpern Engel, 'The Womanly Face of War: Soviet Women Remember World War II', in Nicole Ann Drombowski, ed., *Women and War in the Twentieth Century: Enlisted with or without Consent* (London and New York: Routledge, 1999), p. 142 on the rifle, p. 140 on decorations.

12. Krylova, *Soviet Women*, p. 291.

13. Ibid., p. 118.

14. A. E. Griesse and R. Stites, 'Russia: Revolution and War', in Goldman, ed., *Combatants or Noncombatants?*, p. 70.

15. Britain mobilised 2 per cent of women and the United States 0.13 per cent. The Soviets mobilised only 0.8 per cent of women. Fieseler, Hampf and Schwarzkopf, 'Gendering Combat', p. 116.

16. Krylova, *Soviet Women*, p. 27.

17. Ibid., p. 28.

18. Markwick and Cardona, *Soviet Women*, p. 98.

19. Krylova, *Soviet Women*, p. 93.

20. Alexievich, *Unwomanly Face*, p. 78.

21. Ibid., p. 86.

22. See Wendy Z. Goldman, *Women, the State and Revolution: Soviet Family Policy and Social Life* (Cambridge: Cambridge University Press, 1993).

23. Thomas G. Schrand, 'Soviet "Civic-minded Women" in the 1930s: Gender, Class and Industrialization in a Socialist Society', *Journal of Women's History* 11, no. 3 (1999), p. 130.

24. Ibid., p. 131.

25. Markwick and Cardona, *Soviet Women*, p. 88.

26. Melanie Ilic, *Women Workers in the Soviet Interwar Economy: From 'Protection' to 'Equality'* (New York: Springer, 1998), p. 37.

27. Thomas G. Schrand, 'The Five-Year Plan for Women's Labour: Constructing Socialism and the "Double Burden", 1930–1932', *Europe-Asia Studies* 51, no. 8 (1999), pp. 1455–78.

28. Ilic, *Women Workers*, p. 140.

29. Sue Bridger, 'The Heirs of Pasha: The Rise and Fall of the Soviet Woman Tractor Driver', in Linda Edmondson, ed., *Gender in Russian History and Culture* (London: Palgrave Macmillan, 2001), pp. 195, 196.

30. Krylova, *Soviet Women*, p. 52.

31. Alexievich, *Unwomanly Face*, p. 27.

32. Reina Pennington, '586th Fighter Aviation Regiment', in Pennington and Higham, eds, *Amazons to Fighter Pilots*, vol. 2, p. 521.

33. Reina Pennington, 'Litviak, Lidiia Vladimirovna', in Pennington and Higham, eds, *Amazons to Fighter Pilots*, vol. 1, p. 261.

34. Markwick and Cardona, *Soviet Women*, p. 114.

35. Kazimiera J. Cottam, '46th Taman'sky Guards Bomber Aviation Regiment', in Pennington and Higham, eds, *Amazons to Fighter Pilots*, vol. 2, p. 513.

36. Alexievich, *Unwomanly Face*, p. 194.

37. Cottam, 'Taman'sky', pp. 513–14.

38. Markwick and Cardona, *Soviet Women*, p. 97.

39. Douglas Martin, 'Nadezhda Popova, WWII "Night Witch," Dies at 91', *New York Times*, 14 July 2013, https://www.nytimes.com/2013/07/15/world/europe/nadezhda-popova-ww-ii-night-witch-dies-at-91.html

40. Alexievich, *Unwomanly Face*, p. 194.

41. Ibid., p. 195.

42. Markwick and Cardona, *Soviet Women*, p. 98.

43. Ibid., p. 153.

44. Ibid., p. 154.

45. Ibid., p. 243.

46. Alexievich, *Unwomanly Face*, p. 66.

47. Krylova, *Soviet Women*, p. 174.

48. Alexievich, *Unwomanly Face*, p. 213.

49. Markwick and Cardona, *Soviet Women*, p. 217.

50. Krylova, *Soviet Women*, p. 163.

51. Markwick and Cardona, *Soviet Women*, p. 473.

52. Ibid.

53. Yulia Zhukova, *Girl with a Sniper Rifle*, trans. David Foreman [Kindle edn] (London: Greenhill Books, 1995), p. 131.

54. Alexievich, *Unwomanly Face*, p. 307.

55. Ibid., pp. 307–8.

56. Quoted in Markwick and Cardona, *Soviet Women*, p. 466. The translation in Markwick and Cardona is more fluent than the more recent English-language version of Zhukova's memoir *Sniper*.

57. Alexievich, *Unwomanly Face*, pp. 191–2.

58. Roger R. Reese, *Why Stalin's Soldiers Fought: The Red Army's Military Effectiveness in World War II* (Lawrence: University Press of Kansas, 2011), p. 299.

59. Alexievich, *Unwomanly Face*, p. 235.

60. Ibid., p. 241.

61. Markwick and Cardona, *Soviet Women*, p. 199.

62. Alexander Hill, *The Red Army and the Second World War* (Cambridge: Cambridge University Press, 2016), p. 329.

63. Alexievich, *Unwomanly Face*, p. 236.

64. Ibid., p. 237.

65. 'Natalia Peshkova', I Remember, 2010, https://iremember.ru/en/memoirs

66. Engel, 'Womanly Face', p. 143.

67. 'Mariana Milyutina', I Remember, 2010, https://iremember.ru/en/memoirs

68. Alexievich, *Unwomanly Face*, p. 238.

69. Ibid., p. 86.

70. Ibid., p. 14.

71. See Reina Pennington, '"Do Not Speak of the Services You Rendered": Women Veterans of Aviation in the Soviet Union', *Journal of Slavic Military*

Studies 9, no. 1 (1996), pp. 120–51; Markwick and Cardona, *Soviet Women*, p. 234.

72. Library of Congress Federal Research Division, *Soviet Union: Country Study*, ed. Raymond E. Zickel, Area Handbook Series (Washington, DC: US Government Publishing Office, 1991), p. 119.

73. Pennington, 'Do Not Speak', p. 144.

74. Engel, 'Womanly Face', p. 149.

75. Mark Edele, *Soviet Veterans of the Second World War: A Popular Movement in an Authoritarian Society, 1941–1991* (Oxford: Oxford University Press), pp. 139–40.

76. Suzanne Conze and Beate Fieseler, 'Soviet Women as Comrades-in-Arms: A Blind Spot in the History of War', in Robert W. Thurston and Bernd Bonwetsch, eds, *The People's War: Responses to World War II in the Soviet Union* (Urbana, OH: University of Illinois Press, 2000), p. 225.

77. The Moscow victory parade was entirely male. Carmen Scheide, 'Unstintingly Master Warfare: Women in the Red Army', in Melanie Ilic (ed.), *The Palgrave Handbook of Women and Gender in Twentieth-Century Russia and the Soviet Union* (London: Palgrave Macmillan, 2018), pp. 223–38; Conze and Fieseler, 'Comrades-in-Arms', p. 226.

78. Markwick and Cardona, *Soviet Women*, p. 233.

79. Alexievich, *Unwomanly Face*, pp. 248–9.

80. Ibid., p. 329.

81. Quoted in Engel, 'Womanly Face', p. 154.

82. The speech, of 26 July 1945, is reproduced in Mikhail Kalinin, 'Glorious Daughters of the Soviet People', in *On Communist Education: Selected Speeches and Articles* (Moscow: Foreign Languages Publishing, 1950), pp. 455–60.

83. Engel, 'Womanly Face', p. 149.

84. George H. Quester, 'Women in Combat', *International Security* 1, no. 4 (1977), pp. 80–91.

85. The United States government commissioned multiple inquiries into the question of women in combat beginning in 1982, and recurring until 2013 when combat roles were opened to women. These inquiries will be analysed in greater depth in Chapters 12 and 13 below.

86. Reese, *Stalin's Soldiers*, p. 305.

87. Herres and Members of the Commission, *Assignment of Women*, p. 46.

88. Ibid., p. C-29.

89. Cottam, *Women in War*, p. 232.

90. Markwick and Cardona, *Soviet Women*, pp. 52–3.
91. Herres and Members of the Commission, *Assignment of Women*, p. 46.
92. Ibid.

Chapter 8: Britain in the Second World War

1. Susan Ottaway, *Violette Szabo: The Life That I Have* (Annapolis: Naval Institute Press, 2002), p. 115.
2. Noakes, *British Army*, p. 92.
3. Vera Di Campli San Vito, 'Allen, Mary Sophia (1878–1964), Police Officer', in *Oxford Dictionary of National Biography* [online edn], 8 October 2020, https://doi.org/10.1093/ref:odnb/39176
4. Nina Boyd, *From Suffragette to Fascist: The Many Lives of Mary Sophia Allen* (New York: The History Press, 2013), p. 6.
5. Jeremy A. Crang, 'The Revival of the British Women's Auxiliary Services in the Late Nineteen-Thirties', *Historical Research* 83, no. 220 (2010), pp. 343–57.
6. Jeremy A. Crang, *Sisters in Arms* (Cambridge: Cambridge University Press, 2020), p. 12.
7. Noakes, *British Army*, p. 99.
8. Urquhart, 'Stewart, Edith Helen Vane-Tempest'.
9. Crang, *Sisters in Arms*, p. 11.
10. Quoted in Noakes, *British Army*, p. 96.
11. Quoted in Crang, *Sisters in Arms*, p. 14. 'Leslie the Lion' was also a member of Lady Londonderry's Ark society.
12. Ibid., p. 22.
13. Crang, 'Revival', p. 356.
14. Quoted in Noakes, *British Army*, p. 100.
15. Quoted ibid.
16. Ibid., p. 101.
17. Winston Churchill, Prime Minister, Hansard, HC vol. 376, col. 1036 (2 December 1941).
18. Crang, *Sisters in Arms*, p. 68.
19. Ibid., p. 20.
20. Ibid., p. 237.
21. Anne De Courcy, *Debs at War 1939–1945: How Wartime Changed Their Lives* (London: Weidenfeld & Nicolson), p. 220.
22. Jo Stanley, *A History of the Royal Navy: Women and the Royal Navy* (London:

I. B. Tauris, 2019), p. 90. The WRNS gained military status in April 1941.

23. Ibid., p. 89.

24. Hannah Roberts, *The WRNS in Wartime: The Women's Royal Naval Service, 1917–1945*, 1st edn (London: I. B. Tauris, 2019), p. 78.

25. Ibid., pp. 78, 110.

26. De Courcy, *Debs at War*, p. 66.

27. Crang, *Sisters in Arms*, p. 36.

28. 'Recruiting for the A.T.S.', *The Times*, 21 November 1941.

29. Noakes, *British Army*, p. 108.

30. Mass Observation Archive, File Report 955 – ATS (November 1941), 4.

31. Ibid., 3.

32. Ibid., 16.

33. Ibid., 17.

34. Ibid.

35. Noakes, *British Army*, p. 114.

36. Quoted in Gerard J. DeGroot, 'Whose Finger on the Trigger? Mixed Anti-Aircraft Batteries and the Female Combat Taboo', *War in History* 4, no. 4 (1 October 1997), p. 434.

37. Agnes Hardie, MP for Glasgow, Springburn, Hansard, HC vol. 376, col. 1079 (2 December 1941).

38. Eleanor Rathbone, MP for Combined English Universities, Hansard, HC vol. 376, col. 1088 (2 December 1941).

39. Noakes, *British Army*, p. 115.

40. Crang, *Sisters in Arms*, p. 95; Roberts, *WRNS*, ch. 4.

41. Thelma Cazalet-Keir, MP for Islington East, Hansard, HC vol. 377, col. 1042 (3 February 1942).

42. Quoted in Crang, *Sisters in Arms*, p. 26.

43. Helen Jones, 'Markham, Violet Rosa (1872–1951), Public Servant', in *Oxford Dictionary of National Biography* [online edn], 23 September 2004, https://doi.org/10.1093/ref:odnb/34881

44. Violet Markham et al., *Report of the Committee on Amenities and Welfare Conditions in the Three Women's Services* (London: HM Stationery Office, 1942), p. 49.

45. Gerard J. DeGroot, '"I Love the Scent of Cordite in Your Hair": Gender Dynamics in Mixed Anti-Aircraft Batteries during the Second World War', *History* 82, no. 265 (1997), p. 81.

46. De Courcy, *Debs at War*, p. 159.

47. Ibid., p. 216.

48. Ibid., p. 95.

49. Whittell, *Spitfire*, p. 54.

50. Julie Fountain, '"The Most Interesting Work a Woman Can Perform in Wartime": The Exceptional Status of British Women Pilots During the Second World War', *Cultural and Social History* 13, no. 2 (2016), pp. 215–16.

51. Shelley Saywell, *Women in War* (New York: Viking, 1985), p. 8.

52. Helena Schrader, *Sisters in Arms: The Women Who Flew in World War II* (Philadelphia: Casemate Publishers, 2006), p. 188.

53. Saywell, *Women in War*, p. 5; Nigel Fountain, 'Lettice Curtis Obituary', *Guardian*, 27 July 2014, https://www.theguardian.com/world/2014/jul/27/lettice-curtis

54. Whittell, *Spitfire*, p. 97.

55. Ibid., pp. 98–9.

56. Fountain, 'Curtis'.

57. Saywell, *Women in War*, p. 7.

58. Fountain, 'Interesting Work', p. 217.

59. Jonathan Glancey, 'Diana Barnato Walker', *Guardian*, 8 May 2020, https://www.theguardian.com/uk/2008/may/08/military.gender; Fountain, 'Interesting Work', p. 218.

60. Saywell, *Women in War*, p. 4.

61. De Courcy, *Debs at War*, p. 225.

62. Saywell, *Women in War*, p. 21.

63. Diana Barnato in De Courcy, *Debs at War*, p. 224.

64. Saywell, *Women in War*, p. 1.

65. Ibid., p. 9.

66. Whittell, *Spitfire*, p. 196.

67. Saywell, *Women in War*, p. 21.

68. Fountain, 'Interesting Work', p. 213.

69. Glancey, 'Walker'.

70. Saywell, *Women in War*, p. 19.

71. Ibid., p. 20.

72. Ibid.

73. Ibid.

74. Whittell, *Spitfire*, p. 193.

75. 'Gen. Sir Frederick Pile Dies; Led British Antiaircraft in War', *New York Times*, 15 November 1976, https://www.nytimes.com/1976/11/15/archives/gen-sir-frederick-pile-dies-led-british-antiaircraft-in-war.html

76. General Sir Frederick Pile, *Ack-Ack: Britain's Defence against Air Attack during the Second World War* (London: George G. Harrap, 1949), p. 186.

77. Ibid., p. 187.

78. Ibid., p. 188.

79. D'Ann Campbell, 'Women in Combat: The World War II Experience in the United States, Great Britain, Germany and the Soviet Union', *Journal of Military History* 57, no. 2 (1993), p. 306; Jutta Schwarzkopf, 'Combatant or Non-combatant? The Ambiguous Status of Women in British Anti-Aircraft Batteries During the Second World War', *War & Society* 28, no. 2 (2009), p. 111.

80. Winston S. Churchill, *The Second World War*, vol. 3, *The Grand Alliance* (London: Cassell, 1971), p. 754.

81. Noakes, *British Army*, p. 119.

82. Pile, *Ack-Ack*, p. 188.

83. Schwarzkopf, 'Combatant or Non-combatant?', p. 112.

84. Ibid., p. 119.

85. Pile, *Ack-Ack*, p. 187.

86. Ibid., p. 189.

87. Ibid., p. 192.

88. Saywell, *Women in War*, p. 18.

89. Campbell, 'Women in Combat', p. 306.

90. Saywell, *Women in War*, p. 18.

91. Ibid., p. 17.

92. J. W. Naylor, 'Mixed Batteries', *Journal of the Royal Artillery* 69, no. 3 (1942), p. 200.

93. Ibid.

94. Ibid., p. 206.

95. Crang, *Sisters in Arms*, p. 237.

96. De Groot, 'Whose Finger?', p. 436.

97. Quoted ibid., p. 446.

98. Ibid., p. 447.

99. Saywell, *Women in War*, p. 24.

100. Ibid., p. 11.

101. Ibid.

102. *Yorkshire Post and Leeds Intelligencer*, 21 April 1942.

103. Sarah E. Paterson, *The Auxiliary Territorial Service in the Second World War* (London: Imperial War Museum, 2003), p. 1, http://archive.iwm.org.uk/upload/pdf/Info42.pdf

104. Pile, *Ack-Ack*, p. 193.

105. De Groot, 'Whose Finger?', p. 436.

106. Ibid., p. 95.

107. Crang, *Sisters in Arms*, p. 69.

108. De Groot, 'Whose Finger?', p. 445.

109. Pile, *Ack-Ack*, p. 226.

110. DeGroot, 'Cordite', p. 84.

111. Pile, *Ack-Ack*, p. 194.

112. Ibid., p. 228.

113. M. R. D. Foot, *SOE: An Outline History of the Special Operations Executive, 1940–1946* (London: Pimlico, 1999), loc. 1338. There was in fact nothing specifically illegal about using women in combat operations, but any person (male or female) acting as an irregular combatant would not be subject to the protections usually afforded to soldiers under the laws of war, including prisoner-of-war status.

114. Rita Kramer, *Flames in the Field: The Story of Four SOE Agents in Occupied France* (London: Penguin, 1996), pp. 65–6.

115. Paul Vitello, 'Nancy Wake, Proud Spy and Nazi Foe, Dies at 98', *New York Times* 13 August 2011, https://www.nytimes.com/2011/08/14/world/europe/14wake.html

116. Foot, *Outline History*, loc. 1339.

117. Ibid., loc. 1406.

118. Ibid, loc. 1428.

119. Ibid, loc. 1459.

120. Selwyn Jepson, oral history interview with Conrad Wood, 3 July 1986, Imperial War Museum, no. 9331.

121. David Hebditch, *Covert Radio Agents, 1939–1945: Signals from behind Enemy Lines* (Barnsley: Pen & Sword, 2021), p. vii.

122. Marcus Binney, *The Women Who Lived for Danger* (London: Hodder & Stoughton, 2002), loc. 2751.

123. Ibid., loc. 2777.

124. M. R. D. Foot, 'Witherington [married name Cornioley], (Cecile) Pearl (1914–2008), Special Operations Officer', in *Oxford Dictionary of National Biography* [online edn], 5 January 2012, https://doi.org/10.1093/ref:odnb/99822

125. Ibid.

126. Quoted in Binney, *Women*, loc. 2969.

127. Nancy Wake, *The Autobiography of the Woman the Gestapo Called the White Mouse* (South Melbourne: Macmillan, 1985), p. 148.

128. Graeme Leech, 'Fearless Matriarch of Resistance', *The Australian*, 9 August 2011, https://www.theaustralian.com.au/news/inquirer/fearless-matriarch-of-resistance/news-story/04b8b68e785a9578e2db9dd19d17b702

129. Adam Bernstein, 'Nancy Wake, "White Mouse" of World War II, Dies at 98', *Washington Post*, 9 August 2011, https://www.washingtonpost.com/local/obituaries/nancy-wake-white-mouse-of-world-war-ii-dies-at-98/2011/08/08/gIQABvPT5I_story.html

130. Wake, *White Mouse*, p. 135.

131. Ibid.

132. Leech, 'Matriarch'.

133. Wake, *White Mouse*, p. 142.

134. Bernstein, 'Wake'.

135. M. R. D. Foot, *SOE in France: An Account of the Work of the British Special Operations Executive in France, 1940–1944* (London: HM Stationery Office, 1966).

136. Ibid.

137. Binney, *Women*, loc. 190.

138. Beryl E. Escott, 'Women Agents on Active Service in France (Act. 1942–1944)', in *Oxford Dictionary of National Biography* [online edn], 23 September 2004, 2015, https://doi.org/10.1093/ref:odnb/67691 Towards the end of the war women were permitted to serve overseas.

139. Juliette Pattinson, '"Playing the Daft Lassie with Them": Gender, Captivity and the Special Operations Executive During the Second World War', *European Review of History* 13, no. 2 (2006), p. 276.

140. Escott, 'Women Agents'.

141. M. Tillotson and M. R. D. Foot, *SOE and the Resistance: As Told in* The Times *Obituaries* (London: Bloomsbury, 2011), p. 176.

142. Binney, *Women*, loc. 176.

143. Anastasie told his story to the leader of the resistance group, Philippe Liewer, who passed it to the British authorities. Binney, *Women*, loc 3504.

144. Ibid.

145. Campbell, 'Women in Combat', p. 312.

146. E. H. Carter, 'The Mixed Battery: To the Editor of the Times', *The Times*, 5 July 1943.

147. Crang, *Sisters in Arms*, p. 204.

148. Schwarzkopf, 'Combatant or Non-combatant?', p. 127.

149. Clare Walker, 'Obituary – Lettice Curtis', Royal Aeronautical Society, 15 October 2014, https://web.archive.org/web/20211006163846/https://www.aerosociety.com/news/obituary-lettice-curtis/

150. Fountain, 'Curtis'.

151. Walker, 'Curtis'.

152. Fountain, 'Interesting Work', p. 224.

153. Ibid., p. 225.
154. Ibid., p. 223.

Chapter 9: Germany and the United States in the Second World War

1. Elizabeth D. Heineman, 'Whose Mothers? Generational Difference, War, and the Nazi Cult of Motherhood', *Journal of Women's History* 12, no. 4 (2001), p. 145.

2. Louise Willmot, 'Women in the Third Reich: The Auxiliary Military Service Law of 1944', *German History* 2, no. 1 (1985), pp. 10–20; Perry Biddiscombe, 'Into the Maelstrom: German Women in Combat, 1944–45', *War and Society* 30, no. 1 (2011), pp. 61–89.

3. Adolf Hitler, 'Speech to the National Socialist Women's League', 8 September 1934, German History in Documents and Images (GHDI), https://ghdi.ghi-dc.org/sub_document.cfm?document_id=1557

4. Ute Frevert, *Women in German History: From Bourgeois Emancipation to Sexual Liberation*, trans. Stuart McKinnon-Evans, Terry Bond and Barbara Norden (New York: Berg, 1993), p. 208.

5. Jill Stephenson, 'The Home Front in "Total War": Women in Germany and Britain in the Second World War', in Roger Chickering, Stig Förster and Bernd Greiner, eds, *A World at Total War: Global Conflict and the Politics of Destruction, 1937–1945* (Cambridge: Cambridge University Press, 2004), pp. 212, 27.

6. Lisa Pine, 'German Women and the Home Front in the Second World War: Daily Life, Work and the Impact of War', *Women's History Review* 26, no. 4 (2017), p. 640; Jill Stephenson, *Women in Nazi Germany* (Harlow: Longman, 2001), p. 55.

7. Karen Hagemann, 'Military, War and the Mainstreams: Gendering Modern German Military History', in Karen Hagemann and Jean H. Quataert, eds, *Gendering Modern German History: Rewriting Historiography* (New York: Berghahn Books, 2007), p. 74. Stephenson, 'Home Front', p. 155.

8. Edward B. Westermann, *Flak: German Anti-Aircraft Defenses 1914–1945* (Lawrence: University Press of Kansas, 2001), p. 186.

9. Biddiscombe, 'Maelstrom', p. 68.

10. H. W. Koch, *The Hitler Youth: Origins and Development 1922–45* (New York: Stein & Day, 1976), p. 240.

11. Quoted in Westermann, *Flak*, p. 239.

12. Willmot, 'Women in the Third Reich', p. 12.

13. Ibid., p. 18.

14. Ibid., p. 17.

15. Ibid.

16. Quoted in Campbell, 'Women in Combat', p. 315 n. 45.

17. Biddiscombe, 'Maelstrom', pp. 69, 71.

18. Ibid., p. 71.

19. Ibid.

20. Ibid.

21. Ibid.

22. David K. Yelton, *Hitler's Volkssturm: The Nazi Militia and the Fall of Germany, 1944–1945* (Lawrence: University Press of Kansas, 2002), p. 47.

23. Antony Beevor, *Berlin: The Downfall 1945* (London: Penguin, 2007), p. 180.

24. Koch, *Hitler Youth*, p. 249.

25. Biddiscombe, 'Maelstrom', p. 72.

26. Westermann, *Flak*, p. 282.

27. Biddiscombe, 'Maelstrom', p. 68.

28. Ibid., p. 74; Campbell, 'Women in Combat', p. 317 n. 55.

29. Koch, *Hitler Youth*, p. 248.

30. Campbell, 'Women in Combat', p. 317.

31. Biddiscombe, 'Maelstrom', p. 87.

32. Ibid., p. 72.

33. Campbell, 'Women in Combat', p. 317.

34. Biddiscombe, 'Maelstrom', p. 62.

35. Quoted in Stephenson, *Women in Nazi Germany*, p. 175.

36. Atina Grossmann, *Reforming Sex: The German Movement for Birth Control and Abortion Reform, 1920–1950* (Oxford: Oxford University Press, 1995), p. 139; see also Pascale R. Bos, 'Feminists Interpreting the Politics of Wartime Rape: Berlin, 1945; Yugoslavia, 1992–1993', *Signs: Journal of Women in Culture and Society* 31, no. 4 (2006), pp. 995–1025.

37. Biddiscombe, 'Maelstrom', p. 74.

38. Ibid., p. 81.

39. Laurie Scrivener, 'US Military Women in World War II: The SPAR, WAC, WAVES, WASP and Women Marines in US Government Publications', *Journal of Government Information* 26, no. 4 (1999), pp. 361, 364. The organisations had superb names – SPAR, for example, was the women's coast guard auxiliary, and got its name from *Semper aratus*, the US Coast Guard motto of 'Always ready'. Marine women were known as Marinettes and Yeomanettes.

40. The Women's Army Auxiliary Corps (WAAC) was first set up in 1941 and became the Women's Army Corps (WAC) in 1943, when it came under full military control.

41. Dr Joseph Earle Moore, speaking before the Joint Army and Navy Committee, 28 February 1941, quoted in Marilyn Hegarty, *Victory Girls, Khaki-Wackies, and Patriotutes: The Regulation of Female Sexuality during World War II* (New York: New York University Press, 2008), p. 88.

42. Quoted in Mattie E. Treadwell, *The Women's Army Corps* (Washington, DC: Office of the Chief of Military History, Department of the Army, 1954), p. 17.

43. Quoted ibid.

44. Fieseler, Hampf and Schwarzkopf, 'Gendering Combat', p. 119; Treadwell, *Army Corps*, pp. 113–21.

45. Quoted in Treadwell, *Army Corps*, p. 18.

46. Quoted ibid., p. 22.

47. Quoted ibid., p. 24.

48. *Congressional Record*, vol. 88, no. 55, 17 March 1942, p. 2592.

49. Ibid., p. 2593.

50. Ibid., p. 2606.

51. Treadwell, *Army Corps*, p. 15.

52. Molly Merryman, *Clipped Wings: The Rise and Fall of the Women Airforce Service Pilots (WASPs) of World War II* (New York: New York University Press, 1998), p. 36. Women in the WAC were the only American servicewomen to serve outside the United States during the war. Judith Bellafaire, *Women in the United States Military: An Annotated Bibliography* (London: Taylor & Francis, 2010), p. 63.

53. Campbell, 'Women in Combat', p. 320.

54. Treadwell, *Army Corps*, p. 209; Elizabeth Jane Tencza, 'Serving Two Masters: The Women's Army Auxiliary Corps and the Slander Campaign of 1943', DPhil thesis, George Washington University, 2006.

55. Scrivener, 'US Military Women', 365. In fact, the WAAC had almost no cases of venereal disease (Treadwell, *Army Corps*, p. 193). See also Leisa D. Meyer, 'Creating G.I. Jane: The Regulation of Sexuality and Sexual Behavior in the Women's Army Corps During World War II', *Feminist Studies* 18, no. 3 (1992), p. 587.

56. Hagemann, 'History and Memory', p. 481.

57. Bellafaire, *Women in the US Military*, p. 63.

58. Treadwell, *Army Corps*, p. 17.

59. Ibid., p. 301.

60. Campbell, 'Women in Combat', p. 303.

61. Quoted ibid.

62. Ibid.

63. Quoted ibid., p. 304.

64. Ibid., p. 305.

65. Ibid.

66. Ibid., p. 313.

67. Eleanor Roosevelt, 'My Day', 1 September 1942, Eleanor Roosevelt Papers Project, https://erpapers.columbian.gwu.edu/my-day

68. Amy Shira Teitel, *Fighting for Space: Two Pilots and Their Historic Battle for Female Spaceflight* (New York and Boston: Grand Central Publishing, 2020), pp. 8–9.

69. Amy Goodpaster Strebe, 'The American Women Airforce Service Pilots and Soviet Airwomen of World War II', MA thesis, San Jose State University, 2003, p. 8.

70. Ibid., p. 9; Doris Brinker Tanner, 'We Also Served', *American History Illustrated* (November 1985), p. 13.

71. Katherine Elizabeth Sharp Landdeck, 'Pushing the Envelope: The Women Airforce Service Pilots and American Society', DPhil thesis, University of Tennessee, 2003, p. 78.

72. Ibid., p. 79.

73. Merryman, *Clipped Wings*, p. 11.

74. Marianne Verges, *On Silver Wings: The Women Airforce Service Pilots of World War II 1942–1944* (New York: Ballantine Books, 1991), p. 78.

75. Landdeck, 'Pushing the Envelope', p. 63. See also Verges, *Silver Wings*, p. 51. Verges points out that while Cochran kept the public eye away from the WASPs, Nancy Love's precursor organisation, the WAFS, was more publicity oriented.

76. Rita Victoria Gomez, '"Angels Calling from the Sky"': The Women Pilots of World War II', in Paula Nassen Poulos, ed., *A Woman's War Too: U.S. Women in the Military in World War II* (Washington, DC: National Archives and Records Administration, 1996), p. 105.

77. Merryman, *Clipped Wings*, p. 21.

78. Verges, *Silver Wings*, p. 131; Merryman, *Clipped Wings*, p. 27.

79. Landdeck, 'Pushing the Envelope', p. 83.

80. Merryman, *Clipped Wings*, p. 63; Tanner, 'We Also Served', p. 48.

81. Merryman, *Clipped Wings*, p. 64.

82. Quoted in Tanner, 'We Also Served', p. 70.

83. Merryman, *Clipped Wings*, p. 70.

84. Ibid.
85. Goodpaster Strebe, 'American Women', p. 21.
86. Quoted in Tanner, 'We Also Served', p. 47.
87. Landdeck, 'Pushing the Envelope', p. 86.
88. Merryman, *Clipped Wings*, p. 138.
89. See Megan MacKenzie, *Beyond the Band of Brothers: The US Military and the Myth That Women Can't Fight* (Cambridge: Cambridge University Press, 2015).
90. Bellafaire, *Women in the US Military*, p. 63.

Chapter 10: Post-war Transitions

1. Hagemann, 'History and Memory', p. 489.
2. Ibid.
3. Corinna Peniston-Bird, 'War and Peace in the Cloakroom: The Controversy over the Memorial to the Women of World War II', in Stephen Gibson and Simon Mollan, eds, *Representations of Peace and Conflict* (London: Palgrave Macmillan, 2012), pp. 263–84.
4. Quoted in Jill Elaine Hasday, 'Fighting Women: The Military, Sex and Extrajudicial Constitutional Change', *Minnesota Law Review* 93, no. 1 (2008), p. 106.
5. Marilyn A. Gordon and Mary Jo Ludvigson, 'The Combat Exclusion for Women Aviators: A Constitutional Analysis', *US Air Force Academy Journal of Legal Studies* 1 (1990), p. 63.
6. Hagemann and Campbell, 'Post-1945', p. 705.
7. Linda K. Kerber, 'A Constitutional Right to Be Treated Like . . . Ladies: Women, Civic Obligation and Military Service', *University of Chicago Law School Roundtable* 1, no. 1 (1993), pp. 112–13.
8. Jeanne Holm, *Women in the Military: An Unfinished Revolution*, rev. edn (Novato, CA: Presidio Press, 1992), p. 273.
9. Noakes, *British Army*, p. 151; Hagemann and Campbell, 'Post-1945', p. 709.
10. Crang, *Sisters in Arms*, p. 226; Noakes, *British Army*, p. 150.
11. Sandra Carson Stanley and Mady Wechsler Segal, 'Military Women in NATO: An Update', *Armed Forces & Society* 14, no. 4 (1988), p. 569; Biddiscombe, 'Maelstrom', p. 63.
12. Ulrike Liebert, *Europeanizing the Military: The ECJ and the Transformation of the Bundeswehr*, CEuS Working Paper 2002/7 (Bremen: Jean Monnet Centre for European Studies (CEuS), 2002), p. 15.

13. James Pierotti, 'Barriers to Women in the Canadian Armed Forces', *Canadian Military Journal* 20, no. 4 (2020), p. 25.

14. Donna Bridges and Ben Wadham, 'Gender under Fire: Portrayals of Military Women in the Australian Print Media', *Feminist Media Studies* 20, no. 2 (2020), p. 222.

15. Hagemann and Rose, 'Global Cold War', p. 659.

16. Anna Krylova, 'Neither Erased nor Remembered: Soviet Women "Combatants" and Cultural Strategies of Forgetting in Soviet Russia, 1940s–1980s', in Frank Biess and Robert G. Moeller, eds, *Histories of the Aftermath: The Legacies of the Second World War in Europe* (New York: Berghahn Books, 2010), pp. 83–101.

Chapter 11: Women Rebels

1. Sandra C. Taylor, *Vietnamese Women: Fighting for Ho Chih Minh and the Revolution* (Lawrence: University Press of Kansas, 1999), p. 81.

2. Karen G. Turner, '"Vietnam" as a Woman's War', in Marilyn Blatt Young and Robert Buzzanco, eds, *A Companion to the Vietnam War* (Malden, MA: Blackwell, 2002), p. 93.

3. Elizabeth D. Herman, 'The Women Who Fought for Hanoi', *New York Times*, 6 June 2017, https://www.nytimes.com/2017/06/06/opinion/vietnam-war-women-soldiers.html

4. Turner, 'Woman's War', p. 94.

5. John Mueller, 'The Obsolescence of Major War', *Bulletin of Peace Proposals* 21, no. 3 (1990), pp. 321–8.

6. Martin van Creveld, 'The Great Illusion: Women in the Military', *Millennium* 29, no. 2 (2000), p. 440.

7. Eva Sohlman, 'Overlooked No More: The Russian Icon Who Was Hanged for Killing a Czar', *New York Times*, 30 May 2018.

8. Kurt Schilde, *Jugendopposition 1933–1945: Ausgewählte Beiträge* (Berlin: Lukas Verlag, 2007), p. 98.

9. Quoted in Taylor, *Vietnamese Women*, p. 47.

10. Paige Whaley Eager, *From Freedom Fighters to Terrorists: Women and Political Violence* (Farnham: Ashgate, 2008), p. 94.

11. Ibid., p. 27.

12. Jessica T. Darden, Alexis Henshaw and Ora Szekely, *Insurgent Women: Female Combatants in the Civil Wars* (Washington, DC: Georgetown University Press, 2019), p. 3.

13. Reed M. Wood, *Female Fighters: Why Rebel Groups Recruit Women for War* (New York: Columbia University Press, 2019), p. 2.

14. Data on the number of states that use women in combat is opaque as many states officially have combat roles open to women but in practice have no women in them, and many states allow women in the air force but not in ground combat roles. The number of states where women's combat participation can be verified is twenty, 10 per cent of all states. Sarah Percy, 'What Makes a Norm Robust: The Norm against Female Combat', *Journal of Global Security Studies* 4, no. 1 (2019), p. 132.

15. Alexis Leanna Henshaw, *Why Women Rebel: Understanding Women's Participation in Armed Rebel Groups* (London and New York: Routledge, 2017), p. 99.

16. The FARC had 30–45 per cent; the FSLN and FLMN had 30 per cent.

17. Wood, *Female Fighters*, p. 2. The LTTE and EPLF have used forced conscription, a point discussed further below.

18. Ibid., p. 102.

19. Reed M. Wood and Jakana L. Thomas, 'Women on the Frontline: Rebel Group Ideology and Women's Participation in Violent Rebellion', *Journal of Peace Research* 54, no. 1 (2017), p. 41.

20. Natalia Herrera and Douglas Porch, '"Like Going to a Fiesta" – the Role of Female Fighters in Colombia's FARC-Ep', *Small Wars & Insurgencies* 19, no. 4 (2008), p. 618.

21. Miranda Alison, '"In the War Front We Never Think We Are Women": Women, Gender, and the Liberation Tamil Tigers of Eelam', in Laura Sjoberg and Caron E. Gentry, eds, *Women, Gender and Terrorism* (Athens, OH: Ohio University Press, 2011), p. 141.

22. Wood, *Female Fighters*, p. 66.

23. Henshaw, *Why Women Rebel*, p. 13.

24. Jakana L. Thomas and Kanisha D. Bond, 'Women's Participation in Violent Political Organizations', *American Political Science Review* 109, no. 3 (2015), p. 495.

25. Quoted in Ilja A. Luciak, *After the Revolution: Gender and Democracy in El Salvador, Nicaragua, and Guatemala* (Baltimore: Johns Hopkins University Press, 2001), p. 20.

26. Margaret Randall, *Sandino's Daughters: Testimonies of Nicaraguan Women in Struggle*, ed. Lynda Yanz (Vancouver: New Star Books, 1981), pp. 123–5.

27. Wood and Thomas, 'Frontline', p. 42.

28. Wood, *Female Fighters*, p. 67.

29. Ibid., p. 106.

30. India Rakusen et al., 'Who Is the "Angel of Kobane"?', BBC Trending, Twitter post, 3 November 2014, https://www.bbc.com/news/blogs-trending-29853513

31. Alison, 'War Front', p. 134.

32. Wood, *Female Fighters*, p. 72.

33. Herrera and Porch, 'Fiesta', p. 618.

34. Ibid., p. 631.

35. Maureen Orth, 'She Was Colombia's Most-Feared Female Revolutionary. Can She Help It Find Peace?', *Vanity Fair*, 2 August 2018, https://www.vanityfair.com/news/2018/08/colombia-civil-war-farc-female-revolutionary

36. Ibid.

37. Murat Haner, Francis T. Cullen and Michael L. Benson, 'Women and the PKK: Ideology, Gender, and Terrorism', *International Criminal Justice Review* 30, no. 3 (2020), p. 293.

38. Quoted in Swati Parashar, *Women and Militant Wars: The Politics of Injury* (London: Taylor & Francis, 2014), p. 26.

39. Maneshka Eliatamby, 'Searching for Emancipation: Eritrea, Nepal, and Sri Lanka', in Sandra I. Cheldelin and Maneshka Eliatamby, eds, *Women Waging War and Peace: International Perspectives of Women's Roles in Conflict and Post-Conflict Reconstruction* (London: Bloomsbury Academic, 2011), p. 40.

40. Rita Manchanda, 'Maoist Insurgency in Nepal: Radicalizing Gendered Narratives', *Cultural Dynamics* 16, no. 2–3 (2004), p. 242.

41. Karen Gottschang Turner, 'Vietnam's Martial Women: The Costs of Transgressing Boundaries', in Boyd Cothran, Joan Judge and Adrian Shubert, eds, *Women Warriors and National Heroes: Global Histories* (London: Bloomsbury Academic, 2020), p. 238.

42. Karen Gottschang Turner, *Even the Women Must Fight: Memories of War from North Vietnam* (New York: Wiley, 1998), p. 27.

43. Quoted ibid., p. 42.

44. Ofra Bengio, 'Game Changers: Kurdish Women in Peace and War', *Middle East Journal* 70, no. 1 (2016), p. 32.

45. Alisa Stack-O'Connor, 'Lions, Tigers and Freedom Birds: How and Why the Liberation Tigers of Tamil Eelam Employ Women', *Terrorism and Political Violence* 19, no. 1 (2007), p. 47.

46. Wood, *Female Fighters*, p. 114.

47. Güneş Murat Tezcür, 'A Path out of Patriarchy? Political Agency and Social Identity of Women Fighters', *Perspectives on Politics* 18, no. 3 (2020), p. 728; Wood, *Female Fighters*, p. 103.

48. Wood, *Female Fighters*, p. 43.

49. Jakana L. Thomas and Reed M. Wood, 'The Social Origins of Female Combatants', *Conflict Management and Peace Science* 35, no. 3 (2018), pp. 215–32.

50. Wood, *Female Fighters*, p. 111; Alison, 'War Front', p. 39.

51. Joanne Payton, *Honor and the Political Economy of Marriage: Violence against Women in the Kurdistan Region of Iraq* (New Brunswick: Rutgers University Press, 2020), pp. 36–7.

52. Abdullah Öcalan, *Liberating Life: Women's Revolution* (Cologne: International Initiative Edition, 2013), p. 51.

53. Haner, Cullen and Benson, 'Women', p. 292.

54. Wood, *Female Fighters*, p. 101.

55. Bengio, 'Game Changers', p. 33.

56. Quoted ibid., p. 40.

57. Stack-O'Connor, 'Lions, Tigers', p. 50.

58. Quoted in Alison, 'War Front', p. 138.

59. Quoted in Tezcür, 'Patriarchy', p. 726.

60. Haner, Cullen and Benson, 'Women', p. 727; Tezcür, 'Patriarchy', p. 727.

61. Stack-O'Connor, 'Lions, Tigers', p. 50.

62. Tezcür, 'Patriarchy', p. 727.

63. Stack-O'Connor, 'Lions, Tigers', p. 51.

64. Herrera and Porch, 'Fiesta', p. 613.

65. Orth, 'Female Revolutionary'.

66. Ibid.

67. Ibid.

68. Mia Kazman, *Women of the FARC* (Washington, DC: William J. Perry Center for Hemispheric Defense Studies, 2019), p. 22.

69. Henshaw, *Why Women Rebel*, p. 99.

70. Quoted in Luciak, *After the Revolution*, p. 12.

71. Quoted ibid., pp. 18–19.

72. Ibid., p. 21.

73. Haner, Cullen and Benson, 'Women', p. 286.

74. Ibid., p. 291.

75. Parashar, *Militant Wars*, p. 52.

76. Quoted ibid, p. 136.

77. Stack-O'Connor, 'Lions, Tigers', p. 44.

78. Turner, 'Martial Women', p. 234.

79. Quoted in Turner, *Even the Women*, p. 16.

80. Quoted in Luciak, *After the Revolution*, p. 72.

81. Shobha Gautam, Amrita Banskota and Rita Manchanda, 'Where There Are No Men: Women in the Maoist Insurgency in Nepal', in Kamala Visweswaran, ed., *Perspectives on Modern South Asia: A Reader in Culture, History, and Representation* (Malden, MA: Wiley-Blackwell, 2011), p. 345.

82. Karen Kampwirth, *Women and Guerrilla Movements: Nicaragua, El Salvador, Chiapas, Cuba* (University Park: Pennsylvania State University Press, 2021), p. 9.

83. Herrera and Porch, 'Fiesta', p. 616.

84. Herman, 'Hanoi'.

85. Tezcür, 'Patriarchy', p. 723.

86. Kazman, *FARC*, p. 13.

87. Alison, 'War Front', p. 136.

88. Quoted in Luciak, *After the Revolution*, p. 71.

89. Tezcür, 'Patriarchy', p. 732.

90. Ibid.

91. Ibid., p. 729.

92. Quoted in Lorina Sthapit and Philippe Doneys, 'Female Maoist Combatants during and after the People's War', in Ashild Kolas, ed., *Women, Peace and Security in Nepal* (New York: Routledge, 2017), p. 40.

93. Quoted in Manchanda, 'Maoist Insurgency', p. 244.

94. Dyan Mazurana, 'Women, Girls and Non-State Armed Opposition Groups', in Carol Cohn, ed., *Women and War* (Cambridge: Polity Press, 2013), p. 150.

95. Dyan Mazurana and Susan McKay, 'Child Soldiers', *Bulletin of the Atomic Scientists* 57, no. 5 (2001), p. 31.

96. Kampwirth, *Women and Guerrilla Movements*, pp. 78–9.

97. Alison, 'War Front', p. 138.

98. Amelia Hoover Green, *The Commander's Dilemma: Violence and Restraint in Wartime* (Ithaca, NY: Cornell University Press, 2018), p. 625.

99. Wood, *Female Fighters*, p. 101; Amelia Hoover Green, 'Armed Group Institutions and Combatant Socialization: Evidence from El Salvador', *Journal of Peace Research* 54, no. 5 (2017), p. 695; Sara Dissanayake, 'Women in the Tamil Tigers: Path to Liberation or Pawn in a Game?', *Counter-Terrorist Trends and Analyses* 9, no. 8 (2017), p. 3.

100. Emanuela C. Del Re, 'Female Combatants in the Syrian Conflict, in the Fight against or with the IS, and in the Peace Process', in Seema Shekhawat, ed., *Female Combatants in Conflict and Peace: Challenging Gender in Violence and Post-Conflict Reintegration* (New York: Palgrave Macmillan, 2015), p. 86.

101. Stack-O'Connor ('Lions, Tigers', p. 52) notes this in relation to the LTTE.
102. Kampwirth, *Women and Guerrilla Movements*, p. 33.
103. Parashar, *Militant Wars*, p. 132.
104. Luciak, *After the Revolution*, p. 30.
105. Quoted in Turner, *Even the Women*, p. 20.
106. Quoted in Turner, 'Martial Women', p. 247.
107. Quoted ibid., p. 246.
108. Turner, *Even the Women*, p. 153.
109. Ibid., p. 182.
110. Ibid., p. 153.
111. Quoted in Sthapit and Doneys, 'Maoist Combatants', p. 40.
112. Luciak, *After the Revolution*, p. 49.
113. Randall, *Sandino's Daughters*, p. 56.
114. Parashar, *Militant Wars*, p. 118.
115. Alison, 'War Front', p. 146.
116. Alexis Leanna Henshaw, 'Why Women Rebel: Greed, Grievance, and Women in Armed Rebel Groups', *Journal of Global Security Studies* 1, no. 3 (2016), p. 210.
117. Kampwirth, *Women and Guerrilla Movements*, p. 6.
118. Inigo Gilmore, 'Women Hold the Line in Africa's Forgotten War' (2 May 1999), Dehai News Mailing List Archive, http://www.dehai.org/conflict/news/eltel-5-2-9.htm
119. Helen Kidan, 'From Empowerment During War, Eritrean Women Must Fight Gender Discrimination in a New Peace', Inter Press Service News Agency, 15 April 2019, https://www.ipsnews.net/2019/04/161175/
120. Human Rights Concern – Eritrea, 'Report on Women's Rights Violations in Eritrea – HRCE Report 1/2017', 8 March 2017, https://hrc-eritrea.org/report-on-womens-rights-violations-in-eritrea-hrce-report-12017/

Chapter 12: Gender Equality and the Combat Exclusion

1. Denise M. Hulett et al., 'Enhancing Women's Inclusion in Firefighting in the USA', *International Journal of Diversity in Organizations, Communities, and Nations*, annual review (2008), DOI: 10.188848/1447-9532/CGP/Vo8102/39562
2. 'Taking the Heat: Gender Discrimination in Firefighting', *American University Journal of Gender, Social Policy, & the Law* 17, no. 3 (2009), p. 725.

3. Jane LaTour, *Sisters in the Brotherhoods: Working Women Organizing for Equality in New York City* (New York: Palgrave Macmillan, 2008), p. 141.

4. Sarah Vee Moseley, 'Women's Entrance into the Fire Department: A Theory of Collaboration and Crisis', thesis, Old Dominion University, 2017, p. 100.

5. 'Taking the Heat', p. 720.

6. Moseley, 'Fire Department', p. 100. See also 'Taking the Heat' for a summary of Berkman's experiences.

7. Judy Klemesrud, 'In Coal Mine No. 29, Two Women Work Alongside the Men', *New York Times*, 18 May 1974, p. 9, https://www.nytimes.com/1974/05/18/archives/in-coal-mine-no-29-two-women-work-alongside-the-men-kin-tried-to.html?searchResultPosition=1

8. Terese M. Floren, 'History of Women in Firefighting' (2007), Women in Fire, https://www.womeninfire.org/firefighters/history-of-women-in-firefighting/

9. Kerber, 'Constitutional Right', p. 114.

10. Anthony King, *The Combat Soldier: Infantry Tactics and Cohesion in the Twentieth and Twenty-First Centuries* (Oxford: Oxford University Press, 2013), p. 415.

11. Elizabeth Broderick et al., *Review into the Treatment of Women in the Australian Defence Force: Phase 2 Report* (Sydney: Australian Human Rights Commission, 2012), p. 178.

12. Lance Janda, 'A Simple Matter of Equality: The Admission of Women to West Point', in De Groot and Peniston-Bird, eds, *Soldier and Woman*, p. 305.

13. Quoted in Janda, 'Equality', p. 309.

14. Ibid., p. 312.

15. John Black, 'What Special Forces Means to the Real First Female Green Beret', *SOFREP*, 8 March 2021, https://sofrep.com/news/an-exclusive-interview-with-katie-wilder-the-first-female-green-beret/

16. John Ismay, 'The True Story of the First Woman to Finish Special Forces Training', *New York Times*, 28 February 2020, https://www.nytimes.com/2020/02/28/magazine/woman-special-forces-green-beret.html

17. 'First Woman Fails Green Berets, but Threatens Sex-Bias Lawsuit', *New York Times*, 23 August 1980, https://www.nytimes.com/1980/08/23/archives/first-woman-fails-green-berets-but-threatens-sexbias-lawsuit.html?searchResultPosition=1

18. Ismay, 'True Story'.

19. Mady Wechsler Segal, 'Women's Military Roles Cross-Nationally Past, Present, and Future', *Gender & Society* 9, no. 6 (1995), p. 766.

20. Committee on Women in NATO Forces, *Year-in-Review* (Brussels: Office on Women in NATO Forces, International Military Staff, 2001), p. 15.

21. Alma Persson and Fia Sundevall, 'Conscripting Women: Gender, Soldiering, and Military Service in Sweden 1965–2018', *Women's History Review* 28, no. 7 (2019), p. 1043.

22. Gwyn Harries-Jenkins, 'Women in Extended Roles in the Military: Legal Issues', *Current Sociology* 50, no. 5 (2002), p. 747.

23. Segal, 'Military Roles', p. 762.

24. Jessica M. Frazier, *Women's Antiwar Diplomacy During the Vietnam War Era* (Chapel Hill: University of North Carolina Press, 2017), p. 124.

25. Cynthia Enloe, 'Women – the Reserve *Army* of Army Labor', *Review of Radical Political Economics* 12, no. 2 (1980), p. 51.

26. Rachel Gaddes et al., *A Historical Review of the Influence of the Defence Advisory Committe on Women in the Services (DACOWITS) from 1951 to Present: A 70-Year Review* (Arlington: Insight Policy Research, 2020).

27. Kerber, 'Constitutional Right', p. 102.

28. Ibid., p. 116.

29. Senate Armed Services Committee, S. Rep. No. 96–226 (1979), at p. 9, quoted in *Rostker v Goldberg*, 453 US 57 (1981), at 81.

30. *Rostker v Goldberg,* 453 US 57 (1981), at 77–8.

31. MacKenzie, *Brothers*, pp. 35–40.

32. Phyllis Schlafly, 'What's Wrong with "Equal Rights" for Women?', *The Phyllis Schlafly Report*, vol. 5, no. 7 (February 1972), p. 2.

33. Testimony of Mrs Phyllis Schlafly, President, Stop ERA, *House of Representatives, Committee on Armed Services, Military Personnel Subcommittee*, 96th Congress, 1st Session, 16 November 1979, (Washington: US Government Printing Office), p. 236.

34. Testimony of Hon. Larry McDonald, Representative from Georgia, *House of Representatives, Committee on Armed Services, Military Personnel Subcommittee*, (Washington: US Government Printing Office, September 22, 1980, pp. 42–3.

35. Jane Mansbridge, 'Who's in Charge Here? Decision by Accretion and Gatekeeping in the Struggle for the ERA', *Politics & Society* 13, no. 4 (1984), pp. 343–82.

36. *Angela Maria Sirdar v The Army Board and the Secretary of State for Defence* (C-273/97), [1999] ECR I-7403.

37. *Canadian Human Rights Tribunal*, 'Tribunal Decision 3/89 between: Isabelle Gauthier, Joseph G. Houlden, Marie-Claude Gauthier, Georgina Ann Brown (Complainants) And Canadian Armed Forces (Respondent)' [1989].

38. Joel Greenberg, 'Israeli Woman Sues for Chance to Be a Combat Pilot', *New York Times*, 3 November 1994, p. 12.

39. HCJ 45941/94 *Alice Miller v Minister of Defence* [1995–6] IsrLR 1, at 12.

40. Ibid., at 23.

41. Testimony of Colonel John Ripley, 26 June 1992, available at https://www.tfp.org/testimony-of-col-john-w-ripley-to-the-presidential-commission-on-the-assignment-of-women-in-the-armed-forces/ [accessed 30 January 2023]

42. Joel Greenberg, 'Ruling Expands Women's Roles in the Israeli Military', *New York Times*, 3 January 1996, p. 5.

43. Greenberg, 'Israeli Woman'.

44. Ian Black, 'EU Court Grants German Woman Right to Be Soldier', *Guardian*, 12 January 2000, https://www.theguardian.com/world/2000/jan/12/ianblack

45. *Tanja Kreil v Bundesrepublik Deutschland* [2000] ECR I-69, at 77.

46. Black, 'Right to Be'.

47. *Kreil v Bundesrepublik Deutschland*, at 76.

48. Ibid., at 92.

49. *Canadian Human Rights Tribunal*, 'Tribunal Decision 3/89', at 25.

50. Ibid., at 17.

51. Ibid., at 27.

52. Ibid., at 5.

53. Ibid., at 17, 27, 5 and 9 respectively.

54. Ibid., at 28.

55. Testimony of William Westmoreland, *House of Representatives, Committee on Armed Services, Military Personnel Subcommittee*, 96th Congress, 1st Session, 16 November 1979, on *Women in the Military*, p. 78.

56. Testimony of Hon. Larry McDonald, in *Women in the Military*, p. 44.

57. Herres and Members of the Commission, *Assignment of Women*, p. 26. The Commission also mentions Germany but has an apparently confused understanding of the role of women in Germany in the Second World War, acknowledging later that women served in traditional support and air defence roles (p. 29).

58. Senate Armed Services Committee, S. Rep. No. 96–226 (1979), p. 157 quoted in *Rostker v Goldberg*, at 92.

59. Harold Braswell and Howard I. Kushner, 'Suicide, Social Integration, and Masculinity in the U.S. Military', *Social Science & Medicine* 74, no. 4 (2012), p. 533.

60. Victoria Basham, *War, Identity and the Liberal State: Everyday Experiences*

of the Geopolitical in the Armed Forces (Abingdon: Taylor & Francis, 2013), p. 57.

61. King, *Combat Soldier*, p. 377.

62. MacKenzie, *Brothers*, pp. 140–1.

63. The data can be found in a Google Ngram, which measures the frequency of use of a term in books published during the period in question. https:// books.google.com/ngrams/graph?content=organizational+cohesion&year_ start=1850&year_end=2019&corpus=en-2019&smoothing=0#

64. Gregory Newbold, 'What Tempers the Steel of an Infantry Unit', War on the Rocks, 9 September 2015, https://warontherocks.com/2015/09/ what-tempers-the-steel-of-an-infantry-unit/

65. Rachel Woodward and Patricia Winter, 'Discourses of Gender in the Contemporary British Army', *Armed Forces & Society* 30, no. 2 (2004), p. 290.

66. Ministry of Defence (UK), 'Report on the Review of the Exclusion of Women from Ground Close-Combat Roles' (November 2010), para. 1.

67. Rutgers Institute for Women's Leadership, 'Women in the U.S. Military Services', fact sheet, 2009, https://iwl.rutgers.edu/documents/ njwomencount/Women%20in%20Military%202009%20Final.pdf.

68. 'Let 'Em Be Grease Monkeys', *New York Times*, 3 August 1983, p. A22.

69. Holm, *Women in the Military*, p. 395.

70. Shira Eini Pindyck, 'Innovation and Inclusion in the Armed Forces', DPhil thesis, University of Pennsylvania, 2021.

71. Grammar *sic*. Quoted in Donna V. Bridges, 'The Gendered Battlefield: Women in the Australian Defence Force', DPhil thesis, University of Western Sydney, 2005, p. 2.

72. Nick Madigan, 'Women in the Army: Still No Combat', United Press International, 14 December 1983, https://www.upi.com/Archives/1983/ 12/14/Women-in-the-Army-Still-no-combat/3364440226000/

73. Ibid. The article misspells Wright's first name as Anne.

74. Ibid.

75. Ann Wright, 'The Roles of US Army Women in Grenada', *Minerva* 2, no. 2 (1984), p. 103.

76. Military Personnel and Compensation Subcommittee of the Committee on Armed Services, *An Overview of U.S. Commitments and the Forces Available to Meet Them*, House of Representatives, 98th Congress, 1st Session, 395 (1984).

77. The US spent 27 per cent of GDP on the military in 1988; the military had 2,135,900 members in 1985. The UK spent 16 per cent of GDP on

the military in 1985 and that year had a military of 334,000. Australia spent 10 per cent of its GDP on the military in 1988 and that year had a military of 70,400. (Australia's population was 15.76 million in 1988; Canada had a population of 25.84 million and in 1985 had a military of 72,700.) GDP numbers from the *CIA World Factbook* (1988); military size taken from macrotrends.net. Based on average military personnel numbers between 1980 and 1999, the US had the world's third largest force, with the UK ranking twentieth and Australia sixty-ninth. In terms of average military expenditure during the same period, the US was placed first, the UK fourth and Australia fifty-third. National Material Capabilities (NMC) Data Documentation, Correlates of War Project, 28 June 2021.

Chapter 13: The Gulf War, Iraq, Afghanistan and the End of the Combat Exclusion

1. Niel L. Golightly, 'No Right to Fight', *Proceedings: A Magazine of the US Naval Institute* 113, no. 12 (December 1987), https://www.usni.org/magazines/proceedings/1987/december/no-right-fight

2. 'Comment and Discussion', *Proceedings: A Magazine of the US Naval Institute* 114, no. 2 (1988), https://www.usni.org/magazines/proceedings/1988/february/comment-and-discussion

3. Greg Sheridan, 'Women Have No Place in Combat', *The Australian*, 28 September 2011, https://www.theaustralian.com.au/national-affairs/opinion/women-have-no-place-in-combat/news-story/dcf8dc784bd3766a3cc60948fafcf1da

4. Jenny Gross, 'Boeing Communications Chief Resigns over 33-Year-Old Article', *New York Times*, 8 July 2020, https://www.nytimes.com/2020/07/08/business/boeing-resignation-niel-golightly.html

5. Sheridan, 'Combat'.

6. Greenberg, 'Israeli Woman'.

7. Dafna N. Izraeli, 'Gendering Military Service in the Israel Defence Forces', in De Groot and Peniston-Bird, eds, *Soldier and Woman*, p. 261.

8. Quoted in Joyce Robbins and Uri Ben-Eliezer, 'New Roles or "New Times"? Gender Inequality and Militarism in Israel's Nation-in-Arms', *Social Politics* 7, no. 3 (2000), p. 317.

9. Ibid., p. 319.

10. Ibid., p. 321.

11. Izraeli, 'Gendering Military Service', p. 262.

12. Robbins and Ben-Eliezer, 'New Roles', p. 322.

13. Ibid., p. 324.

14. Izraeli, 'Gendering Military Service', p. 267.

15. Robbins and Ben-Eliezer, 'New Roles', p. 331.

16. Izraeli, 'Gendering Military Service', p. 268.

17. See articles cited ibid., p. 269.

18. Robbins and Ben-Eliezer, 'New Roles', p. 335.

19. Izraeli, 'Gendering Military Service', p. 274.

20. Robbins and Ben-Eliezer, 'New Roles', p. 337.

21. Ibid.

22. Ibid.

23. Ibid., p. 338.

24. Ibid., p. 104.

25. Itamar Eichner, 'IDF Chief: I Don't Foresee Women Serving at Army's Vanguard', *Ynetnews*, 2 May 2018, https://www.ynetnews.com/articles/0,7340,L-5089566,00.html

26. Anne Fieldhouse and T. J. O'Leary, 'Integrating Women into Combat Roles: Comparing the UK Armed Forces and Israeli Defence Forces to Understand Where Lessons Can Be Learnt', *British Medical Journal: Military Health* (2020), p. 1.

27. Shannon Collins, 'Desert Storm: A Look Back', news report, U.S. Department of Defense, 11 January 2019, https://www.defense.gov/News/Feature-Stories/Story/Article/1728715/desert-storm-a-look-back

28. Darlene M. Iskra and Vincent W. Patton, *Women in the United States Armed Forces: A Guide to the Issues* (Santa Barbara: ABC-CLIO, 2010), p. 22. The number of women in the Army was 26,000. See the website Women in the Army: History, https://www.army.mil/women/history/,

29. Christopher Dandeker and Mady Wechsler Segal, 'Gender Integration in Armed Forces: Recent Policy Developments in the United Kingdom', *Armed Forces & Society* 23, no. 1 (1996), p. 32.

30. Leela Jacinto, 'The Cost of Women in Combat', *ABC News*, 7 January 2003, https://abcnews.go.com/International/story?id=79646&page=1

31. *Women in the Military: Deployment in the Persian Gulf War* (Washington, DC: US General Accounting Office, 1993), p. 26.

32. Michelle Tan, '3rd Woman, and 1st Female Reservist, Dons Ranger Tab', *Army Times*, 17 October 2015, armytimes.com/news/your-army/2015/10/16/3rd-woman-and-1st-female-reservist-dons-ranger-tab/

33. Jacinto, 'The Cost of Women'.

34. Joseph F. Sullivan, 'Army Pilot's Death Stuns Her New Jersey Neighbors', *New York Times*, 7 March 1991, https://www.nytimes.com/1991/03/07/nyregion/army-pilot-s-death-stuns-her-new-jersey-neighbors.html

35. Rhonda Cornum and Peter Copeland, *She Went to War: The Rhonda Cornum Story* (Waterside Productions, 2020), p. 228.

36. 'A Woman's Burden', *Time* magazine, 28 March 2003, http://content.time.com/time/nation/article/0,8599,438760,00.html

37. Iskra and Patton, *Guide*, p. 23; Jacinto, 'The Cost of Women'.

38. Quoted in Alistair R. Mack, 'Women in Combat: The British and American Experience in the Gulf War 1991', *RUSI Journal* 138, no. 5 (1993), p. 34.

39. Research Task Group, *Integration of Women into Ground Combat Units* (Brussels: NATO Science and Technology Organization, 2021), p. 28.

40. 'Crossing Milestones for Female Marines: Examining the Maria C. Villescas Collection', Library of Congress, American Folklife Centre and Veterans History Project blog, 26 July 2018, https://blogs.loc.gov/folklife/2018/07/crossing-milestones-for-female-marines-examining-the-maria-c-villescas-collection/

41. Maureen Murdoch et al., 'Women and War: What Physicians Should Know', *Journal of General Internal Medicine* 21, no. S3 (2006), pp. S5–S10.

42. Quoted in Kyleanne Hunter, 'Shoulder to Shoulder yet Worlds Apart: Variation in Women's Integration in the Militaries of France, Norway and the United States', DPhil thesis, University of Denver 2019, p. 205.

43. Amy Eskind, 'A Post-Gulf Memorial Day, 1991: Arms and the Woman', *Washington Post*, 26 May 1991, https://www.washingtonpost.com/archive/opinions/1991/05/26/a-post-gulf-memorial-day-1991-arms-and-the-woman/194133cb-7fbb-4e24-a20d-9a5671a74cc3/

44. Beverly G. Steinberg, 'Women as Warriors After the Gulf War: A Call for the Repeal of All Combat Exclusion Laws', *St John's Law Review* 66, no. 3 (1992), pp. 829–46, n. 845.

45. Eric Schmitt, 'Senate Votes to Remove Ban on Women as Combat Pilots', *New York Times*, 1 April 1991, https://www.nytimes.com/1991/08/01/us/senate-votes-to-remove-ban-on-women-as-combat-pilots.html Perhaps surprisingly in 1991, the Senate had forty-eight men and only two women.

46. Herres and Members of the Commission, *Assignment of Women*, p. 26.

47. Ibid., p. 24.

48. *Women in the Military*, p. 41.

49. 'Women in Combat', C-Span, 28 April 1993, https://www.c-span.org/

video/?40217-1/women-combat. The first women were assigned to navy combat ships in March 1994. https://www.history.navy.mil/content/history/nhhc/browse-by-topic/diversity/women-in-the-navy/women-in-combat.html

50. Morgan Smith, 'A Woman's Right to Fly and Fight', *Smithsonian Magazine* (August 2020), https://www.smithsonianmag.com/air-space-magazine/right-fly-and-fight-180975332/

51. Molly Moore, 'Women on the Battlefield', *Washington Post*, 16 June 1991, https://www.washingtonpost.com/archive/politics/1991/06/16/women-on-the-battlefield/9b65a7fc-7447-4f7e-bf8f-0184736a6b15/

52. Ellen Haring, 'Gender and Military Organizations', in Chantal de Jonge Oudraat and Michael E. Brown, eds, *The Gender and Security Agenda: Strategies for the 21st Century* (London: Routledge, 2020), p. 95.

53. 'Assignment of Army and Marine Corps Women under the New Definition of Ground Support', in *Hearings before the Military Forces and Personnel Subcommittee of the Committee on Armed Services, House of Representatives* (Washington, DC: US Government Printing Office, 6 October 1994).

54. 'Gulf War', National Army Museum website, https://www.nam.ac.uk/explore/gulf-war. See also Mack, 'Women in Combat', p. 33.

55. Dandeker and Wechsler Segal, 'Gender Integration', p. 33.

56. Ibid.

57. Hugh Smith and Ian McAllister, 'The Changing Military Profession: Integrating Women in the Australian Defence Force', *Australian and New Zealand Journal of Sociology* 27, no. 3 (1991), p. 374.

58. Woodward and Winter, 'Discourses of Gender', p. 285.

59. Ministry of Defence (UK), 'Report on the Review of the Exclusion of Women from Ground Close-Combat Roles', paras 3 and 4.

60. Australia has a relatively small number of fighter pilots, and this leads to a very high rate of competition for these roles. James Purtill, 'Inside the Royal Australian Air Force School Preparing Fighter Pilots for Likely Combat', *ABC News*, 14 May 2005, https://www.abc.net.au/news/2015-05-14/royal-australian-air-force-fighter-school-prepares-pilots-combat/6467286

61. Charles Guthrie, 'The New British Way in Warfare', Annual Liddell Hart Centre for Military Archives Lecture, 12 February 2001, King's College London, https://www.kcl.ac.uk/library/assets/archives/2001-lecture.pdf

62. Simon Walters, 'Defence Chief Under Siege by Col. Muppet; Top Female Army Officer Joins Margaret Hodge to Demand Women in Front Line', *Mail on Sunday*, 29 October 2000.

63. Jason Burke, 'Women to Fight on Front Line: Army's Secret Trials Reveal Female Soldiers Perform as Well as Men in Combat', *Observer*, 24 December 2000, https://www.theguardian.com/society/2000/dec/24/uknews.theobserver1

64. Joseph Fletcher and Jennifer Hove, 'Emotional Determinants of Support for the Canadian Mission in Afghanistan: A View from the Bridge', *Canadian Journal of Political Science* 45, no. 1 (2012), pp. 36–7.

65. Claire Turenne-Sjolander and Kathryn Trevenen, 'Constructions of Nation, Constructions of War: Media Representations of Captain Nichola Goddard', in Bruno Charbonneau and Wayne S. Cox, eds, *Locating Global Order: American Power and Canadian Security after 9/11* (Vancouver: UBC Press, 2010), p. 129.

66. Maya Eichler, 'Gender and the Canadian Armed Forces: Does Change Mean Feminist Progress?', *Atlantis: Critical Studies in Gender, Culture & Social Justice* 41, no. 2 (2020), pp. 3–8.

67. Department of the Army (US), 'Fm 3–24 Mcwp 3–33.5: Insurgencies and Countering Insurgencies', 13 May 2014, para. 1-85.

68. King, *Combat Soldier*, p. 395.

69. Ibid.

70. Matthew Rosenberg and Dave Philipps, 'All Combat Roles Now Open to Women, Defense Secretary Says', *New York Times*, 3 December 2015, https://www.nytimes.com/2015/12/04/us/politics/combat-military-women-ash-carter.html

71. Charley Keyes, 'Women Facing the Same Risks as Men in Wars, Mullen Says', *CNN*, 4 November 2010, http://edition.cnn.com/2010/US/11/04/women.in.war/index.html

72. Ethan E. Rocke, 'A Woman Completed Special Forces Training: These Officers Have Some Thoughts', *Coffee or Die* magazine, 15 July 2020, https://coffeeordie.com/first-woman-special-forces/

73. Sara Wood, 'Female Soldier Receives Silver Star in Iraq', US Army website article, 17 October 2011, https://www.army.mil/article/1645/female_soldier_receives_silver_star_in_iraq

74. Ann Scott Tyson, 'Woman Gains Silver Star – and Removal from Combat', *Washington Post*, 1 May 2008, https://www.washingtonpost.com/wp-dyn/content/article/2008/04/30/AR2008043003415.html?sid=ST2008043003513

75. Ibid.

76. Ibid.

77. Ibid.

78. Felicia R. Lee, 'Battleground: Female Soldiers in the Line of Fire', *New*

York Times, 4 November 2008, https://www.nytimes.com/2008/11/05/arts/television/05lion.html?searchResultPosition=

79. Ibid.

80. Lolita C. Baldor, 'Death Highlights Women's Role in Special Ops Teams', Associated Press, 25 October 2011, https://www.sandiegouniontribune.com/sdut-death-highlights-womens-role-in-special-ops-teams-2011oct25-story.html

81. Elisabeth Bumiller, 'Letting Women Reach Women in Afghan War', *New York Times*, 6 March 2010, https://www.nytimes.com/2010/03/07/world/asia/07women.html

82. Ibid.

83. Ibid.

84. Keally McBride and Annick T. R. Wibben, 'The Gendering of Counterinsurgency in Afghanistan', *International Journal of Human Rights* 3, no. 2 (2012), p. 205.

85. Elisabeth Bumiller, 'For Female Marines, Tea Comes with Bullets', *New York Times*, 2 October 2010, https://www.nytimes.com/2010/10/03/world/asia/03marines.html

86. Pindyck, 'Innovation', p. 188.

87. McBride and Wibben, 'Gendering', p. 207.

88. Bumiller, 'Letting Women'.

89. Bumiller, 'Female Marines'.

90. Brenda Oppermann, 'Women and Gender in the US Military: A Slow Process of Integration', in Robert Egnell and Mayesha Alam, eds, *Women and Gender Perspectives in the Military: An International Comparison* (Washington, DC: Georgetown University Press, 2019), p. 132.

91. Sippi Azarbaijani-Moghaddam, *Seeking out Their Afghan Sisters: Female Engagement Teams in Afghanistan* (Bergen: Chr. Michelsen Institute, 2014), p. 2.

92. Ann Jones, 'Woman to Woman in Afghanistan: Female Engagement Teams Join the Counterinsurgency', *The Nation*, 15 November 2010, https://www.thenation.com/article/archive/woman-woman-afghanistan/

93. Pindyck, 'Innnovation', p. 49.

94. Bumiller, 'Female Marines'.

95. Robert U. Nagel, Kinsey Spears and Julia Maenza, *Culture, Gender and Women in the Military: Implications for International Humanitarian Law Compliance* (Washington, DC: Georgetown Institute for Women, Peace and Security, 2021), p. 10.

96. Haring, 'Gender', p. 96.

97. Bumiller, 'Letting Women'.

98. Bumiller, 'Female Marines'.

99. Ibid.

100. McBride and Wibben, 'Gendering', p. 209–10.

101. Bumiller, 'Female Marines'.

102. Office of the Under Secretary of Defense Personnel and Readiness, 'Report to Congress on Women in the Services Review', Department of Defense (US), July 2013, http://wiisglobal.org/wp-content/uploads/2013/05/Report-to-Congress-on-WISR-August-20131.pdf

103. Richard Sisk and Bryant Jordan, 'Panetta Opens Combat Roles to Women', Military.com, 23 January 2013, https://www.military.com/daily-news/2013/01/23/panetta-opens-combat-roles-to-women.html

104. On casualties, see 'A Timeline of Women in the Army', National Army Museum, https://www.nam.ac.uk/explore/timeline-women-army; for numbers served see Berkshire Consultancy, 'Study of Women in Combat – Investigation of Quantitative Data', June 2010, https://webarchive.nationalarchives.gov.uk/ukgwa/20110414121925mp_/http://www.mod.uk/NR/rdonlyres/49C587F5-5815-453C-BEB5-B409BD39F464/0/study_woman_combat_quali_data.pdf; on honours see Louisa Brooke-Holland, 'Women in Combat', Briefing Paper 7521, 4 March 2016, House of Commons Library, https://researchbriefings.files.parliament.uk/documents/CBP-7521/CBP-7521.pdf

105. Brendan Nicholson, 'ADF Women are Already "In Combat"', The Strategist, 24 March 2017, https://www.aspistrategist.org.au/adf-women-already-combat/

106. Sisk and Jordan, 'Panetta Opens Combat Roles'.

107. Susan Harris Rimmer, 'The Case of Australia: From "Culture" Reforms to a Culture of Rights', in Robert Egnell and Mayesha Alam, eds, *Women and Gender Perspectives: An International Comparison* (Washington, DC: Georgetown University Press), p. 182.

108. Michael Inman, 'Guilty Verdict in ADFA Skype Sex Case', *Canberra Times*, 28 August 2013, https://www.canberratimes.com.au/story/6152422/guilty-verdict-in-adfa-skype-sex-case/

109. Quoted in Ben Wadham, 'The Minister, the Commandant and the Cadets: Scandal and the Mediation of Australian Civil–Military Relations', *Journal of Sociology* 52, no. 3 (2016), p. 560.

110. Burke, 'Front Line'.

111. Employment of Women in the Armed Services Steering Group, *Women*

in the Armed Forces (May 2002), https://webarchive.nationalarchives.gov.uk/ukgwa/20031006082902/http://www.mod.uk:80/linked_files/ewaf_full_report.pdf.

112. Ministry of Defence (UK), 'Report on the Review of the Exclusion of Women from Ground Close-Combat Roles', November 2010, https://webarchive.nationalarchives.gov.uk/ukgwa/20110414121923mp_/http://www.mod.uk/NR/rdonlyres/831909C3-F443-49AE-A245-EB5C528AE5F7/0/Report_review_excl_woman_combat_pr.pdf

113. Berkshire Consultancy, 'Qualitative Report for the Study of Women in Combat', 13 November 2009, p. 2, https://webarchive.nationalarchives.gov.uk/ukgwa/20110414121925mp_/http://www.mod.uk/NR/rdonlyres/49C587F5-5815-453C-BEB5-B409BD39F464/0/study_woman_combat_quali_data.pdf

114. Ministry of Defence (UK), 'Report on the Review of the Exclusion of Women from Ground Close-Combat Roles', Annex D.

115. Berkshire Consultancy, 'Qualitative Report', at p. 1.

116. 'Female British Soldier Reveals Why She Killed in Combat', *BBC Newsbeat*, 5 December 2011, https://www.bbc.com/news/newsbeat-16039666

117. 'First Female Military Cross Recipient Marks 15th Anniversary', British Army news, 15 June 2021, https://www.army.mod.uk/news-and-events/news/2021/06/first-female-military-cross-recipient-marks-15th-anniversary/

118. Ministry of Defence (UK), 'Women in Ground Close Combat (GCC) Review Paper', 19 December 2014, para. 19, https://assets.publishing.service.gov.uk/government/uploads/system/uploads/attachment_data/file/389575/20141218_WGCC_Findings_Paper_Final.pdf

119. Matthew Weaver, 'Women Could Get Combat Roles in British Army by 2016', *Guardian*, 19 December 2014, https://www.theguardian.com/uk-news/2014/dec/19/women-combat-roles-british-army-infantry-armoured-units

120. Rowena Mason and Ewan MacAskill, 'UK to Lift Ban on Female Soldiers Serving in Close Combat Frontline Roles', *Guardian*, 9 July 2016, https://www.theguardian.com/uk-news/2016/jul/08/uk-army-female-soldiers-close-combat-ground-role-ban-to-be-lifted

121. Steven Morris, 'All Roles in UK Military to Be Open to Women, Williamson Announces', *Guardian*, 26 October 2018, https://www.theguardian.com/uk-news/2018/oct/25/all-roles-in-uk-military-to-be-open-to-women-williamson-announces

122. Oppermann, 'Women and Gender', p. 119.

123. Meredith Kleykamp and Molly Clever, 'Women in Combat: The Quest for Full Inclusion', in Mariam M. Kurtz and Lester R. Kurtz, eds, *Women, War and Violence: Topography, Resistance and Hope* (Santa Barbara: Praeger, 2015), p. 362.

124. Sisk and Jordan, 'Panetta Opens Combat Roles'; Sage Santangelo, 'Fourteen Women Have Tried, and Failed, the Marines' Infantry Officer Course. Here's Why', *Washington Post*, 28 March 2014, https://www. washingtonpost.com/opinions/fourteen-women-have-tried-and-failed-the-marines-infantry-officer-course-heres-why/2014/03/28/24a83ea0-b145-11e3-a49e-76adc9210f19_story.html

125. Haring, 'Gender' p. 100; Hope Hodge Seck, 'Marines' Combat Test Period Ends without Female Grad', *USA Today*, 8 April 2015, https:// www.usatoday.com/story/news/nation/2015/04/08/last-ioc-marine-experiment-women/25478813/

126. Richard A. Oppel and Helene Cooper, '2 Graduating Rangers Aware of Their Burden', *New York Times*, 20 August 2015, https://www.nytimes. com/2015/08/21/us/military-weighs-role-of-women-army-ranger-graduates.html

127. Rosenberg and Philipps, 'All Combat Roles Now Open'.

128. Katie Rogers, 'Kristen Griest on Course to Become First Female Army Officer Trained to Lead Troops into Combat', *New York Times*, 28 April 2016, https://www.nytimes.com/2016/04/29/us/kristen-griest-on-course-to-become-first-female-army-officer-trained-to-lead-troops-into-combat. html

129. Haley Britzky, 'Meet the First Woman to Lead Elite Army Rangers in Combat', Task & Purpose, 7 September 2021, https://taskandpurpose. com/news/army-shaina-coss-75th-ranger-regiment/

130. Tan, 'Ranger Tab'.

131. Ellen Haring, 'Meet the Quiet Trailblazers', *Army Times*, 4 May 2020, https://www.armytimes.com/opinion/commentary/2020/05/03/meet-the-quiet-trailblazers/

132. Thomas Gibbons-Neff, 'First Woman Set to Pass Special Forces Training and Join Green Berets', *New York Times*, 25 February 2020, https://www. nytimes.com/2020/02/25/us/politics/first-women-special-forces-green-berets.html?searchResultPosition=2

133. Lolita C. Baldor, '1st Female Sailor Completes Navy Special Warfare Training', Associated Press, 15 July 2021, https://www.military.com/daily-news/2021/07/15/1st-female-sailor-completes-navy-special-warfare-training.html

134. Haring, 'Gender', p. 94.

135. Ibid.

136. Wadham, 'Scandal', pp. 553–4.

137. Helen Benedict, *The Lonely Soldier: The Private War of Women Serving in Iraq* (Boston: Beacon Press, 2009), p. 7.

138. Rimmer, 'Case of Australia', p. 180.

139. Holly Honderich, 'Canada Apologises for "Scourge" of Military Sexual Misconduct', *BBC News*, 13 December 2021, https://www.bbc.com/news/world-us-canada-59632657; Marie Deschamps, 'External Review into Sexual Misconduct and Sexual Harassment in the Canadian Armed Forces', 27 March 2015, https://www.canada.ca/en/department-national-defence/corporate/reports-publications/sexual-misbehaviour/external-review-2015.html

140. Honderich, 'Canada'.

141. Andrew R. Morral, Kristie L. Gore and Terry L. Schell, *Sexual Assault and Sexual Harassment in the U.S. Military* (Santa Monica: RAND Corporation, 2015), vol. 2, pp. 21, 90.

142. Megan MacKenzie, 'Why Do Soldiers Swap Illicit Pictures? How a Visual Discourse Analysis Illuminates Military Band of Brother Culture', *Security Dialogue* 51, no. 4 (2020), pp. 340–57.

143. Elisabeth Jean Wood and Nathaniel Toppelberg, 'The Persistence of Sexual Assault within the US Military', *Journal of Peace Research* 54, no. 5 (2017), pp. 620–33.

144. Sandra Whitworth, 'Militarized Masculinity and Post-Traumatic Stress Disorder', in Jane L. Parpart and Marysia Zalewski, eds, *Rethinking the Man Question: Sex, Gender and Violence in International Relations* (London: Zed Books, 2008), p. 120; MacKenzie, *Brothers*, p. 151.

145. Megan MacKenzie and Eda Gunaydin, 'Does Raising the Combat Exclusion Lead to Equality? Measuring the Recruitment, Retention, and Promotion of Women in Canada and New Zealand's Defence Forces', *Journal of Military and Strategic Studies* 21, no. 2 (2021), https://jmss.org/issue/view/5315

146. Rachel Olding, 'Unlikely Feminist Hero: Army Chief's Video Message Draws Plaudits', *Sydney Morning Herald*, 14 June 2013, https://www.smh.com.au/politics/federal/unlikely-feminist-hero-army-chiefs-video-message-draws-plaudits-20130614-2086b.html

Conclusion: Buried History

1. Leszek Gardeła, *Women and Weapons in the Viking World: Amazons of the North* (Oxford and Philadelphia: Oxbow Books, 2021), ch. 4; on weapons see p. 236, quote at p. 423.

2. Mayor, *Amazons*, pp. 63–4.

3. Gardeła, *Women and Weapons*, p. 148.

4. Anahit Y. Khudaverdyan et al., 'Warrior Burial of the Late Bronze Age and Early Iron Age: The Phenomenon of Women Warriors from the Jrapi Cemetery (Shirak Province, Armenia)', *International Journal of Osteoarchaeology* 32, no. 2 (2022), pp. 524–35.

5. David Letts, 'Allegations of Murder and "Blooding" in Brereton Report Now Face Many Obstacles to Prosecution', The Conversation, 19 November 2020, https://theconversation.com/allegations-of-murder-and-blooding-in-brereton-report-now-face-many-obstacles-to-prosecution-145703

6. Iryna Matviyishyn, 'A Two Front Battle: How Ukrainian Military Women Are Fighting for Equality', Ukraine World, 10 March 2021, https://ukraineworld.org/articles/russian-aggression/how-ukrainian-military-women-are-fighting-equality

7. Koh Ewe, '"We Are Not Afraid of Death": The Ukrainian Women Taking up Arms against Russia', Vice, 4 March 2022, https://www.vice.com/en/article/qjbndq/ukrainian-women-soldiers-russia

8. Peter Beinart, 'The New Authoritarians Are Waging War on Women: Donald Trump's Ideological Cousins around the World Want to Reverse the Feminist Gains of Recent Decades', *The Atlantic* (January/February 2019), https://www.theatlantic.com/magazine/archive/2019/01/authoritarian-sexism-trump-duterte/576382/

9. Elizabeth A. Wood, 'Hypermasculinity as a Scenario of Power', *International Feminist Journal of Politics* 18, no. 3 (2016), pp. 329–50.

10. Valerie Sperling et al, 'Vladimir Putin, the Czar of Macho Politics is Threatened by Gender and Sexuality Rights', The Conversation, 12 April 2022, https://theconversation.com/vladimir-putin-the-Zczar-of-macho-politics-is-threatened-by-gender-and-sexuality-rights-180473

11. Kay Rollins, 'Putin's Other War: Domestic Violence, Traditional Values and Masculinity in Modern Russia', *Harvard International Review*, 3 August 2022, https://hir.harvard.edu/putins-other-war/

12. Rahul Garg, 'Russia's Sexist List of Banned Professions for Women Must End', LSE Social Policy blog, 18 January 2021, https://blogs.lse.ac.uk/socialpolicy/2021/01/18/russias-sexist-list-of-banned-professions-for-women-must-end/

13. Percy, 'Female Combat'.

Select Bibliography

Abbott, Carmeta, 'Madame de Saint-Balmon (Alberte-Barbe d'Ernecourt)', in Anne R. Larsen and Colette H. Winn, eds, *Writings by Pre-Revolutionary French Women*, pp. 257–88, New York and London: Routledge, 2017

Abraham, Richard, 'Mariia L. Bochkareva and the Russian Amazons of 1917', in Linda Edmondson, ed., *Women and Society in Russia and the Soviet Union*, pp. 124–44, Cambridge: Cambridge University Press, 1992

Ailes, Mary Elizabeth, 'Camp Followers, Sutlers, and Soldiers' Wives: Women in Early Modern Armies (*c.*1450–*c.*1650)', in Barton C. Hacker and Margaret Vining, eds, *A Companion to Women's Military History*, pp. 61–91, Leiden: Brill, 2012

——, *Courage and Grief: Women and Sweden's Thirty Years' War*, Lincoln: University of Nebraska Press, 2018

Alexievich, Svetlana, *The Unwomanly Face of War*, trans. Richard Pevear and Larissa Volokhonsky, London: Penguin, 2017

Alison, Miranda, '"In the War Front We Never Think That We Are Women": Women, Gender, and the Liberation Tamil Tigers of Eelam', in Laura Sjoberg and Caron E. Gentry, eds, *Women, Gender and Terrorism*, pp. 131–55, Athens, OH: Ohio University Press, 2011

Alpern, Stanley B., *Amazons of Black Sparta: The Women Warriors of Dahomey*, London: Hurst, 1998

'Annette Drevon', *Droits des Femmes: Revue Internationale du Mouvement Feminin* 14, no. 208 (1882): 41–2

Applewhite, Harriet B., and Darline G. Levy, 'Women and Militant Citizenship in Revolutionary Paris', in Sara E. Melzer and Leslie W. Kabine, eds, *Rebel Daughters: Women and the French Revolution*, pp. 79–101, New York: Oxford University Press, 1992

Bay, Edna, *Wives of the Leopard: Gender, Politics and Culture in the Kingdom of Dahomey*, Charlottesville: University of Virginia Press, 1998

Beatty, Bessie, 'Classic Dispatches: The Battalion of Death', *Quarterly Journal of Military History* 32, no. 2 (2020): 78–81

Bell, George, *Rough Notes by an Old Soldier: During Fifty Years' Service*, London: Day & Son, 1867

Bellafaire, Judith, *Women in the United States Military: An Annotated Bibliography*, London: Taylor & Francis, 2010

Bengio, Ofra, 'Game Changers: Kurdish Women in Peace and War', *Middle East Journal* 70, no. 1 (2016): 30–46

Berkin, Carol, *Revolutionary Mothers: Women in the Struggle for America's Independence*, New York: Knopf, 2006

Biddiscombe, Perry, 'Into the Maelstrom: German Women in Combat, 1944–45', *War and Society* 30, no. 1 (2011): 61–89

Binney, Marcus, *The Women Who Lived for Danger*, London: Hodder & Stoughton, 2002

Blanton, DeAnne, and Lauren Cook Wike, *They Fought Like Demons: Women Soldiers in the American Civil War*, Baton Rouge: Lousiana State University Press, 2002

Boak, Helen, *Women in the Weimar Republic*, Manchester: Manchester University Press, 2013

Bochkareva, Maria, *Yashka: My Life as Peasant, Exile and Soldier*, London: Constable, 1919

Bourke, Joanna, *An Intimate History of Killing: Face-to-Face Violence in Twentieth-Century Warfare*, London: Granta, 1999

Burke, John, *A Genealogical and Heraldic History of the Commoners of Great Britain and Ireland*, vol. 3 of four volumes, London: Henry Colburn, 1837

Burton, Richard F., *Mission*, vol. 1 of two volumes, London: Tinsley Brothers, 1864

Calendar of the Manuscripts of the Marquis of Bath Preserved at Longleat, Wiltshire, vol. 1, London: Mackie & Co. for HM Stationery Office, 1904

Campbell, D'Ann, 'Women in Combat: The World War II Experience in the United States, Great Britain, Germany and the Soviet Union', *Journal of Military History* 57, no. 2 (1993): 301–23

Cardoza, Thomas, '"Habits Appropriate to Her Sex": The Female Military Experience in France During the Age of Revolution', in Karen Hagemann, Gisela Mettele and Jane Rendall, eds, *Gender, War and Politics: Transatlantic Perspectives, 1775–1830*, pp. 188–205, London: Palgrave Macmillan, 2010

——, *Intrepid Women: Cantinières and Vivandières of the French Army*, Bloomington: Indiana University Press, 2010

Cardoza, Thomas, and Karen Hagemann, 'History and Memory of Army

Women and Female Soldiers', in Hagemann, Dudink and Rose, eds, *Gender, War and the Western World*, pp. 176–200

Carrier, Hubert, 'Women's Political and Military Action during the Fronde', in Christine Fauré, ed., *Political and Historical Encylopedia of Women*, pp. 34–55, London: Routledge, 2003

Cavazzi, Giovanni Antonio, *Missione evangelica nel Regno de Congo. c.1668*, trans. John K. Thornton, Maria Luisa Martini and Carolyn Beckingham, two volumes, Boston: Boston University Press, *c.*1668

Conze, Suzanne, and Beate Fieseler, 'Soviet Women as Comrades-in-Arms: A Blind Spot in the History of War', in Robert W. Thurston and Bernd Bonwetsch, eds, *The People's War: Responses to World War II in the Soviet Union*, pp. 211–34, Urbana: University of Illinois Press, 2000

Cornum, Rhonda, and Peter Copeland, *She Went to War: The Rhonda Cornum Story*, Waterside Productions, 2020

Crang, Jeremy A., 'The Revival of the British Women's Auxiliary Services in the Late Nineteen-Thirties', *Historical Research* 83, no. 220 (2010): 343–57

——, *Sisters in Arms*, Cambridge: Cambridge University Press, 2020

Crankshaw, Edward, *Maria Theresa*, London and Harlow: Longmans, Green, 1969

Crim, Brian, 'Silent Partners: Women and Warfare in Early Modern Europe', in De Groot and Peniston-Bird, eds, *Soldier and Woman*, pp. 18–33

D'Orléans, Duchesse de Montpensier Anne-Marie-Louise, *Against Marriage: The Correspondence of La Grande Mademoiselle*, trans. Joan DeJean, Chicago: University of Chicago Press, 2002

Dandeker, Christopher, and Mady Wechsler Segal, 'Gender Integration in Armed Forces: Recent Policy Developments in the United Kingdom', *Armed Forces & Society* 23, no. 1 (1996): 29–47

Darden, Jessica Trisko, Alexis Henshaw and Ora Szekely, *Insurgent Women: Female Combatants in Civil Wars*, Washington, DC: Georgetown University Press, 2019

Darrow, Margaret H., 'French Volunteer Nursing and the Myth of War Experience in World War I', *American Historical Review* 101, no. 1 (1996): 80–106

——, *French Women and the First World War: War Stories of the Home Front*, Oxford: Berg, 2000

Davies, Christian, 'The Life and Adventures of Mrs Christian Davies', in Dugaw, ed., *Memoirs of Scandalous Women*, pp. 6–203

Davis, Rodney O., 'Private Albert Cashier as Regarded by His/Her Comrades', *Illinois Historical Journal* 82, no. 2 (1989): 108–12

De Courcy, Anne, *Debs at War 1939–1945: How Wartime Changed Their Lives*, London: Weidenfeld & Nicolson, 2005

De Groot, Gerard J., '"I Love the Scent of Cordite in Your Hair": Gender Dynamics in Mixed Anti-Aircraft Batteries during the Second World War', *History* 82, no. 265 (1997): 73–92

——, 'Whose Finger on the Trigger? Mixed Anti-Aircraft Batteries and the Female Combat Taboo', *War in History* 4, no. 4 (1 October 1997): 434–53

De Groot, Gerard J., and C. Peniston-Bird, eds, *A Soldier and a Woman: Sexual Integration in the Military*, London: Routledge, 2000

De Houssay, Louise Françoise, 'A Narrative of the Sufferings of Louise Francoise de Houssay, de Bannes', in Dugaw, ed., *Memoirs of Scandalous Women*, pp. 406–53

DePauw, Linda Grant, *Battle Cries and Lullabies: Women in War from Prehistory to the Present*, Norman: University of Oklahoma Press, 1998

——, 'Women in Combat: The Revolutionary War Experience', *Armed Forces & Society* 7, no. 2 (Winter 1981): 209–26

DeJean, Joan, 'Violent Women and Violence against Women: Representing the "Strong" Woman in Early Modern France', *Signs: Journal of Women in Culture and Society* 29, no. 1 (2003): 117–47

Dekker, Rudolf M., and Lotte C. van de Pol, 'Republican Heroines: Cross-dressing Women in the French Revolutionary Armies', *History of European Ideas* 10, no. 3 (1989): 353–63

DeVries, Kelly, *Joan of Arc: A Military Leader*, Stroud: Alan Sutton, 1999

——, 'The Use of Gunpowder Weaponry by and Against Joan of Arc During the Hundred Years War', *War & Society* 14, no. 1 (1996): 1–15

Dio Cassius, *Roman History, Volume VIII: Books 61–70*, trans. Earnest Cary and Herbert B. Foster, Loeb Classical Library 176, Cambridge, MA: Harvard University Press, 1925

Dorr, Rheta Childe, *Inside the Russian Revolution*, New York: Macmillan, 1917

Duffy, Christopher, *The Army of Frederick the Great*, New York: Hippocrene Books, 1974

——, *The Army of Maria Theresa: 1740–1780*, New York: Hippocrene Books, 1977

Duffy, James, *Portuguese Africa*, 3rd edn, Cambridge, MA: Harvard University Press, 2013

Dugaw, Dianne, 'Female Sailors Bold: Transvestite Heroines and the Markers of Gender and Class', in Margaret Creighton and Lisa Norling, eds, *Iron Men, Wooden Women: Gender and Seafaring in the Atlantic World, 1700–1920*, pp. 34–55, Baltimore: Johns Hopkins University Press, 1996

——, *Warrior Women and Popular Balladry 1650–1850*, Cambridge: Cambridge University Press, 1989

Dugaw, Dianne, ed., *Memoirs of Scandalous Women*, London: Routledge, 2011

Duncan, John, *Travels in Western Africa, in 1845 & 1846*, vol. 1 of two volumes, 2nd edn, London: Richard Bentley, 1847

Durova, Nadezhda, *The Cavalry Maid: The Memoirs of a Woman Soldier of 1812*, trans. John Mersereau Jr and David Lapeza, Ann Arbor: Ardis, 1988

Eager, Paige Whaley, *From Freedom Fighters to Terrorists: Women and Political Violence*, Farnham: Ashgate, 2008

Easton, Fraser, 'Gender's Two Bodies: Women Warriors, Female Husbands and Plebeian Life', *Past & Present* 180, no. 1 (2003): 131–74

Edgerton, Robert B., *Warrior Women: The Amazons of Dahomey and the Nature of War*, Boulder: Westview Press, 2000

Eliatamby, Maneshka, 'Searching for Emancipation: Eritrea, Nepal, and Sri Lanka', in Sandra I. Cheldelin and Maneshka Eliatamby, eds, *Women Waging War and Peace: International Perspectives of Women's Roles in Conflict and Post-Conflict Reconstruction*, pp. 37–51, London: Bloomsbury Academic, 2011

Elshtain, Jean Bethke, *Women and War*, Chicago: University of Chicago Press, 1987

Engel, Barbara Alpern, 'The Womanly Face of War: Soviet Women Remember World War II', in Nicole Ann Drombowski, ed., *Women and War in the Twentieth Century: Enlisted With or Without Consent*, pp. 138–61, London and New York: Routledge, 1999

Enloe, Cynthia, 'Combat and "Combat": A Feminist Reflection', *Critical Studies on Security* 1, no. 2 (2013): 260–3

——, 'Women – the Reserve *Army* of Army Labor', *Review of Radical Political Economics* 12, no. 2 (1980): 42–52

Eran-Jona, Meytal, and Carmit Padan, 'Women's Combat Service in the IDF: The Stalled Revolution', *Strategic Assessment* 20, no. 4 (2018): 95–107

Eriksson, Brigitte, 'A Lesbian Execution in Germany, 1721: The Trial Records', *Journal of Homosexuality* 6, no. 1–2 (1981): 27–40

Fatherly, Sarah, 'Tending the Army: Women and the British General Hospital in North America, 1754–1763', *Early American Studies* 10, no. 3 (2012): 566–99

Fell, Alison S., *Women as Veterans in Britain and France After the First World War*, Cambridge: Cambridge University Press, 2018

Fieseler, Beate, M. Michaela Hampf and Jutta Schwarzkopf, 'Gendering Combat: Military Women's Status in Britain, the United States, and the Soviet Union during the Second World War', *Women's Studies International Forum* 47 (2014): 115–26

Foot, M. R. D., *SOE: An Outline History of the Special Operations Executive, 1940–1946*, London: Pimlico, 1999

Forbes, Frederick E., *Dahomey and the Dahomans*, two volumes, London: Longman, Brown, Green, & Longmans, 1851

Fountain, Julie, '"The Most Interesting Work a Woman Can Perform in Wartime": The Exceptional Status of British Women Pilots During the Second World War', *Cultural and Social History* 13, no. 2 (2016): 213–29

Fraser, Antonia, *Warrior Queens: Boadicea's Chariot*, Salisbury: Phoenix, 1988

——, *The Weaker Vessel: Woman's Lot in Seventeenth-Century England*, London: Weidenfeld & Nicolson, 1984

Goldman, Nancy Loring, ed., *Female Soldiers – Combatants or Noncombatants?: Historical and Contemporary Perspectives*, Westport: Greenwood Press, 1982

Goldman, Nancy Loring and Richard Stites, 'Great Britain and the World Wars', in Goldman, ed., *Combatants or Noncombatants?*, pp. 21–46

Goldstein, Joshua, *War and Gender*, Cambridge: Cambridge University Press, 2001

Goodpaster Strebe, Amy, 'The American Women Airforce Service Pilots and Soviet Airwomen of World War II', MA thesis, San Jose State University, 2003

Gordon, William W., 'Count Casimir Pulaski', *Georgia Historical Society Quarterly* 13, no. 3 (1929): 167–227

Grayzel, Susan R., *Women and the First World War*, London: Routledge, 2002

Green, Amelia Hoover, 'Armed Group Institutions and Combatant Socialization: Evidence from El Salvador', *Journal of Peace Research* 54, no. 5 (2017): 687–700

Greene, Diana, 'Mid-Nineteenth-Century Domestic Ideology in Russia', in Rosalind J. Marsh, ed., *Women and Russian Culture: Projections and Self-Perceptions*, pp. 78–97, New York: Bergahn Books, 1998

Gwynne-Vaughan, Helen, *Service with the Army*, London: Hutchinson, 1941

Hacker, Barton C., 'Women and Military Institutions in Early Modern Europe: A Reconnaissance', *Signs: Journal of Women in Culture and Society* 6, no. 4 (1981): 643–71

Hacker, Barton C., *Reformers, Nurses, and Ladies in Uniform: The Changing Status of Military Women (c.1815–c.1914)*, in Barton Hacker and Margaret Vining, eds, *A Companion to Women's Military History*, pp. 137–87, Leiden: Brill, 2012

Hagemann, Karen, '"Heroic Virgins" and "Bellicose Amazons": Armed Women, the Gender Order and the German Public During and After the Anti-Napoleonic Wars', *European History Quarterly* 37, no. 4 (2007): 507–27

——, 'History and Memory of Female Military Service in the Age of World Wars', in Karen Hagemann, Stefan Dudnik and Sonya O. Rose, eds, *The Oxford Handbook of Gender, War and the Western World Since 1600*, pp. 470–97, Oxford: Oxford University Press, 2020

——, 'Home/Front: The Military, Violence and Gender Relations in the Age of the World Wars', in Hagemann and Schüler-Springorum, eds, *Home/Front*, pp. 1–41

——, 'Military, War and the Mainstreams: Gendering Modern German Military History', in Karen Hagemann and Jean H. Quataert, eds, *Gendering Modern German History: Rewriting Historiography*, pp. 63–85, New York: Berghahn Books, 2007

Hagemann, Karen, and D'Ann Campbell, 'Post-1945 Female, Gay and Lesbian Soldiers', in Hagemann, Dudnik and Rose, eds, *Gender, War and the Western World*, pp. 698–728

Hagemann, Karen, Stefan Dudnik and Sonya O. Rose, eds, *The Oxford Handbook of Gender, War and the Western World Since 1600*, Oxford: Oxford University Press, 2020

Hagemann, Karen, and Sonya O. Rose, 'War and Gender in the Global Cold War and Beyond', in Hagemann, Dudnik and Rose, eds, *Gender, War and the Western World*, pp. 635–76

Hagemann, Karen, and Stefanie Schüler-Springorum, eds, *Home/Front: The Military, War and Gender in Twentieth-Century Germany*, Oxford: Berg, 2002

Hale, J. R., *War and Society in Renaissance Europe*, Leicester: Leicester University Press, 1985

Haner, Murat, Francis T. Cullen and Michael L. Benson, 'Women and the PKK: Ideology, Gender, and Terrorism', *International Criminal Justice Review* 30, no. 3 (2020): 279–301

Haring, Ellen, 'Gender and Military Organizations', in Chantal de Jonge Oudraat and Michael E. Brown, eds, *The Gender and Security Agenda: Strategies for the 21st Century*, pp. 90–112, London: Routledge, 2020

Harley, Brilliana, and Thomas Taylor Lewis, *Letters of the Lady Brilliana Harvey: Wife of Sir Robert Harley, of Brampton Bryan, Knight of the Bath*, London: Printed for the Camden Society, 1854

Hedenstierna-Jonson, Charlotte, et al., 'A Female Viking Warrior Confirmed by Genomics', *American Journal of Physical Anthropology* 164, no. 4 (2017): 853–60

Helfferich, Tryntje, *The Iron Princess: Amalia Elisabeth and the Thirty Years War*, Cambridge, MA: Harvard University Press, 2013

Hendrix, Scott N., 'In the Army: Women, Camp Followers, and Gender

Roles in the British Army in the French and Indian Wars, 1755–1765', in De Groot and Peniston-Bird, eds, *Soldier and Woman*, pp. 33–48

Henshaw, Alexis Leanna, *Why Women Rebel: Understanding Women's Participation in Armed Rebel Groups*, London and New York: Routledge, 2017

Herodotus, *The History of Herodotus*, trans. G. C. Macaulay, London: Macmillan, 1890

Herrera, Natalia, and Douglas Porch, '"Like Going to a Fiesta" – the Role of Female Fighters in Colombia's FARC-Ep', *Small Wars & Insurgencies* 19, no. 4 (2008): 609–34

Heywood, Linda M., *Njinga of Angola*, Cambridge, MA: Harvard University Press, 2017

Holm, Jeanne, *Women in the Military: An Unfinished Revolution*, 1982, revised edn, Novato: Presidio Press, 1992

Hopkin, David, 'The World Turned Upside Down: Female Soldiers in the French Armies of the Revolutionary and Napoleonic Wars', in Alan Forrest, Karen Hagemann and Jane Rendall, eds, *Soldiers, Citizens and Civilians: Experiences and Perceptions of the Revolutionary and Napoleonic Wars, 1790–1820*, pp. 77–95, London: Palgrave Macmillan, 2009

Hurl-Eamon, Jennine, ed., *Women, Families and the British Army 1700–1880*, vol. 1, *From Marlborough's Reforms to the Outbreak of War with Revolutionary France*, London: Routledge, 2020

Ilic, Melanie, *Women Workers in the Soviet Interwar Economy: From 'Protection' to 'Equality'*, New York: Springer, 1998

Irvine, Margot, 'Imagining Women at War: Jane Dieulafoy's 1913 Campaign', *Women in French Studies* 27, no. 1 (2019): 119–30

Iskra, Darlene M., and Vincent W. Patton, *Women in the United States Armed Forces: A Guide to the Issues*, Santa Barbara: ABC-CLIO, 2010

Izraeli, Dafna N., 'Gendering Military Service in the Israel Defence Forces', in De Groot and Peniston-Bird, eds, *Soldier and Woman*, pp. 256–74

Janda, Lance, 'A Simple Matter of Equality: The Admission of Women to West Point', in De Groot and Peniston-Bird, eds, *Soldier and Woman*, pp. 305–19

Jensen, Kimberly, *Mobilizing Minerva: American Women in the First World War*, Urbana: University of Illinois Press, 2008

Kampwirth, Karen, *Women and Guerrilla Movements: Nicaragua, El Salvador, Chiapas, Cuba*, University Park: Pennsylvania State University Press, 2021

Kazman, Mia, *Women of the FARC*, Washington, DC: William J. Perry Center for Hemispheric Defense Studies, 2019

Keegan, John, *A History of Warfare*, London: Pimlico, 1993

Kelly, Christine, *Mrs Duberly's War: Journal and Letters from the Crimea, 1854–6*, Oxford: Oxford University Pres, 2007

Kerber, Linda K., 'A Constitutional Right to Be Treated Like . . . Ladies: Women, Civic Obligation and Military Service', *University of Chicago Law School Roundable* 1, no. 1 (1993): 95–128

Knox, Alfred William Fortescue, *With the Russian Army, 1914–1917: Being Chiefly Extracts from the Diary of a Military Attaché*, vol. 2, London: Hutchinson, 1921

Koch, H. W., *The Hitler Youth: Origins and Development 1922–45*, New York: Stein & Day, 1976

Krylova, Anna, 'Neither Erased nor Remembered: Soviet Women "Combatants" and Cultural Strategies of Forgetting in Soviet Russia, 1940s–1980s', in Frank Biess and Robert G. Moeller, eds, *Histories of the Aftermath: The Legacies of the Second World War in Europe*, pp. 83–101, New York: Berghahn Books, 2010

——, *Soviet Women in Combat: A History of Violence on the Eastern Front*, Cambridge: Cambridge University Press, 2011

Landdeck, Katherine Elizabeth Sharp, 'Pushing the Envelope: The Women Airforce Service Pilots and American Society', DPhil thesis, University of Tennessee, 2003

Larsen, Lynne Ellsworth, 'Wives and Warriors: The Royal Women of Dahomey as Representatives of the Kingdom', in Janell Hobson, ed., *The Routledge Companion to Black Women's Cultural Histories*, pp. 225–35, London: Routledge, 2021

Law, Robin, 'The "Amazons" of Dahomey', *Paideuma* 39 (1993): 245–60

Lebra-Chapman, Joyce, *The Rani of Jhansi: A Study of Female Heroism*, Honolulu: University of Hawai'i Press, 1986

Lee, Janet, 'A Nurse and a Soldier: Gender, Class and National Identity in the First World War Adventures of Grace Mcdougall and Flora Sandes', *Women's History Review* 15, no. 1 (2006): 83–103

Lehfeldt, Elizabeth A., 'The Queen at War: Shared Sovereignty and Gender in Representations of the Granada Campaign', in Barbara F. Weissberger, ed., *Queen Isabel I of Castile: Power, Patronage, Persona*, pp. 108–19, Woodbridge: Boydell & Brewer, 2008

Lewis, John Frederick, 'Casimir Pulaski', *Pennsylvania Magazine of History and Biography* 55, no. 1 (1931): 1–23

Lovell, Mary S., *A Rage to Live: A Biography of Richard and Isabel Burton*, London: Abacus, 2012

Lowe, Thomas, *Central India During the Rebellion of 1857 and 1858*, London: Longman, Green, Longman & Roberts, 1860

Luciak, Ilja A., *After the Revolution: Gender and Democracy in El Salvador, Nicaragua, and Guatemala*, Baltimore: Johns Hopkins University Press, 2001

Lynn, John, *Women, Armies, and Warfare in Early Modern Europe*, New York: Cambridge University Press, 2008

McBride, Keally, and Annick T. R. Wibben, 'The Gendering of Counterinsurgency in Afghanistan', *International Journal of Human Rights* 3, no. 2 (2012): 199–215

MacKenzie, Megan, *Beyond the Band of Brothers: The US Military and the Myth That Women Can't Fight*, Cambridge: Cambridge University Press, 2015

Maggio, Rosalie, *Marie Marvingt, Fiancée of Danger: First Female Bomber Pilot, World-Class Athlete and Inventor of the Air Ambulance*, Jefferson: McFarland, 2019

Manchanda, Rita, 'Maoist Insurgency in Nepal: Radicalizing Gendered Narratives', *Cultural Dynamics* 16, no. 2–3 (2004): 237–58

Markwick, Roger D., and Euridice Charon Cardona, *Soviet Women on the Frontline in the Second World War*, London: Palgrave Macmillan, 2012

Martyn, Frederic, *Life in the Legion, from a Soldier's Point of View*, New York: Scribner's, 1911

Massey, Mary Elizabeth, *Women in the Civil War*, Lincoln: University of Nebraska Press, 1994

Mayer, Holly A., *Belonging to the Army: Camp Followers and Community during the American Revolution*, Columbia: University of South Carolina Press, 1996

Mayor, Adrienne, *The Amazons: Lives and Legends of Warrior Women Across the Ancient World*, Princeton: Princeton University Press, 2016

Merryman, Molly, *Clipped Wings: The Rise and Fall of the Women Airforce Service Pilots (WASPs) of World War II*, New York: New York University Press, 1998

Miller, Joseph C., 'Nzinga of Matamba in a New Perspective', *Journal of African History* 16, no. 2 (1975): 201–16

Miller, Louise, *A Fine Brother: The Life of Captain Flora Sandes*, Richmond, Surrey: Alma Books, 2012

Monro, Robert, *Monro, His Expedition With the Worthy Scots Regiment Called Mac-Keys*, vol. 1 of two volumes, London: William James, 1637

Monter, William, *The Rise of Female Kings in Europe, 1300–1800*, New Haven: Yale University Press, 2012

Montpensier, Mademoiselle de, *Memoirs of Mademoiselle de Montpensier (La Grande Mademoiselle)*, trans. P. J. Yarrow and William Brooks, Cambridge, MA: Modern History Research Association, 2010

Moore, Lisa L., Joanna Brooks and Carol Wigginton, 'Pauline Léon', in Lisa

L. Moore, Joanna Brooks and Carol Wigginton, eds, *Transatlantic Feminisms in the Age of Revolutions*, pp. 242–4, Oxford: Oxford University Press, 2012

Mortimer, Geoff, *Eyewitness Accounts of the Thirty Years War 1618–1648*, London: Routledge, 2002

Moseley, Sarah Vee, 'Women's Entrance into the Fire Department: A Theory of Collaboration and Crisis', DPhil thesis, Old Dominion University, 2017

Mosse, George L., *Fallen Soldiers: Reshaping the Memory of the World Wars*, New York and Oxford: Oxford University Press, 1990

Naylor, J. W., 'Mixed Batteries', *Journal of the Royal Artillery* 69, no. 3 (1942): 199–206

Noakes, Lucy, *Women in the British Army: War and the Gentle Sex, 1907–1948*, London: Routledge, 2006

Ogilby, John, *Africa Being an Accurate Description of the Regions of Ægypt, Barbary, Lybia, and Billedulgerid, the Land of Negroes, Guinee, Æthiopia and the Abyssines . . . Translated from Most Authentick Authors and Augmented with Later Observations: Illustrated with Notes and Adorn'd with Peculiar Maps and Proper Sculptures*, London: Tho. Johnson, 1670

Oppermann, Brenda, 'Women and Gender in the US Military: A Slow Process of Integration', in Robert Egnell and Mayesha Alam, eds, *Women and Gender Perspectives in the Military: An International Comparison*, pp. 113–40, Washington, DC: Georgetown University Press, 2019

Orr, Andrew, *Women and the French Army: During the World Wars, 1914–40*, Bloomington: Indiana University Press, 2017

Parashar, Swati, *Women and Militant Wars: The Politics of Injury*, London: Taylor & Francis, 2014

Pattinson, Juliette, '"Playing the Daft Lassie with Them": Gender, Captivity and the Special Operations Executive during the Second World War', *European Review of History* 13, no. 2 (2006): 271–92

Pennington, Reina, and Robin Higham, eds, *Amazons to Fighter Pilots: A Biographical Dictionary of Military Women*, two volumes, Westport: Greenwood Press, 2003

Percy, Sarah, 'What Makes a Norm Robust: The Norm against Female Combat', *Journal of Global Security Studies* 4, no. 1 (2019): 123–38

Pile, General Sir Frederick, *Ack-Ack: Britain's Defence against Air Attack During the Second World War*, London: George G. Harrap, 1949

Pindyck, Shira Eini, 'Innovation and Inclusion in the Armed Forces', DPhil thesis, University of Pennsylvania, 2021

Plowden, Alison, *Women All on Fire: The Women of the English Civil War*, Stroud: Allan Sutton, 1998

Price, Neil, et al., 'Viking Warrior Women? Reassessing Birka Chamber Grave Bj.581', *Antiquity* 93, no. 367 (2019): 181–98

Proctor, Tammy M., *Civilians in a World at War, 1914–1918*, New York: New York University Press, 2010

Pula, James S., 'Whose Bones Are Those?: The Casimir Pulaski Burial Controversy', *Georgia Historical Quarterly* 100, no. 1 (2016): 68–87

Randall, Margaret, *Sandino's Daughters: Testimonies of Nicaraguan Women in Struggle*, ed. Lynda Yanz, Vancouver: New Star Books, 1981

Reese, Roger R., *Why Stalin's Soldiers Fought: The Red Army's Military Effectiveness in World War II*, Lawrence: University Press of Kansas, 2011

Riley, Sandy, *Charlotte de la Trémoïlle*, Newcastle upon Tyne: Cambridge Scholars, 2017

Rimmer, Susan Harris, 'The Case of Australia: From "Culture" Reforms to a Culture of Rights', in Robert Egnell and Mayesha Alam, eds, *Women and Gender Perspectives: An International Comparison*, pp. 173–206, Washington, DC: Georgetown University Press, 2019

Robbins, Joyce, and Uri Ben-Eliezer, 'New Roles or "New Times"? Gender Inequality and Militarism in Israel's Nation-in-Arms', *Social Politics* 7, no. 3 (2000): 309–42

Robert, Krisztina, 'Gender, Class, and Patriotism: Women's Paramilitary Units in First World War Britain', *International History Review* 19, no. 1 (1997): 52–65

Roberts, Hannah, *The WRNS in Wartime: The Women's Royal Naval Service, 1917–1945*, 1st edn, London: I. B. Tauris, 2019

Roberts, Michael, 'The Revolt of Boudicca (Tacitus, Annals 14.29–39) and the Assertion of Libertas in Neronian Rome', *American Journal of Philology* 109, no. 1 (1988): 118–32

Robson, Fergus, 'Siege Warfare in Comparative Early Modern Contexts: Norms, Nuances, Myth and Massacre during the Revolutionary Wars', in Alex Dowall and John Horne, eds, *Civilians Under Siege from Sarajevo to Troy*, pp. 83–105, New York: Springer, 2018

Rublack, Ulinka, 'Wench and Maiden: Women, War and the Pictorial Function of the Feminine in German Cities in the Early Modern Period', *History Workshop Journal* 44 (Autumn 1997): 1–21

St John Williams, Noel T., *Judy O'Grady and the Colonel's Lady: The Army Wife and Camp Follower Since 1660*, London: Brassey's, 1988

Sandberg, Brian, '"Generous Amazons Came to the Breach": Besieged Women, Agency and Subjectivity During the French Wars of Religion', *Gender & History* 16, no. 3 (2004): 654–88

Sandes, Flora, *The Autobiography of a Woman Soldier: A Brief Record of Adventure with the Serbian Army, 1916–1919*, London: H. R. & G. Witherby, 1927

——, *An English Woman-Sergeant in the Serbian Army*, London: Hodder & Stoughton, 1916

Saywell, Shelley, *Women in War*, New York: Viking, 1985

Schönberger, Bianca, 'Motherly Heroines and Adventurous Girls: Red Cross Nurses and Women Auxiliaries in the First World War', in Hagemann and Schüler-Springorum, eds, *Home/Front*, pp. 87–114

Schrader, Helena, *Sisters in Arms: The Women Who Flew in World War II*, Philadelphia: Casemate Publishers, 2006

Schrand, Thomas G., 'The Five-Year Plan for Women's Labour: Constructing Socialism and the "Double Burden", 1930–1932', *Europe-Asia Studies* 51, no. 8 (1999): 1455–78

——, 'Soviet "Civic-Minded Women" in the 1930s: Gender, Class and Industrialization in a Socialist Society', *Journal of Women's History* 11, no. 3 (1999): 126–50

Schwarzkopf, Jutta, 'Combatant or Non-combatant? The Ambiguous Status of Women in British Anti-Aircraft Batteries during the Second World War', *War & Society* 28, no. 2 (2009): 105–31

Scrivener, Laurie, 'US Military Women in World War II: The SPAR, WAC, WAVES, WASP and Women Marines in US Government Publications', *Journal of Government Information* 26, no. 4 (1999): 361–83

Segal, Mady Wechsler, 'Women's Military Roles Cross-Nationally Past, Present, and Future', *Gender & Society* 9, no. 6 (1995): 757–75

Shipton, Elisabeth, *Female Tommies: The Frontline Women of the First World War*, Cheltenham: History Press, 2014

Silva, Daniel, '(Anti-)Colonial Assemblages: The History and Reformulations of Njinga Mbande', in Janell Hobson, ed., *The Routledge Companion to Black Women's Cultural Histories*, pp. 75–85, London: Routledge, 2021

Simonton, Deborah, 'Surviving the Siege: Catastrophe, Gender and Memory in La Rochelle', in Deborah Simonton and Hannu Salmi, eds, *Catastrophe, Gender and the Urban Experience, 1648–1920*, pp. 17–41, New York: Routledge, 2017

Singh, Harleen, *The Rani of Jhansi: Gender, History and Fable in India*, Delhi: Cambridge University Press, 2014

Snell, Hannah, 'The Female Soldier', in Dugaw, ed., *Memoirs of Scandalous Women*, vol. 5, pp. 203–399

Stack-O'Connor, Alisa, 'Lions, Tigers and Freedom Birds: How and Why the Liberation Tigers of Tamil Eelam Employ Women', *Terrorism and Political Violence* 19, no. 1 (2007): 43–63

Staller, Jared, *Converging on Cannibals: Terrors of Slaving in Atlantic Africa 1509–1670*, Athens, OH: Ohio University Press, 2019

Stanley, Jo, *A History of the Royal Navy: Women and the Royal Navy*, London: I. B. Tauris, 2019

Stanley, Sandra Carson, and Mady Wechsler Segal, 'Military Women in NATO: An Update', *Armed Forces & Society* 14, no. 4 (1988): 559–85

Stephens, Matthew, *Hannah Snell: The Secret Life of a Female Marine, 1723–1792*, Sutton: Ship Street Press, 1997

Stephenson, Jill, 'The Home Front in "Total War": Women in Germany and Britain in the Second World War', in Roger Chickering, Stig Förster and Bernd Greiner, eds, *A World at War: Global Conflict and the Politics of Destruction, 1937–1945*, pp. 207–31, Cambridge: Cambridge University Press, 2004

——, *Women in Nazi Germany*, London: Longman, 2001

Sthapit, Lorina, and Philippe Doneys, 'Female Maoist Combatants During and After the People's War', in Ashild Kolas, ed., *Women, Peace and Security in Nepal*, pp. 33–49, New York: Routledge, 2017

Stites, Richard, *The Women's Liberation Movement in Russia: Feminism, Nihilism, and Bolshevism, 1860–1930*, Princeton: Princeton University Press, 1991

Stockdale, Melissa K., '"My Death for the Motherland Is Happiness": Women, Patriotism, and Soldiering in Russia's Great War, 1914–1917', *American Historical Review* 109, no. 1 (2004): 78–116

Stoff, Laurie, 'They Fought for the Homeland: Russia's Women Soldiers of the First World War', PhD thesis, University of Kansas, 2002

Tacitus, Publius Cornelius, *Annals: Books 13–16*, trans. John Jackson, Loeb Classical Library 322, Cambridge, MA: Harvard University Press, 1937

——, 'Annals', ed. and trans. Arthur Murphy, in *The Works of Cornelius Tacitus with an Essay on His Life and Genius*, Philadelphia: Thomas Wardle, 1844

Tallett, Frank, *War and Society in Early Modern Europe*, London: Routledge, 2010

Taylor, Larissa Juliet, *The Virgin Warrior: The Life and Death of Joan of Arc*, New Haven and London: Yale University Press, 2009

Taylor, Sandra C., *Vietnamese Women: Fighting for Ho Chi Minh and the Revolution*, Lawrence: University Press of Kansas, 1999

Teitel, Amy Shira, *Fighting for Space: Two Pilots and Their Historic Battle for Female Spaceflight*, New York and Boston: Grand Central Publishing, 2020

Tezcür, Güneş Murat, 'A Path out of Patriarchy? Political Agency and Social Identity of Women Fighters', *Perspectives on Politics* 18, no. 3 (2020): 722–39

Thomas, Jakana L., and Reed M. Wood, 'The Social Origins of Female Combatants', *Conflict Management and Peace Science* 35, no. 3 (2018): 215–32

Thornton, John K., 'The Art of War in Angola 1575–1680', *Comparative Studies in Society and History* 30, no. 2 (1988): 360–78

——, *A History of West Central Africa to 1850*, Cambridge: Cambridge University Press, 2020

——, 'Legitimacy and Political Power: Queen Njinga, 1624–1663', *Journal of African History* 32, no. 1 (1991): 25–40

Tillotson, M., and M. R. D. Foot, *SOE and the Resistance: As Told in* The Times *Obituaries*, London: Bloomsbury, 2011

Turner, James, *Pallas Armata: Military Essayes of the Ancient Grecian, Roman and Modern Art of War Written in the Years 1670 and 1671*, London: Richard Chiswell, 1683

Turner, Karen Gottschang, *Even the Women Must Fight: Memories of War from North Vietnam*, New York: Wiley, 1998

——, 'Vietnam's Martial Women: The Costs of Transgressing Boundaries', in Boyd Cothran, Joan Judge and Adrian Shubert, eds, *Women Warriors and National Heroes: Global Histories*, pp. 233–51, London: Bloomsbury Academic, 2020

Van Creveld, Martin, *The Changing Face of War: Combat from the Marne to Iraq*, New York: Presidio Press, 2008

——, 'The Great Illusion: Women in the Military', *Millennium* 29, no. 2 (2000): 429–42

Van Slyke, Gretchen, 'The Sexual and Textual Politics of Dress: Rosa Bonheur and Her Cross-Dressing Permits', *Nineteenth-Century French Studies* 26, no. 3–4 (1998): 321–35

——, 'Who Wears the Pants Here? The Policing of Women's Dress in Nineteenth-Century England, Germany and France', *Nineteenth-Century Contexts* 17, no. 1 (1993): 17–33

Verges, Marianne, *On Silver Wings: The Women Airforce Service Pilots of World War II 1942–1944*, New York: Ballantine Books, 1991

Wadham, Ben, 'The Minister, the Commandant and the Cadets: Scandal and the Mediation of Australian Civil–Military Relations', *Journal of Sociology* 52, no. 3 (2016): 551–68, https://journals.sagepub.com/doi/abs/10.1177/1440783316655637

Wake, Nancy, *The Autobiography of the Woman the Gestapo Called the White Mouse*, South Melbourne: Macmillan, 1985

Warner, Marina, *Joan of Arc*, London: Vintage, 1981

Westermann, Edward B., *Flak: German Anti-Aircraft Defenses 1914–1945*, Lawrence: University Press of Kansas, 2001

Wheelwright, Julie, '"Amazons and Military Maids": An Examination of Female

Military Heroines in British Literature and the Changing Construction of Gender', *Women's Studies International Forum* 10, no. 5 (1987): 489–502

Whittell, Giles, *Spitfire Women of World War II*, London: Harper Perennial, 2008

Willmot, Louise, 'Women in the Third Reich: The Auxiliary Military Service Law of 1944', *German History* 2, no. 1 (1985): 10–20

Wilson, Peter H., 'German Women and War, 1500–1800', *War in History* 3, no. 2 (1996): 127–60

Woodward, Rachel, and Patricia Winter, 'Discourses of Gender in the Contemporary British Army', *Armed Forces & Society* 30, no. 2 (2004): 279–301

Yelton, David K., *Hitler's Volkssturm: The Nazi Militia and the Fall of Germany, 1944–1945*, Lawrence: University Press of Kansas, 2002

Zhukova, Yulia, *Girl with a Sniper Rifle*, trans. David Foreman [Kindle edn], London: Greenhill Books, 2019

Index

Stephen Heath Photography

Sarah Percy is associate professor at the University of Queensland. The author of *Mercenaries*, she completed her MPhil and DPhil as a Commonwealth Scholar at Balliol College, Oxford. She lives in St. Lucia, Australia.